I0762532

MIGHTY REAL

MIGHTY REAL

A History of LGBTQ Music, 1969–2000

Barry Walters

VIKING

VIKING
An imprint of Penguin Random House LLC
1745 Broadway, New York, NY 10019
penguinrandomhouse.com

Photo on p. 427 courtesy of the author.

Designed by Alexis Sulaimani

ISBN 9798217059829 (hardcover)
ISBN 9780525506416 (ebook)

Printed in the United States of America

1st Printing

The authorized representative in the EU for product safety and compliance is Penguin Random House Ireland, Morrison Chambers, 32 Nassau Street, Dublin D02 YH68, Ireland, eu-contact.penguin.ie.

To my husband Jim Salveson,
the light at the Frankenstein place of my life

Contents

Preface *xi*

ONE The Velvet Underground and Lou Reed *1*

TWO Laura Nyro *10*

THREE Janis Joplin *14*

FOUR Motown *17*

FIVE The Kinks *33*

SIX David Bowie and Glam *37*

SEVEN Bette Midler *43*

EIGHT Labelle *48*

NINE Elton John *51*

TEN Lavender Country *55*

ELEVEN Olivia Records and Women's Music *59*

TWELVE Queen *74*

THIRTEEN Patti Smith *80*

FOURTEEN *The Rocky Horror Picture Show* 85

FIFTEEN Disco's Birth 88

SIXTEEN Donna Summer 98

SEVENTEEN Village People and Their LGBTQ Kin 106

EIGHTEEN Sylvester 114

NINETEEN Blondie and Punk 121

TWENTY The B-52s 131

TWENTY-ONE Talking Heads and Post-Punk 137

TWENTY-TWO Judas Priest 143

TWENTY-THREE Prince and Wendy & Lisa 146

TWENTY-FOUR Joan Jett and the Go-Go's 153

TWENTY-FIVE Diana Ross and Luther Vandross 160

TWENTY-SIX Grace Jones 171

TWENTY-SEVEN Michael Jackson 179

TWENTY-EIGHT Wendy Carlos and Kraftwerk 194

TWENTY-NINE Iggy Pop and David Bowie in Berlin 198

THIRTY Gary Numan 203

THIRTY-ONE Duran Duran and the New Romantics 206

THIRTY-TWO Kate Bush *217*

THIRTY-THREE Dolly Parton *221*

THIRTY-FOUR Soft Cell and Eurythmics *225*

THIRTY-FIVE Frankie Goes to Hollywood and Bronski Beat *236*

THIRTY-SIX Boy George *247*

THIRTY-SEVEN R.E.M. *250*

THIRTY-EIGHT The Smiths and Morrissey *260*

THIRTY-NINE Hüsker Dü and Bob Mould *269*

FORTY *Grease* and Olivia Newton-John *276*

FORTY-ONE ABBA *281*

FORTY-TWO Cher *286*

FORTY-THREE Cyndi Lauper *292*

FORTY-FOUR Madonna *297*

FORTY-FIVE Wham! and George Michael *319*

FORTY-SIX Whitney Houston *330*

FORTY-SEVEN Depeche Mode, Yaz, and Erasure *346*

FORTY-EIGHT New Order *354*

FORTY-NINE Pet Shop Boys, Dusty Springfield, and Liza Minnelli *358*

FIFTY Tina Turner and Bonnie Raitt *370*

FIFTY-ONE Phranc and k.d. lang *376*

FIFTY-TWO Sinéad O'Connor *385*

FIFTY-THREE Tracy Chapman *388*

FIFTY-FOUR Indigo Girls *392*

FIFTY-FIVE Melissa Etheridge *399*

FIFTY-SIX Nirvana and Hole *408*

FIFTY-SEVEN C+C Music Factory, Deee-Lite, and House Music *410*

FIFTY-EIGHT Bikini Kill, Green Day, Pansy Division, and Suede *413*

FIFTY-NINE Queen Latifah and Hip-Hop *418*

SIXTY RuPaul (and a little more Sylvester) *421*

Acknowledgments *429*

Discography *431*

Notes *459*

Preface

If you're reading this, it's almost certain you've taken heterosexual songs and made them homo. If you're a gay guy, you've likely heard songs by women addressed to men as coming from your own perspective and mentally switched the gender of the subjects of male-sung songs. If you're lesbian, you've done the opposite. If you're bi, or trans, or somewhere on the spectrum of queer or questioning, you've also heard music in a way that makes sense to you. Like all art, music is to be interpreted and enjoyed any way that pleases us—even those of you who are straight but so culturally allied that you picked up this book.

LGBTQ people know this because most music isn't designed for us—not even music *by* us. Our musicians face the scrutiny and commercial pressures of mostly straight, white, male music-industry execs who, fifty-seven years after Stonewall, despite countless award-winning LGBTQ films, TV shows, books, and plays, still find reasons to nix or marginalize undisguised queer content in most pop unless it comes from a juggernaut like Chappell Roan. I hope things have changed by the time you read this, but that's the way it's always been.

To get around this, LGBTQ musicians have made an art out of saying what can't overtly be said, just as LGBTQ listeners have learned to hear what others can't. Sometimes a song's context makes it gay for us via visual cues, the performer's persona, or the queer spaces where we hear it. Those cues can also come in the way some songwriters avoid specifying gender while stressing themes of alienation, rejection, melancholy, rebellion, survival, liberation, transcendence, and, above all, uncommon love.

It's not incidental or accidental that these themes are the crux of rock 'n' roll, which, since the days of Sister Rosetta Tharpe and Little Richard—the very beginning—has often been implicitly gay. Straight white people tend to think everything is about them, and the game is rigged to perpetuate that perception. But that doesn't mean that plenty of rock—and soul, pop, disco, hip-hop, house, and techno—isn't, to our ears at least, a little bit queer.

"When I used to watch *Xena: Warrior Princess*," Emily Saliers of the lesbian folk-rock duo Indigo Girls told me, "Xena and Gabrielle were so hot because I didn't have anything else. Whether it's a live concert or someone on the screen, you don't project your sexuality onto them, but you do experience it when there's any element of queerness and you're a queer person."

Over the past seventy years or so, pop's subtly gay tints grew into a rainbow of musical expression foregrounded by our increasing cultural presence, self-awareness, and empowerment. But when I was still figuring out who I was, it was a Big Deal when someone voluntarily said they were LGBTQ. The first out person in my life was a social studies instructor who began teaching at my high school in 1971. To support him, his fellow faculty didn't tolerate antigay language and behavior—a revolutionary policy when the religious far-right had just started making gay teachers its earliest enemy. This helped us students, too. I went from being rightly afraid of junior high buses and locker rooms to having plenty of friends and feeling like the world outside my suburb might welcome me. In 1985, that teacher, Tim Mains, became New York State's first openly gay elected official. He served as a Rochester City Councilmember for twenty years.

My professional career began in 1984, at *The Village Voice*, just as gay male participation in twentieth century pop peaked. I wrote about mainstream sounds, forward-leaning rock, R&B, club music, LGBTQ artists, and queer paragons, not realizing I was creating the Venn diagram of overlapping interests and involvement that would shape this book.

In 1986, when the *Voice* assigned me to review Pet Shop Boys' *Please*, it dawned on me that I couldn't fully write about it without acknowledging its gayness—as well as my own. Back then, unless an LGBTQ musician was also an activist, their sexuality wasn't addressed. I aimed to join *Voice* trailblazers such as Arthur Bell, Jill Johnston, and my mentor, Vince Aletti, who all wrote from a viewpoint that was often LGBTQ for an audience that was not solely or expressly gay. This was a new thing, and few at the time had the opportunity to do it elsewhere. I aimed to give readers what Tim Mains gave to me.

So, I came out in that review, and learned to supportively identify LGBTQ themes in pop without committing what is still considered libel. As a staffer for the *San Francisco Examiner*, columnist for *The Advocate*, senior critic at *Rolling Stone*, and regular contributor to *Spin, Out, Entertainment Weekly*, NPR, *Pitchfork*, and other outlets, I've been doing this for decades. During the worst of the AIDS epidemic, I tried to be as political as possible, much to the exasperation of some editors. Since then, my "gay agenda" advises but does not dominate my writing. In this book, however, LGBTQ life and music is everything.

Yet *Mighty* Real isn't foremost about who is and who isn't same-sex attracted. Unless I've identified someone as gay, their inclusion here shouldn't be considered conclusive evidence of their sexuality: Ambiguity is built into queerness. Although I'm emphasizing gay artists here, not everyone I've written about is thoroughly queer or completely out. Just as non-celebrity LGBTQ people may initially share their orientation or gender with only their families and/or close friends, many gay musicians first come out to us through codes in their songs and presentation while courting a largely straight, and often oblivious, audience. Some never fully come out but still speak to us. And some of our most beloved stars are straight in bed but pack their art full of queer curves. The closet and disclosure aren't completely binary. Neither are heterosexuality and homosexuality.

Rather than attempting to cover *every* LGBTQ or gay-friendly musician, I've tried to do justice to quite a few. I've omitted many personal favorites and, undoubtedly, plenty of yours. Some included here have said or done bad things, and if the fallout significantly impacted their work or the way we've received it, I've often said so. My interpretations are, in some cases, bound to rankle. "I will sue the next media organization, or anyone else, that falsely suggests 'Y.M.C.A.' is somehow about illicit gay sex," warned Village People cop, and the song's sole surviving co-writer, Victor Willis in 2020. He reiterated that warning in 2024 after President Donald Trump's reelection. That's how strong the impulse to mute us remains.

Some songs are unintentionally queer, like the Partridge Family's 1970 smash "I Think I Love You." Although it was released on a label run by a gay man, Bell Records' president Larry Uttal, it launched a fictional family rock group designed for mass consumption via a TV sitcom. That show begat the early '70s' defining teen idol, David Cassidy. But once you consider "I Think I Love You" as an LGBTQ song, it's hard to hear it any other way. In a dream, lead singer Cassidy is struck by unexpected, overwhelming emotion. "I'm afraid that I'm unsure of/A love there is no cure for," he realizes. Keep in mind that, at the time, the American Psychiatric Association hadn't yet declassified homosexuality as a mental illness. The character Cassidy is playing resolves to hide and silence these feelings yet can't stop himself from fretting over them. After much apprehension, Cassidy confronts the person he loves and makes his confession. When they echo his admission, consternation shifts to celebration. Against all odds, this bubblegum ditty sums up the first step to coming out in an accidental but oddly articulate nutshell, depicting both the angst and the elation of going public with private truths.

Although I've included some songs from the 1950s and '60s that impacted what followed, *Mighty Real*'s focus is music after the Stonewall riots of late June and early July 1969, because that's when LGBTQ pop started to become less coincidental or covert. I've covered every persuasion but favored queer musicians who wrote their own material and/or evolved our culture the furthest, especially those who expressed themselves through multiple mediums, such as video, which I've also examined when relevant. I've put myself into the narrative as an example, but I've also asked Black, female, straight, and trans musicians for help so this story isn't told solely through my perspective. Through a few hundred revolutionary songs and singers, I've told the history of how we shaped pop in the late twentieth century, and how it shaped us.

I've used the pronouns "we" and "us" throughout as a construct to welcome LGBTQ readers and flip the script of those who downplayed or denied our contributions in so many other music histories. When I write "we," it's with the understanding that not every L, G, B, T, and Q person is alike—not even within our respective letters. Believe me, as someone who was constantly told I was "different" while growing up, I still see difference everywhere, and sometimes it alienates me, even from my fellow G's.

For the sake of this book and its narrative, I've focused on the things we lesbian, gay, bisexual, trans, and queer/questioning folks share so I can describe what, in all this varied and often not stereotypically "gay" music, holds us together. I've discussed pro-female pop, not only because feminism and lesbianism are parallel expressions of the same impulse (women loving women), but also because gay and bisexual men, as well as many trans people, embrace femininity in ways that society says we shouldn't. Either way, LGBTQ pride is inherently feminist.

Straight critics have been telling us how to hear our music for ages, so I'm simply offering a queer alternative—based on forty years of professional research and two prior decades of fandom, with insights gleaned not only from when these records were new and we experienced them in the moment but also from retrospection and insider information. Although most of them capture widely relatable truths, more of them than you might think are specifically about ours.

My aim has been to demonstrate how we, as a coalition, make sense of the sometimes initially underground but often ultimately mainstream culture we built as artists and listeners despite often overwhelming opposition. Moreover, I've attempted to capture the community these nurturing songs give us—especially when we think we're most alone.

MIGHTY REAL

⏭

Chapter One

The Velvet Underground and Lou Reed

Shortly before Stonewall sowed the seeds of LGBTQ political revolution, the Velvet Underground led a similarly queer and freethinking musical one. Its leader was Lou Reed, a Jewish, middle-class Long Islander who wrote about undergoing electroshock as a teen on his highest-charting album in the US, 1974's *Sally Can't Dance.* Its "Kill Your Sons" describes how doctors "cured" those like us with electroconvulsive therapy before we fought back. "That's what was recommended . . . to discourage homosexual feelings," Reed said of his treatment. While in high school, Reed worked at the Hayloft, a local gay club. At Syracuse University, the budding writer tried heroin and contracted hepatitis but still made the dean's list. Even then, Reed's poetry focused on gay life's illicitness, like restroom sex. "If it's not dark and it's not degrading, it's not hot and it's not sex," a childhood friend quoted Reed.

Named after a trashy 1963 survey of sexual "aberrance," the Velvet Underground grew out of Reed's alliance with John Cale, a Welsh classical-music student with ties to the maverick art collective Fluxus, as well as to two leading lights of the American classical world, both gay, Leonard Bernstein and Aaron Copland. Cale's background was, like Reed's, heretical. He'd been molested as a child and, upon arrival in New York, collaborated with the top musical avant-gardist, also gay, John Cage. Along with bass and keyboards, the heterosexual but not-at-all-straight musician played viola, then antithetical to rock. This erudition complimented the minimalism of androgynous drummer Maureen "Moe" Tucker—who beat out primal rhythms, often while standing—and guitarist Sterling Morrison, who doubled on bass. Like many 1960s innovators, Cale favored drones over melody.

The Velvet Underground had both, as well as Andy Warhol, its early manager, who featured the band in his multimedia roadshow, Exploding Plastic Inevitable. For their 1967 debut, *The Velvet Underground & Nico*, Warhol devised the seminal cover art featuring a banana sticker on the original pressings that, when peeled off, revealed a phallic pink fruit beneath. Credited as the album's producer, Warhol instead functioned as anti-producer. His name, notoriety, and queerness—not voiced for public record but spoken through his art—gave the band permission to make seditious music.

A notable exception was the album's opening track, "Sunday Morning." Supervised by Bob Dylan's early producer Tom Wilson, who was Black, this uncharacteristically relaxed ballad glistens like Simon and Garfunkel, whom Wilson also oversaw. But even that gloss has an artistic purpose, as it offsets what's lyrically to come. A celesta twinkles like a xylophone through a tune as serene as Reed's sighing delivery, but two phrases subtly scrape up against their dewy wonder. "Watch out, the world's behind you," Reed warns. Maybe he stayed up all Saturday night chasing dreams or sex or distraction, and now he's returned to a world where we don't fit in, not in broad daylight. With the carnival over and his drugs worn off, the dawn exposes his estrangement. "I've got a feeling I don't want to know," Reed admits. That feeling is *him*, and it sums up where LGBTQ people were in 1967.

Inspired by the 1870 novella *Venus in Furs* by Leopold von Sacher-Masoch, the Austrian nobleman for whom masochism was named, "Venus in Furs" describes an S&M interaction as if relating religious pageantry: "Downy sins of streetlight fancies . . . Ermine furs adorn the imperious." Reed dignifies what then would've been considered demeaning—just like photographer Robert Mapplethorpe, a decade later, gilded BDSM with dramatic lighting and exacting focus. Unlike the era's soft-core pornography, Reed doesn't assume a pseudo-documentary tone; the song's perspective shifts from that of a sympathetic narrator, to an unnamed dominatrix, to the supplicant Severin, and back again. What makes "Venus in Furs" pioneering is that it comes from a loving place.

"I'll Be Your Mirror" is even more empathetic. The deep contralto of its singer, the German model Nico, is as striking as her looks. Her heavily accented delivery—not the least bit feminine—puts a little bitterness into Reed's sweet song to make it profound. In lending support to someone who can't see their own beauty because they've been fed condemnation, she's comforting the electroshocked Reed as well as all of us who have been told we're skewed and mean. "Please put down your hands," Nico sings, "'Cause I see you." Before Stonewall, when coming out was impossible for most of us, being seen and loved this way was lifesaving.

Frustrated by minimal sales, the Velvet Underground split from Warhol and Nico after that first record, which freed it to pursue a louder, harder, and crueler direction in 1968's *White Light/White Heat*, especially on its closing cut. "I like to think of Sister Ray as a transvestite smack dealer," Reed once explained about that song's titular character. "The situation is a bunch of drag queens taking some sailors home with them, shooting up on smack, and having this orgy when the police appear."

Cishet people with no exposure to gay life may miss the LGBTQ content of "Sister Ray." For us, it's as blatant as the song's title, which is a product of a time when we had to obscure gender to avoid arrest. It's still a term of endearment for one LGBTQ person to call another "sister," regardless of their sex. The same goes for giving one another silly, feminine, and comically sibilant nicknames. In the song, while Duck and Sally cook up some heroin, Rosie and Miss Rayon, aka Sister Ray, await an unnamed-but-hung country seaman. Gay-for-pay guys like him can be dangerous for us. That may be why Cecil shoots him. Reed's reaction isn't one of shock. Instead, he dryly reprimands, "Don't you know you'll stain the carpet?" Back then, detailing intravenous drug use with first-person pronouns in an oft-repeated refrain was one thing. But the similarly repeated line, "She's busy sucking on my ding-dong" is even now a humdinger, particularly since "she" most likely has one herself. When the cops arrive, Reed can't be bothered—he's focused on his fix and fellatio.

The instrumental squall accompanying all this doesn't relent for seventeen-and-a-half minutes. Legend has it that the engineer merely pressed record and walked out, capturing the one-take results with no overdubs but plenty of mistakes. Out of control *and* proportion, the band reach for something akin to the free jazz of queer bandleader Sun Ra. But as loud and lurid as it is, the composition itself is simple and static in the manner of Warhol films such as 1964's *Blow Job*, which features a single unmoving shot of actor DeVeren Bookwalter's face as he allegedly gets a BJ beneath the camera's view. The repetition and length of "Sister Ray" make it a kindred test of not just endurance but of concentration and perception. With what's now known as "noise rock," the lyrically queerest band in the land also became the most musically queer, as well, and did it while most of its contemporaries uncomplicatedly preached peace and love.

Later in 1968, Van Morrison released "Madame George" on his acclaimed album *Astral Weeks.* Tranquil and sincere where "Sister Ray" is caustic and noxious, it, too, presents an impressionistic scene around a gender-blurred character whose presence prompts a police raid. Morrison denied his epic had anything to do with LGBTQ people, despite its lyric about "playing dominos in drag" and, indeed, its title. Reed made no such disavowals.

Adversarial stances aren't built to last. Reed replaced Cale with Doug Yule, an orthodox multi-instrumentalist. Now the sole bandleader, Reed emphasized this change by having Yule sing the opening of 1969's far quieter but incandescent *The Velvet Underground.* "Candy Says" speaks stirringly for Candy Darling, one of Warhol's "superstars," a coterie of bohemian and largely queer artists, actors, musicians, models, and hustlers who hung out at his studio, the Factory, and improvised his films. As art historian Benjamin H. D. Buchloh observed, Warhol subverted rank as he predicted "the hierarchy of subjects worthy to be represented will someday be abolished." In Warhol's world, poor trans women were as worthy of screen time as wealthy debutantes—hence his oft-quoted prophecy, "In the future, everyone will be world-famous for fifteen minutes." He meant even us.

"Candy says, 'I've come to hate my body/And all that it requires in this world,'" Yule croons straight away—a soft alarm. This statement gains more substance if you know that Darling was a trans actor who received hormone injections, a far riskier prospect then than today. Aside from the title's refrain, every word comes from her aspect, her body—the very thing she longs to escape. Like the other members of the band, Yule lacks vocal finesse, but when he reaches for a falsetto note, his fragility devastates. The jump to that note accentuates the distance between Candy's male body and her feminine spirit, which gently cries out.

Years later, scientists would diagnose this rift as gender dysphoria: the distress a trans person feels regarding their birth-assigned sex. The song doesn't spell this out. Reed makes his understated hymn delicate, like its subject, while leaving its lyric open and relatable. If you were hip enough to have heard the Velvet Underground in 1969, you might've known this is the Candy who had recently acted in *Flesh*, the Warhol-produced answer to *Midnight Cowboy*. If you didn't, the song still works. Who hasn't wished they could change something about their body or step outside of it to see what others see? Who doesn't sometimes seek prohibited knowledge? Or dread silence? Or worry that our chances for a better life might be passing us by?

Yet Reed's song offers more clarity as a groundbreaking depiction of trans experience. Yule sings of Candy's struggle to make up her mind, and it's likely that the big decision causing endless mental revisions involved surgery. Darling resisted this, but Reed coaxes the listener into identifying with a trans person contemplating that process by giving her an internal life while couching her dilemma in universal emotions. This vagabond who died of lymphoma five years later, at age twenty-nine—likely from carcinogenic hormones—is just like everybody else.

"No kinds of love are better than others," Reed similarly reminds in "Some Kind of Love." He's hiding his intent to cajole a reluctant partner into doing what they "fear most"—anal intercourse. There's no hierarchy of sexual orientation *or* practices, he more than implies, so you might as well, as the song recommends, use that jelly and turn thought into expression. What's often thought of as nasty is here presented as wondrous.

That's gayness itself. We do things with one another that repulse straight people. They pretend to not understand the mechanics. "Who's the girl?" they say. "Who's the guy?" Furthermore, we dare to feel things that we're taught are sinful. Yet these very interactions elevate us, and the resistance we're forced to endure for effecting them only heightens their heavenliness.

Nevertheless, Reed pulled out of his own band, leaving it leaderless right before the release of what he designed to be its commercial breakthrough, 1970's undeserved flop, *Loaded.* Although Reed's previous Velvets output predated Stonewall, it belongs here because of its delayed yet lasting impact on glam, punk, alternative rock, and LGBTQ culture itself. So many more listeners heard these VU albums years or decades later because Reed's greatest student, David Bowie, and so many others raved about them, and because that rising star oversaw Reed's second solo disc of 1972.

Few could've predicted that this album, *Transformer,* would be so of its time that it landed Reed on AM radio with an aesthetic even queerer than Bowie's. According to Reed biographer Victor Bockris, "David had shown him a way to be a star and carry his bisexuality as a weapon rather than a burden." "You hit me with a flower," goes "Vicious," which Reed built up from a Warhol recommendation. Repurposing the artist's deadpan camp, he quips, "You must think I'm some kinda gay blade," while projecting that persona—fagged out yet stiletto sharp. Implying his bed partner is trans, "Make Up" only slightly paraphrases the "Out of the closet and into the streets!" rallying cry of the Gay Liberation Front. "The gay life at the moment isn't that great," Reed said in 1973. "I wanted to write a song which made it terrific."

Co-producer Mick Ronson—the guitarist who helped Bowie forgo folk—rocks out alongside Reed on Velvety tracks but also contributes plush piano and string arrangements that act as heightened counterparts to Reed's reserve.

"Perfect Day" epitomizes their pairing. It describes what might be an ordinary Sunday for most people: sangria in the park, the zoo, a movie, then home. But for Reed, this scenario is resuscitative, as if he'd never experienced such relaxation. For an LGBTQ person in 1972 with a history of electroshock, psychological reprogramming, familial damage, and addiction, a regular date like this might be a rare occurrence. It's what those in the closet dream of—a day when they can be themselves with a likeminded lover. Reed often unexcitedly spoke his way through songs. Here, he emotes. His voice even cracks. "I thought I was someone else," he continues, now soberly, "someone good." What makes him bad is never identified, only inferred, as if too terrible to mention. "He should forget this artsyfartsy homo stuff," Nick Tosches of *Rolling Stone* advised in his 1973 review.

"Perfect Day" would be the zenith of anyone's album if it didn't share space with the hit that puts the trans in *Transformer*. "Walk on the Wild Side" began as the theme to Reed's never-completed musical adaptation of Nelson Algren's 1956 novel, *A Walk on the Wild Side*, but was rewritten into a trans-heavy depiction of Factory hustling. According to her autobiography, *A Low Life in High Heels*, Holly Woodlawn hitchhiked as a teenager in 1962 to New York City, where she hatched a career out of her new identity. In Reed's version, she transitions en route: "Shaved her legs and then he was a she." Today's listeners might consider that line crude. But hearing it on Top Forty radio back in 1973 when I was only eleven was like picking up an alien transmission from a friendlier planet. To me, back then, it was fabulous, and still is.

In the second verse, Reed again writes of Candy Darling, who subsists on her fellatio skills but remains unflappable. The third is devoted to Joe Dallesandro, the pulchritudinous actor whose crotch adorns the Rolling Stones' Warhol-designed cover for 1971's *Sticky Fingers*. Dallesandro, who had also escaped home, supported himself as a nude model for Bob Mizer, a pioneering beefcake photographer whose Athletic Model Guild generated homoerotica. Dallesandro's verse is based on his fictional hustler persona in

Flesh, even though Reed called him Little Joe, which was the actor's role in Warhol's other 1968 film, *Lonesome Cowboys*.

Sugar Plum Fairy, the subject of the fourth verse, could be Joe Campbell, an early lover of Harvey Milk, the gay San Francisco supervisor who helped pioneer LGBTQ politics. Warhol's 1965 film, *My Hustler*, credits the actor as "S.P. Farry." But Factory archivist Billy Name claims Sugar Plum Fairy was less of an identity and more of a title bestowed upon drug dealers for making magic happen. The fifth and final verse is pegged to actor/playwright Jackie Curtis, whose fluid gender and love of glitter helped inspire glam.

Reed's monotone delivery, spartan composition, and reportorial descriptions of trans and gay life in "Walk on the Wild Side" mirror the minimalism of Warhol's own queer-demimonde documentation. But unlike most Reed classics, guitar isn't central—it's the funky bottom that matters. Herbie Flowers doubles on upright bass and a fretless Fender electric bass, sliding between low notes as if to represent lithe bodies sashaying through alleyways. Bowie's own sax teacher, Ronnie Ross, takes a jazz solo that grants these superstars the elegance Warhol denied them.

Because mainstream awareness of LGBTQ life was low at the time, the easily offended didn't recognize the song's trans theme, and so its sexual content wasn't a deal-breaker. Instead, it was the record's racial aspect that caused controversy. Reed instructs, "and the colored girls go" at the beginning of the doot-doot chorus—a spoof of white musical colonization. Although "Walk on the Wild Side" simulates the street sophistication of blaxploitation soundtracks, none of its musicians are Black—not even Thunderthighs, the backing singers. Like the rest of *Transformer*, this apotheosis of pre-gentrification Manhattan was recorded in London. What the Brits bring is far more florid than what our textbook New Yorker matter-of-factly contributes. They make Reed's grit glam.

Reed soon fell hard for a real-life transformer: Mexican American trans woman Rachel Humphreys, whom he namechecks in 1975's soothing "Coney Island Baby." His partner, assistant, drug buddy, and muse from *Sally Can't Dance* through 1978's *Street Hassle*—that's her with Reed on the cover of

1977's *Walk on the Wild Side: The Best of Lou Reed*—Humphreys lived with Reed in the longest, most stable relationship of the singer's drug-heaviest years. Toward the end of his life, Reed married Laurie Anderson, the first notable musician to defy gender through vocal electronic pitch modulation. Reed was as far from flawless as his subjects, perhaps more so, but he raised the visibility of LGBTQ life's most suppressed aspects more than anyone else here, and did it first, when it was hardest to do.

⏭

Chapter Two

Laura Nyro

Much of the intricate, intimate side of 1970s music began in the 1960s with one of its most unorthodox yet influential musicians, Laura Nyro. With stormy music so masterful and far-reaching that it encapsulated the twentieth century well before it was over, this maverick exuded the otherworldliness of LGBTQ experience at the time of Stonewall. Long before she lived her final decades with another woman, Nyro was one of us.

This Bronx-born, Jewish Italian singer-songwriter didn't resemble a revolutionary. On the sleeves of 1967's *More Than a New Discovery* and 1968's *Eli and the Thirteenth Confession*, Nyro looks like a Caravaggio portrait of the Virgin Mary, while the music inside recalls the painter's pronounced contrasts. She sang as she wrote, with sometimes jarring but always riveting variations between loud and quiet, fast and slow, and darkness and light that, undiluted, proved too much for the mainstream. Her augmented chords emphasized the emotionality of her lyrics and came in peculiar patterns, foregrounding expansive melodies that showcased her three-octave range. She sometimes toured, but even onstage, she went on an inner journey—not something for show. Managed by David Geffen and signed by Clive Davis, who'd both find same-sex lovers, Nyro never reached AM radio on her own. Yet her albums were embraced by fellow musicians and inspired an LGBTQ-slanted cult following.

Nyro's *Eli and the Thirteenth Confession* features the first recognizably lesbian *or* gay love song released by a major label in the rock era: "Emmie." Starting with vibraphone, a concert harp, and girl-group ooh-la-las, this aerial ballad captures a transition from cavalier adolescence to discerning adulthood, the album's core theme. As inferred by the song's opening image of a heart carved on a tree, Nyro aches for Emmie to change her from girl to grownup. After she sings of designing a woman, the song pauses, and then tympani count time as Nyro steps toward her in our mind's eye. To the most rapturous melodic line in a songbook overflowing with them, Nyro sings, "Touch me, oh wake me/Emily, you ornament the earth for me" as her backing vocals merge with her lead—a move that mirrors her alignment with Emily. Suggesting but then withholding a key change, a slow vibraphone passage allows listeners to fully digest the meaning of this movement, one that implies a tender embrace. Nyro's music says even more than her lyrics.

Those don't hold back either. Nyro calls Emily the natural snow, the unstudied sea. There's nothing abnormal about her or about Nyro's attraction. Like Walt Whitman, Nyro sees nature's beauty in her beloved. She swears Emily was born to love a weaver—another daring declaration, because weavers are typically women—then affirms their affection by quoting Neil Diamond's 1966 hit "Cherry, Cherry." Diamond's song isn't about sisterly solidarity—it's a dance tune about sex, and maybe even female sex parts, so quoting it shifts "Emmie" further from merely platonic pleasantries. Like Cherry "grooves" Diamond, Emily *moves* Nyro. Their bond is divine but corporeal, too.

Until late in her career, Nyro wrote amorously about the men with whom she partnered early in her life, but she retained what was forbidden. On "Gibsom Street," from 1969's *New York Tendaberry,* she's given a strawberry and sings, "I sucked its juices." On that album's "The Man Who Sends Me Home," she offers proof of her thirst but also of how much the guy wants her, which evens their power dynamic: "When I touch the man/Lord I rise to the rooftops in his eyes." Her eroticism was intellectual, physical, and spiritual, all at once—broadening not only what it meant to be a female singer-songwriter but also what it meant to be human, because men and women alike had been taught to be those things separately. She brought them together.

Nyro released her music to critical acclaim but few sales. Others flourished with the very tunes radio wouldn't accept directly from her. In 1969, Blood, Sweat & Tears and Three Dog Night scored Top Ten hits with "And When I Die" and "Eli's Coming," respectively. Barbra Streisand did the same with the title track of 1971's *Stoney End*, which includes two other Nyro-written singles: "Time and Love" and "Flim Flam Man." Most of all, the 5th Dimension became a Nyro-fueled airwave fixture with its harmonious renditions of "Stoned Soul Picnic," "Sweet Blindness" (both 1968), "Wedding Bell Blues," "Blowing Away" (each 1969), and "Save the Country" (1970). And those were just the hits!

After a sabbatical during which she married, moved to the country, divorced, and lost her mother to ovarian cancer—the disease from which she'd also die, at forty-nine in 1997—Nyro returned with 1976's *Smile*. There she covers the Moments' steamy 1974 R&B hit "Sexy Mama." Softened with acoustic guitar, fluctuating rhythms, and her own inimitable chords, Nyro's version omits or paraphrases some of the original's raciest lyrics but retains key ones. "I wanna open up the love gates," she sings. "There's gonna be a love explosion." A single masculine pronoun officially maintains the original's heterosexuality, yet her rendition still sounds like an avowal of lesbian love.

When Nyro broke another long silence with 1984's *Mother's Spiritual*, she was raising her only child while living with her female partner. Still, men don't entirely vanish from her lyrics. She calls out the patriarchy on "Man in the Moon": "You know you're the old world/And I'm the new world." Addressing maternity, feminism, and goddesses throughout the album, Nyro divulges a sexual shift. "I'm not waiting for Miss or Mister Right," she admits on "Melody in the Sky."

I attended one of the 1988 shows documented on 1989's *Laura: Live at the Bottom Line*. What I most remember was the love flowing between the songwriter and her significantly LGBTQ audience, as if the Greenwich Village event was more reunion than concert. This love—and the humor that went with it—lingers through 1993's *Walk the Dog and Light the Light.* Set to a soulful strut, "The Descent of Luna Rosé" pays comic tribute to her menstrual cycle. Feminism informs everything, from how she sees herself to the way she covers oldies of her youth, such as the Impressions' "I'm So Proud," and presents them through motherhood's prism.

Nyro's intricacies primed the public for psychedelic soul, progressive rock, and all sorts of pop figures who, in her wake, forsook straightforward folk for compositions unshackled by genre and lyrics unbound by literal meaning. Todd Rundgren, later a producer for several queer acts, was so impacted by Nyro that his rock band, Nazz, had to split. "I stopped writing songs like the Who and started writing songs like Laura Nyro," he explained. There's early Carole King in Nyro, but also early Nyro in King: "(You Make Me Feel Like) A Natural Woman"—the 1967, Aretha Franklin–sung, King–Gerry Goffin anthem that King reclaimed on 1971's monumental *Tapestry*—is so much a Nyro number that she covered it in concert. But most important, Laura Nyro's sensual and musical fluidity helped make possible many of the subsequent LGBTQ artists in this book.

Chapter Three

Janis Joplin

Growing up overweight and miserable in Port Arthur, Texas, Janis Joplin lived as an LGBTQ archetype before she ever made a record. Voted the "Ugliest Man on Campus" at Austin's University of Texas, she hitched to San Francisco in 1963. There she met Jae Whitaker, an androgynous Black woman, at a gay bar in North Beach, then a hub of the Beats and a growing LGBTQ community. Their relationship lasted a year, but Joplin still fantasized about settling down with a guy. "I think she wanted kids," Whitaker said, "but I also think she really felt very good with a woman, yet she punished herself for that feeling. She didn't think it was right."

Joplin's legendary self-destruction may have been both compensation for and an escape from that guilt. Her drinking and drugging escalated so quickly that her new friends sent her home. Back in Port Arthur, she aimed to go straight in both senses of the word. But in San Francisco, word of her talents spread to Big Brother and the Holding Company, an early psychedelic band that asked her to join as a second singer. The resulting quintet played at 1967's nearby Monterey International Pop Festival, alongside Jefferson Airplane and Jimi Hendrix, during San Francisco's fabled Summer of Love. This changed everything.

You can see why in D. A. Pennebaker's 1968 documentary *Monterey Pop*. Like most hippie bands, Big Brother thought of itself as a democracy without stars. But when Joplin sings Big Mama Thornton's "Ball and Chain," the director captures her awe-striking articulation of soul-searing doom in extreme closeup: There's no point in paying attention to anything else. Few at America's first major rock fest were aware of her, yet Joplin already belts with paradigm-shifting force. Because her alienation, anguish, and talent went way deeper than that of the average white musician drawing from Black culture, and because she belonged to a sexual minority only beginning to find its voice, Joplin lacked the affectation and ill-fitting appropriation of the era's many white blues musicians. Her outsider stance was both authentic and personal, as if she were ripping out all the thorny damage she'd endured and sharing it with a stadium full of instant intimates.

What Joplin suffered was so devastating that she could never find freedom. Love ideally sends hearts in flight, but, for Joplin, it was shackling. For an LGBTQ person trained to keep their hunger hidden, exposing that level of torment can be both terrifying and liberating. Joplin's pain is evident, yet she practically flies off the stage. Through reaction shots of the Mamas and the Papas singer Cass Elliot, you can imagine other unconventional women, particularly lesbians, seeing possibility in Joplin's deviation from the skinny, Swinging Sixties ideal.

Joplin soon proved herself a master of reinterpretations so drastic she nearly conceived new compositions. Originally a Negro spiritual, "Down on Me," in Big Brother's 1967 revision, describes searching for love when everyone seems out to get us. Have faith and reciprocate caring when offered, Joplin suggests in this testimony of one outcast to another. The resistance implied by her delivery and the din of Big Brother's overdriven guitars—particularly on their raucous *In Concert* rendition—rebuts any religious martyrdom.

In her final self-written song, "Move Over" from 1971's solo *Pearl,* Joplin pleads for sexual and spiritual equilibrium. The singer enacts the indecision of a relationship in limbo via extreme shifts between her tense verses and explosive choruses. Replacing the looseness of her previous work, a rock-steady rhythm drives home the conflicts of bisexual hippiedom. Does she want a stable relationship or unlimited freedom? Escape through drugs or acceptance and genuine connections? Mainstream success or countercultural integrity? Men or women? She's struggling to reconcile choices that, even in San Francisco at its free-loving peak, were often mutually exclusive. "Make up your mind!" she bawls.

Joplin's opportunity to resolve those tensions never arrived. When the Grateful Dead's road manager Richard Hundgen showed her a Bay Area paper that claimed she was a lesbian, the singer told him, "You fly up there tomorrow and tell this bitch that Janis has slept with thousands of men and a few hundred women."

"That was her way of proving she was straight," Hundgen reasoned.

Evidence suggests these conquests were a product of her lingering insecurities, not liberation. It's likely that one of the reasons Joplin's other notable girlfriend, Peggy Caserta, lasted longer than the others was because they often shot up before sex. "I was stark naked, stoned out of my mind on heroin, and the girl lying between my legs giving me head was Janis," goes the memorable first line of Caserta's 1973 memoir *Going Down with Janis*. That gave us something to think about, yet the story didn't end well. While recording *Pearl*, Joplin arranged for her fiancé, Seth Morgan, and Caserta to meet for a threesome, but neither showed up. That October 1970 weekend, Joplin fatally overdosed.

In Joplin's wake, the record industry craved a replacement—not because the suits welcomed female musicians, but because she proved wild women could be hugely profitable. Like Jimi Hendrix and the Doors' Jim Morrison, Joplin sold far more dead than alive. But the music business didn't know what to do with queer rockers. Few of them got past the gatekeepers, and, for years, those who did couldn't achieve success commensurate with their skills or influence.

⏭

Chapter Four

Motown

The softening and broadening of masculinity in post-Stonewall soul started with Motown and Smokey Robinson. This vocally androgynous crooner was the Black-owned and -staffed Detroit label's earliest star to sing, write, and produce major hits, doing so for his group, the Miracles, and many others. As far as we know, Robinson isn't gay. Throughout Motown's long reign in both the mainstream and in LGBTQ culture, this issue would not be discussed. A contemporary—such as trailblazing trans soul singer Jackie Shane, who had a long-gestating 1967 Canadian hit with her 1962 cover of William Bell's "Any Other Way," on which she sings, "Tell her that I'm happy/Tell her that I'm gay"—would let her art speak for her. Back then, anything beyond that would be used against us.

Nevertheless, Robinson broke gender rules from the beginning. In 1960's "Shop Around," Motown's first million-seller, he sings almost entirely from his mother's perspective, not only doling out love advice that would've traditionally been handed down from father to son, but also leaping up to hit feminine notes that suggest he's the medium of his mom's authority.

"The Sound of Young America," as the label accurately described itself, was particularly popular among LGBTQ people before, during, and after Stonewall. Common ground between show-tune gays and rock 'n' roll queers, Motown crossed Broadway's perky melodiousness with R&B's ingenuities of harmony and meter. The Miracles and what followed showed us how to thrive in the straight world while being true to ourselves.

Consider the Cheshire cat smile of the Motown singer most revered by many LGBTQ listeners, Diana Ross. Like all Black women, Ross carries the weight of both racism and sexism on her shoulders as she hits her notes with utmost precision. Flawless in wigs, baubles, and costuming designed to open doors ordinarily closed to her people and ours, she makes love to the cameras and, therefore, everyone as she sashays, gesticulates, and STOP!s in the name of love. Acutely feminine yet steely, Ross sustains her smile—even in the music itself—with almost unnerving steadfastness. Occasionally, you can spot a strain that not even her immaculate professionalism covers. In those rare instants, Ross is most like us: We know kindred pains, even as we also strive to conceal them. Just like her, we crave entry into that world of not merely attainment and acceptance but also vindication.

I don't know what it's like to be Diana Ross or Smokey Robinson. But I do know what it's like to be scrutinized and thought of as substandard simply because of my sexuality, or because my presentation of gender hasn't always been military-grade male. As a result, like many LGBTQ folks, I've endured physical and psychological violence. Sometimes queer people blend in with straights, which lends us a modicum of safety, yet that makes us more likely to witness bigotry that punctures our inviolability. Even if we haven't been beaten up and laughed at, every single LGBTQ person has heard "faggot," or "dyke," or "tranny" so many times that we don't often fully acknowledge this when it happens because that reminds us of our second-class status. Like other minorities, we're akin on the outside to those who conceive and raise us, yet, in our case, dissimilar within. This attunes us to difference and leads us to build cultural alliances that help us feel less brutalized. Just as Motown modeled how to rise above racism for Black America, Ross, Robinson, and the rest unknowingly advised us on how we could transcend homophobia.

Through its many girl groups and the grace that etiquette instructor Maxine Powell nurtured in Motown's men and women, classic Motown stresses inclusivity as it projects youthful upward mobility born of faith in both Blackness and femininity. The label polished every element of its disciplined acts, from the meticulousness of their coiffed hair to the mirror shine of their shoes, just short of dulling their edge. Slickly synced, they exuded both exuberance and restraint that, together, crossed racial and gender lines in what was then a largely segregated society. This barrier-breaking élan made them attractive to us and other minorities, as well as to women, who are feted as "sunshine on a cloudy day" in the Robinson-crafted Temptations classic "My Girl." Femininity in a Motown lyric is like God in a gospel song: the organizing principle around which all else orbits. It's the solution, not the problem.

The flipside is that Motown's love lyrics are often deliriously dysfunctional. In 1963's "Forever," the Marvelettes vow, "I'll be your slave for the rest of my days"—a loaded phrase for Black women to sing during the same year that Betty Friedan unleashed *The Feminine Mystique*, which inspired second-wave feminism, and King led protesters through segregated Birmingham, Alabama.

Set to the steps of marching feet, 1964's "Where Did Our Love Go"—the first of five consecutive pop chart-toppers for the Supremes—introduced a prouder paradigm. Soon to become one of the decade's most televised groups, the Supremes gave suffering a dignified dance beat and trancelike simplicity while focusing on the elation of having loved, not the heartache of being dumped. That's the Motown way: rising above the pain that makes pleasure more satisfying. It's the Black experience of the 1960s sublimated into a romantic context.

Like every smash for the Supremes' original incarnation, as well as most 1960s hits for the Four Tops, "Where" was written by Lamont Dozier and brothers Brian and Eddie Holland. Sometimes the trio produced unambiguously upbeat records, but even ecstatic Motown hits often cast shadows that accentuated their light. Mart Crowley used that contrast in his pioneering play and movie about pre-Stonewall self-loathing, *The Boys in the Band*, by setting a comic-relief dance routine to Martha and the Vandellas' musically jubilant but lyrically conflicted 1963 hit "Heat Wave," on which Martha

Reeves testifies of love's burn. "I can't keep from crying/Tearing me apart," she sings. Holland–Dozier–Holland capture the confusion of what it means to be young, infatuated, and lacking the courage to walk away from unrequited love. "Please don't do me this way," Ross sings in 1964's "Baby Love" as she alternates between resolutions of devotion and pleas for better treatment. LGBTQ people, who were so abhorred that our very existence was illegal, could relate.

In early 1968, Dozier and the Holland brothers left Berry Gordy's empire. They soon set up their own Detroit-based labels, Invictus and Hot Wax, for which they co-wrote and produced LGBTQ-ratified smashes, such as Freda Payne's gay-insinuating 1970 chart-topper "Band of Gold." While the Temptations got funkier via the psychedelic soul of producer Norman Whitfield, the late '60s Supremes vacillated between blatant attempts to prove their crossover cred on albums like 1968's *Diana Ross & the Supremes Sing and Perform "Funny Girl,"* and streetwise affairs like that same year's *Love Child*. Co-written by Tommy Chong before he formed the stoner comedy duo Cheech & Chong, *Love Child*'s "Does Your Mama Know About Me" ranks among the most universal songs about bigotry. Its narrator belongs to an unspoken group, one difficult for some to countenance at the dinner table. Are they a convict? A different race? Queer? Ross inhabits what's left open to interpretation with startling force and feeling. "We've got to be strong/For love that's so right," the usually reserved singer belts. There's no wrongness.

Even more relevant to LGBTQ experience are two Miracles songs addressing Robinson's central theme of love's illusions. "The Tracks of My Tears," from 1965, rides pop's conventional, squared-off rhythms until its chorus, which pulls against that regimentation at the end of every line with quarter-note triplets that trip up the composition's creaminess to evince how Robinson's outward assurance masks his inner turmoil. At the bridge's end, there's an onslaught of these triplets: "My smile is my makeup/I wear since my breakup with you." The effect is that the singer seems to break down, as if suddenly choking, momentarily unable to maintain the front he so eloquently describes. That's how a master singer-songwriter conveys the broadest definition of queerness. In this case, it's not just the words—it's in the very physics of his music.

Composed by Stevie Wonder and his early producer Hank Cosby but completed by Robinson's lyrics, "The Tears of a Clown" illustrates further LGBTQ relevance. First appearing on the Miracles' 1967 album *Make It Happen* but remixed in 1970 for what became a chart-topping single, "Clown" reprises the concealed-crying theme of "Tracks." Yet it also exudes a cheer that exemplifies Robinson's message. "Clown" starts with contrapuntal orchestral riffs that mimic a steam-driven calliope before kicking into an archetypal Motown rhythm of insistent drum whacks. Electric bass interacts with a bassoon—a woodwind not frequently heard in R&B—to form a synergy that makes the bottom even more energized than the label's standard. When the beat cuts in half, as if steam is literally being let out, rolling drum fills suggest the narrator's unsteadiness. The other Miracles chant of sadness before the song's circus-like riff returns and that steady snare snaps the tension back in again. "Just like Pagliacci did/I try to keep my sadness hid," Robinson confesses.

Every LGBTQ person trapped in some kind of closet understands that devastating rhyme—and so did much of America. The Vietnam War exploited young male masculinity, and those who managed to survive often came back so traumatized that they couldn't shed tears. Many queer men let themselves be drafted to avoid acknowledging their sexuality, which carried the threat of electroshock and mental hospitals. Other LGBTQ people fought a war at home for their right to live a fuller range of sexuality and emotions. Straight folks were only okay with us if we made them laugh. On 1970s daytime TV, intrepidly gay comics like Paul Lynde (who battled alcoholism) or Charles Nelson Reilly (who survived the 1944 Hartford circus fire that killed 167 people) defined what it meant to be recognizably gay, and that meant having a pithy comeback for any innuendo-packed game show question volleyed in their direction. Even they were sometimes glib about the butchness of the era's lesbian stereotype, but if you were both female and homosexual then, wouldn't another layer of emotional veneer help you withstand the weight of twofold discrimination? We understood why Robinson put on a show, as he explains throughout "Clown." We sometimes followed suit, but not always, and not for long.

In 1973, when the Miracles regrouped for their post-Robinson comeback, the loss of their star singer loomed large. But the songwriter's status as Motown's vice president gave his replacement, Billy Griffin, and longtime Miracles member Warren "Pete" Moore the leverage to conceive and write 1975's *City of Angels*. Ambitious by even Stevie Wonder's standards, *Angels* tells the story of a rube who follows his girlfriend to Los Angeles, where she aims to become a star.

This plotline mirrored Motown's own. Following Holland–Dozier–Holland's departure and the 1967 Detroit riot—a bloody showdown between Black people and police in the wake of a speakeasy raid, akin to what would soon happen at Stonewall—Gordy shifted his sights to Hollywood, and, in 1972, finalized the company's move to L.A. Like most acts that stayed with the label, the Miracles migrated with Motown. Griffin's colorful observations of his new home inspired the album's concept, including his likely false impression that fully half of his acquaintances there were just like us.

So he wrote about his new friends in one of the most literal and merry LGBTQ-themed songs of its era, "Ain't Nobody Straight in L.A." Chockablock with cha-cha rhythms, Spanish guitars, bilingual lyrics, and flutes, it's unmissably Latino and gay—like a penis-shaped piñata filled with rainbow glitter exploding over the group. While Griffin chirps flabbergasting lines like "homosexuality is a part of society" and "bisexuals on a loving spree" in a Smokey-like falsetto, the arrangement's extravagance conveys queer culture's lack of inhibition. Being similarly righteous and free-spirited men of soul, the Miracles stand beside their Latino and LGBTQ brothers and sisters who express themselves without censure. The track culminates with a spoken interlude in which the group contemplates clubbing. One member suggests returning to a place on Hollywood Boulevard, while another counters that it's a gay bar. But hey, gay people are nice, too, they conclude, so one of

America's most successful and respected R&B groups of all time drives off to party with us.

Another surprising thing happened with that album. A risqué disco number, "Love Machine," was released as the lead single, sold 4.5 million copies internationally, which made it the biggest Miracles single ever, and helped the album go platinum. No doubt some sales came from us. According to Griffin, "Ain't Nobody Straight in L.A." prompted interviews with the gay press, then a rare occurrence for R&B giants. The Miracles broke ground by reminding straight listeners that knee-jerk hostility isn't a required response to LGBTQ culture. Everyone can appreciate one another's company—even in our own spaces. For context, note that the highest-charting 1970s US pop single to address gay life then had turned us into a lousy punchline. Released the previous year, Jim Stafford's "My Girl Bill" outlines what seems to be a tense discussion between two male lovers who turn out to be friends competing for the same babe. "She's my girl [pregnant pause, implied comma] Bill," Stafford grumbles at its god-awful end.

Meanwhile, Robinson's suave 1975 solo album, *A Quiet Storm,* helped inspire a new R&B radio format started by a pioneering gay DJ. Originating in 1976 on Howard University's WHUR, Melvin Lindsey's late-night show, *The Quiet Storm,* focused on amorous soul and jazz ballads sometimes sourced from the Washington, DC, jock's own collection. Lindsey's support breathed new life into seasoned soul and even older jazz, such as Nancy Wilson's silky yet stropped "Guess Who I Saw Today" from 1960. Kindred shows swept the country. For a time in 1979, San Francisco's KBLX extended the quiet storm format around the clock. New York's WBLS still has its own weekday nighttime program of slow jams. After Lindsey was diagnosed with AIDS, he came out. When he died in 1992, those he championed, including Jean Carn and Phyllis Hyman, sang at his funeral. Robinson's understatement permeates quiet storm, conveying both masculine and feminine manifestations of love and rendering them equal. We can all hear our own beleaguered hearts beating to it.

The bridges Motown built between racial and sexual minorities didn't end with the Miracles. The Dynamic Superiors also specialized in plush harmonies and prominent falsetto vocals. The difference was that Tony Washington, the leader of this Washington, DC, quintet, was unquestionably gay. His eyebrows were plucked, he wore makeup and false eyelashes, and in practically every group photo, he strikes a feminine pose; either his wrist is limp, or his hip is cocked, as if to say, "Yeah, I'm queer—what are *you* going to do about it?" Another Superior was gay but not out, not like this.

On the cover of the quintet's eponymous 1975 debut, the group is surrounded by pink; butterflies hover. Washington is coiffed and rouged and lipsticked to such an extent that his face suggests he might be a woman, but his partially exposed torso is clearly a man's. The sleeve of that year's *Pure Pleasure* features two brown legs surrounded by bath bubbles. The legs are hairy, but the hands resting on them feature a girly ring and red painted nails; all are likely Washington's.

"The first time I saw the group walking down the street, I didn't know what we had gotten ourselves into, because they all had on loud fur coats in pastel colors," said Valerie Simpson, who, with her late husband Nick Ashford, wrote and produced most of Marvin Gaye's duets with Tammi Terrell, some of Diana Ross's best work, and their own hits, such as 1984's "Solid," as well as the Dynamic Superiors' aforementioned albums. "I was like, 'I don't know *what* this is.' But whatever it is, I want to see it expressed. I think that's what brings out the best performances. When people can find themselves, they're singing their truths."

Venerated by LGBTQ listeners—particularly Black ones—for their melodic sophistication, consonant arrangements, and philosophical lyrics, Ashford & Simpson stressed the Superiors' classicism, which paid off immediately. Their nostalgic first single, "Shoe Shoe Shine," clicked on R&B radio in 1974, and *The Dynamic Superiors* sold well for an act so gay that it covered Billy Paul's infidelity-confessing Philly soul classic "Me and Mrs. Jones" in concert as "Me and *Mr.* Jones." Judging by their *Soul Train* appearance, haters were kept in check.

"I might walk up to a guy and stand between his legs and sing to him," Washington told *The Advocate* in 1977. Washington expresses that audacity on *Pure Pleasure*'s "Nobody's Gonna Change Me," a rebellious funk number in which the frontman sounds enraged.

"We were just intending to give Tony a first-person-singular lyric that he could sing proudly," Simpson explained of the song. "You could look at him and see that lyric—*nobody* was gonna change him. The Temptations had falsetto singers, but Tony had another quality. He was more piercing, a little stronger. We weren't really concerned with [Washington's sexuality]. We were just trying to come up with material that would showcase his particular talent. If people love it, they'll love it, and you don't have to worry about a few naysayers."

After four albums, Motown dropped the Superiors, and Washington reportedly died of AIDS in 1989. But the label's commitment to gay expressions and audiences set the stage for the boldest LGBTQ anthem of the 1970s to get major music-industry muscle.

In 1971, Bunny Jones opened, in East Harlem, what *Billboard* believed was the first major US recording studio owned and operated by a Black woman. As the proprietor of several Harlem hair salons, she wanted to help her gay employees. "I began to feel that gays are more suppressed than Blacks, Chicanos, or other minorities," she explained. "You hear of great designers or famous hairdressers, and that's about as far as society will let gays go."

She found Charles Valentino performing in a revival of the 1960s' definitive hippie musical, *Hair*. "Do you feel brave?" she asked him. "Do you know who you are spiritually? Do you know what you're supposed to do here?" Jones considered herself a metaphysician. "I have this song I'm gonna write for you, and it's gonna be an anthem," she predicted. Jones then got together with Chris Spierer, a white rock musician she met at an aquarium shop. Addressing homophobia as it honors LGBTQ identity, self-esteem, and perseverance, their "I Was Born This Way" is the gay equivalent of earlier civil rights anthems. But unlike nearly all of those, it springs from songwriters outside the minority it honors: Jones was straight, and so is Spierer. Yet it remains one of the greatest songs about LGBTQ experience and helped inspire Lady Gaga's 2011 monster hit "Born This Way."

Valentino watched Jones and Spierer arrange the song in the studio. Then Stevie Wonder showed up. Jones's son was Wonder's road manager, and the superstar wanted to rework the track. "You're not touching my song!" she told him, knowing that if Wonder got too involved, it would delay her record's release. Therefore, Wonder simply plays drums—skipping triplets that reinforce the lyric's giddiness. "I'm happy, carefree, and I'm gay/I was born this way," Valentino belts with a gusto that straddles R&B and Broadway. Jones's lyric goes on to insist that same-sex attraction is not only compatible with religion but also determined by biology. In 1975, it was revolutionary to assert that homosexuality is not a choice but a predetermined orientation. Spelling this all out in song was profound.

Even more groundbreaking was that millions of people, straight and gay alike, heard it. One of Jones's many associates was Frankie Crocker, the program director and top DJ of WBLS, New York's trendsetting, Black-owned R&B station. Crocker pioneered his suave blend of R&B, funk, disco, jazz, reggae, salsa, gospel, and rhythmic pop as a new radio format: "urban contemporary," which shaped big-city Black radio programming throughout the 1970s and '80s. Urban contemporary is Afrocentric, yet overlaps with the taste of New York's gay cognoscenti, as it shares their love of cosmopolitan soul. When Crocker decided that Kraftwerk, the Clash, or even more obscure dance music championed at Manhattan's largely gay and Black disco Paradise Garage fit his mix, those records would often spread to other R&B- and dance-radio playlists. Many future club classics got their first airwave exposure via WBLS.

Crocker made Valentino's "I Was Born This Way" a Top Twenty WBLS hit. After Jones sold fifteen thousand singles out of the back of her car, Motown picked it up for distribution. At Jones's insistence, Motown only put its name on promo copies—she wanted everyone to know that her record was Gaiee, her label's name. Even the UK pressing, which major-label giant EMI distributed through Motown, is Gaiee. Motown's motivations were more conventional. Its vice president Suzanne de Passe wrote in one press release, "We didn't purchase this record because it was socially controversial, but because it sold enormously in New York and is, we think, a hit record." She'd eventually become president of Motown Productions.

Yet the industry giant also understood the potential political impact of the record, and how it fit with the label's own history of fighting prejudice with proud positivity. "Upon bringing this record home we score a greater victory than just another hit" went another Motown press release. "We walk in the light of establishing yet another personal freedom, strengthening all existing ones." That one was written by Tom DePierro, a gay Motown promo man.

Shortly after the single was released, Valentino performed the tune at the Continental Baths, in San Francisco's gay march, and at Oakland's Paramount Theatre with Gloria Gaynor, Disco Tex & the Sex-O-Lettes, and Sylvester. The record got some club play and even a UK buzz. Its triplet rhythms, however, made it difficult for DJs to mix. Jones also made the miscalculation to move both her and Valentino to Las Vegas, where this gambler believed the entertainment world soon would be headed. She was right but a few decades too early, and her bad timing alienated Valentino, who eventually toured as the scarecrow in *The Wizard of Oz*'s "Super Soul Musical," *The Wiz*—the same role played in the 1978 film version by Michael Jackson. So Motown financed a rerecording of the song with a left-field but inspired choice of vocalist: Carl Bean.

"Gospel has always been predominantly lesbian and gay," Bean told me on the eve of his seventy-fifth birthday. "It's the best-kept *known* secret of the biz. Everyone knows that the organist, the choir director, and the kid who, as we used to say, 'set the church on fire,' is gay, but it's never spoken about." Big-voiced and resplendent, Bean was precisely that kind of singer. Discovered by gay gospel titan Alex Bradford while singing along to Martha and the Vandellas on the jukebox at the Harlem gay club the Fantasia in the early 1960s, this Baltimore native grew up in Martin Luther King Jr.'s scholarly and progressive Black high church. Bean didn't experience antigay attitudes within it—after all, he was surrounded by his own kind. Nor did he weather it in Harlem, where in his experience police didn't regularly raid and arrest LGBTQ people like they did in Greenwich Village. The gay Black dancers he met at the Apollo were welcome. But when Bean toured the fundamentalist churches where preachers decried homosexuality in public, yet privately aimed to sleep with him, he knew he had to quit the gospel circuit.

Marvin Gaye's epochal 1971 album *What's Going On* suggested to Bean that his destiny was in "message music"—soul shaped by civil rights, jazzy innovation, and gospel's emphasis on noble action. So he left for Gaye's adopted home, Los Angeles. There, Bean met Lee Young, who signed Bean's group, Universal Love, to ABC Records. Released by that label's gospel subsidiary, Peacock, 1974's *All We Need Is Love* shows Bean wearing a dashiki and skullcap, as did many Black brothers who represented the African diaspora. There were other gay ones like him, but the world didn't know it yet.

Berry Gordy hired Young, who knew Bean was the right guy for "I Was Born This Way." "When I saw the lyric, I thought, 'Oh, this is bull—they ain't gonna let me sing this!'" Bean remembered. "Then I found out how real it was. I said, 'I gotta do what Ray Charles did with "I've Got a Woman" and others he changed from gospel to R&B. I've gotta turn this Broadway-sounding song into something that will make Black people wanna dance their butts off.'"

Motown paired Bean with Hal Davis, who had recently scored with Diana Ross's "Love Hangover" and Thelma Houston's "Don't Leave Me This Way," which both topped the US pop, R&B, and disco charts. That's how much Motown believed in the singer and the song. But Bean—who was respected in the gospel and Broadway fields through shows like Bradford's *Your Arms Too Short to Box with God*—told Motown, "I don't think it's gonna work out with this cat."

The label then enlisted Philadelphia producers Norman Harris, Ron Kersey, and T. G. Conway to recast the tune in a roof-raising arrangement akin to that team's creations for the Trammps, who'd been packing dancefloors with "That's Where the Happy People Go," a Pentecostal-styled praise song in which disco's community-building cheer saves souls. Like the Trammps' Earl Young, who pioneered disco's heavy bass drum and hissing high-hat, Harris, Kersey, and Conway played on dozens of '70s soul and disco hits, including those released by Philadelphia International, the label that bore the message-music mantle built by Gaye and Curtis Mayfield. The Sweethearts of Sigma contribute prominent choral parts that make this not merely a man's record—it speaks for all LGBTQ people. Harris had produced two albums with former Temptations singer Eddie Kendricks that similarly combined gospel-disco with social commentary, but Motown went one better here by hiring disco's hottest mixer, Tom Moulton, who'd mixed the Trammps' hits, to give "I Was Born This Way" his sheen.

Bean preaches gay love and self-esteem during the MFSB band's closing vamp. "When I started, as they say, 'going to church on it,' that's what sold the song," Bean said. "'From a little bitty boy'—that's my creation at the microphone." Even as a small child, Bean knew he was gay. So did many of his neighbors and family members—an uncle took advantage and molested him. Yet none of this caused a fuss until a friend's parents discovered their son had been having sex with Bean, who was more identifiably gay and, therefore, considered the seducer. Suddenly this A-student became a pariah. He attempted suicide.

It's this wounded boy who heals himself and finds his calling at the record's momentous peak when he prays to the Lord and asks him to spread the word that he was born gay. Then he begs listeners to love him and, by extension, all

LGBTQ people the way he does them. If that can be achieved, anything's possible. On Motown—the African American musical ambassador to all races—Bean announces that he's a Black gay man who believes in God. In doing so, he unites secular and religious worlds kept apart via selective misapplications of biblical passages. Even today, church remains the institution in which communities self-segregate the most. Nevertheless, Bean's version of "I Was Born This Way" became both Motown's gayest *and* most gospel hit.

Although Bean had been singing with Black gay men all his life, he hadn't sung for a white audience until he debuted the track one afternoon at L.A.'s Circus Disco for a gathering of club DJs. "The whole place stopped," he remembers. "People started screaming, jumping up and down. Any intimidation or fear I had was gone. I had an army to walk with me down this journey of gay liberation."

At his insistence, Bean's first public performance of the cut was at Jewel's Catch One, a disco opened by Black lesbian Jewel Thais-Williams that, even today, draws a gay and largely Black audience. But the night that most shaped Bean's fate was when he sang at Studio One, West Hollywood's top disco. He was still singing in the same unapologetically Black gospel style, but here it served LGBTQ liberation, and the combination made white gay guys also weep and whoop. This behavior was frowned upon in the high church that nurtured Bean. Yet it was the very response Bean generated in the storefront churches where his Black LGBTQ peers were meant to feel hypocritical, homophobic shame. After the show, Bean told DePierro that he needed a stroll to calm down. He had a lot to process.

"I remember walking down the street, and this guy, very preppy—with the tennis sweater around his neck, probably just coming out—called out to me," the singer said. "What he said to me on that corner of Santa Monica and La Peer was so real and heartfelt that, when he left, shaking my hand and hugging me, I cried for about two blocks. 'You don't know what you did for all those guys and especially for me,' he said. 'I can be okay and do things.' I had to stop and recognize, 'Carl, this is not just show business. What you're doing is going to have a profound effect upon the era. You knew you wanted to do message music—you just didn't know it would be this kind of message.'"

Soon after, Bean met with the Motown brass. The response was positive but did not align with Bean's growing sense of himself as a gay, Black emissary of truth.

"Man, the jockeys are loving you," he recalled Motown telling him in early 1978. Bean had the strange luck of singing on disco's gayest record right when this Black- and queer-led movement suddenly amassed millions of white, straight followers courtesy of *Saturday Night Fever.* "You're climbing the charts, and David is messing up with these drugs, so Berry wants to take David's voice off these songs, put your voice on, and release the album in your name," a Motown exec told him.

"'David? David who?'" Bean replied. They meant the Temptations' former lead singer David Ruffin. "I remember saying to Iris Gordy, 'I'll have to get back to you.' I went home and listened [to Ruffin's unreleased album]. Now I'm gonna sing 'girl' and 'hey baby'? I went back and said, 'That's not who I am.' Everything I learned about social justice and civil rights didn't fit me becoming that person. I came out to be honest, and I felt good about that, so I had to ask for a release."

Bean left the label without a plan. Then his friends in New York started getting sick. He learned what he could and created the Minority AIDS Project. DePierro became one of Bean's many music-biz clients before dying of the plague.

As all this was happening, "I Was Born This Way" experienced a second wave of popularity in New York when crucial club-music figures Shep Pettibone, Bruce Forest, Boyd Jarvis, and Timmy Regisford remixed the track. Bean's social work needed funding, so the singer stipulated a one-thousand-dollar fee for every East Coast gig to promote its mid-1980s rerelease. Bean flew back home with nearly thirty thousand dollars in a brown paper bag. This grew MAP into a fifty-person agency serving thousands of AIDS patients, often otherwise neglected, and funded Dignity House, a West Los Angeles AIDS shelter. One Easter, Bean's patients asked him if they could have a worship service because they didn't feel comfortable attending their usual churches looking unwell. This led to Bean founding the Unity Fellowship Church, the first expressly for LGBTQ African Americans.

Bean died in 2021. Yet his message far eclipses his hit's beginnings, which were simple but never humble. In 1975, Bunny Jones aimed to help gay people through music, just like Black singers elevated their own. "I Was Born This Way" does both.

Chapter Five

The Kinks

Before I discovered the queerest band of the British Invasion, I couldn't get enough of the Beatles. I didn't have a conventional crush on them, like my sister, who is twelve years older and was the ideal age for a Beatlemaniac. Instead, like many gay kids, I saw in them who I could become: a gender-noncompliant gent who could frolic with other fellows and win worldwide approval. Well, maybe I had a *little* bit of a crush. I was captivated by the back cover of 1967's *Sgt. Pepper's Lonely Hearts Club Band*, which showed John Lennon with his hands stuffed into the waist of his satin trousers. My mother told me it was bad to touch yourself down there, so I thought John was doing something naughty. I knew I shouldn't look, but the album's lyrics were printed right on top of him, even on his crotch, where I really wasn't supposed to stare. But this was *the Beatles*. How bad could just looking be? The fact that I fixated on this image yet felt guilty about it was my first clue that I wasn't like other boys.

Rock 'n' roll taught me that things ordinarily considered bad were often wonderful—like the Kinks. I didn't know what their name implied; only that it was something cool. This London band kick-started heavy metal with the distortion generated by their teenage guitarist Dave Davies, whose hair was nearly longer than my sister's, and the insistent beat of Mick Avory, whose drums were sometimes louder than Ringo's. Following their bulldozing 1964 breakthroughs "You Really Got Me" and "All Day and All of the Night," leader Ray Davies's songs grew more delicate and observational, like those of the Beatles, who were also raising rock's compositional bar on ballads, such as *Help!*'s "You've Got to Hide Your Love Away." That one was later speculated to be about Brian Epstein. Back then, we didn't know the Beatles' manager—and those of the Who, the Yardbirds, the Bee Gees, the Honeycombs, and others—was gay and understood that straight teen girls like many of the same things that gay men do. Before Stonewall, you had to be "in the life" yourself to know that anyone besides the usual suspects was queer. Back then, these things were mysterious.

The Kinks' wistful tunes and wry social commentary voiced what would not ordinarily be uttered. As illustrated by the Velvet Underground, Western songwriters sometimes draw from Eastern music when evoking something special or cryptic, and that's what Ray does on "See My Friend," which, in 1965, was among the earliest rock hits to mimic Indian drones, even in its minimal lyrics. He sings of pals prone on a river's other side and his companion's absence, which culminates in a subtle shift. "She is gone and now there's no one else to love/'Cept my friend," he croons with a gentleness far removed from the group's initial bluster. "The song is about homosexuality," Davies notified London's *Evening Standard* when the song was new. This was, for rock, an unprecedented announcement. But most of us missed his message, especially since the single was renamed for international release as "See My Friends" and flopped in North America. Yet it impressed Mick Jagger and Paul McCartney, and its exoticism launched psychedelic rock.

Participating in what was then a substantially gay English entertainment industry meant most British Invasion acts were queer-adjacent. During their press conferences, each Beatle could ad-lib a quip with the tongue-in-cheekiness of Oscar Wilde. It's likely that they didn't learn this only from Epstein. In the class-fixated UK, where popular culture provided a rare opportunity for working class people to better their station, drollery was imperative as theatricality. And for LGBTQ people of that era, inventive language meant survival. If you're required to speak in code to convey sexual intentions without getting assaulted or arrested, you'd better be clever. London gays even used Polari—a slang developed over centuries by entertainers, sailors, gangsters, and other groups—to avoid arrest, because sex between men was illegal in the UK until 1967.

Even more than Paul McCartney, Ray Davies drew from the pre-rock thespian traditions of music hall, the UK equivalent of vaudeville, especially on 1966's "Dedicated Follower of Fashion," which lampoons Carnaby Street's androgynous dandies with a mincing delivery. Grounded by the menace of nonconformist odes like that year's Dave-sung B-side "I'm Not Like Everybody Else," Ray could wander into hammy and even homoerotic territory while maintaining the quartet's recalcitrant profile. On "David Watts," from 1967's *Something Else by the Kinks*, Davies plays the part of a student besotted with another lad. Admitting he wants *to be* David Watts, Davies also implies he wants *to do* David Watts. "He is so gay and fancy free," he sighs. Straight listeners might've assumed Davies meant his boy-crush is merely jolly. But as revealed by the group's gay biographer Jon Savage, David Watts was a concert promoter hot for Dave Davies. The Jam's 1978 cover made the song a UK punk hit.

Following the Kinks' chaotic 1965 US tour—during which Ray punched, in the face, an official from the American Federation of Television and Radio Artists who called the group "fairies"—the American Federation of Musicians refused the band permits at the peak of its popularity. The Kinks' US audience subsequently declined so drastically that 1967's UK smash "Waterloo Sunset"—rightfully a Brit-pop classic—failed to chart in North America. Most groups would've pursued a comeback by writing something universally relatable. Instead, Ray devised a surefire hit about falling in love with a trans woman. Engaging and enlightening a mass audience by making an off-limits subject thoroughly approachable, both lyrically and musically, Davies's disarming song starts with a commanding acoustic guitar and clanging Dobro, and culminates with a sing-along. This contagious, communal positivity makes the Kinks' "Lola," from 1970, the first crucial post-Stonewall smash.

Accounts conflict as to its inspiration. Ray claims it was Kinks manager Robert Wace. "In his apartment, Robert had been dancing with this Black woman, and he said, 'I'm really onto a thing here.' And it was okay until we left at six in the morning and then I said, 'Have you seen the stubble?' He said 'Yeah,' but he was too drunk to care." Avory thinks he sparked "Lola" by patronizing the drag clubs of Earl's Court, London's gay district. "All the Kinks were a bit versatile," he said. In his autobiography, Dave writes of affectionate and sometimes sexual connections with men like Long John Baldry, the singer Elton John backed in his pre-stardom band Bluesology. "Lola" is likely Ray's embellished composite.

Deftly leading the listener along a gradual avenue of discovery, Davies aptly sets the scene of "Lola" in Soho, the home of rock and the sex industry in London, where things are not what they seem: Champagne tastes like cola; candlelight is electric. A woman advances who seems feminine, but her voice and strength are masculine. There's gender-based humor as they drink, dance, and stare into each other's eyes, but it's as gentle as Lola is mighty. Only in the song's harmonically contrasting bridge does the narrator's confusion create conflict. At Lola's place, the guy shoves her away. But he's the one who falls—she's no pushover. On his knees, Davies sees eternity embodied in Lola's magnificence. In that moment, the melody returns to its hypnotic lilt, all vocal anxiety vanishes, and Lola's gender becomes as genuine as their affection. Davies isn't looking down on her. He's looking up.

Perhaps all desire is naive; certainly this singer is. Newly on his own, he'd never even kissed a woman, so it's Lola who makes him a man. Thirteen years before the musical *La Cage aux Folles* declared "I Am What I Am," Davies's famous closing line plays with language, just like Polari, to portray queer ascension: "I know what I am and I'm glad I'm a man/And so is Lola." That may read like a joke, but it's not played as one. Live Kinks clips capture when Ray is clearly adopting a theatrical character, but when he sings "Lola," you never see him wink in any way or distance himself through a campy delivery. He means every word, and that makes all the difference. At the song's end, there's a rumble, as if they're rocketing to the heavens for one of rock's happiest endings, fueled not by what haters consider *amour fou*, but by what this pair knows is wise and true love.

⏭

Chapter Six

David Bowie and Glam

Even before he started releasing records, David Bowie subverted gender. In a 1964 BBC TV interview, seventeen-year-old David Jones (his real name) fronted his Society for the Prevention of Cruelty to Long-Haired Men, a brotherhood fed up with enduring emasculating insults simply because they resembled various Kinks and Rolling Stones. Was it a publicity stunt? Or was he serious?

Bowie raised those questions throughout his long career—particularly when, in an early 1972 interview with the English music weekly *Melody Maker*, he said, "I'm gay, and always have been, even when I was David Jones." Having earlier spoken to *Jeremy*, England's first gay mag, and reclined in a dress for the UK cover of 1970's *The Man Who Sold the World,* Bowie took glam's sexual ambiguity and androgyny further than his main competition: bisexual Londoner Marc Bolan, whose about-face from elfin psych-folk to cocky rock made his band, T. Rex, teen idols in Europe with not particularly teeny hits like 1972's "Children of the Revolution."

"David's present image is to come on like a swishy queen, a gorgeously effeminate boy," the *Melody Maker* article reports before noting Bowie's limp wrist and use of Polari. "The important fact is that I don't have to drag it up," Bowie asserted. "I want to go on like this for long after the fashion has finished."

As we soon learned, the restless musician—who was married to a woman and had an infant son—routinely reinvented himself. Now in a trendsetting mullet and unisex jumpsuit as tight as his bell-bottoms on the long-haired back cover of late 1971's just-released *Hunky Dory* were baggy, he no longer resembled the Bowie he was publicizing. It's an overstatement to claim this article turned a one-hit-wonder into the 1970s' most influential rocker, but only a mild one. "I'm going to be huge, and it's quite frightening in a way," this immaculate creature predicted.

When enthusiastic press helped catapult Bowie up the charts that summer, another act of willful queerness transfigured the singer into a national phenomenon. This was when Bowie sang 1972's "Starman" on the widely viewed, massively influential weekly British TV show *Top of the Pops*. In terms of impact, Bowie's *TotP* dramatics are up there with the Beatles shaking their mop tops on *The Ed Sullivan Show*. "It was such a seminal moment for my generation," said Spandau Ballet's Gary Kemp. "For the Apollo kids, like I was, it was rock music from another planet, and I wanted to go to that planet."

When, on *TotP*, a particularly androgynous incarnation of Bowie twice draped his left arm over the shoulders of his similarly stunning guitarist, Mick Ronson, the pair presented nearly carnal familiarity. Was their unhesitant gaiety hip? Horrifying? A nation had to decide.

The already ever-changing rocker had been waiting for this moment. He'd released several singles under different names as well as his 1967 debut LP, *David Bowie*, while in his teens. He'd also studied mime with Lindsay Kemp, who briefly became his lover, and staged and danced in the star's 1972 UK tour. Yet nothing clicked beyond "Space Oddity." Issued in 1969 to coincide with that year's moon-walking Apollo 11 mission, it conjures a cosmic journey gone wrong through a tense string arrangement by future Elton John collaborator Paul Buckmaster. A UK hit, "Space Oddity" went largely unheard in North America until its 1973 US reissue, when it seemed to imitate Elton's "Rocket Man" rather than the other way around. Nevertheless, this single introduced David Bowie to Top Forty North American radio.

I remember the first time I saw Bowie's name in print, because it was the first time I encountered the word *bisexual*—I was eleven and just learning what sex was. If this guy with blazing hair and luminous outfits was bisexual, bisexual had to be good. "Space Oddity" became the first record I bought before hearing it.

I was born on the day the US first sent a person into space, and grew up with astronaut toys like Major Matt Mason and his blond buddy Sgt. Storm. What Bowie presented suited my childhood imagination: a countdown, a musical blastoff, and then a weightlessness that shifts from exhilaration to loneliness. "Planet Earth is blue/And there's nothing I can do," he sang. Even as a child, I struggled to accept things as they were. I didn't know I was gay, just "special." That isolated me in ways typical of my LGBTQ generation. So before I could name what I was, Bowie represented it. His space oddity was much like my own. And as it turned out, like a whole lot of other people's, too.

Simultaneously reaching ahead and behind, the glam that Bowie epitomized also found inspiration in the sybaritic art and nightlife of Germany's Weimar Republic, a sexually enlightened era between the end of World War I and Nazism's rise. Just in time for glam, 1972's Oscar-winning *Cabaret*, starring Liza Minnelli, summed up the Weimar epoch. Based on gay novelist Christopher Isherwood's quasi-autobiographical novellas *Mr. Norris Changes Trains* and *Goodbye to Berlin* and featuring tunes by Broadway's gay John Kander and Fred Ebb, director and choreographer Bob Fosse's voluptuously queer portrait of Germany at its freest is to glam and LGBTQ people what *Hair* was to psychedelia and flower children: a mainstream summation of subcultural currency. You can see it in *Transformer*'s cover, where a mascaraed Lou Reed resembles Minnelli's Sally Bowles, and hear it in Reed's 1973 follow-up, *Berlin*. "All that filters into punk rock as well," Pet Shop Boy Neil Tennant later noted. "It was a big popular culture moment, Liza Minnelli in *Cabaret*."

Like the punk movement it preceded, glam rejected the hippies who were still dominating youth culture, as affirmed by Mott the Hoople's "All the Young Dudes," a 1972 glam canticle Bowie wrote, produced, and sang backup on to prevent this rowdy band from breaking up. Whereas hippies honored depth and naturalism, glam embraced not only gaudy surfaces and willful artificiality but also those who couldn't conform to what culture dictates as real, which implicitly meant heteronormative identity and sexuality. "Dudes" rejects both in one verse. "Now Lucy looks sweet 'cause he dresses like a queen," sings Mott's Ian Hunter before acknowledging Lucy's fortitude and implicating himself with the lyric, "*Oh yes*, we can love."

"It's a Gay Anthem!" Lou Reed enthused. "A rallying call for all the young dudes to come out in the streets and show that they were beautiful and gay and proud of it."

Bowie drew directly from Reed and his queer peers. On *Hunky Dory*'s "Queen Bitch," he acknowledges both the Velvets and the Factory superstars who populated their overlapping worlds, repurposing an old Eddie Cochran riff much like Warhol silkscreened newspaper headlines. Unlike "Lola," "Queen Bitch" requires knowledge of gay culture to fully comprehend what's happening in it. Back in 1971, only LGBTQ listeners and a few other Warhol/Velvets fans would've known that Sister Flo is a trans, and likely Black, prostitute about to fuck Bowie's friend and that the singer wishes he were fucking this dude himself. "It could've been me!" Bowie bemoans.

Whereas *Hunky* reflects the songwriter's multifariousness—a thread borne out by *Hunky*'s US hit, "Changes"—1972's *The Rise and Fall of Ziggy Stardust and the Spiders from Mars* achieves far greater coherence. It's the defining Bowie album because it's the most fictional. Rather than just rocking out, he's playing the part of an alien rock messiah. It introduces itself as a concept album set "Five Years" before Earth's death, yet interrupts its plot with songs that blur the lines between Bowie and Ziggy, the savior this singer actualizes and praises.

Pop, particularly pre-Stonewall, is all about female objectification, so it was jolting for a man to praise another guy's physique, as Bowie does in "Ziggy Stardust." His protagonist is "well-hung . . . the nazz with God-given ass." In the album's "Moonage Daydream," this "mama-papa" yields aggressively, power-bottom-style: "I'll be a rock 'n' rollin' *bitch* for you." If you were a baby gay like me, these were among the many alluringly degenerate lines on the album that you hoped your parents wouldn't hear but inevitably did.

In a 1974 *Rolling Stone* interview, Bowie attempted to unravel *Ziggy*'s tangled yarn to queer Beat Generation novelist William S. Burroughs, whose "cut-up" technique of arbitrarily rearranging texts influenced Bowie's even more dystopian album that year, *Diamond Dogs*. More cogent were the singer's thoughts about how he guided his fans. "A song has to take on character, shape, body, and influence people to an extent that they use it for their own devices," Bowie explained. "It must affect them not just as a song, but as a lifestyle."

Bowie didn't tell us how to live, yet he set an LGBTQ-relevant example in reinvention. For boomers who adopted free love when it fit heteronormativity's confines, his oblique but bluntly homoerotic songs were both threatening and tantalizing. Even straight dudes who couldn't contemplate sex with other guys had to admit glam brought genuine danger to rapidly softening rock. Could they explain what *Ziggy*'s "Suffragette City" meant, or its relation to feminism? Maybe not. Could they get with lines like "this mellow-thighed chick just put my spine out of place" when the music was this volatile? Hell yeah!

Bowie gave permission. Along with Argent's "Hold Your Head Up" (1971) and Everyday People's "I Like What I Like" (1972), "Suffragette City" ranked among the relevant songs spun during fundraising dances held at the Firehouse, the Gay Activists Alliance's SoHo headquarters in New York City. Even its sleeve advised "TO BE PLAYED AT MAXIMUM VOLUME." You can't get more rock 'n' roll than that.

Ziggy arrived when analogous "gender-fuck" costuming spread through San Francisco, where the Cockettes and the Angels of Light donned dumpster drag in shambolic shows. Bowie similarly swaggers as sci-fi savior. But he also swoons with the theatricality of Anthony Newley on *Ziggy*'s "Lady Stardust," which uses masculine nouns to celebrate a graceful, long-haired "Lady" with whom Bowie is infatuated. This combination of lovely melody and at times howling delivery—another gender game—anticipates pop power ballads but with none of their bad taste. Abandoning Bowie's naturalistic femininity of the previous two years, Ziggy was audaciously queer, not a sissy. He and the Spiders sound as though they'd cut you if you blew them a kiss the wrong way.

Yet Bowie offered affinity on "Rock 'n' Roll Suicide." Much of his song cycle documents Ziggy's rise, but this captures his fall. As explained in "Ziggy Stardust," the Starman's fans have turned on him, and his band has broken up, leaving him on Earth to face its brutal normality in solitude. Bowie offers a helping hand to both his alter ego and to the misfit fans he knew would come with this album. Like a deity, he forgives their faults while acknowledging their shared bond. The track's pressure builds to the suspenseful moment when all instrumentation abruptly halts and the singer yelps, "You're *NOT* alone!"

This is the scream of the Other reaching out for another. It's the moment when Bowie's imaginary self breaks rock's theatrical fourth wall and bleeds into the bedrooms of besieged kooks just like him. Ziggy speaks to them, for them, because he *is* them. Outsiders the world over knew what Bowie's grandstanding gesture meant: He's proclaiming our estrangement and owning it. His conviction is undeniable, and LGBTQ fans, for decades, have taken it to heart. We're *not* alone.

⏭

Chapter Seven

Bette Midler

A plainly Jewish gal raised in Honolulu, Bette Midler struggled with—but was also motivated by—a sense of otherness and isolation akin to that of pre-Stonewall LGBTQ people. To overcome her shyness, she did what many of us still do, and compensated with outsized bawdiness. It has since grown commonplace to characterize plucky divas like Lady Gaga as gay men trapped in women's bodies. Indeed, before she morphed from cult hero to Disney luminary, Midler presented herself as a bigger, more outrageous fag than most of us. Check her early talk show appearances for proof.

Midler wasn't mellow or introspective or any other trait common to the women musicians who emerged in the early 1970s. This fulsome figure belted with more chutzpah than any pop star since Barbra Streisand. At the start, Midler's technique wasn't always elegant, which was okay, because that roughness offset her sweetness. Formidable lung power and personality allowed her to project forceful femininity so staged it constituted commentary on female representation.

Remarkably, Midler and some of her musicians got their breaks in a bathhouse designed to give men a safe space for spontaneous trysts. Opened in 1968 by bisexual entrepreneur Steve Ostrow, the Continental Baths—a sex club in the basement of the Ansonia, a residential hotel on Manhattan's Upper West Side—facilitated gay liberation in New York by making it far easier to have man-on-man intercourse. Bathhouses, like the Continental and the Everard Baths, offered refuge from the condemning eyes of the outside world as well as an immersive, nonstop sensual experience in which physical pleasures could overlap endlessly, like one record segued into another through a seamless DJ mix. Bathhouses were like discos of the flesh—often sordid, but still oases.

Along with a restaurant and other health-club amenities, the Continental added entertainment. When Ostrow's initial musicians split in 1969, he found their replacement at the Improv. According to him, Midler didn't initially wow patrons the way her comedy cohort Liz Torres did, but in her then-unknown gay accompanist, Barry Manilow, a jingle writer and trained pianist, Midler found her foil. Together with her backing singers the Harlettes, which included fellow future star Melissa Manchester, they combined girl-group oldies, contemporary rock, and then-passé Great American Songbook selections like their dumpster-diving drag sisters pieced together outfits. While embracing the side of herself non-fans considered freaky, Midler learned to treat young male patrons in towels as though their intimacy and mutual outlander status made them instant pals. That is proper bathhouse etiquette, and it cracked the code to the crowds' hearts. Midler's charisma exploded as she became far raunchier and realer than previous gay goddesses. Having reinvented cabaret for a post-Stonewall world, she generated electrifying gay buzz. Patrons arrived anticipating familiarity and camaraderie from not just other near-naked guys but also this female likeness of themselves. Midler and context became one.

Yet like most Manhattan establishments that attracted a gay clientele, the Continental was regularly raided—attractive undercover cops hit the steam room to entrap patrons. Ostrow claimed to have collected 250,000 signatures to change the state's antiquated laws on homosexuality and entrapment, but the raids continued until the Gay Activists Alliance negotiated to remove restrictions on men drinking and dancing together, which finally occurred in December 1971. Once Ostrow hired Fire Island's Bobby "DJ" Guttadaro, the Continental's disco also took off. When a spread in the February 1972 issue of *Women's Wear Daily* trumpeted the Baths as "the steamiest spot in town," gay chic truly arrived. So did Midler-curious squares, who alienated the Continental's core audience. In 1977, the Baths became Plato's Retreat, a sex club for hetero swingers at which gay male contact was forbidden. Midler moved on to her Oscar-nominated role in *The Rose*, a smash 1979 quasi-biopic about a Janis Joplin–esque rocker that would mark Midler's transition to Middle American mainstay.

Her *Rose* role fit a barnstormer who thrilled audiences by teetering on the precipice of control as if driven by emotions too vast for temporal existence, but even this didn't suit Midler as well as the part she played throughout her first and by far greatest album, 1972's *The Divine Miss M.* Like Ziggy, Miss M substantiated bold gay culture as it leaped out of the closet and into the public eye. Like Bowie, Midler masked her introversion behind a persona so confident it satirized itself as camp.

In Stonewall's wake, camp's mainstream presence grew, and Midler popularized it like no one since Liberace. As the theorist Susan Sontag, who was bisexual, wrote in her 1964 essay "Notes on 'Camp,'" "Camp sees everything in quotation marks. It's not a lamp, but a 'lamp'; not a woman, but a 'woman.' To perceive Camp in objects and persons is to understand Being-as-Playing-a-Role. It is the farthest extension, in sensibility, of the metaphor of life as theater." Midler pitted her womanly curves against her voice's manly firmness while exuding the bygone extravagance of such gay-endorsed artists as Carmen Miranda and Busby Berkeley, even on the Continental's small stage. Like her toweled fans, who sought romance in rented rooms the size of closets, she reached for glamour's brass ring within unglamorous circumstances. Yet she could also disengage with a vulgar joke. Midler isn't physically masculine, but her moxie defies and defiles gender all the same.

Miss M opens with her first hit, a slinky slide through Bobby Freeman's "Do You Want to Dance." Unlike his naive 1958 original, Midler's version exudes a been-there, done-that-and-want-more adult knowingness that early 1970s women were just beginning to voice. She sings it as if she'd smoked a joint, spotted a fine hunk of man, and savored time standing still in lustful anticipation. The melody wordlessly ascends, and with her "ah-ah-ah-ahhhhhhhhh" comes a key change, as if she and her squire have attained a heavenly plane of earthly satisfaction.

Midler approaches "Chapel of Love" with the optimism of the Dixie Cups' original but faster, more confident, and gospel, as if her belief in the sanctity of marriage was religion itself. Ponder the significance of Midler's reviving a matrimonial girl-group oldie in a bathhouse designed for instant gay male sex. To honor marriage for queer spectators, who, right there, could enjoy as much sex as possible with as many partners as they pleased, was not only nostalgic but also willfully perverse. In the Continental's context, heterosexual monogamy is artifice, while gay promiscuity is natural. That, my darlings, is camp, but also poignancy: She lionized what we could not yet do.

Pre-rock oldies rarely clicked with the counterculture until Midler lent them the levity Streisand progressively downplayed. Radio bypassed the A-side of Midler's "Delta Dawn" single in favor of her allegiant rendition of the Andrew Sisters' World War II anthem "Boogie Woogie Bugle Boy" on the B-side, making the latter a Top Ten hit. The album's other jazz standard, "Am I Blue," attests to Midler's queer allegiance as she asks, "Am I gay?"

The emerging star found what would become her theme song among the album's newest material. "Friends" appears twice: first with jazz pros, then closing the album with her looser, Manilow-led stage band. Each time, Midler's alone and making the best of it. Solitude means there's "no one to deride me"—a line that resonates with those of us called some of the slang dictionary's worst words. Midler parlays her Bathhouse Betty exoticism into approachability, as if gaining pals with every sprightly chorus.

Two "Friends" lines have aged disturbingly: "I had some friends, but they're gone/Something came and took them away." By the time Midler's popularity peaked in the late 1980s and early '90s, through unironic easy listening like *Beaches*'s 1989 hit "Wind Beneath My Wings," AIDS had indeed taken away many of Midler's friends and fans. Once a subtle element in its flavor profile, the bittersweetness of "Friends" abounded as it became a song of mourning and survival that honors the deceased. In the LGBTQ world, where so many of us have been abandoned by relatives, friends remain paramount.

"It wasn't bizarre," Midler said of the Continental Baths. "I could understand how other people would think it was odd. But I was in community theater growing up and I understood that world." She's never been a mere songbird. This pivotal figure, who united the legendry of showbiz with the latitude of counterculture, is nothing less than an LGBTQ community builder, and that all began in the gayest venue imaginable. There, in her untamed prime, Bette Midler was fantastical and fabulous—the Stonewall generation's queerest straight diva.

⏭

Chapter Eight

Labelle

Glam's biggest Black female proponent had queer connections even before David Bowie. While touring the UK in the 1960s as Patti LaBelle and the Bluebelles, this vocal quartet befriended *Ready Steady Go!* producer Vicki Wickham, future domestic partner of the group's Nona Hendryx. Its backing band there, Bluesology, included Elton John. Just as Aretha would make *West Side Story*'s "Somewhere" hers, the Bluebelles covered "Over the Rainbow," an eventual solo Labelle showstopper. After Cindy Birdsong left for the Supremes, the remaining trio—LaBelle, Hendryx, and Sarah Dash—took on Wickham as its manager, moved to London, grew Afros, shortened its name to Labelle, and appeared on Laura Nyro's *Gonna Take a Miracle*, which introduced the threesome to queer aficionados who followed the songwriter.

Labelle's rock-soul fusion is much like Nyro's own: vivid and individual. The group's primary songwriter, Hendryx, favors sociology over simple love songs. This emphasis on collectivity fosters sisterhood while showcasing LaBelle's biting soprano within gospel's call-and-response framework. No matter how low you set the volume, these women won't settle into the background. They wail, and you must pay attention.

The mainstream did just that when Labelle caught its eye with the help of Larry LeGaspi, the queer costumer for Kiss, Parliament-Funkadelic, and many others. LeGaspi formulated an Afro-futuristic look for the threesome that mixed feathers, studs, tiny mirrors like those on a disco ball, and synthetic silvery spacesuits. Introducing its tinselly new look, the trinity publicized its 1974 concert at NYC's Metropolitan Opera House with ads that recommended attendees "wear something silver" to mimic LeGaspi's garb. This formalized how David Bowie disseminated his own extraterrestrial glam through similarly attired disciples.

"If one wanted to be catty about it," wrote *The New York Times*'s John Rockwell, "one could suggest that Sunday's crowd was the Met's opera audience come out of the closet: There can rarely have been so many bearded gentlemen in dresses, razzle-dazzle sequins and arched eyebrows at a Met performance before."

Disco's earliest platinum album, 1974's *Nightbirds,* proved how big a record could get if overlapping LGBTQ and Black audiences got behind it. Labelle's ferocity finds flattering compliment in producer Allen Toussaint's New Orleans funk, which grounds Hendryx's inclusive rock 'n' soul as the Meters' propulsive accompaniment sprinkles gumbo spice in disco's melting pot. Written by Kenny Nolan and Bob Crewe, the latter the gay co-writer/producer behind most of the Four Seasons' hits, the album's "Lady Marmalade" sums up disco's spirit of sexual and racial fluidity. First recorded by Crewe and Nolan's the Eleventh Hour, it tells a New Orleans tale of a john who meets a Creole prostitute. She solicits her customer with pop's most infamous foreign language lyric: "Voulez-vous coucher avec moi ce soir," which translates as, "Do you want to sleep with me tonight?" Even in French, that chorus was *très* daring in the mid-'70s—particularly for a song that makes more sense if the guy hungry for her chocolatey good stuff is understood to be white. Returning to his drab existence, he can't shake the memory of their down-low encounter. Even in his sleep, the hapless john craves more, More, MORE!

From the syncopations of the Meters' rhythms to the punch of Toussaint's horns, Labelle's revision of the Eleventh Hour original is so soaked in Creole marmalade that it clearly sides with the sex worker. It imparts this shift with an additional "Soul sister, go sister" refrain that sets a drastically different tone. Right away, we're in a Black, feminine world where Labelle, free from judgment, encourages one of its own. Strutting onstage *as* her, the trio practically tells Lady M to take that white man's money and leave him begging. You *go*, sister!

Labelle proved just as flagrant on 1976's literally climactic, seven-minute ballad, "Going Down Makes Me Shiver." "I forget all my lost years/When I am kneeling," LaBelle sings; Dash and Hendryx emphasize that final word by joining her on it. Harmonizing like a sapphic gospel choir while wading in the waters of a lover's "river" as if being baptized, the trio leave little doubt that they're praising and participating in cunnilingus from a first-person perspective. Until the twenty-first century, no other mainstream R&B act would honor lesbian love this intensely and lucidly.

Later that year, the group split and pursued solo careers. LaBelle upheld her R&B presence and, in 1984, achieved her first solo pop hit, "New Attitude," with the sound of gay '80s clubland "hi-NRG," a form of accelerated electronic disco that's typically more pop than R&B and often features an octave-jumping bassline. Dash elaborated on the forbidden-love theme of "Marmalade" with 1978's disco hit "Sinner Man" before singing with the Rolling Stones. Hendryx hit her songwriting stride on 1983's *Nona,* which blends vanguard post-disco flavors to express LGBTQ themes. Although she confesses much about herself in "Keep It Confidential," she never assigns a gender to the lover who gives her newfound awareness, and so it feels as though her secret admissions correlate to sexual orientation: What goes unsaid speaks loudest of all. Co-written by the lesbian-led Canadian new wave band Rough Trade, "Transformation" enumerates alterations—including one R&B ordinarily avoids: "Cash a check, change your sex." Like Lou Reed, Hendryx sings for the transformer in all LGBTQ people.

⏭

Chapter Nine

Elton John

"It's a little bit funny, this feeling inside/I'm not one of those who can easily hide" goes the opening of Elton John's introductory 1970 hit "Your Song," but hide Sir Elton initially did. Forget for a moment everything you know about his trademark garishness and contemplate his first few album jackets. There's lots of beige and denim—little gaiety. For much of his early '70s catalog, the songs within were also earth-toned, yet rarely autobiographical. Even when paying tribute to Americana in 1970's conceptual country album *Tumbleweed Connection*, his sidekick lyricist and fellow Englishman Bernie Taupin imparts mythic, even gothic otherworldliness to the Old West and bygone South. Conjuring detailed imaginary worlds through compositionally rich and sumptuously symphonic talents rarely exceeded in pop, the piano man makes their reveries seem conversely real because he serves them with surreal levels of feeling. The bounty of Taupin's wordy poesy and the fulsomeness of Gus Dudgeon's production pull each album further into an extroversion rare for singer-songwriters. As word spread of Elton's showmanship, his presentation grew far larger than the personal life he avoided discussing.

Aside from "Razor Face" on 1971's *Madman Across the Water*, which offers love to a grizzled and quite possibly gay elder gent who's "looking for a place to lay down," someone who "needs a young man to walk him around," there isn't much tangible queerness to Elton's earliest records. Tentative steps to a pop-art presentation are taken on 1972's *Honky Château,* and its singles proved relatable to LGBTQ people. "Rocket Man" is sung by an astronaut removed from ordinary existence. When society kept most of us closeted, its axial line "I'm not the man that they think I am at home" voiced our secrets by proxy. "Honky Cat" tells the story of an outland lad who, like many of us, finds salvation in the big city's bright lights. *Don't Shoot Me I'm Only the Piano Player* furthered this evolution in 1973. Sung from one brother to another, "Daniel" was the closest we got to a ubiquitous '70s same-sex love song.

It's that same year's subsequent *Goodbye Yellow Brick Road* that flicked the switch from sepia to Technicolor for good. Rather than merely paraphrasing old-time boogie-woogie, as he did on *Don't Shoot*'s kitschy "Crocodile Rock," Elton becomes a genuine rocker here, yet simultaneously show tune-y—a combo that would influence queer rock musicals like *Hedwig and the Angry Inch,* as well as theatrically inclined LGBTQ rockers like Scissor Sisters. For the first time, Elton consistently captures the exuberance of his piano-pounding, Little Richard–inspired concerts, which chafed against his early earnestness. Recorded with the working title "Silent Movies and Talking Pictures," *Goodbye* serves as his musical coming out—a prelude to his personal one in *Rolling Stone,* first as bisexual in 1976, then as gay in 1988.

You can see that shift in *Goodbye*'s artwork. Clad in a pink-satin bomber jacket, Elton abandons the monochromatic drabness of ordinary existence and follows the bluebird of happiness into the dawning of a far-brighter, Hollywood-inspired reverie over the rainbow. He's not forgoing *The Wizard of Oz*'s yellow brick road, as the title suggests, but stepping right onto it in glittery, crimson platform shoes—the '70s male equivalent of Dorothy's ruby-red slippers. Its symbolism couldn't be clearer: The musician flees the drab reality he was born into as Reg Dwight, his birth name, and trades it for the emerging LGBTQ dream of a multicolor utopia he could only reach as Elton John. He's even wearing rose-colored glasses.

You can hear this transition in the music, too, right in the opening medley. A dirgelike overture, "Funeral for a Friend" can be heard as a eulogy for Elton's former closeted self, summing up the seriousness of his previous albums before slamming into "Love Lies Bleeding." This stately swell of rock 'n' roll shifts Elton away from a softy singer-songwriter into a genre-crossing genuine rocker.

The third of six consecutive chart-topping albums, *Goodbye* marks when Elton attained the cultural centrality of the Rolling Stones, whose muck he mimics on "Dirty Little Girl." More unexpected is the specter of Slade—glam's butchest best-selling louts—on the double LP's shout-along lead single, "Saturday Night's Alright for Fighting," and even Alice Cooper on "All the Girls Love Alice," which eulogizes a well-bred but licentious sixteen-year-old lesbian.

The latter song's illustration in *Goodbye*'s triple-gatefold sleeve further draws from *The Killing of Sister George*, a 1968 film that also features a queer Alice. Like Elton's 1974 hit "The Bitch Is Back," which set a precedent for the b-word's popularity in pop but bypasses its usual misogyny (because the singer calls himself a bitch and owns it), *Sister George* isn't remotely PC. Its lesbians live cruel, mutually destructive lives, and the song goes even further to suggest—as did many other LGBTQ movies of the era—that if you act on queer passions, you'll wind up dead. Still, a catchy, hard-rocking, lesbian-themed tune on a number one album was a breakthrough that spoke to LGBTQ listeners hungry for *any* likeness of our lives. Although Taupin's lyric shows little understanding of gay experience, Elton's music feels firsthand. Punctuated by pregnant pauses and peaking in a vortex of stabbing guitars, pounding piano, zip-zapping synths, and ricocheting sound effects, it's Elton's sexiest song. "If I give you my number, will you promise to call me?/Wait till my husband's away," he pleads from the perspective of Alice's female admirers. Here was a likely gay superstar singing about same-sex relations with first-person pronouns—*and it's hot.* When lesbians had no mainstream voice, this spoke volumes. I played this track obsessively at age twelve while reading the lyrics and studying the illustration to figure out what they could mean—about Elton, and me.

Goodbye set the musician's compositional identity. Even in its most contrasting moments, Elton sounds more like himself here than on any other album. His choice of chords and the notes he accentuates are as intrinsic to his sonic stamp as the jumps in his voice from baritone to falsetto, especially on the ascending title track. He fought against the single release of his most Elton-y song ever, "Bennie and the Jets," because he didn't believe it would be successful. Instead, it became, for decades, his biggest US hit. His exaltation of an electric-booted, mohair-suited singer who empowers fans to fight their parents' outdated morality couldn't be more glam. Given the masculine moniker and female pronouns, Bennie—spelled "Benny" on the UK single—might even be a guy Elton calls "she" in the arch gay way before vamping girlishly. Its slow and funky groove made "Bennie" an R&B radio hit, set a precedent for 1975's Philly soul tribute "Philadelphia Freedom," and helped land Elton on *Soul Train*.

Aretha gave her approval even earlier: Her 1970 gospel rendition of Elton's "Border Song" charted higher than his own. But Elton's connection to outsiders goes deeper than his R&B skills. *Goodbye* pays tribute to Hollywood through Marilyn Monroe in *Goodbye*'s original "Candle in the Wind." He rerecorded the song in 1997 as a tribute to Diana, Princess of Wales, and it became the second-best-selling single of all time. Giving Taupin's archetypes troubled souls, Elton situates both heroines in a lonely place beyond the status quo that's akin to ours. In his rarely straightforward music, you can hear the allied rhythms of their challenging lives.

Identifying with the glamorous and gutsy extremes of *Goodbye*, Elton broke from the middle-of-the-road crooner he was initially perceived to be. Although his queerness wasn't quite explicit yet, it was now thoroughly implicit. Even with Taupin's speaking for him lyrically, there's hardly a moment when this superstar seems straight in any sense of the word. *Goodbye* is where he truly transcends reality—the ultimate, if unspoken, goal of all minorities, and women as well. The dreams Elton John dared to dream really did come true.

⏭

Chapter Ten

Lavender Country

Until hip-hop arrived, no genre polarized LGBTQ people quite like country music. For some gays and lesbians who fled the red states or couldn't leave, it's musical comfort food. But for many of us who came of age in Stonewall's wake, country remains the musical voice of an oppressor still promoting regressive, far-right ideals of sexuality, gender, traditional family, and fundamentalist Christianity.

It's therefore remarkable that the earliest known album solely devoted to gay *and* lesbian experience is a country record. Distributed almost exclusively through mail order, because only a few underground gay bookstores would dare carry it, Lavender Country's eponymous 1973 album sold out its one-thousand-copy pressing—and then vanished from history for decades.

Its leader, Patrick Haggerty, boasts country-and-western cred beyond that of many conservatives. "I grew up in a barn, milking cows, listening to Hank Williams and the other early country women and men," the Seattle songwriter told me. "Country was the only thing I had any basic competence in. A lot of Lavender Country songs are three chords, and I'm certainly telling the truth."

His paraphrase of songwriter Harlan Howard's oft-quoted line about country music being "three chords and the truth" is no overstatement. The first verse in "Waltzing Will Trilogy" is based on Haggerty's time at Western State

Hospital, the Lakewood, Washington, facility where actor Frances Farmer was institutionalized in the 1940s.

"Back then, homosexuality was considered a mental illness," Haggerty said. "In 1966, I joined the Peace Corps and was housemates in Calcutta with another rural guy. Jerry was heterosexual, and we never had a sexual encounter, but I fell in love with him. The Mormon doctor working for the Peace Corps found out, and, 24 hours later, both Jerry and I were on planes back to Washington, DC. The Peace Corps decided that Jerry was not gay and that I was gay, and so they sent Jerry back to India to complete his projects and kicked me out.

"I was trying to get back to India, so I stayed at a Honolulu YMCA, a hotbed of gay activity. I didn't participate, but it caused me to call my mother and say, 'Mom, I gotta come home. I'm in rough shape.' So my mother took me to the family doctor, who decided I had a homosexual encounter in Honolulu I was blocking, which led him to believe I was borderline psychotic. He advised my mother to check me into the mental hospital, and I was too weak to fight. The sidebar to this story is that I never broke off my relationship with Jerry, and we continue to be fabulous friends."

In 1969, Haggerty was living in Missoula, Montana, where he was the only person he knew who came out in response to Stonewall. The resulting anger and isolation fed his activism, and that fueled his music. The two became one.

"What was going on in my mind was, 'Fuck you all. I'm not crawling under a rock for you,'" he said. "I was in the club of people desperate for information, and there wasn't any. God love Alfred Kinsey and Masters and Johnson, the sexologists. They approached the topic scientifically. But everybody else, I'm telling you, were completely fucked up. We had to create our own validity. We took speaking engagements wherever we could get them: libraries, community colleges, churches, radical organizations. We saw ourselves as educators, and Lavender Country grew out of that. It was about us, from us, for us—one of the first times when it was even possible for that to happen."

But the group's forthright queerness ruled out a country career. Only other activists would give the band gigs, and those didn't pay. Even with a graduate degree in social services, Haggerty couldn't get a job. Shortly after the album's release, the lesbian-feminist DJ Shan Ottey was fired from Seattle's KRAB, one of the earliest educational FM stations, for playing the song that would prompt the album's 2014 rerelease, "Cryin' These Cocksucking Tears." You can hear why she'd do such a crazy thing. Aside from the song being *really* queer, it's a clear-eyed critique of straight-white-male privilege, which Haggerty links to homophobia, racism, and misogyny. The sentiment behind its opening line—"I'm fighting for when there won't be no straight men/'Cause you all have a common disease"—wasn't new to 1970s feminists, but a gay guy voicing it so forcefully on a record was unprecedented.

"The point is, if you're heterosexual and white, that you tend to think you're entitled to extra privileges and goodies, that you're better than the rest of us," Haggerty clarifies. "That's what straight means: that sense of entitlement. You get to ride the gravy train. At the time, a lot of white straight men thought exactly that."

The album also includes "To a Woman," a lesbian love song written by the band's violinist, Eve Morris. "You've opened part of me/Made me free," she sang, just as "women's music"—what lesbian feminists had started calling songs exclusively played by and emphatically for women—birthed a separatist movement. Uniting gay and lesbian experience wasn't a mere art project: The year *Lavender Country* was released, Haggerty fathered and raised a daughter with her lesbian mom.

A couple of years after Lavender Country played Seattle's first Pride celebration in 1974, the group dissolved. In 1989, Haggerty ran unsuccessfully for Seattle city council along with three men from the Nation of Islam on a Black/gay unity platform. Haggerty, who spent a decade devoted to Black community issues, also ran unsuccessfully for Washington State representative in 1990. Growing interest in country's concealed queer roots, the official archiving in 1999 of *Lavender Country* by Nashville's Country Music Hall of Fame and Museum, and the inclusion of "Cocksucking Tears" on 2012's

Strong Love: Songs of Gay Liberation 1972–1981 coalesced into the band's 2022 reunion album, *Blackberry Rose.* Lavender Country paved the way for Lil Nas X, whose success means more LGBTQ country *and* hip-hop acts can safely walk down Haggerty's old town road. "He reminds me of me in 1973," Haggerty, who died in 2022, said of Lil Nas X. "This isn't the time to get tame. This is the time to get outrageous."

⏭

Chapter Eleven

Olivia Records and Women's Music

As the independent labels that ignited the 1960s faded, and the majors consolidated into the corporations we know today, record labels in the 1970s started behaving more like banks and less like artistic communities. The only long-running label that solely signed and employed women, Olivia Records, fought back against all that. It originated in 1973 from two groups of Washington, DC–based lesbian feminists: Radicalesbians, who'd attended the University of Michigan and recently moved from Ann Arbor; and the Furies Collective, who'd been publishing a DC newspaper and included Rita Mae Brown, whose 1973 book, *Rubyfruit Jungle,* was the first successful post-Stonewall lesbian novel.

"We thought that if women knew about being lesbian, they would all come out, because why would you want to be in a sexist environment?" Olivia Records cofounder and president of Olivia Travel Judy Dlugacz told me. "Why would you choose the other thing that was putting you down and not allowing you to be who you are? It wasn't like anybody hated men. It was like, 'This is so much *better*!'"

Dlugacz and her friends aimed to form a self-sufficient company that would pay and train women. Among this collective was Meg Christian, a local singer who specialized in a certain kind of cover version. She'd either change the pronouns of women's songs to address other women, or sing guys' songs, like the Temptations' "My Girl," without alteration. A canny choice was the Four Seasons' already-girly oldie "Sherry," with its refrain, "Can you come out tonight?" Christian honed her act at Mr. Henry's, the club where Roberta Flack got her start similarly reframing material in a queer context, like "Ballad of the Sad Young Men," an off-Broadway jazz standard that scans as a summation of pre-Stonewall gay life.

One day, a bargain-bin obscurity caught Christian's eye. The sleeve featured a woman "on a rock by the ocean who had her hands on her hips looking really sexy and tough," as Dlugacz put it. This was Cris Williamson on the back of her self-titled 1971 LP for Ampex, an electronics company that terminated its record label soon after releasing her album. Christian promptly featured Williamson's songs in her set.

Like some songs by Laura Nyro and Joni Mitchell, but few others back then, "Joanna," the album's standout, passes the Bechdel test. Named after the queer cartoonist and author of *Fun Home,* Alison Bechdel, the test is a measure of fictional female representation. For a work to pass, it must contain at least two women who talk to each other about something other than a man. If they do that, even fleetingly, then its female characters aren't solely defined by what they do for dudes. It's estimated that half of all films fail this simple test.

While honoring female friendship in what's ostensibly a conventional country song, "Joanna" also suggests that the title character is more than a little high. "I need to touch you, Joanna/And you need to stand on the ground," Williams sings welcomingly, while swirling strings imply that she's imagining their bodies intertwining in a way that couldn't be put into words. This was incontestably the work of a major talent, and possibly a fellow lesbian. It lit Christian's fire.

Learning Williamson would be coming to DC, Christian alerted her own fans. When Williamson—then without a record label, airplay, or promotion—played Georgetown University, six hundred women showed up, a huge turnout for an otherwise unknown talent. It was a night that altered the lives of this singer and her soon-to-be colleagues.

"Cris had no idea," Dlugacz said. "She just thought she had another event where she was the mysterious woman artist nobody knew. Instead, she comes onstage, and the entire audience went nuts. Cris was so distracted that she forgot the words to 'Joanna,' and out of the audience came Meg's voice singing the words to her." After the show, Williamson agreed to join Christian on *Sophie's Parlor*, a DC public-radio show featuring music and conversation by and for women.

The early to mid-1970s was a time of unprecedented success for female singer-songwriters with feminist material. Carly Simon became an overnight sensation with 1971's "That's the Way I've Always Heard It Should Be," which astutely critiques marriage, and her 1972 Number One, "You're So Vain," pokes holes in male egos with such veracity that the media scrambled to discover its real target. Helen Reddy's gold-certified Grammy-winner, "I Am Woman," was the fourteenth-biggest single of 1972. Having drawn the introspective blueprint for women's music with 1971's *Blue*, Joni Mitchell moved on to jazz with 1974's *Court and Spark*, which includes the gender-bending hit "Free Man in Paris," written from the perspective of her gay manager, David Geffen.

Given this success, the music industry should've prioritized female musicians, but many record companies still wouldn't sign more than one. Cris Williamson spoke of her rejections on *Sophie's Parlor*, and Meg Christian responded that she and her friends had started a feminist organization. Williamson suggested they start a women's record label. Aside from Christian, none of the members had professional music experience, and even Christian wasn't yet writing her own songs. But when this ten-woman aggregate met to discuss the idea, Olivia cofounder Ginny Berson convinced the others that a female-specific label could employ and empower women while elevating their consciousness.

Olivia wasn't the first LGBTQ record label. That distinction likely goes to Camp, an L.A.-based company that in the early to mid-1960s released two albums and several singles that spoofed gay male life and offered same-sex slants on standards. Although Camp's ads bragged that their records featured "well-known Hollywood personalities," records like 1964's *The Queen Is in the Closet* were issued without credit or with clearly arrant pseudonyms, like Max Minty and the Gay Blades. Full of harsh humor and unflattering language, these pre-liberation "party records"—illicit pressings of adult material—seem to be laughing at us, not with us. Yet the specificity of these songs, about cruising, drag, and "rough trade"—straight toughs who hustle to gay gents—suggests this satire is informed by personal experience, so their target audience would've understood they came from within our community. At a time when any LGBTQ content was considered obscene, that was enough. Camp risked arrest just to distribute its silly stuff.

Olivia aimed higher. "Everybody wanted to create something that would change the world," Dlugacz said.

"A socialist venture in a capitalist world" is how Williamson later put it.

Olivia put those progressive ideals into practice throughout every step of the process and maintained those standards for two decades. Considering that the label started when unmarried or divorced women often couldn't even get a credit card, that accomplishment remains monumental.

Almost immediately, Dlugacz quit her job. "'Dear Mom and Dad, I'm not going to law school—I'm starting a lesbian record company!'" she remembered telling her parents. "We called it a *women's* music company because we were smart enough to know that nobody would buy the music if we called it 'lesbian.' But we could reach women through the music and could change their hearts and minds, which we did for hundreds of thousands of women and gentle men."

Epitomizing Christian's gift for repurposing mainstream songwriters to suit a lesbian audience, Olivia's first release, a 1974 single, features her rendition of "Lady" by the City, a late-'60s trio featuring Carole King. "Do you like the one your beauty's been sold to/How does it feel when he holds you?" Christian inquires, as if addressing a lesbian trapped in a loveless marriage. She leans so heavily into the title—then a sexist put-down—that she sets it in quotation marks. Don't conform to an obsolete and false patriarchal construct of what it means to be a "lady," she suggests. Come out and be your authentic self, she's singing without saying.

In the May 1974 issue of the women's music quarterly *Paid My Dues*, Olivia introduced its platform to an audience hungry for it. "We are a group of lesbian/feminists who understand the need for women's music—music that speaks from all our experiences. . . . We expect to employ only women in all aspects of Olivia. . . . We recognize the importance of working out class, race and age differences among all the employees, and we are trying to create a political structure which will make Olivia a non-oppressive institution in which people can grow and create."

Advertised in the underground feminist press, "Lady" sold via mail order for $1.50, but buyers often sent $5 or $10, which financed the $11,000 budget to record and press Christian's full-length debut, 1974's *I Know You Know*. Subsequent Olivia releases would only include songwriting by women, but this one opens with a tune from singer-songwriter Rolf Kempf, "Hello Hooray," a recent hit for Alice Cooper, yet initially popularized by Judy Collins. As she often did, Christian flips its masculine nouns to feminine so the song's ritual of playing and receiving music becomes solely female. She magnifies the feminine affinities of Williamson's "Joanna" via vocal harmonies from its composer and rewrites Linda Lewis's "Goodbye Joanna" as an all-female companion piece, but stays faithful to Jimmy Webb's "The Hive," which describes a wedding as if it were a virgin sacrifice.

Christian's self-written material emphasizes the difficulty of being lesbian back then. "Song to My Mama" sings its way around the topic of coming out, just like its narrator stops short of coming completely clean to Mom. In "Morning Song," Christian lies awake thinking about "how hard it's been to let myself love you." In "Scars," she's haunted by "ghosts lurking in my nightmares that mock our revolution," as if unable to escape the twin traumas of misogyny and homophobia.

Yet it's the album's cheeriest, most "out" cut that remains Christian's signature song. "Ode to a Gym Teacher" pays pithy tribute to the acceptably gender-noncompliant women who are often the first role models for budding lesbians. "She'll always be a player on the ball field of my heart," Christian nearly yodels. Recorded live in San Francisco, with prominent background cheers, it's comically self-deprecating, yet learned: While delivering the nascent movement's first campfire sing-along, Christian name-checks bisexual feminist writer Edna St. Vincent Millay.

"Meg was the interpreter, the librarian, the voice that started it all with her love for women and her understanding of the closet," Dlugacz explained. "She was what I would consider 'old gay,' which was gay before liberation, and brought with her from the South a real poignancy and humor that was unprecedented. No one was gonna tell her not to be a lesbian."

A mainstream platform was not an option, yet *I Know You Know* did equivalent business. Nearly one hundred thousand copies sold via word of mouth, ads, reviews in the lesbian press, feminist and gay bookstores, record stores, and, most important, the singer's then-unusual merch table. Armed with a classical guitar degree, Christian preached the twin gospels of female self-empowerment and lesbian liberation. Although some fans had their consciousness raised only momentarily before going back to their husbands, nearly all recognized a part of themselves their daily existence denied.

"A lot of women were very isolated from each other," Dlugacz reasoned. "They didn't know there were other lesbians. And so they would buy the music, and they wouldn't be alone. Or they'd find out that a concert was happening two hundred miles away. They'd go, and then their life would change. Or there were women who didn't even think that they were lesbian, and because we were calling it 'women's music,' they had access to it. It didn't sound political. It just sounded like music."

Christian's success funded the all-time women's music bestseller. Another LGBTQ milestone with a transformation-themed title, Cris Williamson's *The Changer and the Changed,* cost nearly twice as much as Christian's debut. By 1975, the Olivia crew had shrunk from ten to five, and moved into a communal home/office in Los Angeles, where housing was cheaper yet near the music industry. This proximity didn't make the album's creation easier. Under ordinary circumstances, Williamson—who produced the album with Christian, fellow singer-songwriter Margie Adam, her recent ex, and violinist Marcy Dicterow—could've hired session musicians who can quickly conceive their parts because they're used to playing together. But aside from Carol Kaye—the virtuoso bassist on hits by the Beach Boys and other A-listers—practically every top L.A. session player was a guy. Training instrumentalists not accustomed to professional recording meant more time and money spent at the newly built Martinsound recording studio in nearby Alhambra.

Changer's ambitions paid off, particularly on its most orchestrated track. Written by Williamson, with lyrics based on a poem from her girlfriend, Jennifer Wysong, "Sweet Woman" is classic singer-songwriter pop. Yet within its straightforwardly sentimental message, there's a communal context. "I returned from the first National Women's Music Festival filled with such warmth in my soul," Williamson writes in the liner notes, "and I ran to my piano to capture the beautiful strength of women and its impact on me." Together with Christian and Adam, she sings, "Sweet woman, risin' so fine," not only about her lover but also all womankind. This was crucial, for it meant straight feminists could sing along to a lesbian love song, because it was also about sisterhood ascending.

As befitting a park ranger's daughter, Williamson comingles themes of nature and sensuality in her music. Before she met the Olivia crew, the singer, like so many then, hadn't yet defined her sexuality. She was simply a free spirit. Featuring the album's title, "Waterfall" speaks to that restlessness. It's literally about rain and rivers. Yet there's the suggestion that Williamson is also singing about female sexual response, especially when delving into untried delights. "When you open up your life to the living/All things come spilling in on you," she sings before further manifesting her metaphor in harmony with Christian. Other singers might've stressed eroticism. Instead, Williamson's execution casually flows in that direction, which makes the track more intimate.

Williamson personifies women's music, not merely because she writes about lesbians and looks good in denim. Unlike most folkies, her voice is even stronger than her songs. Throughout *Changer,* she covers a considerable range of notes, as if navigating winding nature trails, the kind that led Williamson to her album cover's literal rock. She sings as though she could move that mountain behind her. Despite years of vocal and piano lessons, Williamson doesn't sound studied. She's not howling, but there's a lone coyote quality to her singing and songs, as if she were calling out to find others like her.

In February 1976, Olivia assembled its first tour, which featured *Changer*'s primary contributors—Williamson, Christian, and Adam—plus Holly Near, a California singer-songwriter who'd begun releasing music on her own Redwood label. Advertised as An Evening of Women's Music but remembered as Women on Wheels, the trek was brief—eight gigs, all in California, encompassing venues as humble as the La Cumbre Junior High School in Santa Barbara, as well as the Oakland Civic Auditorium. But like the women's music festivals that had just begun, Women on Wheels helped popularize a new way of doing things. *Everything*—from the sound to the lights to the production itself—was done solely by gals for other gals. The final concert took place at the California Institution for Women, a prison. Unlike typical rock concerts, Women on Wheels lacked hierarchy—no supporting or headlining act.

"The conceit of the show was there are four soloists who can hold a concert space," Margie Adam explained to me, "and they are all doing something that requires stepping back and accompanying. It was a demonstration of women organizing together and activism as a collegial and collaborative effort. The first thing we did was sing together in four-part harmony." This was "Hello Hooray," which set the tone for varying configurations of accompaniment.

The setlist positioned the most universal material up front, then segued into more lesbian-specific songs, like "Ode to a Gym Teacher," which provoked screams of recognition when Christian embodied the coach's special admirer, the "girl who may grow up to be the *gayest* of all."

Margie Adam, who played and sang on *I Know* and *Changer* and wrote the latter's "Having Been Touched (Tender Lady)," was also central to the growing movement. She debuted in 1973 at the first women's music festival, which was coordinated by *Sexual Politics* author Kate Millet and took place at Sacramento State University. Adam then joined Christian and Williamson for 1974's initial National Women's Music Festival, at the University of Illinois. Like Williamson, Adam had tried to enter the mainstream. "But I learned that if you weren't already Nyro or Mitchell or King, your options remained limited," she said.

When Olivia's commitment to women of color meant that the label's next solo act would be Linda Tillery—who'd recorded for majors without receiving the attention she deserved—Adam and her lover/manager, Barbara "Boo" Price, formed Pleiades Records to self-release 1976's *Songwriter*. Decades before unicorns became LGBTQ culture's mascot, Adam makes that mythological beast a metaphor of her own difference in "Best Friend (The Unicorn Song)." "The others smiled at me and called me crazy/But I was not upset by knowing I did not conform," she sings of her imaginary pal. Peter, Paul and Mary covered it for 1978's *Reunion*, where it serves as a fitting sequel to "Puff (The Magic Dragon)."

At the closing of 1977's watershed National Women's Conference in Houston, Adam sang "We Shall Go Forth!" Although it alludes to lesbian visibility, feminism, and reproductive rights, her civil canticle doesn't name those things, but it demonstrates the communal determination and freshness of women's music as it was being invented, and is now in the Smithsonian's exhibit on US political history.

During the 1970s, women's music got no further on radio than feminist public access shows like *Sophie's Parlor.* With most conventional outlets out of reach, women's music events proved crucial. Lisa Vogel, who would cofound the biggest one, attended some of the earliest gatherings.

"There'd be a concert that would last two or three hours," she remembered, "and then everybody would go to whatever couches they were crashing on. So on the ride home, I started fantasizing, 'Wouldn't it be fabulous if we didn't have to leave?'" In 1976, Vogel, her sister Kristie, and friend Mary Kindig—all barely in their twenties—produced the first Michigan Womyn's Music Festival, which featured Adam, Tillery, and others. "From the very beginning, our vision of a cloistered camping community meant that we had to create the space," she said. "We had to learn how to provide the systems and services that people need when they're in there for several days."

With a two-thousand-person turnout the first year, Vogel learned fast. The second year, a Saturday night storm destroyed their stage. "But someone came forward to help us the next day," she said, "and that woman became our head carpenter for thirty-eight years." Vogel prepped women in all aspects of festival production. This meant hiring, training, and supervising a vast community of employees and volunteers who devised previously neglected services, like wheelchair access, signing for the hearing impaired, childcare, alternative medicine, and other amenities that later shaped Lollapalooza, Coachella, and Burning Man.

Olivia's initial success with Christian and Williamson meant that women's music became synonymous with singer-songwriter folk, which didn't require small armies of backing musicians. One woman with a guitar or piano was enough, and if a companion joined her onstage, that was even better. Yet early on, Olivia sought to diversify its roster, starting with Be Be K'Roche, an all-woman Bay Area funk-rock band produced by Tillery and engineered by

Sandy Stone, a trans woman who, prior to transitioning, had recorded rock royalty like Jimi Hendrix, Van Morrison, and the Byrds. Stone had transitioned in Santa Cruz and opened a stereo-repair business that became a de facto LGBTQ community center. This is where Dlugacz headhunted Stone. At the time, there were few experienced female engineers. Although some of the supporting musicians on Olivia's records are straight, Stone was, at the time—like Olivia's founders and solo acts—a lesbian and, like them, whip-smart, which made her a perfect fit, and a welcome addition to the Olivia household. After engineering albums by Tillery and Teresa Trull, Stone remixed *The Changer and the Changed*.

"It was meant to be a birthday surprise for Cris," Stone reminisced. "We brought in Meg and Teresa to sing an additional background choir and added new instrumental parts. But for some songs, we still didn't have the budget, so I wound up doubling and artificially creating some more strings. If there was a future for lesbian separatism and what that meant, whether it was possible for women to compete on the men's playing field and whether it was possible to touch people emotionally with the work that we were doing—all of that came together with that album. It's still the highest moment of my life so far."

This second version of *Changer* gave Olivia a record with mainstream potential. Yet the label lacked a national distributor or even concert promoters. Instead, Olivia drafted friends to produce concerts at women's centers, schools, libraries, and other nontraditional concert venues, and would scout suppliers in each town. These were fans who would sell Olivia's catalog out of their cars to every possible outlet. Because women believed in this music and the label's purpose, Olivia built up a network so effective that *Changer* sold five hundred thousand copies—far more than out gay men like Jobriath or Steven Grossman with major labels behind them.

The most famous figure adjacent to Olivia, Janis Ian, was living with her girlfriend when she made 1975's chart-topping *Between the Lines*. Its soft-pop anthem of teen disaffection, "At Seventeen," can be heard by LGBTQ people as articulating their own outsider pains, although she didn't design it as such. Shortly before the song won her a Grammy, *The Village Voice* printed a lengthy piece in which she discussed her bisexuality with Cliff Jahr, the gay journalist who would write Elton John's own bi-divulging *Rolling Stone* feature the next year. Ian didn't publicly speak of her sexuality again until 1993's comeback and coming-out album *Breaking Silence*, despite deep cuts like "Maria" on 1977's *Miracle Row*. "Oh, Maria/I envy any man who knows your name," she sang desirously. Yet as Ian told me, "Nobody picked up on it."

Feminist musicians didn't always get a welcome response, even from enlightened critics. *The Village Voice*'s Robert Christgau wrote of the Olivia-like female folk-rock trio the Deadly Nightshade, "I hate them."

"The lesbian movement had one place to go and that was to create our own," Dlugacz said. "We never existed 'out' before. Olivia was instrumental in making that happen. It was like we were all missionaries."

This success soon became a problem. Olivia had been producing women-only events as "a way to develop community so that women would see each other and be with each other," Dlugacz wrote retrospectively in *Hot Wire*, a women's music publication. Some saw this not as pro-woman empowerment but as anti-male discrimination, and the YMCA, the site of several Olivia shows, threatened to sue.

Others doubled down. The 1975 edition of Linda Shear's album *A Lesbian Portrait* bares the hand-stamped, red-ink warning, "TO BE SHARED BY AND SOLD TO WOMEN ONLY!" The 1977 pressing clarifies, "LESBIAN MUSIC FOR LESBIANS ONLY."

In 1977, former pop singer, Florida orange juice spokeswoman, and unctuous Christian crusader Anita Bryant launched the Save Our Children campaign to repeal a Dade County ordinance that prohibited discrimination based on sexual orientation. This caused a national uproar and an effective orange juice "gaycott." That's why the cover of Olivia's 1977 collection *Lesbian Concentrate: A Lesbianthology of Songs and Poems* features an orange juice can adorned with Venus symbols, and why Linda Tillery sings to "a sweet Christian lady preachin' hate" on "Don't Pray for Me." *Lesbian Concentrate* gathers Olivia's queerest material, like Sue Fink's "Leaping Lesbians," which spoofed Bryant's notion that we recruit straight kids.

"We didn't realize it, but every single artist had to make a conscious, important decision about coming out, and they heroically did it," Dlugacz said. Others followed. Right after Women on Wheels, Holly Near began a relationship with Meg Christian that culminated in 1978's *Imagine My Surprise!*, which consecrates lesbian love with contributions from Christian, Tillery, and other Olivia mainstays. Having emerged from the antiwar movement, Near sometimes wrote and sang with a stridency that came to define how the mainstream viewed women's music. "We can all be battered and raped," she chants in "Fight Back."

The dark side of women's music is that many of its practitioners and fans had indeed been battered and raped. Post-traumatic stress disorder wasn't the common topic then that it is today. Then, it was mostly seen as something men suffered after combat. Yet women in a patriarchal society struggle with it, too, and a vocal minority misdirected their anger at Olivia, and particularly Stone.

"She became a very dear friend to me," Dlugacz confided.

"We never had any conflict over my being trans," Stone confirmed.

But once word got out that Stone was assigned male at birth, serious problems arose. "A small part of the community became horrible and made our lives miserable for several years because *they* weren't ready," Dlugacz said.

She's not exaggerating. A letter from a then-unknown writer, Janice Raymond, arrived at the Olivia office with a chapter of her PhD thesis. The topic was transsexuality, which Raymond was very much against. "I suddenly realized that being pre-operative might be a liability," Stone said.

This situation became more daunting right before Olivia's next West Coast journey, which featured Christian, Tillery, and Trull. The engineer had hand-built Olivia's mixing board, which meant she had to tour with them: No one else knew how to run it. Right before leaving, Stone secretly had her gender reassignment surgery at San Mateo General, where she had to room in the hospital's prison ward. Nevertheless, Stone remembers much of the trip fondly. "Women came to those concerts who had not been in a room with that many lesbians before and were blown away by it," she recollected. "Some of them just wanted to come up and touch us to prove we were real. I'd never experienced anything quite like that."

Amid this euphoria, Stone got word that a lesbian separatist group, the Gorgons, had arrived in Seattle to kill her. "Their particular thing was that they shaved their heads and wore camouflage pants, tops, and weapon belts," she explained. Doubling as lighting director, Stone stood vulnerably alone at her soundboard in the middle of the venue. During the Seattle show, someone yelled, "GORGONS!" But no one fired shots, and the concert continued. After the show, Dlugacz hugged Stone, who was rattled by the death threat and weak from her surgery. "The next thing I knew, I was on the ground," she said. The engineer had passed out, but the tour went on.

An open letter to Olivia about Stone ran in the June 1977 issue of the Los Angeles feminist publication *Sister.* Decades before the acronym TERF (trans-exclusionary radical feminist), this missive reveals the hatred one marginalized group can have for another. "We feel that it was and is irresponsible of you to have presented this person as a woman to the women's community when in fact he is a post-operative transsexual. . . . When we did discover the truth about Stone and tried to discuss this with you, we were told that you considered him very much a woman, a lesbian, and that you trusted him more than middle class, heterosexual women. This was very painful to hear and indicated a great lack of respect and love for women and our struggle. . . . We do not believe that a man without a penis is a woman any more than we would accept a white woman with dyed skin as a Black woman." Among the twenty-two signees were women's music pioneers Alix Dobkin and Maxine Feldman, as well as Michfest's Lisa Vogel. Soon, Olivia was boycotted.

"We were being deluged with what looked like form letters about me," Stone said. "Some of our biggest enemies were the people who should've been our biggest fans but were jealous of the fact that we could make things sound better." The official story is that Stone resigned, but Olivia could no longer afford to pay her.

Despite 1978's Varied Voices of Black Women jaunt, which featured Tillery, Gwen Avery, Pat Parker, and Mary Watkins, Olivia's investment in Black artists didn't yield the same financial dividends as their white counterparts. Other labels would've forced their biggest moneymaker to compensate, but despite *Changer*'s success, Williamson rarely performed, because she was addicted to heroin. "There was no way we could build on that album," Stone said. "We couldn't put her on tour. We couldn't do a follow-up. We couldn't do anything."

When the boycott snowballed these challenges, Olivia struggled for survival. In 1979, the label's sole release was comic Robin Tyler's *Always a Bridesmaid Never a Groom*. That year, Raymond published *The Transsexual Empire: The Making of the She-Male*, which accused Stone of generating the divisiveness among women that Raymond herself concocted. Quitting music, Stone studied with Donna Haraway—a feminist pioneer in cyborg studies—to earn her PhD at UC Santa Cruz in the History of Consciousness. Stone's 1987 essay, "The *Empire* Strikes Back: A Posttranssexual Manifesto," is now considered a foundational paper of transgender studies. *The Transsexual Empire*, once admired by some, is now dismissed as hate speech.

Olivia's problems didn't vanish in the next decade: Teresa Trull's juicy 1980 disc, *Let It Be Known,* drew criticism merely because its cover features the singer wearing makeup. That year, Williamson finally released her follow-up to *Changer*, *Strange Paradise*, which ventures further from folk via Bonnie Raitt, who sings and plays on one song, and the record's producer, June Millington, former guitarist for the earlier all-women rock band Fanny. Olivia focused on Williamson and Christian—a label-saving tactic that culminated in two tenth-anniversary shows that sold out Carnegie Hall in 1982. Collectively, Dlugacz and the others sold more than a million records while pioneering DIY strategies that punk unknowingly replicated. Well before the label's innovations became standard practice, Olivia nurtured a generation of lesbians as it educated and employed them for twenty years.

⏭

Chapter Twelve

Queen

It's not often that a band features one charismatic showman, two virtuosos, three good-to-stupendous lead vocalists, and four smash songwriters. Blessed with cultish eccentricities, Queen could play anything and did so, much to the delight of several generations of fans. But this resoundingly British quartet ranks among the greatest and most successful acts to have routinely received some of the worst reviews of its day. The music industry had by Queen's arrival in 1973 sliced rock 'n' roll into tightly formatted pieces along racial and other demographic lines and, therefore, insisted that musicians stay in their lane. Even queers were expected not to deviate. But Queen defiantly did, via prog rock, glam, metal, disco, cabaret pop, and much more. Unfortunately, many of its original critics complied with the industry and penalized the band accordingly. Not until the 1991 AIDS death of lead singer, songwriter, and pianist Freddie Mercury did this change.

Born Farrokh Bulsara in Zanzibar and partially educated in India, Freddie Mercury wasn't white but Parsi-Indian. Nor was he straight. When the original group released its fifth album, 1976's *A Day at the Races*, he came out to his girlfriend, Mary Austin, and soon began living with his lover, Elektra Records executive David Minns. These distinctions sparked an otherness that arena-packing riffs and vocal bravado couldn't drown out. Instead, Mercury wore his queerness like an OBE medal. I'll always remember that horrifying junior high moment when a girl in my homeroom yelled out, "Barry's a *fag*—he listens to Q*UEEEEEEEEEEEN*!" Two years later, everyone else in high school did, too.

Queen's democracy shielded and supported its singer while he exuded fearless flamboyance on tracks like *Queen II*'s "The Fairy Feller's Master-Stroke," a detailed description of Richard Dadd's Pre-Raphaelite painting of that name. Had Mercury been solo, like Joni Mitchell, who was regularly quizzed about her autobiographical content, he would've had to discuss its punning allusions to his sexuality. Guitarist Brian May played vehemently as well as fancifully, yet sang understatedly. Roger Taylor hit the highest notes, yet his drums were engineered to give him some of the era's heaviest bottom-banging beats. Although Mercury wrote and sang most of the band's landmarks, all four musicians formulated substantial hits, even the member who didn't sing on record and left in 1997: bassist John Deacon, writer of Queen's 1980 funk-rock smash "Another One Bites the Dust." The resulting stylistic sweep and compositional aptitude added up to an all-encompassing aural androgyny.

These multifaceted, ever-changing qualities gave Mercury the freedom to express himself and his loves while hiding in plain sight. Queen's first international hit, 1974's "Killer Queen," could theoretically be about a high-class call girl. Yet listeners with musical gaydar can sense that it, much like those early Camp Records 45s, was written about a recognizably queer archetype by someone on the inside. Even before the single was released, Mercury told Eric Hall—Queen's gay record promoter at EMI, the band's UK label—that he wrote the song about him. Hall rightly claims it's irrelevant that the lyric uses feminine pronouns, because Mercury, like many gay men of his era, routinely called everyone "she." The singer chirps with a flirtatiousness that enables him to occupy the killer queen's persona as he sashays across the beat, spitting out tricky lyrical rhythms—"fastidious and precise!"—as if his queen spoke in syncopation, as if he's glorifying his own sexy self. "Drop of a hat, she's as willing as," he skitters like jazz scatting. May's smart-alecky solo culminates in buzzing guitar harmonies that swarm like bees singing barbershop to a nectar-filled flower in a Disney cartoon.

Debuting on the international pop charts with a song this flaming likely emboldened Mercury to take further chances. In *Races*'s music hall–inspired "Good Old-Fashioned Lover Boy," the vocal ping-pongs between Mercury's solo voice and the band's overdubbed harmonies. "Ooh, love, ooh lover boy," the choir sings, seemingly about a chivalrous gent, whom Mercury hammily plays like an actor in a bygone Hollywood romance. Outwardly, this boy is Mercury, who swaps between his solo voice and prominent participation in the choir so deftly that he dissolves distinctions between subject and object even more than on "Killer Queen." From within the safety of the band's sonic trickery, Mercury sings to *his* lover boy.

Few Queen songs have aged as remarkably as 1977's "We Are the Champions." Like its flipside, "We Will Rock You," it was conceived to inspire audience participation. As proven by its ongoing use at sporting events, it's seemingly a song for conquerors. This might be why a venomous *Rolling Stone* pan of 1978's *Jazz* sneered, "Queen may be the first truly fascist rock band." But considering that Mercury's sexuality became common knowledge in the wake of his death, and that students in conservative US towns still fight to perform his songs because he was queer, "Champions" can also be heard as an anthem for the downtrodden: us. The line "I've had my share of sand kicked in my face" certainly refers to Charles Atlas's bygone bodybuilding ads, in which a weakling was humiliated at the beach by a brute. As if addressing generations of bullied kids who would claim the singer as their own, Mercury adds, "but I've come through." Few would argue otherwise.

As he matured, Mercury's assertion of his gayness grew physically. Out went the long hair and flowing floral outfits that situated Queen in '70s rock. In came motorcycle jackets, bulging jeans, sleeveless T-shirts, bandannas, and armbands. When he added a mustache in the early 1980s, Mercury completed the "clone" look that originated in gay ghettos like Manhattan's West Village and San Francisco's Castro District. An inverse of the straight stereotype of gay men as emasculated, preening pansies, the clone is blue-collar, athletic, no-nonsense, and sexually interchangeable: If you can't hook up with one, others can readily replace him. It's a guise that went largely undetected by staunchly straight guys because it appropriated their machismo, repurposing it into costume and camouflage.

But in the video for 1982's "Body Language," Mercury pushed his clone persona too close for mainstream comfort. The set combines the plumbing and dirty tiles of bathhouses with the lit floors of discos as dancers strip and crawl in blatantly sexual configurations. Mercury cavorts among them while the band only briefly drops by, reflecting their nominal involvement in the synth-based track, which draws from both gay club music and *West Side Story*'s finger-snaps. Three big Black women decked out in sequins and feathers—looking just like Sylvester's background singers, Two Tons o' Fun—pull the clip further from rock and into disco. MTV balked.

The video that proved even more detrimental to Queen in the US is the one for Deacon's 1984 emancipation anthem "I Want to Break Free." It spoofs England's long-running soap opera *Coronation Street* and features the band in drag, playing characters hugely familiar to Brits. In 1982, the show's fictional character Hilda Ogden—played by May in the video—was voted the fourth most recognizable woman in Britain; only real-life royalty beat her. Despite the program's popularity in other English-language countries, it never caught on stateside. To US viewers, Mercury's outfit—which parodies the show's chintzy Bet Lynch—simply suggests a stock drag queen: big bosom, bigger wig, short skirt, plenty of pink, plus his own severe 'stache. In another scene, Mercury appears shirtless in black leather pants. During the ballet sequence, he's in makeup and tights. All this gaiety didn't hurt the song overseas: "Free" went Top Ten throughout much of the world and reached Number One in several countries. Here, it meant that MTV and other North American stations barely played the video, if at all. The song that became one of the band's most loved, especially by us, could only get lukewarm North American radio play. "[The video] was viewed as a valid piece of comedy in Europe, but I think in the States it was viewed as something quite shocking," May reflected in 1992. "The hint of it—that we were transvestites, or gay, or whatever."

Queen's earlier single that year, "Radio Ga Ga" (which gave Lady Gaga her name), was its last US Top Forty song. What would turn out to be the band's final North American concert had already taken place in 1982. But during the band's 1985 Live Aid gig in London, which gave 2018's barely queer Queen biopic its requisite happy ending, Mercury repurposed his flouncy "Free" arm-waving in what's now considered one of rock's pinnacle performances.

At the end of Mercury's life, the band further revisited its earlier riches. In its video for 1991's "These Are the Days of Our Lives," Mercury's finale, the singer is frail but vaudevillian, a tear-inducing juxtaposition. Following his demise that year, other Queen songs took on relevant meanings, particularly 1986's "Who Wants to Live Forever." But the Mercury opus that is most significantly reinterpreted in the wake of posthumous information about its creation remains his masterpiece, 1975's "Bohemian Rhapsody."

A truly rhapsodic journey through a cappella choral music, piano balladry, guitar fireworks, operatic balderdash, ramrodding hard rock, and then a subtle variation on its introductory introspection, Queen's quintessential hit—the costliest and most elaborate single of its day—draws from these divergent styles in a madly audacious way that speaks volumes about its era. Nothing tells you more about '70s pop than one of popular music's most essential LGBTQ records.

As its title implies, "Bohemian Rhapsody" is an over-the-top studio spectacular symptomatic of a decade crazed with froufrou. Sporting so many overdubs—allegedly 180 in the opera section—that the master tape turned transparent, it's nevertheless compositionally compact despite lasting nearly six minutes—a pop radio eternity. There's little repetition and no chorus, yet key and tempo changes abound.

But what the bismillah is it all about? For ages, the band guarded its buried treasure, saying only that it was the composer's personal business. "Freddie was a very complex person," May later admitted, "flippant and funny on the surface, but he concealed insecurities and problems in squaring up his life with his childhood. He never explained the lyrics, but I think he put a lot of himself into that song." The superstar's final partner, Jim Hutton, believes it's about Mercury's reconciling himself with being gay and sharing a coded coming-out with the world; an interpretation backed up by Mercury's pal, the knighted lyricist Tim Rice. This admission wasn't unprecedented. Early in Queen's run, Mercury told a journalist he was "gay as a daffodil," and later confided that he slept with "men, women, and cats." Here, cloaked in poetic metaphor and sonic filigree, he confesses far more.

After its choral opening, Mercury questions reality, then confesses to his mother—who was not supportive of his sexuality—that he'd just committed murder. But what he's really destroying is any notion that he's still straight, and he does this by having a transformative gay affair. Through it, Mercury's "trigger" gets "pulled," and his old self is offed. This proves so traumatic that he comes to the same conclusion that many LGBTQ people—who, even today, experience suicide rates far exceeding those of straight folk—still reach: "I sometimes wish I'd never been born at all." The ensuing phantasmagorical operatic interlude externalizes internal turmoil as Mercury struggles to accept his new identity. He cries for escape, but taunting inner voices insist he confront himself.

By vanquishing those internal adversaries, Mercury harnesses their power, escapes their constraints, and plunges himself into a fireball of man-on-man masculinity realized by the kick-ass section that still fires up headbangers. *Wayne's World* captured this adoration in 1992 and put the resurrected song back in heavy rotation. Once derided, the rocker was reborn as AIDS-martyred Saint Mercury. As for the hell that came with being both gay and Parsi, he gets himself right outta there. He skyrockets—as represented by May's ascending guitar solo—to a realm where he can be free. Across all religions, that's the definition of heaven. Rendered by the song's closing calm, it's a beatific place where nothing, not even sexual orientation, really matters. That's why the most ostentatiously odd yet covertly queer hit of all time also ranks among the most universal. It's the story of Mercury's setting self-criticism aside and learning to love himself. Who can't relate to that?

⏭

Chapter Thirteen

Patti Smith

Female rockers rarely drew attention to their difference like queer guys did after David Bowie came out. Just being a woman in what was perceived as a man's game was more than enough otherness. Even in women's music, the emphasis was on unity, not alienation. This is why there were far fewer recognizably queer themes in female rock and pop until the mid-'70s arrival of New York's Patti Smith.

Released on Clive Davis's usually mass-market Arista label, Smith's *Horses* offers an antidote to the aural faultlessness that Queen and so many others had been chasing since Phil Spector's girl-group symphonies. The pivot between classic rock and the oncoming punk revolution, Smith's crude but exhilarated debut draws from the gay Beat Generation writers of the 1950s, applies their jazz-inspired literary liberation to unbolted sounds inspired by the '60s, and becomes a '70s game changer. High art in low-slung jeans, *Horses* is impudently queer rock 'n' roll by a heterosexual ally so enmeshed with LGBTQ life and art that to call her straight would be a disservice.

Credited as "Gloria: in excelsis deo/Gloria (version)," the album's opening combines Smith's previously unpublished 1970 poem "Oath" and "Gloria," an early Van Morrison song first released by his band Them as a 1964 B-side. Because the Shadows of Knight imperceptibly sanitized a risqué lyric, their 1966 version became the biggest of an untold number of covers that made

"Gloria" a garage-rock milestone. But theirs isn't the best. That's Smith's—rock's same-sexiest remake.

The standard "Gloria" is a simple exultation of copulation: three chords in quick succession, over and over, with volume variations suggesting sensual tension and release. The latter arrives when the singer spells out Gloria's name and the band answers as if seeing God in a mutual climax. Smith's version frames this doxology with even more transgression: Heaven manifests itself in her love for another woman.

Over pensive piano provided by her gay keyboardist, Richard Sohl, Smith sing-speaks the album's legendary opening line, "Jesus died for somebody's sins, but not mine"—a paraphrase from "Oath." Years later, this childhood Jehovah's Witness explained that she didn't want Jesus taking responsibility for her sins; she just "wanted to be free." But back in 1975, those were fighting words. As the tempo escalates, society issues her a warning she doesn't heed; this gal moves in circles in which anything goes. As attested in her memoir *Just Kids*, she'd lived romantically in Manhattan's miscreant Hotel Chelsea with the gay photographer Robert Mapplethorpe, who also mixed iconoclasm with reverence. He took *Horses*'s black-and-white cover shot of Smith, her hair tousled like her favorite gay, French, nineteenth-century poet, Arthur Rimbaud. She's casually yet thoroughly gender-neutral at a time when such a look was expected of men but forbidden for women. When she hit the big time with 1978's *Easter*, her armpit hair on its cover proved as controversial as what was within.

In her "Gloria," Smith is stuck at a boring party. She glances out the window, fixates on a woman, and sees God in her face. Anticipating their union, the singer lingers on the details of this angel's journey to her at midnight, just like in every other version of the song. But in hers, Smith doesn't emphasize how this gal merely makes her feel good. Instead, she shifts it into a conquest. Smith takes "the big plunge" and makes her "mine"—an echo of her opening line. This queer act of love and sex and God proves so revelatory that she must tell the world about it, so the scene shifts to a stadium full of adoring girls, like those in 1960s newsreels who went apoplectic in the presence of that decade's deities, the Beatles. In Smith's reverie, they're screaming their own names at the singer. With this very song, Smith willed herself into notoriety. But she can't hear their cries over the bells chiming in her own heart ringing out in praise of her new inamorata, whose name naturally spells G-L-O-R-I-A GLORRRRRR-RI-A! Smith's love for Gloria, like that of her female fans for her, is *not* a sin. Jesus didn't die for it.

Smith later explained that she isn't a lesbian; her intention was to sometimes sing from a male viewpoint. That didn't stop her from telling audiences that the album's next track takes place "where women love other women." This is "Redondo Beach," a lilting, quasi-reggae song set in the real-life locale then popular with Los Angeles lesbians. In the song, an argument has transpired and a girl washes up on the shore, "the victim of sweet suicide." No male onlookers are mentioned, only women. Smith later remarked that she had been inspired by an argument with her sister, but by withholding this information, she suggests a lesbian lover's quarrel turned tragic. "You'll never return into my arms 'cause you were gone-gone," she laments.

What Smith can't achieve through vocal technique, she attains through feeling, cadence, rhythm, and vocabulary—particularly on the album's topper, "Land." What "Howl" is to Allen Ginsberg, "Land" is to Smith—her hallucinatory homoerotic vision. Like "Gloria," the nearly ten-minute track starts slowly. Named after the gay protagonist of ex-Beat William S. Burroughs's 1971 homoerotic novel *The Wild Boys: A Book of the Dead*, Smith's Johnny is cruised and abused by a hood in a school hallway. "He drove it in, he drove it home, he drove it deep in Johnny," Smith chants. Given the context, "it" could be a cock, a knife, a syringe, or, most likely, a narcotic amalgamation of the three. Regardless, some sort of rape has taken place. This traumatizes Johnny, who collapses on his knees, convulses in laughter, and sees equine visions that Smith conjures with such awe she can't always make her nouns and verbs agree.

Then she jump-cuts into another oft-covered oldie, "Land of a 1000 Dances." Unlike "Gloria," there's nothing outrightly sexual about this song that salutes the Pony, the Mashed Potato, the Twist, the Watusi, the Jerk, and other dances. But while seething with the surrealism of supernatural soul, the Patti Smith Group play it like the Velvet Underground might—erotically. This is not by accident: VU co-founder John Cale produced *Horses*. When hiring fellow rock critic Lenny Kaye to accompany her earlier poetic recitations, Smith asked, "Can you play a car crash with an electric guitar?" Kaye here updates the Velvets by scraping his trebly guitar as if clawing at a bug bite swelling with infection, growing itchier and more maddening.

The intensity drops as Smith returns to her original subject. Johnny lies in a coffin of sperm until a cherub taunts him back to life. Switchblades, horses, desire, and blood similarly intertwine "in a sea of possibilities" as the band ebbs and flows while different recordings of the singer's voice drift in and out of the mix, overlapping like ocean waves. Smith enters the narrative, her legs spread like a seaman, as if morphing into one of Burroughs's wild boys in another permissive universe. Johnny's cock hardens in the hand of this guy she's playing as matter merges into an outer-space sea where there's no line between psychic death and sexual rebirth. Finally, her protagonist disintegrates, dissolving back to the album's opening, back to Gloria. Closing the track, Smith shifts to the solemnity of a Greek narrator, summarizing what came before in circular fashion. A man dances—in the sheets, of course—to the simple rock song of which she speaks, supplies, and substantiates.

Primed by Smith's poetry in the rock magazine *Creem*, I bought *Horses* when it was new and I was only fourteen. Much of its subject matter was *way* beyond my lived experience, yet familiar through its references to favorite songs of my older sister. She was a dance teacher, so when I was a tyke, we'd bop in the basement to "Land of 1000 Dances" like those manic go-go girls on TV's *Shindig!* and *Hullabaloo*. I played *Horses* incessantly, not to just enjoy, but also to decode. It became one of the first records my mother hated for reasons I could barely comprehend. Soon after *Horses*'s release, I got a weekend job selling records at House of Guitars, a locus for much that was cool in my mostly uncool hometown. One day, my freshman English teacher showed up with her husband, a dreamy Kris Kristofferson-eque artist/biker type who wanted shopping advice. I suggested *Horses*. He told my teacher, "This kid's special." It was one of the first times I felt seen—and by the kind of guy I wanted to see me.

After she released 1988's "People Have the Power" and other queer-inspiring anthems, I interviewed Smith. I told her how "Land" affected me: I had regularly been shoved against lockers, as her Johnny was, by a bully who later came out. "I wrote that song for people like you," she responded like the mom she'd become.

⏭

Chapter Fourteen

The Rocky Horror Picture Show

Nearly every LGBTQ person of my generation has a story about *The Rocky Horror Picture Show*. Mine starts in 1973, when my local Top Forty station gave a few spins to a crazy glam-rock number about a Transylvanian transsexual. So I tracked down *The Rocky Horror Show*'s UK cast album, which, for me, was a far more fun and relatable *Jesus Christ Superstar*. Two years later, the same musical yielded a movie, so I convinced two older kids who could drive to see it with me. En route, we sniffed from a small bottle labeled "RUSH," a porn-shop approximation of amyl nitrite, that made me feel as though Pop Rocks were going off in my head. I loved it so much that I knew I couldn't ever do it again. Two of the few patrons at the theater turned out to be fellow drama-club chums. We all came back to school dancing "The Time Warp," but the movie had already left town. *Rocky Horror* remained our little secret.

Ordinarily nothing happened in our neighborhood. Theater was big at our high school because the smart/artistic/gay kids had little else to do. Yet when *Rocky Horror* became a midnight Saturday ritual throughout the US in the late '70s, it somehow found a home in our suburb, as did post-film gatherings at the nearby Big Boy. There, we met other misfits dressed in outfits that would've gotten us beaten up elsewhere. When I left for college, in 1979, and saw the film at the Waverly—the Greenwich Village theater where *Rocky*

Horror's audience antics originated—I confirmed what I'd already sensed: This was the first across-the-board LGBTQ pop culture event. It's not a faultless film, but its flaws still invite *Rocky Horror*'s groundbreaking crowd participation. We made it ours when little else was.

Patricia Quinn's Magenta lip-syncs writer/composer/lyricist/actor Richard O'Brien's vocals in mouthy closeup during the opening, "Science Fiction/ Double Feature," a move that subliminally introduces *Rocky*'s gender-blurring theme. Most of the sci-fi and horror films O'Brien lists as inspirations—like *It Came from Outer Space* and *Forbidden Planet*—hail from the repressive 1950s, when Senator Joseph McCarthy's communist-baiting witch hunts enflamed fears that these B-movies dramatized allegorically. Their battles with mutants, androids, and aliens were often secretly scripted by the writers McCarthy blacklisted. As with comic books back then, few adults took these movies seriously, so their criticisms of conformity and totalitarianism went unchecked. By citing those films extensively, O'Brien lets us know that, under *Rocky Horror*'s satirical camp cover, he, too, will invoke a similar beast—the LGBTQ "other." In art, as in real life, we're the so-called monster.

A stylistic descendant of these intruders, *Rocky Horror*'s Dr. Frank-N-Furter hails from Transsexual Transylvania, a planet in a faraway galaxy. Like Mary Shelley's Dr. Frankenstein, Furter creates life. His blond hunk, Rocky, looks like he stepped out of the muscle mags favored by gay men before porn's decriminalization. The humans are stuck in the same McCarthy-era *Rocky Horror* satires, right down to their old-hat songs. But the queer aliens have timeless tunes and foretell tomorrow's rock, in which sex and gender are nonbinary: Even its lesbian couple, Magenta and Columbia, bisexually cavort. Their pale faces, darkened eyes, and dyed hair prognosticate such punk and goth acts as Siouxsie and the Banshees.

Before preexisting pop song catalogs were regularly exhumed for the stage, musicals were theater first and rock 'n' roll second, if at all. *Rocky Horror* was the first since *Hair* that featured genuine rock about queer experience. Without this gay authenticity, no one would've cared enough to yell at the screen or throw toilet paper. In the late '70s, a teenage, pre–R.E.M. Michael Stipe, in full Furter drag, was captured on video by a St. Louis TV-news team. *Rocky*'s fans, he explained, "are all quite normal"—a statement that presaged how he'd later come out.

In the role that made him a star, Tim Curry plays Furter as a supercilious queer, with an upper-class London accent that US ears hear as homo because Hollywood has long given its villains this exact voice to set them (and us) apart from heroic, all-American heteros. When the band drops out in "Sweet Transvestite" and Curry drawls out, "So come up to the la-ab and see what's on the sla-ab," he sounds like every homophobe's perception of how gay men speak—seductively sinister. But he's not weak or submissive. Curry's alluringly haughty authority gave him a lifetime of roles that always retained a trace of Furter's mad queen.

His Charles Atlas–spoofing "I Can Make You a Man" maximizes gay inflections even further when Curry stretches "man" into an orgasmic moan spanning five notes. Furter argues that there's no point in becoming a bodybuilder to seduce other musclemen when he can just make one from scratch. "Don't Dream It, Be It" is not only *Rocky Horror*'s thesis, but also our own mantra.

Like Dorothy in *The Wizard of Oz* or Tony and Maria in *West Side Story*, Furter pines for a promised land, so he sings "I'm Going Home" much like they did with "Over the Rainbow" and "Somewhere." Nevertheless, he and Rocky meet the same cruel fate as many queer heroes that our foes deem monsters. That's why the film ends on a melancholic and not cathartic note. Furter brings liberation to earthlings, but back in 1975, they couldn't do the same for him.

⏭

Chapter Fifteen

Disco's Birth

Today, few of the records played in the earliest post-Stonewall LGBTQ dance clubs would be individually identified as disco, but, collectively, they pointed the way.

Consider what the Stonewall Rebellion Veterans' Association verifies as having been in the Stonewall Inn's jukebox when the riots raged in late June and early July 1969. There was a Motown bounty—several huge hits (including Stevie Wonder's "My Cherie Amour" and Marvin Gaye's "Too Busy Thinking About My Baby") as well as cult favorites (the Four Tops' B-side "Don't Bring Back Memories," an early disco mainstay). There were pop covers from *Hair,* and singles by top-tier divas—Barbra Streisand, Dusty Springfield, and Shirley Bassey; the last of them singing the queer-championed anthem "This Is My Life." There was breezy Latino androgyny (Chris Montez's "The More I See You"), bouncy R&B (Spiral Staircase's "More Today Than Yesterday"), racially integrated funk (Sly and the Family Stone's "Stand!"), righteous gospel (the Edwin Hawkins Singers' "Oh Happy Day"), celluloid symphonics (Nino Rota's theme from *Romeo and Juliet*), and, naturally, the Beatles' "Get Back," which mentions Sweet Loretta Martin, who "thought she was a woman, but she was another man." The Philly soul bravado of Jerry Butler's "Only the Strong Survive," also in the jukebox, would've spoken to Stonewall customers who risked arrest just for shimmying with same-sex partners on the bar's dancefloor, which was for this reason a rarity in LGBTQ joints. Even more relevant was Harry Nilsson's "Everybody's Talkin'" from *Midnight Cowboy*, the soon-to-be Oscar-winning film about fictional NYC hustlers that some Stonewallers would've understood as being about them.

Because jukeboxes could only accommodate seven-inch singles, every song was short, not the lengthy album cuts or twelve-inch remixes that soon dominated disco. They were sequenced by a sonically limited machine, not a sentient selector making musical and lyrical connections between records on high-tech equipment. There were agonizing silences between songs as the machine switched disks, not the continuous beat-matched segues and overlaps that mixers, multiple turntables, and in-house DJs would soon make possible. And despite their stylistic sweep, every selection was mainstream—none of the imports, indie-label rarities, or promo-only pressings that would soon distinguish big-city gay clubs from their straight, suburban imitations. As fine as these songs are, any barkeep could've bought these at Woolworth's.

Yet if one were to combine their exhilarating melodicism, rhythmic dexterity, lavish orchestrations, and lyrical relevance to LGBTQ life, the result would point in disco's direction. Mostly recorded by Black musicians and those inspired by them (even the Beatles here showcase future gay R&B star Billy Preston), these records capture the urbanity, internationalism, and gender parity of gay taste that catalyzed our autonomy.

Before discos, DJs played in discotheques, acting as a jukebox that could read the crowd. Sometimes these clubs were gay, like Times Square's Peppermint Lounge, where Twisters turned a tiny hustler bar into such a celeb magnet that it seduced even Greta Garbo out of seclusion. Like the Pill, the Twist defined the early 1960s, for it was the first phenomenally popular dance in decades that didn't dictate that partners hold one other. It doesn't require a partner at all. You simply swivel your hips, rock in place, and stick out your rear. This was considered delightfully indecorous—a welcome break from the regimented, repressive '50s.

The Twist generated several smashes, but the greatest was Sam Cooke's

"Twistin' the Night Away" from 1962. It wasn't the first rock hit with gay connections. That came in 1955, with the genre's genesis and Little Richard's "Tutti Frutti." Originally, that song extolled the best butts and recommended, "If it don't fit, don't force it/You can grease it, make it easy." Without those lines, "Tutti Frutti" is nearly nonsensical, yet still feels sexual and queer, mostly because a gay, Black, tornado of a man with a towering pompadour and blatant makeup is literally screaming it.

By contrast, debonaire Cooke captures the Peppermint Lounge's innovative nature with double entendres that wink at the in-crowd while bypassing censors. With Tom Wolfe's reportorial flair, soul superstar Cooke summarizes how the Twist began a decade of economic and gender fluidity. In a New York nightspot, "where the people are so gay," dancers dodge the tribulations that lurk beyond the Lounge. Inside it, a man in formal wear dances with a young woman in slacks. This was a no-no in 1962, when straight venues barred women not in ladylike apparel. Even in LGBTQ clubs, before Stonewall, patrons were expected to wear at least three items of clothing then considered appropriate to traditional gender. Fail to reach that threshold, and you could be arrested. Likewise, a denim-clad dude dances "with an older queen" in jewels. Even if she were a biological female, cougars weren't supposed to be this gallant. His voice bouncing and churning as his instrumentation exudes joie de vivre, Cooke comes across supportive, as if he, too, were twisting with androgynous chicks and diamond-rocking queens. The entire song is gay—in both senses of the word.

America's next crucial discotheque brought another innovation. When in *A Hard Day's Night* George Harrison was asked what he called his shaggy, gender-noncompliant hairstyle, the Beatle quipped, "Arthur." Inspired, Sybil Burton subsequently gave that name to a Manhattan nightclub she founded in 1965 with fellow English ex-pat actor Roddy McDowall using divorce settlement money from her ex-husband, Richard Burton. Although the club wasn't gay, McDowall was, and, as at most hotspots, queers and their deities danced at Arthur: Rudolf Nureyev, Truman Capote, Tennessee Williams, Leonard Bernstein, Julie Andrews, and Liza Minnelli all showed up opening night. What distinguished Arthur from previous US nightclubs was that its gay DJ, Terry Noel—previously a professional Peppermint Lounge dancer—mixed records. His use of two turntables to shape continuous collages of sound pioneered a sonic highway. He explained, "Many people would come up to me and say, 'I was listening to the Mamas and the Papas and now I'm listening to the Stones and I didn't even know.'"

Arthur closed a week before the Stonewall riots. But later in 1969, another nightclub became the first queer dance haven where the DJ overlapped beats to maintain tempos, rhythms, and moods. Located in Hell's Kitchen, the Sanctuary was in a former church, complete with stained glass, organ, and pews rearranged around a dancefloor. Its pulpit was a DJ booth. Sanctuary started out straight, but in Stonewall's wake, gay entrepreneurs Seymour Seiden and Shelley Bloom purchased the club and catered to the gay clientele of their West Village bars. Its DJ, Francis Grasso, was straight, but also a dancer, and he understood what emancipated gays wanted to hear: masculine music epitomized by Chicago Transit Authority's "I'm a Man."

Like other long rock tracks that followed Iron Butterfly's seventeen-minute "In-A-Gadda-Da-Vida," this 1969 remake of the 1967 Spencer Davis Group original features a beefy drum workout. But its percussion break also boasts cowbell, claves, and tambourine, which maintain a steady, danceable rhythm. When the rest of the band, soon known simply as Chicago, returns, it doesn't jam digressively like the Grateful Dead. Instead, it's tightly focused, like funk but faster. No one takes a noodling solo—even the group's shared vocal uprears manly collectivity. Although they'd eventually rank among the blandest practitioners of easy listening schlock, these jazz-rock hippies accidentally spawned the first kick-ass proto-disco anthem of the gay-pride era. "I'm a man, yes I am/And I can't help but love you so," they growl, as if speaking for a new generation of queers who refused to hide or apologize for loving each other.

While also playing rock records by Santana and Rare Earth that similarly psychedelicized Latin and African grooves, Grasso favored progressive soul that broke from Noel's pop. Post-Stonewall LGBTQ dancers loved divas and female harmony acts, but preferred them more womanly than girly—as if the lesbian civil rights activist Angela Davis were fronting the Supremes. That's the aura of a 1970 Sanctuary anthem, Little Sister's "You're the One."

Written, produced, and partially played by Sly Stone of Sly and the Family Stone for his actual little sister Vet, "You're the One" captures the transition from 1969's optimistic *Stand!* to 1971's ominous *There's a Riot Goin' On*. Writing from the viewpoint of an excluded Black other, Sly's universally popular Family Stone was Black and white *and* female and male. While many socially conscious songs of the era came from an us-versus-them mentality borne out of the gap between baby boomers and their parents, their sibling group's "You're the One" suggests we all bear the full responsibility of being our own savior or enemy. Vet and two other singers belt mostly in unison for a collective effect that contrasts with a declamatory yet introspective lyric that struck a chord with LGBTQ listeners claiming identities previously considered forbidden: "Now I know I got to look at me/Some things a little hard to see." Its honking horns, chanted vocals, and booming bassline feel assertively festive, like one of the Gay Activist Alliance's protest zaps. In 1981, San Francisco's way-gay Boys Town Gang remade it.

While Grasso entranced midtown dancers within Sanctuary's bloodred walls, an even bolder DJ held court inside his own SoHo home. Having grown up in an orphanage, David Mancuso fathered a wide-ranging family of choice at weekly parties that, in the absence of a designated name, became known as "the Loft." He threw the first one on Valentine's Day 1970. Like most of his patrons, Mancuso was gay, and he hosted friends across the racial, gender, and sexuality spectrum. Because Mancuso's home lacked the space for self-segregation, the usual divisions dissolved. Everyone danced as one.

Mancuso followed that diversity to achieve the cohesion his childhood had failed to provide. Like Grasso, he played soul, jazz, rock, and music from all points between, with a scope far beyond commercial nightlife's usual limitations. Inspired by the daily rise and fall of nature and his own journeys with LSD, Mancuso's international selections took revelers on a spiritual trip.

"You had to climb all these stairs, and then you'd get a tab of acid or a whistle at the door," Judy Weinstein, the Loft's mid-'70s manager, told me. "David played on what looked like a loft bed, and on the other side of the booth, there was salad, fruit, and the punchbowl, which was spiked with acid. You'd dance and be amazed at the sound coming from these Klipschorn speakers that faced the wall, not the dancefloor. On the way home the next day, you'd pick up the records you just heard."

One that initially proved impossible to find was Manu Dibango's "Soul Makossa." Originally the B-side of a French 1972 single Mancuso uncovered at a West Indian record store in Brooklyn, this hypnotically funky track features its Cameroonian saxophonist stretching and stuttering "Makossa"—a Duala word for dance—into hypnotically funky dancefloor Esperanto. After Mancuso shared his discovery with his DJ cronies, WBLS's Frankie Crocker put it in rotation, which triggered demand and nearly two dozen covers. For the first time in history, a gay club DJ made a pop hit happen—the song even earned a Grammy nod. Its impact soon went way beyond the nascent gay network: Kool & the Gang approximated Dibango's polyrhythms and stuttering lyrics in their 1973 pop breakthrough "Jungle Boogie."

Dibango's gay-propelled breakthrough caught the attention of Vince Aletti, who in the May 1972 issue of *Creem* became the first rock critic to come out. The occasion was Ian Mathews's 1972 cover of the Crystals' "Da Doo Ron Ron," on which the former Fairport Convention singer bucked convention by not changing the gender of a female-sung song. This isn't incidental: Mathews's a cappella rendition of the girl-group classic has sixteen instances of masculine nouns. On US pressings, Vertigo Records even added "(When He Walked Me Home)" to the title, emphasizing this breach. Distancing himself from assimilationist gays through derogatory language, Aletti dished, "Too often the songs that many faggots have chosen to identify with in the past have been disgustingly self-pitying songs that have accepted unquestioningly society's definition of homosexual love as not only tragic but doomed." What would become disco was already rejecting all that.

The following September, *Rolling Stone* published another prescient Aletti essay, "Discotheque Rock '72: Paaaaarty!" He wrote that "the hardcore dance crowd—blacks, Latins, gays" now packing dance clubs were already becoming not only "a rapidly spreading social phenomenon" but also "a strong influence on the music people listen to and buy." In the first acknowledgment of the as-yet-unnamed scene, Aletti spotlights DJs as "underground stars" who were "discovering previously ignored albums, foreign imports, album cuts, and obscure singles with the power to make the crowd scream and were playing them overlapped, nonstop so you dance until you drop."

Aletti had been spending his weekends at the Firehouse, the gay but exclusive Tenth Floor, and his favorite, the Loft. "To go to a place where I didn't recognize more than two records in an evening was unexpected and mind-blowing," the critic told me fifty years later. "The more I went, the more I realized how unusual it was that David would be playing Bonnie Bramlett, and Chicago, and Joe Bataan, and all this stuff that was not strictly R&B, along with these jazzy instrumentals. That's what really excited me, this melding together and hearing how one thing fit into another. Little by little, it became a sound—what people call disco. I don't think I would've gotten that if I hadn't been to the Loft."

Disco embraced the multicultural margins and made them central. Played by skilled session musicians across the usual racial and ethnic divides, it often came from countries previously overlooked by the US mainstream, and it was curated by DJs who were usually Black, or gay, or Italian, or Latino, or some amalgamation thereof. But Aletti aside, most media took little notice of these distinctions. Even the Philly divas of First Choice were initially deemed R&B. In *Billboard*, the music industry bible, disco was rarely mentioned until the July 6, 1974, issue, in which the Hues Corporation's "Rock the Boat" topped the pop chart after months of New York club play. "Labels Eye Discos as Hot Spots to Break R&B Product" was that week's feature story, reporting that clubs were making unexpected hits happen even as radio playlists tightened. In its July 1, 1974, feature, *New York* magazine observed, "Today's disco crowd is mixed prole, largely black and gay, and very wild."

Now, the music industry didn't need radio, TV, or print media to promote a record, or even a live band; it only needed support from gay club DJs and dancers. At *Billboard*'s first Disco Forum in early 1976, Florence Greenberg of Scepter Records—the first female-owned label to generate gold-certified hits—reported that her label could sell 150,000 copies of a disco record in New York alone, and without radio. Although this sudden development caught much of the record biz off-guard, labels large and small made pop culture's first effort to court what became known as the gay dollar.

The week that "Rock the Boat" topped the pop chart, another gay disco discovery, George McCrae's "Rock Your Baby," topped the R&B tally. The next week, it, too, reached pop's pole position. It would eventually sell more than eleven million copies internationally—an accomplishment still ranking it among the biggest singles of all time. McCrae's smash was written, produced, and mostly played by Harry Wayne Casey (aka KC) and Richard Finch of KC and the Sunshine Band. This racially integrated act fronted by a white guy initially perceived as Black released its first two albums without group photos before 1976's *Part 3* hid them inside a rainbow jacket. This marketing ploy of intentional anonymity blurred or buried the races, nationalities, ages, and even genders of disco acts that were often little more than overlapping combinations of session musicians, whose contributions were then sold with homoerotic artwork. On the male side, there's Macho's 1978 remake of "I'm a Man," Theo Vaness's *Bad Bad Boy* from 1979, and every LP by Italy's Easy Going. Lesbian eroticism graces the sleeves of Saint Tropez, Tuxedo Junction, Hott City, and others. Wild Fantasy's *Jungle Drums* from 1978 even has a gal couple on the front and a guy pair on the back—both faceless and topless. The danceability of a disco record mattered most, not the identity of those behind it.

These circumstances made disco the safest working environment for LGBTQ music-industry insiders. Back in the 1960s, record companies would hire "house hippies" to clue them in on underground heat. In the '70s, labels employed "homo promo"—gay promotion men able to navigate gay clubs, gay DJs, and gay dancers. From these positions of tastemaker power, gay men could exert and extend their influence without fearing their sexuality would cost them their jobs. Instead, it gave them insider knowledge and clout.

A former promoter for James Brown's first label, King, Tom Moulton followed the lead of early gay club DJs who used two turntables and a mixer to seamlessly combine the Part 1 and Part 2 sides of seven-inch singles like Brown's. In the recording studio, the former model similarly manipulated the mixing board to invent the longer and more forceful "disco mix," as well as the sonically superior twelve-inch single to accommodate it. Further replicating the nonstop, DJ-mixed club experience, Moulton segued the first three songs of Gloria Gaynor's 1975 debut *Never Can Say Goodbye* together for a continuous, eighteen-minute LP side. These achievements secured Moulton's status as disco's most prolific early mixer. He would also become a *Billboard* columnist, Grace Jones's record producer, and the head of his own label, Tom n' Jerry—an offshoot of disco's first crucial record company, Salsoul, which often released his work. "A Tom Moulton Mix" meant certain disco suitability.

Because they possessed the deftest mixing skills at the hottest clubs, gay DJs typically got the top remixing gigs of the disco era. Walter Gibbons mixed the first commercially released US twelve-inch single, Double Exposure's "Ten Percent," in 1976. David Todd went from Fire Island's Ice Palace to an A&R gig at RCA Records, where he mixed, among many others, the twelve-inch version of Evelyn "Champagne" King's 1977 hit "Shame," which replaced the original mix on her gold album *Smooth Talk*. A myriad of gay DJs-turned-remixers followed, including Tom Savarese (Chic's "Dance, Dance, Dance [Yowsah, Yowsah, Yowsah]," 1977), Jim Burgess (Rod Stewart's "Do Ya Think I'm Sexy?," 1978), and Larry Levan (Instant Funk's "I Got My Mind Made Up," 1978).

Their largely extended, club-conscious, and, therefore, more-physical mixes brought the gay experience of disco right into the music itself, which now moved like our bodies on the dancefloor. In a disco remix, string and horn crescendos grow more palatial, boosted bass-guitar runs reverberate even at low volume, and extended drum breaks—disco's orgasmic release—send dancers into fits of fist-pumping and ass-shaking. Once dismissed as "jungle music," R&B, in this heightened setting, further accentuates African and

Latin American syncopation as its disco stepchild beefs up and prolongs the percussion.

Rock critics harped on what they perceived as disco's escapism. But if your main conflict in life is a love that society condemns and tries to stop you from expressing, disco offers the opposite of escape. It's an arrival—one that gave a generation of LGBTQ people permission to be ourselves in a public of our own. Dancing becomes not a prelude to something else, like finding a lifelong mate, but a means to communal, night-long bliss. To dance is to liberate.

Disco codified gay-male taste and ritualized our consumption. We'd been secretly supporting divas for decades, but with disco, we openly worshipped them in our own spaces with the hippest heteros, because our clubs were more forward than theirs. It's not an exaggeration to say that for a solid decade, wherever queers and allies met, there was disco. It soundtracked our revolution like nothing else before or since, and opened the door to broader expression for everyone. Stepping outside your usual orientation at a sports bar could be greeted by a beating or worse. Where bodies do the talking, disco allows straight dancers to not be so narrow. They see us at our best and follow our freer example.

Disco became the first and, for decades, only genre in which women proved more popular than men. *Many* disco divas and soul sisters sang for us, like Candi Staton ("Young Hearts Run Free," 1976), Chaka Khan ("I'm Every Woman," 1978), and Jackie Moore ("This Time Baby," 1979). Articulating an agency that LGBTQ people then rarely possessed, divas facilitated queer emergence and empowerment by privileging liberating femininity. But none have embodied LGBTQ freedoms—as well as their backlash—as much as disco's most complex and contradictory figure.

⏭

Chapter Sixteen

Donna Summer

"I do not sing; I act," Donna Summer wrote in her autobiography. Whereas soul stars are honored as exemplars of authenticity expressing autobiographical pains, disco's prima Donna summoned the sighing pleasure of her breakthrough hit, 1975's apocalyptically carnal "Love to Love You Baby," while pretending she was someone else: Marilyn Monroe. The song's breathy excess made it ripe drag fodder—so much so that this former background singer was rumored to be a man.

These thespian skills enabled Summer to pioneer the role of dance-pop superstar as ever-changing performance artist. Unlike most Black women of her era, Summer co-wrote nearly all her hits. Following her epochal, seventeen-minute version of "Love to Love You Baby," Summer pioneered disco as an album medium, not merely a means to generate singles. Most of her greatest releases are concept LPs that link songs lyrically and musically like the best DJs. Showcasing the similarly whopping sequel "Try Me, I Know We Can Make It," 1976's *A Love Trilogy* amalgamates earthy eroticism and heavenly sanctity; Barry Manilow's best ballad, 1975's "Could It Be Magic," gets reinterpreted as a holy disco hymnal. *Four Seasons of Love* from 1976 contrasts relationship stages, while 1977's *I Remember Yesterday* presents a chronological history of twentieth-century Black music. Aside from her weepy "Can't We Just Sit Down (And Talk It Over)," it's all disco-grounded—especially that single's B-side, which was flipped to popularize one of the most eruptive recordings of all time, "I Feel Love."

This largely nostalgic album's culminating futuristic cut doesn't include much more, lyrically, than another luscious Munich disco concoction, Silver Convention's Grammy-winning "Fly, Robin, Fly" from 1975. Nearly detached from language, her body, and reality, Summer sings in head tones, like male falsettos, to an unspecified "you"—maybe a robot or a full-body vibrator. During the verses, most of her vocal melody descends as she croons triplets at the top of her range against the ticking sixteenth notes of a modular Moog IIIp synthesizer. This generates a rhythmic disjunct between what she sings and her four-squared synth accompaniment. When the chorus comes, everything ascends to the cosmos, or into pure imagination. "I feel laaaaaaaa-haaaaaaaa-haaaaaaaa-haaaaaaaave!" she glides, as if floating on waves so ecstatic they no longer feel terrestrial. "I Feel Love" posits a utopia of spirit that can still fill us with wonder. "I have heard the sound of the future," electronic music pathfinder Brian Eno told David Bowie after hearing it. If we trace *I Remember Yesterday*'s Black pop narrative through jubilant jazz, girl-group heartbreak, Motown rebound, Blaxploitation funk, hedonic disco, and slow-jamming soul, it follows that the sci-fi hereafter represented by "I Feel Love" is Black as well. Summer situated her Valhalla of electro-love in a transatlantic African Tomorrowland and gave us all a one-way ticket.

Magnifying the *Star Wars*–induced intergalactic vibe of 1977, "I Feel Love" blueprinted what was to come in both Black-originated sounds, like techno and house, and in LGBTQ-dominant ones, like synthpop and hi-NRG—styles that, like disco itself, sprang from overlapping Black and queer identities and communities. Her first pop smash since "Love to Love You Baby," it climbed the charts just as LGBTQ culture achieved another landmark: Anti-gay crusader Anita Bryant got a pie in the face. Evoking the street theater of the Gay Activists Alliance, this childish but inspired prank—along with our nationwide Florida orange juice boycott—helped turn sentiment against Bryant and what she represented. Today, this might seem like a small thing, but it marked the first time our protests persuaded much of the US media and public to decry antigay mistreatment. The unexpected popularity of "I Feel Love" similarly propelled Summer's musicality, which grew more chimerical as she moved Top Forty disco closer to the worldly extravagance favored in gay clubs.

Bolstered by her new gay arranger, Bob Esty, 1977's *Once Upon a Time . . .* features Summer's fullest, most gay-coded narrative. It's a modern Cinderella story that contrasts the darkness of day-to-day existence with the vibrance of dreams and salvation of love. Leading the nonstop, side-long Act 1 suite, the title cut sets a jittery tone familiar to those in the closet. "Hiding from reality, treated like a stranger," Summer paints her protagonist. "Faster and Faster to Nowhere" heightens her desperation, and so she flees into a "Fairy Tale High" until plunged back into the reality of "Say Something Nice." No one does.

Act 2 picks up where the synths and strenuousness of "I Feel Love" left off. Accompanied by a somber gothic choir, "Now I Need You" sends out a prayer for a prior lover's help. It doesn't arrive, so "Working the Midnight Shift" emphasizes, through even icier electronics, her protagonist's withdrawal. Portraying an industrious adult through the belabored voice of a bruised inner child, Summer makes producer and co-writer Giorgio Moroder's disco bluesy. "My body still carries on/But I'm dying inside," she sighs. On the chorus, similarly ghostly background vocals lag like a reverberation, as if the city were a cave where only echoes hear her cries. "Queen for a Day" honors disco's liberation by depicting how Summer's heroine transforms herself into royalty. Referencing glass shoes and other finery, the singer poeticizes the LGBTQ experience of the 1970s, when most of us, like Cinderella, could only realize our true selves at night, in secret, on the dancefloor. "Dressed head to toe so you'd never know it's me," she sings suggesting drag. Moroder then swaps his synths for Esty's orchestrations, as if lifting a veil from the true self Summer hid for much of Act 2.

This shift sets up Act 3, when Summer's protagonist further asserts previously veiled passions through the sashaying funk of "If You Got It Flaunt It" to lure her potential prince—who materializes on "A Man Like You"—only to lose him as "Dance into My Life" fades. Although she begins the album with little-girl-lost variations on the sex-kitten purr of "Love to Love You Baby," Summer celebrates her reunion with the prince by belting Act 4's continuous suite ("Rumour Has It," "I Love You," and "Happily Ever After") with the composure of a Broadway leading lady and the power of a gospel gal. This is the ballsy, in-command voice she brings to her hit streak at disco's peak. Forgoing the submissiveness of her earlier material, Summer—if we were to characterize her in sexual role-playing terms—switches from being a musical bottom to a top.

Rather than setting her hopes on a lifelong mate, Summer in 1979 went on a musical manhunt in search of "Hot Stuff." Merging disco's thumps with rock's growling guitars, Summer smashed gender and racial norms with a force unprecedented atop the pop chart. Just as she'd assumed passive modes with such commitment that even *Time* claimed she orgasmed twenty-two times during "Love to Love You Baby," Summer here plays the aggressor with a thirst for immediate sexual satisfaction so transgressive and liberating that she wowed even the stodgy Recording Academy, nabbing the first Best Female *Rock* Vocal Grammy. "Wanna bring a wild man back home!" she whoops.

Summer is loving herself—not necessarily through sex but through self-esteem—a message we heard loud and clear, as if sent directly to us. "I let go long enough to show all the things I've been told since childhood to keep secret," Summer told *Time*. That sums up Summer's LGBTQ appeal. She was referring to "Love to Love You Baby" but could've been talking about her entire disco oeuvre. Through a multitude of voices and personas, she enacted what we were taught to repress.

In one of pop's greatest one-two punches, "Hot Stuff" segues nonstop on *Bad Girls* into the title track. Inspired by a police officer mistaking a Black secretary at Casablanca, her label, for a prostitute, Summer inclines further into soul to describe Black experience. "Now you and me, we're both the same," she sings to her bad girl, the Black female listener, and us—we're bad girls, too. On the bridge, the perspective shifts to first person as Summer struts for potential johns while drawing further parallels between prostitution and pop stardom. As in Labelle's "Lady Marmalade," "Bad Girls" lacks condemnation. Instead, there's solidarity, and in the song's unblushing groove, a defiance that LGBTQ people know well. The song Summer initially shelved, because she refused to give it to Cher, became her biggest hit.

But like so many divas, Summer secretly struggled. Throughout her 2003 autobiography, *Ordinary Girl: The Journey*, Summer bristles at the sexual persona she claims Casablanca foisted upon her. Most of her greatest performances are those in which she's fighting against adversity. In "Last Dance," from the 1978 film *Thank God It's Friday*, romance must be consummated on the disco floor minutes before closing time. In 1979's "No More Tears (Enough Is Enough)," she and Barbra Streisand show jerky dudes the door.

This strife culminates in her LP-side-long rendition of "MacArthur Park," on which Summer and her studio henchmen reshape Richard Harris's already epic Jimmy Webb–penned 1968 hit into an even grander 1978 suite of suffering and transcendence. Adding "One of a Kind" and "Heaven Knows," Summer tries to stitch together a romance that can never be reconciled. Infamously symbolized, by Webb's derided but unforgettable metaphor for lost love, as a cake left out in the rain, the tragedy of this wasted affair is rendered with so much feeling and poise that its beauty is almost overwhelming. When AIDS hit and gay life itself became similarly cataclysmic, this beauty turned to pain. Even now, Summer's "MacArthur Park" can bring a gay dancefloor to tears.

And with AIDS, the singer's relationship to her original audience became that rain-soaked cake. Make no mistake: Summer knew who her fans were. In the January 1976 issue of Andy Warhol's *Interview,* Lance Loud—who in 1973's *An American Family* became the first out gay reality-TV star—told Summer that when "Love to Love You Baby" came on at Manhattan's 12 West, "there was literally an explosion of snapping and popping, just like the Fourth of July." When he clarified that he was talking about the use of amyl nitrite poppers in gay discos, Summer retorts, "GAY DISCOS?!? Honey, I don't believe I've ever been in anything BUT gay discos. There AIN'T any other kind!"

In the July 5, 1983, issue of *The Village Voice*, critic Jim Feldman captured a different side to the singer. He wrote, "Donna Summer made an incredibly rude, gratuitous, and lame antigay crack during her show at Resorts International in Atlantic City June 20—you know, 'Adam and Eve, not Adam and Steve.' Then she added, 'But I love you anyway.'" The singer had just released "She Works Hard for the Money," a feisty fusion of rock, soul, and hi-NRG. Because her feminist lyric insisted "you better treat her right" with a forthrightness that mirrored women's music, the song won approval across the LGBTQ spectrum. I know this, because I danced to it down Fifth Avenue during that June's Pride march. Like your initial sexual experience, you don't forget the first time you publicly proclaim who you are.

The slogan "God made Adam and Eve, not Adam and Steve" goes back at least as far as a picket sign at a 1977 antigay rally covered by *The New York Times*. Shortly after, Anita Bryant paraphrased it, then televangelist Jerry Falwell repeated it ad nauseam. While Summer was feeling suicidal over career pressures, drug reliance, and longtime insecurities, she became born again, sued Casablanca, and left both it and her longtime manager.

Gay music magnate David Geffen made Summer the first artist on his new label, Geffen Records, with 1980's pop-rocky *The Wanderer*, which maintains her relationship with Moroder and co-writer/co-producer Pete Bellotte but begins her break from disco. Geffen canceled its intended successor, *I'm a Rainbow*, before completion and insisted the star change producers. Quincy Jones brought higher R&B peaks to 1982's *Donna Summer*, but the studio legend couldn't maintain the metric he set with Michael Jackson. Yet Summer still sings triumphantly, and on "Lush Life," the standard by Duke Ellington's queer collaborator Billy Strayhorn, aptly. "I used to visit all the very gay places," she serenades.

As the 1980s progressed, unfounded rumors spread that—like Falwell and other fundamentalists—Summer believed AIDS was divine retribution against us. Making matters worse was that she no longer wrote like a renegade. Freed from the sexual provocation she now regretted, Summer toned down her presentation and distanced herself from the songs we loved. "I don't do them the way I used to do them and eventually I will cast them out," she told *The Washington Post* in 1981 with hard to miss biblical language. She found the Christian collaborator she was looking for in *Money*'s soft-rocker Michael Omartian. Another side to Summer emerged via unmissable religiosity in "I Believe in Jesus," "He's a Rebel," and "Forgive Me." Mawkish material like this so rarely engaged gay clubs that boycotts were almost moot. It just wasn't made for us.

Then in 1989, Summer did an about-face. She partnered with Mike Stock, Matt Aitken, and Pete Waterman, the straight British hitmakers who'd been buffing gay hi-NRG and house into international chart-toppers. Some of the acts they've assisted are queer, like Divine, Hazell Dean, Dead or Alive, and Samantha Fox, but all of them are LGBTQ-pleasers. "We make gay records, there's no question about it and we're not afraid to say that," Waterman declared the week in 1986 that Bananarama's camp-tastic version of "Venus," which they produced, reached Number One in the US. Unlike Summer's other '80s albums, which highlight her versatility at the expense of danceability, 1989's *Another Place and Time* is nothing but updated gay disco. Snagging import copies, our DJs made "This Time I Know It's for Real" an instant club smash. You may think I'm being too tough on Summer, but "This Time" kicked off my 2017 wedding reception. It's a fitting song to celebrate finally getting married at age fifty-six.

When the single took off, Summer didn't even have a US record label. Atlantic Records picked up the album after many fans bought the import, but by 1989 AIDS had politicized gay life more than ever. At a Boston Pride party for the Grass Roots Gay Rights Fund, activists appeared from ACT UP (AIDS Coalition to Unleash Power). This largely LGBTQ political group emerged in the late '80s to fight AIDS through education, research, treatment, and other direct action. Activists chanting "SHAME!" tried to stop the DJ spinning Summer. Finally, the singer addressed these conflicts in a long-overdue letter to ACT UP. "I did not say God is punishing gays with aids," she wrote. "I did not sit with ill intentions in judgment over your lives." Then she quoted all of 1 Corinthians 13—not the savviest approach to appease those with a long history of Bible quotations being used against them.

The controversy faded, particularly in light of Summer's AIDS fundraising in the next decade, but it never disappeared: "This Time I Know It's for Real" became her final North American Top Forty hit. Its US follow-up, "Love's About to Change My Heart," harkened back to "Last Dance," back when love didn't often lead to death. It was both heaven and haven.

⏭

Chapter Seventeen

Village People and Their LGBTQ Kin

Our prodigious disco proxy, Donna Summer, had many LGBTQ peers who crashed the mainstream. Disco Tex & the Sex-O-Lettes—a studio group fronted by celebrity hairdresser Monti Rock III—released in 1974 what remains a contender for the campiest record ever to hit the pop Top Ten, "Get Dancin'." It's sung by producer Bob Crewe, co-writer Kenny Nolan, and singer Cidny Bullens, who then, decades before his transition, was known as Cindy. They sing the entire song between Rock's rants, which reprise his conspicuously queeny TV talk show appearances. "My chiffon is wet, darling," he quips like Liberace with the gayness knob set to eleven.

Alicia Bridges's international 1978 hit "I Love the Nightlife (Disco 'Round)" offers subtler commentary that also comes from a queer place. Top gay DJ Jim Burgess maximized its dancefloor potential in a twelve-inch mix so mellow you might not notice that the song is written from the outlook of a neglected woman struggling to leave her womanizing husband. Like so many lesbians then stuck in straight relationships, the song's protagonist longs for liberation—*"ack-shon,"* Bridges memorably sings. Bridges came out following her 1984 album *Hocus Pocus,* on Olivia Records' Second Wave subsidiary, and "Nightlife" enjoyed another round of popularity following its appearance in *The Adventures of Priscilla, Queen of the Desert,* 1994's hit road comedy in which two drag queens and a trans woman parade a myriad of fabulous, Oscar-winning outfits across the Australian outback.

After leaving the Edgar Winter Group, for which he played bass, wrote, and sang 1973's "Free Ride," Dan Hartman became the rocker who made the most full-on disco transition: Being gay, he knew how to do that properly. Following 1978's zippy, gold-certified "Instant Replay," he released a ten-minute track so consummate it culminates the entire genre. Building through multiple tension-building vamps, 1979's "Vertigo/Relight My Fire" plateaus for a whole-souled love song in which Hartman calls on his wayward lover to help him rebuild their faltering relationship. Yet embedded within this narrative is a profound search for queer sanctuary and transcendence. The singer asks not only his partner but also his listeners to "stand up in the name of love" and make the world more like our dreams. Via one of popular music's most stratospherically elevating climaxes, the song shifts into gospel overdrive with the explosive entrance of disco's mightiest, most visceral vocalist, Loleatta Holloway. "You gotta be *strong* enough to *walk* on through the *night*!" she implores. LGBTQ and Black audiences know she's singing about our overlapping adversities. Holloway, Hartman, the background singers, and the orchestration interlock so heartily that the affirmation searched for at the song's start arrives.

In 1993, a cover of "Relight My Fire" by British boyband Take That and Scotland's Lulu went Number One in the UK. Soon after, Hartman died of a brain tumor at a time when AIDS patients, of which he was one, often did. He never came out. Yet "Relight My Fire" lives on as a dancefloor evergreen guaranteed to take our tribe to disco's higher plane.

Although her US presence got no further than the gayest clubs, Amanda Lear achieved major European stardom with a dozen overseas hits that all draw from drag's impish staging of femininity. As suggested by the title of 1977's *I Am a Photograph*, artifice is central to Lear's art and even her life story. Largely because of her own obfuscation, Lear's birthplace, age, ethnicity, nationality, and sex assigned at birth remain blurry. But if we consider her the first transsexual pop star, a title that seems to be substantiated by trans filmmaker Zackary Drucker's 2025 documentary *Enigma*, Lear's continual toying with the autobiographical ambiguity demanded of most LGBTQ VIPs was not only understandable but necessary.

In 2016, Italy's leading newspaper, *La Stampa,* printed Lear's alleged birth certificate, which revealed she was born Alain Tap in Saigon in 1939. Trans activist (and MBE recipient) April Ashley claims that as a fellow performer at the legendary Parisian drag club Le Carrousel, she introduced Tap to the Surrealist painter Salvador Dalí, whose erotic attractions were mostly male. As Dalí's protégé and muse, Tap relocated to London, where she became Amanda Lear and befriended the Rolling Stones. Lear's modeling career apexed in her appearance on the luridly alluring jacket of 1973's Roxy Music album *For Your Pleasure*. Later that year, Lear played a witchy Delilah in David Bowie's futuristic pageant *The 1980 Floor Show*, which was broadcast on *The Midnight Special*. I well remember as a wide-eyed kid watching Bowie sing his then-current single "Sorrow" to Lear, who claims to have been his lover. She was already nearly impossibly ravishing.

Inspired by Dalí's surrealist painting "Honey Is Sweeter Than Blood," Lear's 1977 single "Blood and Honey" introduced her disco template. Whereas most divas of the time were mellifluous and heated, Lear purrs in the cool, near-monotone of the femme fatale she describes. Adding sly gay innuendo to her arsenal, 1977's "Queen of China-Town" trades on her Eurasian background, and on 1979's "Fabulous (Lover, Love Me)," she avows her contradictory mythology with the preeminent gay word, one whose mere pronunciation can make a straight guy sound nelly. "My *fabulous* secret is mine," she taunts.

On 1978's "Follow Me," Lear's mystery fully dovetails with queer reinvention. Playing both ambitious protagonist and satanic temptress in a disco retelling of the Faust legend, she breaks from Lucifer and embraces love's salvation. Despite a lifetime of transsexuality denials, Lear zeroes in on personal transformation. "You'll have a new identity," she beckons as the devil, offering to "change your desssstiny." Gay Toronto DJ Wally MacDonald's twelve-inch remix accentuates the fluttering production's weightlessness and the languid way Lear floats through it, as if she were not a singer but a mist.

"Follow Me" became a must-play at BDSM "black parties," and an ever-changing signature of Bobby Viteritti, San Francisco's top *Billboard*-awarded DJ. He'd regularly re-sequence its peaks and valleys, reinforcing Lear's invitation to trail and trust her naughty lead.

Like Lear, Paul Jabara led multiple lives that converged in gay disco. Appearing in *Hair*, *Jesus Christ Superstar*, and *The Rocky Horror Show*, he brought musical theater opulence to solo material peppered with LGBTQ references. Queer listeners recognize that he sings "she" throughout 1978's "Disco Queen"—from *Thank God It's Friday*, the dancefloor comedy in which he also acts—to represent one of us. "Where'd she get her energy?" Jabara squeaks, rhetorically. He knows the answer is speed; that's how his "first lady of the floor" summons the stamina to reign from L.A. to Fire Island. On the twelve-inch single of "Disco Wedding/Honeymoon (In Puerto Rico)," he's dressed as both bride and groom.

Co-writer of Donna Summer's "Last Dance" and "No More Tears (Enough Is Enough)," as well as Barbra Streisand's own 1979 disco hit, "The Main Event/Fight," Jabara brought this irreverence to a song so jocose no star would touch it. In 1979, he and future *Late Show* bandleader Paul Shaffer wrote "It's Raining Men" for Summer, but the recently born-again singer found it blasphemous and sent Jabara a Bible in response. Further rejections came from Streisand, Cher, and Diana Ross. Jabara finally wore down the resistance of Two Tons o' Fun's Martha Wash and Izora Armstead. Renamed the Weather Girls for the 1982 single release, Wash and Armstead, the latter then known as Redman, fully commit to this simultaneously comical and uplifting, fella-celebrating song. Naturally, it became an instant gay anthem, as well as an international sleeper hit. Buoyed by a low-budget but high-camp video featuring miniaturized monster-movie sets, Busby Berkeley–style choreography, and muscle-bound dancers in Speedos and raincoats, "It's Raining Men" brings a torrent of gayness—the kind that also speaks to straight women. "Rip off the roof and stay in bed!" howl the Girls over co-producer Bob Esty's instrumental thunder. It's Homer Simpson's favorite song.

Morocco-born Frenchman Jacques Morali became disco's most successful and least apologetic Svengali by making music inspired by us. "Morali was openly gay and he had no shyness about it," said his business partner Henri Belolo. "His dream was to bring some of the gay life to the mainstream." In 1975, Morali convinced Belolo to underwrite his Philly-recorded studio project, the Ritchie Family, but only after its "Brazil" became a hit did Morali assemble a girl group to promote it. Enthralled by Felipe Rose, a go-go boy decked out in Native American regalia at the Anvil, a notorious gay Manhattan disco, Morali applied that approach to his next conceptual act, Village People. "I wanted to do something only for the gay market," Morali admitted to *Rolling Stone* in 1978.

Like the Ritchie Family's music, 1977's *Village People* was recorded by session musicians, in this case joined by lead singer Victor Willis. Its four songs are all paeans to LGBTQ communities—"San Francisco (You've Got Me)," "In Hollywood (Everybody Is a Star)," "Fire Island," and "Village People." The first and biggest one is a riot of queer-male semiotics that cites the gayest streets, apparel, transportation modes, and music of a city "known for its freedom." Just as "every gesture there has a meaning," nearly every line sends out a semaphore signal for LGBTQ listeners to decipher. The album topped *Billboard*'s disco chart for seven weeks and went gold—a major achievement given its minimal radio exposure. Again, Casablanca Records captivated disco's core audience.

For the LP sleeve and promotion of 1978's *Macho Man*, other members were assembled, and soon each of the six took on a costume-based persona derived from the blue-collar archetypes made gay in Greenwich Village—Rose the "Indian," Willis the cop, Alex Briley the G.I., David Hodo the construction worker, Glenn Hughes the biker, and Randy Jones the Marlboro Manly cowboy. Once more, the lyrics scream "gay" without using the word, particularly on "I Am What I Am," a rousing pride anthem. "To love is not a sin/I did not choose the way I am!" Willis, who is heterosexual, bawls much like Carl Bean. But the title track—the act's long-lasting pop breakthrough—sends conflicting signals. Straight people can hear it as a straightforward glorification of machismo, whereas gay men know it honors their own performative masculinity—a butch outfit and studly stance to attract sexual attention from other guys. The resulting gold single and platinum album gave the group a mainstream platform that Bean's "I Was Born This Way"—which came out two months earlier—couldn't reach. Still in the suburbs and too young for discos, I lacked access to Bean. But like other LGBTQ teens, I had the Peeps.

When Willis took over as lyricist for 1978's *Cruisin'* and 1979's *Go West,* the group's messaging became less lucidly gay. But the concepts themselves, still Morali-driven, nevertheless broadcast brazen queerness, particularly on pop's gay Rorschach test, "Y.M.C.A." As all-American as circumcision, the Young Men's Christian Association remains a harbor for jocks of every stripe, much like this single, which at twelve million international sales, belongs to everybody. The evidence is its ongoing presence at sporting events, bar mitzvahs, wedding receptions, and even conservative rallies. The fact that, nearly fifty years later, listeners are still debating its implicit yet nearly dogmatic gay meaning proves how deeply coded mainstream-targeted LGBTQ culture had to be back then, and how resistant some straight folk, even today, can be when it comes to seeing the world from any perspective beyond their own.

According to Jones, Village People's classic cowboy, the song was inspired by his own experience at a particular YMCA. "I had a lot of friends I worked out with who were in the adult film industry," said Jones, then a member of the McBurney Y, where he brought his producer. "[Morali] was impressed by meeting people he had seen in the videos and magazines. Those visits with me planted a seed in him, and that's how he got the idea for 'Y.M.C.A.'—by literally going to the YMCA."

Located in Manhattan's gay-intensive Chelsea neighborhood, the McBurney Y then doubled as residential hotel, and its proximity to the Village—and therefore many of New York's gay discos, bars, and bathhouses—meant gay and bi men from the surrounding area rented its cheap rooms for weekend crash pads and hookups. Because Morali, a foreigner, experienced the gayest YMCA in the universe, the Y represented American LGBTQ liberation to him. "You can hang out with all the boys," Willis wails between the *pow-pow-pow-pow* of horny horns that simulate the militaristic marches of John Philip Sousa. Like the group's earlier city-themed songs, "Y.M.C.A." offers queer sanctuary from inhibition.

It doesn't matter that Willis is straight. It doesn't matter that the song lacks any mention of man-on-man sex, an impossibility for a 1978 smash. "Y.M.C.A." glorifies self-actualization within an all-male context. "Young man, you can make real your dreams," it promises. In Village People's gay-empowerment lexicon this means joining a gay community, for true abolition from the slavery of societal/self-loathing cannot be achieved on one's own. So blatantly commercial it sounds like a jingle, "Y.M.C.A" is nothing less than a Broadway-scaled advertisement for LGBTQ life and love. Filmed outside the McBurney Y, the Christopher Street Pier (then throbbing with alfresco gay sex), and its nearby Ramrod leather bar (future site of an antigay massacre), its video looks and feels like a recruitment ad. Don't be depressed, the song tells us. Lift yourself up and find others just like you.

Soon after, my gay best friend from high school stayed at the McBurney Y. One night, we went out clubbing, and rather than going back to my dorm, I slept on his closet-sized floor. The next morning, he snuck me into the showers, where geezers ogled me like the chicken I was. With "Y.M.C.A." stuck in my head, I felt I'd stepped into the seedy reality behind the song's splendiferous fantasy. Years later, I got my own membership at San Francisco's Embarcadero Y, where I was caught trying to make my dreams real with another steam room gent. We were both shown the door.

By 1979, Morali had spread himself too thin with other acts, like his boyfriend Dennis Parker, aka porn star Wade Nichols. Nevertheless, *Grease*'s super-gay co-producer Allan Carr decided Morali's very gay story of masterminding the mostly gay Village People would provide a fitting narrative for what he intended to be Hollywood's first overtly gay musical. *Grease*'s gay screenwriter, Bronté Woodard, scripted a movie that would inexplicably star Steve Guttenberg as Jack Morell, Valerie Perrine as Morell's supermodel roommate, and Olympic gold medalist Caitlyn Jenner (decades before she transitioned) as a Wall Street lawyer who champions the group. In the spring of 1979, Carr's also-inexplicable choice as director, sitcom actor Nancy Walker, started filming what was originally titled *Discoland . . . Where the Music Never Ends* without Willis, who'd left the group.

Released in June 1980, Carr's retitled *Can't Stop the Music* ended up being one of the most entertainingly horrendous movies of all time. Shafting LGBTQ authenticity in favor of straight showbiz corn, it presents every major character as goofily hetero, while the Village People recede into the background of their own movie despite lavishly bumbling dance numbers, such as "Milkshake," which was actually funded with two million dollars from what's now known as the American Dairy Science Association. Only their showstopping "Y.M.C.A." dance sequence, featuring 250 West Hollywood–style male gymnasts, exudes the glorious gayness otherwise withheld. Bombing everywhere but Australia, Japan, and Bali, *Can't Stop the Music* lost eighteen million dollars.

Village People have continued to depreciate their queer legacy so often that President Donald Trump—whose first administration appointed antigay judges, opposed the Equality Act, gutted or blocked LGBTQ protections, and tried to stop trans people from serving in the military—vacated the White House he claimed was still his to the tune of "Y.M.C.A." When he returned in 2025 to do much worse, Willis's reconstituted Peeps performed it at his victory party. Morali couldn't comment, much less stop this disco sacrilege; he died of AIDS in 1991.

⏭

Chapter Eighteen

Sylvester

The most courageously queer disco star to penetrate the mainstream, Sylvester sprang from both the hippie and LGBTQ countercultures of San Francisco with the Pentecostal ferocity of his gospel-singing childhood still intact. Keening in a riveting falsetto while sparkling in sequined gowns that alluded to his full-on drag past, he flared out musical and visual gender fluidity decades before such a term existed. Bringing the purest expression of LGBTQ dancefloor transcendence to an international audience without stinting on the elements ordinarily kept underground, Sylvester was disco personified.

Having left home in his teens, Watts-born Sylvester James Jr. entered gay life early—his first chosen family was the Disquotays, stalwart Black queens of South Central who cross-dressed, even though it was then illegal in California, and stole lipstick, wigs, and hairspray during the Watts riots. Sylvester even took his graduation photo in drag. He moved to San Francisco to join the Cockettes, a street-theater commune that eschewed drag's previous goal of gender illusion. These were guys with beards *and* feminine makeup, or gals who dressed exaggeratedly womanly, like today's faux queens. Sylvester stood apart as a less comical, more historical entertainer who sang Black women's blues, jazz, and cabaret oldies. When the freewheeling, under-rehearsed Cockettes tore up New York nightlife but tanked onstage, the fledgling star, whose professionalism remained intact, refocused on an unorthodox mix of glam and soul.

His 1973 albums *Sylvester and the Hot Band* and *Bazaar* unfurl the singer's interpretive sedition. The former opens with a raging reinvention of "Southern Man," Neil Young's indictment of religious hypocrisy and Confederate racism, made more furious by Sylvester's queer, Black presence and his (white) Hot Band screeching and syncopating like Lynyrd Skynyrd covering Sly and the Family Stone. Steeped in Black music's past, Sylvester was nevertheless a creature of the future. The disco that would properly exhibit his talents and speak to the audience that awaited him was still being invented.

Sylvester lost his shrillness when he dropped the rock, assembled a white R&B band, and added Two Tons o' Fun, whose Black church harmonies complimented his leads to create pan-gender gospel that manifests its god in the amalgamation of their voices. Recorded with ex-Motown producer Harvey Fuqua in what seems like one feverish live take, 1977's *Sylvester* reflects the growing buzz over the group's gigs in the Castro. Although Sylvester exemplified the liberation of LGBTQ San Francisco life, his torrid rendition of Ashford & Simpson's "Over and Over" challenges the gay male pursuit of anonymous sex to achieve freedom. Sylvester, Martha Wash, and Izora Armstead chant "You can't be nobody's lover/Till you're somebody's friend" as if spiraling like whirling Sufis. They know affection—even in friendship—is more important than sex, even for those defined by their sexuality.

Sylvester became the star he was born to be after finding the final missing piece of the disco puzzle: synthesizer wizard Patrick Cowley, whose gay agenda was indeed filled with cruising and hookups. A former electronic-music student, Cowley had been recording experimental electronic tracks, R&B covers, and homemade remixes. His eventually renowned sixteen-minute version of Donna Summer's "I Feel Love" first tantalized local dancers with extra synth passages even more orgasmic and outré than Giorgio Moroder's own. Then a lighting technician at the City disco, Cowley was asked to make similar additions to two songs that would break Sylvester internationally.

In the spoken intro to 1978's US Top Twenty hit "Dance (Disco Heat),"

Sylvester surveys a "fabulous" club full of "fabulous" people—a coded message to his LGBTQ audience that implies he's a gay individual among many. Building on this message of community, Sylvester, Wash, and Armstead sing nearly everything together. Sylvester solos only when repeating "come on and dance" at the bottom of his baritone and ad-libbing lines at the falsetto top. After its first two minutes, the track mostly vamps on one chord magnified by Cowley's rapid synth undulations. When long-delayed changes shift exultant stasis to fervent release, the result feels like a James Brown jam spiked with poppers.

Sylvester and his guitarist, James "Tip" Wirrick, similarly reconfigured what began as a nondescript R&B ballad with disco's hallmarks: hissing hi-hat cymbals and a four-on-the-floor pulse, but also an octave-jumping bass that soon helped define hi-NRG. When Cowley added sequencer lines that would envelop dancers with a bubbling bath of electronics, 1978's "You Make Me Feel (Mighty Real)" took on the modernity of its deeper message—one that's lasted on LGBTQ dancefloors like few others.

Largely ad-libbed, its lyric is, on the surface, as simple as the song's construction. A connection between two lovers intensifies at the disco, and when the pair come home invigorated by music's mettle and dancing's warmth, their spark burns hotter, not only in physical gratification, but also in affirmation. The money shot comes when Sylvester sings, "And I know you'll love me like you/SHOOOOOULD," his falsetto swooping up for a note that, even forty-plus years later, provokes dancefloor screams from nearly everyone, but particularly LGBTQ clubbers.

Like all minorities, we know the pain of being told *we shouldn't.* We shouldn't engage in physical intimacy with those of the same sex. We shouldn't even speak of it, and we sure shouldn't "flaunt it," "rub it in their faces," or "shove it down their throats." We shouldn't get married, or "influence" children, or use the "wrong" restroom, or wear clothes "inappropriate" for our gender, or be too loud, or too soft. Most of all, we shouldn't love each other, or even ourselves. Yet Sylvester, as a gender-blurred Black man, breaks all those rules. He insists with his entire being, but especially with that sky-high shriek, that everything the straight world told us about ourselves is wrong. Our love is right and fated—the ultimate "should." You *should* love Sylvester, the rest of us, *and*, most of all, *yourself*. That's the *real* "real."

In *Paris Is Burning*, the 1990 documentary about Harlem's trans-centered costume ball culture and the largely Black/Latinx LGBTQ community who built it, the film's lesbian director Jennie Livingston quotes the Black drag legend Dorian Corey and her peers on "realness"—a ball category in which contestants compete to present exacting representations of gender, class, race, military bearing, and sexual orientation. "If you can pass the untrained eye, or even the trained eye and not give away the fact that you're gay, that's when it's real," Corey explains. Livingston syncs footage of well-dressed straight men and women walking through Manhattan to Cheryl Lynn's 1978 disco hit "Got to Be Real," as if they, too, stage an elaborate gender show. Emcee Junior LaBeija observes, "When you're gay, you monitor everything you do. You monitor how you look, how you dress, how you talk, how you act. 'Did they see me?' 'What do they think of me?'"

The mighty realness Sylvester sings about is the absence of that self-consciousness. It's freedom from our own censorship; a place where we don't need to perform or adjust, where being ourselves is enough. Sylvester celebrates that "you"—meaning *us*—take him to that unconditionally loving state. In this seemingly straightforward song about dancing and sex, Sylvester honors that most hallowed fulfillment of all. It's hard-won for LGBTQ folks even today, but in the '70s, we routinely lost our jobs, our safety, and our lives pursuing it. This is what we endure all the bullshit to attain. That's how much we need to feel real.

On his next single, Sylvester did something even more revolutionary. He broke the unspoken rule that even LGBTQ people must use pronouns that frame hit songs in a heterosexual context. With his 1979 rendition of "I (Who Have Nothing)," Sylvester constructs a bisexual love triangle. In previous versions, by Ben E. King and others, male singers contrast their devotion against the hollow extravagance of a "he" who showers their paramour with diamonds and other material symbols of devotion. In Sylvester's version, the singer's rival is a "she," and with that elemental switch, the song grows complex. His competition can take his beau to pricey places, but, it's implied, those nighteries would reject the two men together.

When he sings of his "nose pressed against the windowpane," the conflict is no longer just about money but cishet privilege. While a bass drum pounds for eleven minutes, like a fist hammering on a wall erected between gays and straights, he bemoans that his wealthy female rival can give his man everything yet never know what Sylvester intuits—he loves him *more*. In society's eyes, what he offers can never measure up to that of his challenger. But because disco was so big in the first half of 1979, and because the singer embodied it with such singularity, Sylvester managed to do what other gay men could not, and would not, achieve again for many years: He got a grammatically same-sex love song on US radio.

This crest couldn't last. On July 12, 1979, shock jock Steve Dahl staged a Disco Demolition Night promotion in Chicago's Comiskey Park between games of a doubleheader between the Chicago White Sox and the Detroit Tigers. With admission reduced to ninety-eight cents for attendees who brought a disco record, nearly fifty thousand fans showed up—thousands more than the park's capacity. After the first game, Dahl blew up the records in a mock funeral pyre. A full-scale riot ensued, as mostly young, male, and white fans poured onto the playing field, tore up the turf, and set fires, forcing the White Sox to forfeit the second game.

That week, dancefloor smashes by Donna Summer and Anita Ward ("Ring My Bell") occupied the top three positions on *Billboard*'s pop singles chart. Right after Dahl's demolition, radio cut back on disco. Chic's epochal "Good Times" would be the group's last pop Top Forty entry, even though hip-hop's first hit, Sugarhill Gang's "Rapper's Delight," heisted its instrumental hooks. Replacing "Good Times" at Number One, the Knack's "My Sharona"—*Billboard*'s top record of 1979—abruptly shifted the music industry away from disco and toward rock that retained punk's vitality.

There are many theories as to why disco went from the biggest innovation in 1970s entertainment to yesterday's mashed potatoes almost overnight, but the most legit one is from Tom Moulton, who told me, "Radio was sick and tired of being forced to play records they didn't want to play." Disco's nearly planetary popularity post–*Saturday Night Fever* forced radio's hand to broadcast records already favored by LGBTQ and Black audiences, which undermined the airwaves' hit-making power. No wonder Dahl's on-air disco-destruction gimmicks spread throughout the US courtesy of radio consultant Lee Abrams.

Disco similarly diminished the authority of record companies, which catered to and even hired us during disco's peak, but were rarely run by us, and resented our clout. The most successful solely LGBTQ-owned label of the '70s, Larry Uttal's Private Stock, released several disco smashes, including Frankie Valli's "Swearin' to God" (1975), Walter Murphy's "A Fifth of Beethoven" (1976), and the Michael Zager Band's "Let's All Chant" (1977). In 1978, Uttal shuttered Private Stock to pursue film ambitions right when RSO Records—co-owned by gay mogul Robert Stigwood—hit its movie-propelled stride. RSO released monumental soundtracks to 1977's *Saturday Night Fever*, 1978's *Grease*, and 1980's *Fame*; disco pips by Andy Gibb, David Naughton, Linda Clifford, and Festival; and countless blue-chip hits by the Bee Gees, the brothers behind most of RSO's biggest successes. The label folded a few years after those titans smacked it with a two-hundred-million-dollar lawsuit in 1980. In 1993, Uttal died of AIDS.

But why did those Chicago kids hate disco so much? There hadn't been such an outcry against music since 1966, when John Lennon said the Beatles had become "more popular than Jesus," an offhand remark that inspired radio bans, record burnings in the South, and protests by the Ku Klux Klan, which criticized the Fab Four's support of civil rights and claimed they were communists.

Masses don't riot over mere music. A symbolic burning at the stake of all the Black, brown, female, and LGBTQ people who conceived and cultivated our music, Dahl's Disco Demolition gave the radio programmers and record execs reluctantly riding our bandwagon an excuse to claim "Disco Sucks," the antigay battle cry of the disco disenfranchised assembled against us so-called sodomites and trannies.

A year later, the only pure disco song still in the Top Forty was Lipps Inc.'s

"Funkytown." Yet it was joined by club-friendly acts sold as something else: nostalgic soul (the Spinners), uptown funk (Jermaine Jackson, the S.O.S. Band), classic rock (the Rolling Stones), synthpop (Gary Numan), and new wave (Blondie). However, disco never died in liberal cities with sizable LGBTQ and non-white populations. In New York, dance radio stations like WKTU, Kiss FM, and WBLS kept pumping thumps into stores, hair salons, and taxis for years. Illustrating how central club culture remained in urban life, from 1981 to '84, *Saturday Night Live*'s opening montage of NYC signifiers featured Roy Thode spinning at Studio 54. A day before *SNL*'s seventh season finished, in May 1982, the DJ, who spun at such hallowed gay spaces as the Saint and the Ice Palace, was found lifeless from an overdose.

But in the big picture, disco's death proved as fleeting as the furor over Lennon's remark. Just as the Beatles released their revolutionary *Sgt. Pepper* and were once again canonized, disco absorbed punk's brashness and was rebranded as "dance music"—a genre linked to most everything nearly everyone loves about the 1980s, from John Hughes movies to moonwalking.

⏭

Chapter Nineteen

Blondie and Punk

In olden queer parlance, *punk* wasn't the bratty, mid-1960s garage rock that started the genre. *Punk* was like *chicken*—a gay man's younger partner, or a sexually submissive prison inmate. Nevertheless, there's ample homoeroticism in punk rock—the kind that shows up whenever tough guys emphasize their masculinity so much it becomes a performance, like in professional wrestling. The more fundamental and transgressive rock gets, the closer it comes to its Black queer origins in Sister Rosetta Tharpe, Esquerita, and Little Richard. Given that *all* rock 'n' roll is an extended metaphor for intercourse, the best punishingly hard bands playing "in the pocket" sound as though their members are physically and psychically conjoined in musical sex. This was especially true of the New York Dolls, a polarizing early 1970s ensemble that briefly wore the in-crowd crown in the Velvet Underground's wake.

When prog's overcooked virtuosity filled arenas, the Dolls arrived as a raw antidote—the Stones swathed in hot pink instead of the blues. Squeezed onto a couch with their hair teased and faces painted, the quintet are only falsies away from full drag on the cover of 1973's *New York Dolls*. Everyone not on *Creem*'s mailing list presumed the group were homos or hookers or both. Equivocally queer songs like "Frankenstein" and "Jet Boy" didn't discourage this, nor did campy quotations from girl-group goodies like the Shangri-Las' "Give Him a Great Big Kiss."

Producer Todd Rundgren positioned guitarist Sylvain Sylvain in the left speaker and guitarist Johnny Thunders in the right, each noisier than normal rock. While David Johansen mangles his arrant poetry in the center, chewing on words like *kiss* and *trash* until they take on extra syllables, Sylvain and Thunders vie for attention, shooting off in different directions, then rub up against each other to generate friction, sparks, sweat, and spunk so thuggishly it feels like *you*'re the punk at the center of a prison throuple. Every sonic hole is filled.

I was a junior high punching bag, invariably picked last for the team along with the kid who ate his boogers. Too young to have experienced the Velvet Underground in real time, I asked for and got this album as a Christmas present from my dad when it was new and I was twelve. My mother said I should turn the other cheek like Jesus, but this made me feel as though I could take a hit, for I had the Dolls, the scrappiest sissies, and my bullies did not. I'd discovered the secret of life, or at least my survival. They proved the so-called bad things about myself were actually good.

Soon after, an all-girl rock band did the same in Los Angeles. Like the Dolls, the Runaways drew from sources too varied to be purely punk in sound, but they were always that in spirit. Even when Lisa Ford's showy solos steered them in heavy metal's direction, these teen girls, doing what was then thought to be a grown guy's job, signaled disruptive dissent. As Joan Jett sang in 1977's "I Love Playin' with Fire," the Runaways announced their allegiance to all that's inflammatory.

The band burned out two years later, but its impact lives on in a 1976 song more enduring than most gold records. "Cherry Bomb" crams everything indispensable about the group into 140 snotty seconds. Written by Jett and the band's seedy manager Kim Fowley, it taunts guys while inviting other girls to the party, not merely as observers, but as core participants: "Get down ladies, you got nothing to lose!" Having absorbed the androgyny of glam bands like Sweet, who proved how tough it could be while trilling girlish harmony, the Runaways similarly chuck the gender script by yelling like guys. "I'm the *fox* you've been *waiting for*" reads laughably, but the way Cherie Currie roars it feels righteously feminist. She doesn't need a man to make her desirable: She already knows she is. Explosive feminine power has since been the theme of many hits, but back then, out of the mouth of a bottle-blond teen in satin underwear, it was an event. This song is so stutteringly catchy that it broke the language barrier in Japan and turned the group into national superstars.

"Secrets" addresses the band's undisclosed sexuality. Written by Currie, Fowley, drummer Sandy West—whose primary relationships were with women—and Kari Krome, one of Jett's early girlfriends, the song captures the compromises demanded by L.A.'s rock scene. Bowie's influence meant bisexuality—especially by women—was considered cool, but "it was not okay for women to completely reject men," as band biographer Evelyn McDonnell has pointed out. "They were gay and I wasn't," Ford told her. As a result, "Secrets" is openly covert. "We speak in codes and no one knows/'Cause we're living a double life," Currie sings over bedrock riffs. For the sinister bridge, she trades lines with Jett as if in a lover's duet, both vowing to deny everything if caught. Then a jaunty piano part comes out of nowhere, as if momentarily releasing what they refuse to completely conceal. The next year, the entire group was thrown out of Disneyland for "lesbian behavior." According to Jett, they were merely walking arm-in-arm for a photo. Nevertheless, this ejection got a mention in *Rolling Stone* back when their music didn't.

Also in 1976, another band spat out a debut so vital and unprecedented it singlehandedly forged punk's template. Co-managed by Danny Fields, one of the first LGBTQ rock insiders to come out, the Ramones were the fastest and most notorious band at punk's headquarters, CBGB, as well as Mother's, a gay bar near the Chelsea Hotel. Replicating their short and speedy live sets, 1976's *Ramones* features fourteen distortion-driven cuts in twenty-nine minutes. Referencing horror films, bubblegum pop, urban life, and pervasive violence, all imparted with deadpan humor, this patently dumb yet ingenious record brought rock back to its rudimentary roots while making a pop-art statement akin to Andy Warhol out of minimalism and mass-market brutality. Almost overnight, the album's impact spread, and the label that released it, Sire, became a pillar of what its queer co-founder Seymour Stein coined "new wave." Through Sire, Stein became rock's most influential LGBTQ tastemaker.

Ramones's fleshiest narrative, "53rd & 3rd," describes bassist Dee Dee Ramone's real-life experience of hustling himself to guys. It's set on a Manhattan corner then popular with male prostitutes and johns, the same spot where the gay protagonist of Rod Stewart's "The Killing of Georgie (Part I and II)," from that same year, is killed by a roughneck. That song is compassionate, but this one is heartless. After being rejected by johns, the hustler—played by Dee Dee himself, who sings the song's bridge—takes out his razor and does "what god forbade" to prove he's "no sissy."

Time has proven that "53rd & 3rd" is accurate about homophobia. Having been gay-bashed in San Francisco back in 1977, the gay Asian American filmmaker Arthur Dong in his 1997 documentary *Licensed to Kill* confronted several real-life murderers of gay men to uncover their motivations. Their rationalization was that society told them to do away with us. In their minds, particularly of those who had queer experience or attractions, the act vouched for their masculinity and proved that they're not gay. In 1996, researchers writing in the *Journal of Abnormal Psychology* found that the men in their study who'd expressed antigay attitudes showed a positive genital response when presented with male homosexual imagery. In 2012, researchers Richard and William Ryan wrote an op-ed in *The New York Times* about their study that also provided evidence that homophobia can be a by-product of the suppression of same-sex attraction. They illustrate this hypothesis with examples of politicians and religious leaders who led campaigns against LGBTQ rights and were then arrested for allegedly soliciting sex in public toilets, like former Senator Larry Craig, or in the case of megachurch leader Ted Haggard, exposed by a masseur he paid for sex and meth.

I'll admit something awkward, because I'm certain some of you can relate. Shortly after entering my teens, I thought I was straight because I had a major crush on Debbie Harry. I couldn't get enough of Blondie. I would put their music on, stare at the record sleeves, and imagine myself in their downtown Manhattan, the one Madonna would soon inherit. I wouldn't say I was conventionally turned on by Harry, although I did have blond quasi-girlfriends in high school. But I was physically captivated by all that she and the band represented. That pull was so strong it felt sexual, and so I kidded myself that this meant I was hetero and not simply that I adored Blondie in the same way as other LGBTQ kids I had yet to meet.

"The 'Blondie' character I created was sort of androgynous . . . some kind of transexual creature," Harry writes in 2019's *Face It: A Memoir.* "To be an artistic, assertive woman in girl drag, not boy drag, was then an act of transgression. I was playing up the idea of being a very feminine woman while fronting a male rock band in a highly macho game. . . . My Blondie character was an inflatable doll but with a dark, provocative, aggressive side. I was playing it up yet I was very serious."

Punk—like LGBTQ culture—empowers those who are estranged. Growing up where the legal drinking age was eighteen, I was carded only once, unsuccessfully, when in 1978 the Ramones played the Penny Arcade, a Rochester biker bar. No amount of pleading could get me and my underage pal entrance through the front, so we went around the back, and knocked on the stage door. When Dee Dee ushered us in, it felt as though we'd passed through a gateway of adult opportunity. Taller friends concealed us until we couldn't stop ourselves from pogoing. This made us visible to the bouncer, who grabbed us by our collars and threw us out. We briefly lost our dignity but forever won the game: New York City was nearly ours.

But as much as the Ramones gave pent-up outsiders like us catharsis, they proved too aggressive for others. Punk's queer-friendly entrée became Blondie, who was initially also on a gay-owned label, Private Stock. As all-encompassing as the Ramones were single-minded, Blondie personified NYC's multiplicity. A childhood tomboy, former Playboy bunny, actor, philanthropist, and pop eidolon, Harry has been so many things thought mutually exclusive that she's done more than any other rock star to destroy the notion that female singers must fit narrow hetero expectations. Drawing simultaneously from high art and mass-market camp, punk and disco, uptown and downtown, Harry *became* Blondie—so much so that many thought it was her name. If Warhol had constructed a band, it would've been this one.

Queers comprehend the sci-fi weirdness of daily life that remains Blondie's throughline. TV transmits cosmic hallucinations in 1978's "Fade Away and Radiate." The protagonist of "Shayla," from the following year, works in a factory until extraterrestrials claim her. Hungry Martians play upon the biblical connotations of 1981's "Rapture," in which dancing occurs "man to man." Harry sings of aliens because, like us, she's been alienated. After an early CBGB gig, Harry and her personal/professional partner, Blondie guitarist Chris Stein, were accosted while entering Stein's apartment. The intruder tied them up, stole Stein's guitars, and raped Harry. More than any other mainstream act, Blondie addressed the inequity that provoked punk, feminism, and gay activism alike. During the band's appearance at New York's 1977 Gay Liberation Day festivities, Harry dedicated "Rip Her to Shreds" to Anita Bryant.

The co-producer and co-writer of many UK glam hits, Mike Chapman made an inspired strategic decision while overseeing Blondie's 1978 breakthrough, *Parallel Lines*. He realized the zingiest rhyme of what would become the first new wave record to hit Number One in the US, "Heart of Glass," could impede airplay, so he held back "Once I had a love and it was a gas/ Soon turned out to be a pain in the ass" until the final verse. That couplet is brilliantly gay on many levels; no one knows how much love can be a pain in the ass more than us. Some still consider the song's disco arrangement a sell-out, but that, too, springs from punk. "We used to do 'Heart of Glass' to upset people," keyboardist Jimmy Destri admitted. While pissing off the purists, Blondie welcomed us.

Queer Blondie favorites like "Heart of Glass" exude so much urbane wit that it seemed implausible that the group didn't have at least one LGBTQ member. Sure enough, Harry divulged in 2014 that she's been bisexual, believing "women are more sensual"—a statement foreshadowed by songs like 1976's "Kung Fu Girls," 1978's "Pretty Baby" and "Sunday Girl," and 1999's comeback "Maria," in which she lauds a Latina with not a small amount of lust. None of these are explicitly erotic, but neither are they entirely platonic. Because Harry is a presumed hetero who doesn't resemble what cishet people define as lesbian, the affection shown in these songs went largely undetected—but not by those of us who've claimed Harry as kin. "If you're a boy or if you're a girl/I love you just the same," she and her queer stylistic stepchild Beth Ditto sing on Blondie's "A Rose by Any Name" from 2013. That alone makes Harry more punk than the band's detractors.

One of the earliest UK punk bands, Manchester's Buzzcocks, flagged queerness on its very first single, 1977's "Orgasm Addict." A former employee at a store that sold sex toys—literally buzzing cocks—the quartet's bisexual frontman Pete Shelley rhymes "dirty magazines" with "stains on your jeans" to broadcast what's now diagnosed as sex addiction over Ramones-style punk clamor. With double the guitarists, a tighter drummer, a tenor singer, and way more words, the effect is exponentially more effusive. Shelley gasps punk's wackiest simulated sex spasm, which triggers a key change as his protagonist shifts from masturbation to sexual couplings not limited by age, class, or gender. Nowhere is there faultfinding. Instead, there's old-fashioned gaiety.

What followed was even more startling: Buzzcocks had UK hits. Shelley sang nearly all his songs to a "you" who is both the object of his affection and us, the listeners. This was his strategy to reach everyone. "Rather than going into the rock clichés of 'Oh baby, be my girl' and things like that, it's easier if you just leave it open," Shelley explained, "because then it's more honest." Since they're nearly all fast and frantic, few Buzzcocks songs seem sad, but many match the euphoric melancholy of Motown while pitting cheery instrumentation against lyrical anguish.

This duality reached its apogee in 1978's "Ever Fallen in Love (With Someone You Shouldn't've)," which reached the US mainstream a decade later via Fine Young Cannibals' cover. Everyone experiences infatuations that can't be reciprocated, but LGBTQ people know this more than most because much of the world's population is physically off-limits. Because of the stigmas attached to just being us, we're more likely to encounter condemnation when voicing our attractions. In crossing that line ordinarily not breached, Shelley fears desolation. "And we won't be together much longer/Unless we realize that we are the same," he reasons. This universal statement takes on more meaning in an LGBTQ context, as if Shelley's flame couldn't face the consequences of their intimacy, as if he can't accept that he, too, is queer. While the song builds, Steve Diggle plays a nagging guitar figure that's innate to Buzzcocks yet atypical of first-generation punk. He repeats it as if articulating the persistence of Shelley's allegiance until John Maher clobbers out a drum fill that feels like a final frustrated knock on a closed door. Years later, Shelley divulged that he'd written the song about his relationship with another male musician.

Soon after Buzzcocks split for several years, solo Shelley released 1981's "Homosapien," an unprecedented mix of programmed synths, acoustic guitar, and the chugging beats of a brand-new Linn LM-1 drum machine that would soon propel the Human League and other proudly plastic poppers. Written in 1974, before Buzzcocks, it's a product of young Shelley's David Bowie fixation. In our unpublished 1986 interview, the singer revealed the rhyme that triggered a BBC ban for an assumed reference to gay sex—"Homo superior in my interior"—was inspired by Bowie's 1971 song "Oh! You Pretty Things." Shelley references its lyric "Gotta make way for the homo superior," which draws from Fredrich Nietzsche's "Übermensch," or Superman.

Given Bowie's coming out, "homo superior" also holds LGBTQ implications, and unlike Shelley's Buzzcocks material, "Homosapien" genders its subject as male. Like Nietzsche, Shelley wanted to advance humanity and transcend his mortality, both in this relationship and the song itself. Weary of sexual labels, he refrains from classifying his boyfriend, or even us, "like an animal in the zoo." But, on the single sleeve and LP jacket as well as in the video, the singer wears a green carnation—a Victorian-era homosexual proclamation popularized by Oscar Wilde. Shelley and Diggle did both marry women. Yet when *Outpunk* magazine interviewed the pair in 1996, the Mancunians confirmed they'd been lovers.

Twisting a placard slogan with British irony, the Tom Robinson Band's "Glad to Be Gay" from 1978 is as happy as a miner's strike and sounds like one, too. It opens with a sarcastic spoken dedication to the World Health Organization, which then still defined homosexuality as a disorder. Its first verse describes barbaric gay club raids. The second protests the hypocrisy of UK tabloids, which featured topless women while deeming the gay press obscene. The third decries the dangers queer folks were forced to withstand, and the fourth complains of complacent LGBTQ people who betray their own kind. "Sing if you're glad to be gay/Sing if you're happy that way" goes the chorus, its drunken music-hall lilt embittered by Robinson's gritted-teeth delivery. Added to US pressings of *Power in the Darkness*, it received mainstream distribution because Robinson seemed poised for US success with 1977's "2-4-6-8 Motorway." Closer to Bruce Springsteen than the Ramones, its accessibility masks that he'd modeled its driving-themed chorus on a gay lib chant: "Two, four, six, eight/Gay is twice as good as straight/Three, five, seven, nine/Lesbians are mighty fine."

⏭

Chapter Twenty

The B-52s

The B-52s sprang from the queer bohemia of Athens, Georgia, to exemplify the queer aesthetic of the LGBTQ collector. These pop culture connoisseurs are the gay elders who own the antique stores and run the swap meets, estate sales, and auctions. They live for castoffs, for they—and we too—are cast off. We surround ourselves with souvenirs from a childhood often taken from us once we start showing our underappreciated otherness. We're the unwanted junk we know has value.

The B-52s revive a thread of gay-beloved, mid-century modernism that is sometimes faultlessly elegant—the once-abandoned Eames chair now worth thousands, the sensual curves of Scandinavian design, and much of Palm Springs—and at others such kitsch that it becomes cultural commentary when amassed. The latter is what the B-52s exalt—the Polynesian geegaws, tiki lamps, and shellacked porcupine fish that once adorned suburban basements and brightened backyard luaus. Their music is the new-wave version of exotica LPs by Martin Denny, Esquivel, and Les Baxter. You can hear Denny's ersatz world music emulated in the B-52s' David Byrne–assisted *Mesopotamia* cut "Deep Sleep" from 1982.

Cold War–era design delineates the B-52s' jet-streamed space. Named after the sky-touching bouffant that Southern women wore long after their Northern counterparts favored droopy bangs, the Bs also reference Boeing's B-52

Stratofortress bomber. Like the plane, the band is an aerodynamic marvel. For years, its genius—and queerness—flew over everyone's heads but ours and our allies'. Even today, the Bs are men and women who have always manifested their difference with rollicking glee. That's their political statement.

Achieving a telepathy that hierarchical bands never attain, these kindhearted kooks turn friendship and shared biology into kinetic art that tells those who need it most that no matter where you're from, you can be queer, weird, and safe together in your mutual aberration. As singer Fred Schneider sagely counsels in 1979's "There's a Moon in the Sky (Called the Moon)," "If you're in outer space, don't feel out of place/'Cause there are thousands of others like you." You don't need a leader, and you don't need to lead just to stand out and stand tall in your community. You can be yourself and belong—even in the South.

Self-taught, the B-52s' Ricky Wilson, who was gay, became rock's most remarkable rhythm guitarist of his generation by inventing tunings and even stringings. Haranguing in a Southern variant of "gay voice," Schneider, also gay, rarely holds notes or attempts melodies. Fred, Ricky's sister Cindy, Keith Strickland, who too is gay, and Kate Pierson, who is lesbian, all swap instruments with primarily percussive results that are simultaneously retro and modish. Pop-art magpies yet innovators, they prove themselves punk through cooperative DIY selfhood. No one has ever sounded like, or as queer as, these Bs.

Without bass guitar or slick production, 1979's *The B-52's* encapsulates the band's thrift-store methodology. Kate's howl doubles her Farfisa organ to evoke a theremin—the early electronic instrument heard in superannuated sci-fi flicks. A toy piano pinks and plonks on one track, and a walkie-talkie beeps on another. For "Planet Claire," Ricky repurposes the virile guitar riff from TV's private eye series *Peter Gunn*. Many have heard Yoko Ono in Kate's and Cindy's birdcalls, but a better comparison is Yma Sumac, the 1950s' Peruvian goddess whose ability to encompass a seemingly glass-shattering soprano and growling baritone set a world record. Women routinely find themselves forced into making themselves smaller and softer in support of men, but Kate and Cindy don't do that. Their good vibrations are big and brassy, because that's how they harmonize.

Animated by the girls' screaky impersonations of marine life and a guitar part so badass its creator thought it stupid, "Rock Lobster" is a Dada take on cinema's campiest genre: the beach-party movie. From 1963's *Beach Party* to 1967's *Thunder Alley*, American International Pictures cranked out a dozen of these, most starring heartthrob Frankie Avalon and buxom ex-Mouseketeer Annette Funicello. These teensploitation cheapies were designed for the straight male gaze, but their plethora of cute boys in swim trunks meant beach party movies provided women and pre-Stonewall gay men a rare and socially acceptable means to check out objectified males before Andy Warhol's *Blue Movie* kicked off the "Golden Age of Porn" the same summer as the Stonewall riots.

Like the films it spoofs, "Rock Lobster" doesn't make much literal sense, so Fred's gender reversals ("Boys in bikinis/Girls in surfboards") get camouflaged like seahorses in a kelp forest. Playing a conventional guitar stripped of two middle strings and then down-tuned so it suggests a bass, Ricky drives the groove as forcibly as Fred's cowbell and ranting vocal. Because they were so queer and danceable, the B-52s became the first new wave band to get disco play with songs that weren't disco.

There's nothing concretely gay going on in "Party Out of Bounds" from 1980's *Wild Planet*, but neither does its fete seem straight—certainly not Fred's reaction to it spiraling. "Who's to blame when situations degenerate?/ *Disgusting* things you'd never anticipate!" he gasps, Paul Lynde–style. Crying with preternatural urgency, Cindy implores seabirds to help her find and revive her drowned inamorato on *Planet*'s "Give Me Back My Man." She's doing her woolly rendition of the torch-carrying heroine we gays love, yet it's much more than schtick, especially when she leaps up for the song's title, pleading not with just her voice but with everything she's got. Fred's and Kate's combined glockenspiel and keyboard countermelody provides so much hopefulness that singing to seagull Cupids seems viable. When AIDS took away so many of our men, Cindy's prayer became ours.

On 1983's synthpoppier but still guitar-gritty *Whammy!*, "Legal Tender" reflects frustration with rock's glass ceiling. Despite gold-certified albums and sold-out shows, the B-52s couldn't yet crack US Top Forty radio. "We're in the basement," the girls sing metaphorically of their cult status. To remedy the situation, they print counterfeit cash and "try to pass that trash." Women and LGBTQ people get the repeated message that we're not as authentic as straight men. When we satirize this second-class status with secondhand clothes, we're considered cheeseballs. As of early 2026, the B-52s, like most queer acts, still aren't in the Rock and Roll Hall of Fame.

Ricky came down with AIDS but hid his illness from everyone except Keith until dying in 1985, aged thirty-two. Held back until 1986, *Bouncing Off the Satellites* suffers from Ricky's decreased involvement, but blazes his warmth on its opening "Summer of Love," and ends awestruck on "She Brakes for Rainbows," another stellar Cindy showcase. Awash with candy-coated synth hues, it sounds like she's stopping to watch her brother's specter shoot across the sky. Grieving and unsure how to continue without their primary player, the band went on indefinite hiatus.

Having switched from drums to guitar, Keith rallied his bandmates to write new material with him. Now with production assistance from Don Was and Chic's Nile Rodgers, 1989's *Cosmic Thing* rebirthed the band through counterculture. Rodgers had been a Black Panther. Lesbian bassist Sara Lee had played with the radical post-punks Gang of Four. Was's art-funk outfit, Was (Not Was), had recently hit pop radio, but the band's bread-and-butter was underground dance jams like 1981's Paradise Garage favorite "Tell Me That I'm Dreaming," which samples and skewers President Ronald Reagan. Rather than reviving 1960s magic-carpet-ride vibes for mere memorabilia, the band repurposes them in groovy guitars, lyrical goodwill, and earthy femme energy heightened by the rural Woodstock, New York, settings in which the album was written and partially recorded. *Cosmic Thing* is sentimental, nature-loving, and sociological for good reason: AIDS forced many of us to renew our activism twenty years after Stonewall. To hear this utopianism from our own shindig standbys, who'd lost a cohort and brother to the epidemic, was like a reassuring hug from a reenergized nightlife pal presumed gone for good.

Although the group draws much of its manic zing from vintage TV, 1980s television had grown antagonistic to LGBTQ viewers via the cable-enabled rise of virulently antigay televangelists, the Reagan-emboldened far right, and news media that either ignored AIDS or demonized its casualties. "Gettin' nothin' but static," the group summarizes on "Channel Z." Given all the "politicrits pushin' dope," it became an act of defiance just to walk out the door queer. I learned this firsthand on October 6, 1989, when a battalion of San Francisco cops in riot gear attacked ACT UP protesters in the Castro's heart. I'd merely left a restaurant, but had to sneak along storefronts to reach home without getting arrested.

A tender reminiscence of LGBTQ otherness, "Deadbeat Club" praises bohemian wellsprings secluded beyond major municipalities. Drawing from their shared outsider history and memories of their departed teammate, the group honor the camaraderie that fed their dreams. The "Normaltown" they crash is a real-life Athens neighborhood that harbored Allen's, a nightclub home to both the Bs and R.E.M. That's why Fred's fellow University of Georgia alumnus Michael Stipe appears in the song's misty-eyed music video. Amid horses, convertibles, and other Southern signifiers, the camera captures the closeness Keith and Fred share with their male friends. Their deadbeat club is likely a lot like yours.

"Love Shack" follows the tradition of songs like the Temptations' 1969 hit "Psychedelic Shack" that consecrate clubs offering shelter from the squares who subjugate us. "Sign says, 'Stay away, fools'/'Cause love rules at the Love Shack," Fred warns. It's situated where bohos need it most—in the boondocks. As the 2006 documentary *Small Town Gay Bar* reminds, LGBTQ life in the pre-internet Bible Belt took place in rural sanctuaries like this one. Unlike urban nightspots, which attract some tribes and exclude others, rural

LGBTQ bars, by necessity, are mixed. In this shack, every kind of body—including those of drag queens, as signified by pre-fame RuPaul's inclusion in the video—moves and grooves as one glitter-trailing party animal.

An imperishable smash that tipped the band into multiplatinum status, "Love Shack" united generations and nations of fans as the Bs became grade A queer ambassadors, a role varying incarnations of the group have continued into the twenty-first century. This GOAT LGBTQ band remains proof that the surest way to dissolve homophobia and its damage is to openly have more fun than your oppressors.

⏭

Chapter Twenty-One

Talking Heads and Post-Punk

When I was sixteen, I met a band for the first time, a heterosexual but queer one: Talking Heads. Their bassist, Tina Weymouth, said something that's stuck with me. I had asked the New York quartet what they listened to, expecting its members to mention the punk bands that enchanted edgy rock fans that year, 1977. Instead, Weymouth enthused about Brian Eno, with whom they'd later record their most intrepid work, but also Parliament-Funkadelic and Al Green. She might've even included Bohannon, Bob Marley, and the other Black giants who'd be name-checked by Tom Tom Club—her forthcoming splinter band with her sisters and husband, Heads drummer Chris Frantz—in 1981's "Genius of Love." Some pundits before Talking Heads' MTV-fueled, early '80s mainstream breakthrough thought punk and Weymouth's favorites were antithetical, but after speaking with her, I fathomed the punk-ness of funk. Women, queer people, and other subordinates would soon bring both together to make rock more jagged and rhythmic, yet inclusive, even intellectual, like urban life.

Take Talking Heads on "The Girls Want to Be with the Girls" from 1978's *More Songs About Buildings and Food*, their first with Eno. Whereas most punk features guitars distorted into a constant blur of chords, Talking Heads' punchy staccato approach pulls from James Brown. But because its members wore preppy duds and started at CBGB like their Sire label mates the

Ramones, few initially noticed this. As in soul, there's little instrumental hierarchy in the Heads; Weymouth's bass is just as prominent and important as everything else. She'd met drummer Frantz and guitarist/singer David Byrne at the Rhode Island School of Design and thought the former was gay because of the company he kept. The group—especially when completed by fellow art student Jerry Harrison on keyboards and guitar—made their avant-garde elements approachable because they were outstandingly taut. With excitable, explosive yelps that give "Psycho Killer" believability, Byrne moves the rhythm vocally. Despite its brains, this is a physical band.

In "The Girls," Byrne examines differences between men and women the way a visitor from a distant galaxy might. Lines such as, "Well, there's just no love/When there's boys and girls" imply he's observing lesbian feminism's rise. Other observations suggest he's studying the socialist ambitions of matriarchal enterprises like Olivia Records. Yet this chipper song's meaning remains open-ended. Do these gals want to be with each other because they're on the same wavelength, or because they're gay? Either way, Byrne acknowledges that men can be threatened by what they can't cognize, especially when it comes to women not desiring them. He isn't angry; just puzzled. Alix Dobkin—the singer-songwriter behind Lavender Jane's *Lavender Jane Loves Women*, which in 1973 was the first album to focus on lesbian life—covered "Girls" on 1990's *Yahoo Australia! Alix Live from Sydney*. She was among the staunchest separatists of women's music, the sort who wouldn't ordinarily approach a man's song without satire. Yet she sings this one sincerely. She knows from experience what Byrne merely speculates about.

Just as gay and bisexual men like Tom Robinson and Pete Shelley infiltrated the UK pop mainstream via punk's noncompliance, queer and allied women like Switzerland's LiLiPUT crashed alternative dance clubs with disobedient guitars that declared underground affiliations. The B-side of a 1980 UK single, "Die Matrosen"—German for "The Sailors"—is delivered in broken English. Guitarist Marlene Marder came out of a lesbian-feminist scene influenced by Olivia Records. But every ragged thing about this post-punk favorite, from its browbeating bassline to its whistling chorus, is compulsively catchy, and the band wallops them all, as if they were the sailors aiming to impress the girls. Book of Love—a New York synthpop foursome fronted by Susan Ottaviano and Ted Ottaviano, not related yet both gay—covered "Die Matrosen" on the group's eponymous 1986 debut, which is packed with dance hits like "Boy," on which Susan sings of being unable to enter Boy Bar, a real-life East Village gay hotspot that barred women.

Several early '80s mixed-gender groups materialized with women in the driver's seat. Like LiLiPUT, they evolved out of punk yet took arrangement cues from the build-ups and drop-outs of disco. Au Pairs' 1981 alternative club corker "It's Obvious" politicizes the personal by placing the simplest egalitarian message—"You're equal, but different"—in a relationship context and repeating it as one would in a rally. Yet this Leeds, England, quartet plays with crackling tension that transcends agitprop. Suspense mounts from each instrumental element, withholding release until the chorus, which adds just enough choppy variation to propel the groove. In the verses, leader Lesley Woods's languid vocal hints that this parity extends to equal-opportunity orgasms. Her lover scrubs her back in the bathtub, and cooks breakfast, too, and she reports this all as if basking in post-coital felicity, while guitarist Paul Foad follows her lead, showing solidarity. Today, Woods identifies as polysexual, and her concerns extend beyond orientation even here.

New York yielded Bush Tetras, who got their start when ex-Contortions guitarist Pat Place went out with bassist Laura Kennedy, a former schoolmate of singer Cynthia Sley. This isn't a ladylike band: Graffiti near Sley's apartment renamed them "Butch Tetras." Their debut single on 99 Records, 1980's "Too Many Creeps," remains a snapshot of downtown Manhattan at its challenging peak. "I just don't wanna go/Out on the streets, no more!" Sley proclaims. Women are told that their life's purpose is to consume, but these

Tetras don't care to because nothing's worth the price they'd pay. The negativity fueling NYC's paradigmatic post-punk club hit protests that women are rarely entirely safe; something LGBTQ people also grok. Yet cohesion comes out of this pressure cooker. While Place hacks out cranky chords, Kennedy scales across her bass, as drummer Dee Pop (a guy) keeps immovable time. Everything's equal, but different, and functioning as one. At the end of every chorus in which the title is reiterated, there's a one-word affirmation: "Yeah!" Even on a petulant record built on noncompliance, that sliver of positivity acknowledges that we've dodged the garbage tossed our way.

"Too Many Creeps" soundtracked my wedding's spotlight dance, featuring me and my final female ex, Liz, a New York–born Latina with whom I shared a male ex, my first boyfriend, Mike. Liz taught me a crucial lesson. Not being able to make things work with her meant I wasn't bi like Mike; I was gay. She brought her son to the wedding, where he danced with my stepdaughter. This surreal occurrence marked the fact that Liz and I beat the odds and made it through, surviving the creeps, and even ourselves.

Contemporaries of LiLiPUT and Bush Tetras, two lesbian-fronted new wave bands cracked the Canadian mainstream in the first half of the 1980s. Toronto's Rough Trade didn't only pick up where *Rocky Horror* left off musically; the liner notes of its 1976 debut *Rough Trade Live!* explain that the band "celebrates and satirizes those regions of carnal knowledge that society prefers to keep underground." These hidden strata went overground across Canada in 1981 with "High School Confidential," which is likely the first mainstream lesbian hit anywhere in the world. Broadcasting unrepentant lust for a "cool blonde scheming bitch" still in secondary school, Carole Pope more than hints that her narrator is a girl infatuated with a classmate who "makes me cream my jeans when she comes my way." While lip-syncing this line in the video, Pope reaches between her legs and pulls upward—a gesture that predates crotch-grabbing by Michael Jackson, Madonna, and a million rappers.

This success greenlighted more queer themes. The video for 1981's "All Touch" features a lavender triangle that frames Pope and reinforces the queer signaling of the band's name. The next year, when British Invasion star Dusty Springfield lived with Pope and covered her songs, Neil Bogart's Boardwalk Records, then doing big business with Joan Jett, released *For Those Who Think Young*, the album containing "All Touch," in the US. MTV helped make the single a minor US hit, but Bogart died, Boardwalk folded, and no US label dared to release the band's next domestic triumph, 1982's "Crimes of Passion," in which a different kind of gay triangle meets a deadly end enacted in an even more explicitly queer video. Rough Trade faded soon after, but its legacy was already assured.

The Parachute Club broke from the darkness that defined Rough Trade and much LGBTQ life. This mixed-gender Toronto septet's "Rise Up"—a 1983 Canadian pop and US dance hit—radiates so much sunny positivity that it feels like a lesbian-led Pride parade, and that's exactly what its video looks like. With lines like "We want freedom to love who we please" and "Woman's time has come," this soca-fueled empowerment call comes from a lesbian-feminist perspective that's unmistakable for those with ears to hear it. "Rise Up" won the 1984 Grammy-equivalent Juno for Single of the Year over smashes by Bryan Adams and Men Without Hats. In 2022, the group's leader, lesbian activist and filmmaker Lorraine Segato, was named to the Order of Canada.

Women weren't the only rockers advocating for change. With their 1982 MTV hit "Love My Way," the Psychedelic Furs became LGBTQ allies. "It's basically addressed to people who are fucked up about their sexuality and says, 'Don't worry about it.' It was originally written for gay people," singer Richard Butler explained. Unlike Todd Rundgren's 1973 track "You Don't Have to Camp Around," which offers support but also criticism, Butler stands with us.

This was an unusual move for a brooding London post-punk band known for sneering social commentary and sarcastic anti-love songs. Ordinarily, Butler's voice drips withering disdain, like on 1981's "Pretty in Pink," which inspired John Hughes's same-titled 1986 film. But on "Love My Way," he softens his rasp to a purr and eliminates his usual distance from his subjects. Butler describes an enemy to freedom but doesn't designate what that opposition wants to squash. "Love my way, it's a new road/I follow where my mind goes," he repeats. This liberty is threatening to those who aim to subjugate and separate "us." Butler's use of this collective, inclusive pronoun is notable, for he usually sets himself apart from the crowd. Rather than concluding by repeating the chorus, like most pop tunes, Butler segues from the morale-boosting third verse into a wordless sigh that ascends over producer Rundgren's buoyant marimba riff to imply the singer attains enlightenment by loving who he wants.

By the early twenty-first century, the seeds Weymouth planted had grown into a forest. Post-punk returned through chiefly female and/or queer bands like Gossip and Le Tigre that drew not only from the genre's fractured and often female-articulated funk but also its feminist back talk. The teen protagonist of 2017's *Call Me by Your Name*—among the most viewed and acclaimed LGBTQ films ever—watches his crush dance to "Love My Way." Inflamed by fear, jealousy, and fervor, he throws up, and they kiss. That's love their way—and ours.

⏭

Chapter Twenty-Two

Judas Priest

Punk wasn't merely a genre: Like the LGBTQ movement, it changed wardrobes, hairstyles, and lives. In their leather jackets, skimpy T-shirts, dark sunglasses, and worn jeans, all of which became massively imitated punk signifiers, the Ramones may have drawn inspiration from Marlon Brando in *The Wild One*, but to us they looked like sketchy rough trade. In England, the link between punk and queer presentation was more direct. Aspiring London fashion designers Malcolm McLaren and Vivienne Westwood had fabricated red patent leather costumes for the New York Dolls, whom McLaren briefly managed before the band split, and sold their own apparel out of a boutique that routinely changed its name. While known as SEX, their shop specialized in fetish gear and goading T-shirts that often had a gay slant, like Westwood's "Cowboys," which appropriated Colt Studio co-founder Jim French's drawing of two pants-free buckaroos with cocks nearly touching. Those who worked or hung out there formed the future of UK punk: all four original Sex Pistols plus members of Siouxsie and the Banshees, Adam and the Ants, Generation X, and the Pretenders.

As this antiestablishment movement threatened to render all preexisting rock obsolete, other insurgent musicians were forced to confront a daunting question: How could they still seem rebellious in a world where these punk upstarts preached anarchy?

Judas Priest took this issue zealously. Formed among the same Birmingham factories that birthed Black Sabbath, this quintessential British heavy metal band switched record labels, costumes, drummers, and styles for several years with limited success. Like Queen, the fivesome features an operatic singer, Rob Halford, who can sing anything. The band even covered Joan Baez's "Diamonds and Rust," which the pioneering feminist folkie loved, but it didn't make Judas Priest stars. What cracked the quintet in the UK was even more improbable. Halford buzzed off most of his hair, traded his silks and sashes for leathers and studs, and performed "Take on the World" on England's *Top of the Pops* in 1979 looking like he'd just walked out of a Tom of Finland illustration. The sing-along outlined Priest's plans for an audience that to this day remains almost exclusively male: "We're gonna ride ya/We're gonna get right inside ya."

The album that "Take on the World" comes from, *Hell Bent for Leather*, is remembered for its speed-metal title track. For years, Halford made his entrances to it on a Harley. He'd pantomime fucking that motorcycle, and crack a whip at his bandmates. But even before manifesting this queerness, he sang of it. "Raw Deal" from 1977 describes a bar overflowing with macho men. There's no mention of women. Instead, Halford references Fire Island. As his character drinks, his narration grows impressionistic, suggesting an orgy with the singer at its center. "I was barely holding on to this flying body symphony," he reports as if drifting out of reality before snapping back to deliver the clearest lyric: "The true free expression I demand is human rights." Although few noticed at the time, Halford averred his sexuality and stood up for us.

In 1978's "Beyond the Realms of Death," Halford describes a catatonic patient at a psychiatric hospital, the kind in which LGBTQ people, even those not mentally ill, were still sequestered like inmates. The subject detaches from everything, "Until one day he smiled/It seemed as though with pride," and then dies, finally achieving the sovereignty denied him. Shrieking his way through earthly emotional barriers, Halford metaphorically describes what he dared not directly address: the spiritual death that is life in the closet.

In 1985, the Parents Music Resource Center sought to regulate music deemed violent, drug-related, or sexually explicit. Number three on the PMRC's "Filthy Fifteen" list was Judas Priest's "Eat Me Alive." Tipper Gore—wife of future Vice President Al Gore—believed the track from 1984's *Defenders of the Faith* advocated rape through lyrics like "I'm going to force you at gunpoint to eat me alive." Like most Priest songs, it doesn't mention gender, but lines like "You're well-equipped to take it all" suggest rough but consensual gay sex. As with that album's "Jawbreaker," Halford's weapon is almost certainly just a big dick.

Halford fully came out in 1998 while promoting his industrial metal duo 2wo. Hiding at that point would've been ridiculous: 2wo's fetish-intensive "I Am a Pig" music video revels in queerness orchestrated by Chi Chi LaRue, a trans director of gay and bi porn. Halford reunited with Judas Priest in the twenty-first century, and the six albums the band recorded after his announcement charted higher in the US and/or the UK than anything the band released while he was closeted. As confirmed by his 2020 autobiography *Confess*, Halford defies the codes of silence expected in a hypermasculine scene. When Dolly Parton was inducted into the Rock & Roll Hall of Fame in 2022, he sang "Please don't take away my man" during her "Jolene." Through gestures like this, Halford attains the human right to freedom of expression he earlier demanded.

⏭
Chapter Twenty-Three

Prince and Wendy & Lisa

Like Rob Halford, Prince evolved into one of the world's most magnetic yet defiant superstars by introducing LGBTQ auras into a genre ordinarily seen as inimical to queer influence. Although he would integrate practically every single style of the twentieth and early twenty-first centuries, his core was funk, which, like metal, is largely performed and consumed by ostensibly straight guys. But unlike Judas Priest, Prince was never butch. A compact, soft-spoken, sensitive, and wildly prolific Black man who challenged racial and gender norms as routinely as most humans change their underwear, Prince put the Q in LGBTQ. "Am I Black or white?/Am I straight or gay?" he asked in 1981's "Controversy," the first hit to scrutinize his unconventional persona while perpetuating it.

But don't take my word. Here's an excerpt of the 2009 interview I conducted for *Out* with guitarist Wendy Melvoin and keyboardist Lisa Coleman, the lesbian couple at the heart of his greatest and most popular band, the Revolution.

> MELVOIN: I was frequenting the Starwood, a famous L.A. rock club on one side and a disco on the other. The summer of '78, I snuck into the disco and heard "Soft and Wet." I thought it was a girl. I ran up to the DJ and the guy said, "It's this kid out of

> Minneapolis. His name is Prince." And then I get this phone call from my darling Lisa Coleman, who had been flown to Minneapolis to do the *Dirty Mind* record. She had no idea who he was. I didn't think he was a gay guy—I just had a sense about him because of my own gayness.
>
> COLEMAN: He was little and kinda prissy, but he's so not gay.
>
> MELVOIN: He doesn't have that kind of playfulness. He's a girl for sure, but not gay.
>
> COLEMAN: I think you had said that he looked at me like a gay woman would look at another woman.
>
> MELVOIN: Yeah, exactly right.
>
> COLEMAN: Totally. He's like a fancy lesbian.

Singing nearly all his earliest songs in a falsetto even more feminine than Sylvester's, Prince, particularly at the beginning, epitomized the kind of guy that heterosexuals at least initially perceive as gay. On *American Bandstand,* in early 1980, he lip-synced his pop breakthrough "I Wanna Be Your Lover" while shaking his Farrah Fawcett hair with Mick Jagger–level assurance, yet he could barely speak above a whisper when interviewed by host Dick Clark. Even then Prince was complex and contradictory, sometimes to a fault. On 1979's hard rock "Bambi," he attempts to seduce a lesbian by asserting "it's better with a man" and "maybe you need to bleed."

Prince ramped up this provocation on the masterstroke that established his outré preeminence while blueprinting Black '80s pop: 1980's slow-jam-free *Dirty Mind.* Decked out on its cover in a flasher's raincoat, black bikini underwear, cowboy bandanna, and assless leggings, Prince projected a hypersexual otherness that raised more questions than it answered.

Featuring a synth redolent of Blondie's cheap organs, *Dirty Mind*'s title track swells and constricts one melodic line over disco's four-on-the-floor steadfastness. "I may not be your kind of man," he admits, but that doesn't stop his seduction, which flaunts submission as a form of domination. "You got me on my knees," he genuflects, power-bottom style. An ascending churchy organ offsets descending key changes—a Princely juxtaposition of god-fearing Christianity and low-down lasciviousness. Ending with agitated repetition, the arrangement denies consummation in favor of suspended anticipation. You can almost hear its singer salivating.

These kinks buttressed Prince's new wave cred, particularly on "When You Were Mine." There's the clothes-sharing, his fixation on his replacement, and that zinger about not making a fuss when this guy slept between his honey and him. In "Uptown," a passing hottie asks, "Are you gay?" Never losing his sangfroid, Prince reasons, "She's just a victim of society and all its games."

In 1981, Prince launched the first of many side projects in which he was the principal songwriter, player, and producer, often under false names. Singing together with frontman Morris Day throughout to bolster his song's unmissable man-on-man flavor, Prince gives the Time's "Get It Up" enough ambiguity to make it an R&B hit, but its lyric makes most anatomical sense if its seduction is directed at another guy. "I'm gonna try to blow your mind," Day insinuates. On Prince's own *Controversy*, the rising star sings "Private Joy" lovingly to his penis, declares "I'm gonna let my body be free" on "Sexuality," and concludes by offering to "Jack U Off."

After these humdingers, Prince recalibrated his presentation's queerness to prioritize women in homoerotic formulations, like his girl group Vanity 6, and then his own band. The video for 1982's "1999" features Coleman and backing vocalist Jill Jones singing while undulating body to body. Following this, guitarist Melvoin joined Coleman, then her lover, in what Prince aptly named the Revolution, which situated a lesbian couple at pop's artistic and commercial forefront. Recorded in part with Coleman and Melvoin, 1984's *Purple Rain* became the best-selling album of its year, topped the US pop chart for six months, and moved twenty-five million copies worldwide. Its accompanying movie was the year's eleventh-biggest film. In both, lesbians played a part by design.

"We had a photo shot for the *Purple Rain* poster," Coleman said of the foldout that came with *Purple Rain*'s vinyl. "We were all in our different positions, and Prince walked over to me and Wendy, lifted my arm up, put my hand around Wendy's waist, and said, 'There.' That's how precise he was about how he wanted the image of the band to be."

For the opening of that album's "Computer Blue," a circuitous groove the duo helped compose, Prince handed them a brief and nearly nonsensical script that suggests that the two bathed together and that this ritual generated the music. To some degree, it did. Melvoin and Coleman's intimacy helped make the Revolution—who were black and white and male and female, just like Sly's Family Stone—creatively and culturally fertile. Their contributions as lesbians expanded the band's possibilities while suggesting that different kinds of people could create something definition defying while coming together.

This message wasn't merely for show, and that's because these women play better than many men. Their fathers ranked among L.A.'s session-player elite—Melvoin's arranged and played on the Partridge Family's hits, while Coleman's contributed to loads of 1970s Motown—and properly trained their daughters. Soon after Melvoin joined his band, Prince rigorously incorporated jazz, psychedelic pop, folk, and other styles far beyond funk while widening his arrangements and advancing his melodies. This inclusivity continued through Prince's most Melvoin and Coleman–shaped album, 1986's frolicsome psych-soul excursion *Parade*. He assembled another, *Dream Factory*, soon after, but held on to it. Then he recorded a disc of artificially pitched-up vocals—a sonic gender reassignment—for an album he intended to release under the name Camille. Trimming and combining both, he assembled what's considered his capstone, 1987's *Sign "O" the Times*.

Its title track marks the first time a US superstar tackled AIDS in a hit. He clarifies that the epidemic was not, as then often believed, a gay-specific malady. "In France a skinny man died of a big disease with a little name/By chance his girlfriend came across a needle and soon she did the same" begins the album that inverts Melvoin and Coleman's lushness through stark funk infused with spiritual distress.

The pair play on three tracks, but their influence lingers throughout, particularly on *Sign*'s Camille-intended "If I Was Your Girlfriend." It's been written that it reveals Prince's jealousy of Melvoin's closeness to her twin Susannah, his former fiancée, who sang in the Family, a group he assembled for her and was the first to release "Nothing Compares 2 U." Yet it might be inspired by Melvoin's rapport with Coleman. Sung in a pitch-raised plea from the perspective of a man wishing he were a woman so he could be a confidant in a way Prince believed only women can achieve with other women, it's his smartest lyric.

Rather than telling this lover who might already be his ex what to do, as a man would, Prince asks provocative questions, the way a gal-pal might. But his queries soon escalate beyond dressing, shampooing, breakfast-making, and chick-flick-watching to indicate the musician wishes he were more than girl-friendly. "I want to be all of the things you are to me," he continues as the instrumentation undergoes unorthodox harmonic shifts and key changes, as if his own gender is remodeling. Abandoning his platonic proposal, he monologues, "We don't have to make children to make love." The song concludes as he imagines them both undressing as women, having sex, and basking in the afterglow. In other words, Prince wishes both he and his girlfriend were lesbians.

In the Revolution's wake, Melvoin and Coleman relaunched as Wendy & Lisa. Whereas Prince effortlessly crossed genres, color lines, and genders, in part because colossal popularity gave him leverage, Wendy & Lisa struggled against an industry that didn't know what to do with lesbian lovers who shape-shifted like their former collaborator because they helped him do it. That friction is played out in the artwork for 1987's *Wendy and Lisa*. Whereas the European release resembles the famously sapphic shot in Ingmar Bergman's *Persona*, the US cover soft-pedals their intimacy. The closest they came to a domestic hit, that album's "Waterfall" resembles expansive UK rock fusions, not the narrow lingerie-funk the US record biz required.

The duo pushed back. Both feminine and gallant, 1990's *Eroica* includes k.d. lang guesting on "Mother of Pearl," which foreshadows the panoramic haze of their subsequent indie discs after a preliminary album with UK superproducer Trevor Horn got scrapped. While they aimed to flex their creative brawn, Horn wanted them to be the Spice Girls and, as they testified to me, treated them homophobically. Playing backup for lang, Madonna, and Meshell Ndegeocello before pivoting to TV and film, Melvoin and Coleman won an Emmy in 2010 for their *Nurse Jackie* theme.

It's an oversimplification to say that Prince never recovered from their departure, but he couldn't sustain his brilliance and best-selling run. He recorded the untitled *Black Album* as a butch counterpart to *Camille,* only to withdraw it at the last moment, in late 1987, and replaced it with 1988's *Lovesexy*, which features the superstar in a girly nude pose on its cover, which might've hindered US sales. For the next few years, he alternated flops like 1990's *Graffiti Bridge* film with hits that sometimes recertified his place on the LGBTQ spectrum. "Cream" celebrates bottoming as it rhymes "get on top" with "you will cop." Prince joked that he wrote this 1991 hit while looking in the mirror—likely to downplay that he directs it at a guy.

Then Prince waged war with his record company, changing his name to an unpronounceable symbol, which embellishes the combined male and female glyph he had employed for the previous decade—another gender disobedience that recalls his opening lyric to *Purple Rain*'s "I Would Die 4 U": "I'm not a woman, I'm not a man/I am something that you'll never understand." Floppy discs containing the font were sent to critics like me so we could avoid typing "the artist formerly known as Prince." During a stretch of angry, hypermasculine music, Prince self-released 1994's "The Most Beautiful Girl in the World," a supplicating falsetto tribute to his dancer and future wife Mayte Garcia that emanates femininity and became his final pop hit.

Yet Prince's showmanship persevered. Throughout 2016's strictly solo Piano & a Microphone Tour, he improvised labyrinthine medleys of hits and deep cuts, substantiating what can truly be described as genius. Had I not witnessed it myself, I wouldn't have believed it. A week after the outing's end, Prince overdosed on a painkiller that masked years of rigorous dancing in high heels. This was the price he paid for being funk's greatest musician, producer, songwriter, and gender-bender. Prince broke so many rules that he broke his body—the paramount transgression LGBTQ people know all too well.

⏭

Chapter Twenty-Four

Joan Jett and the Go-Go's

When the Runaways imploded in 1979, their rhythm guitarist and sometime singer Joan Jett didn't seem destined to eclipse her idol, Detroit-born, UK-based Suzi Quatro. Most Americans remember Quatro as Leather Tuscadero on TV's nostalgic sitcom *Happy Days*. But in England, the bassist became a glam star, a female version of the genre's requisite gender reversal, as typified by her screaming 1973 cover of the Beatles' early Ringo Starr–sung rocker "I Wanna Be Your Man." Like Starr did in his band's 1963 cover of the Shirelles' "Boys," on which he sings that they're "a bundle of joy," Quatro announced that gender and even heterosexuality's rules didn't apply to her, nor to rock 'n' roll.

As her costuming and choice of covers have proven for fifty years, Jett still follows Quatro's recusant example. Her first post-breakup move was to produce 1979's notoriously noisy *(GI)*, the only studio album by the Germs, an L.A. band that invented hardcore punk before its gay singer, Darby Crash, intentionally overdosed on heroin. Despite the help of industry veteran Kenny Laguna, Jett's eponymous 1980 solo debut was rejected by twenty-three labels before Jett, like many in women's music, released it on her own label, Blackheart Records. Drawing from punk, glam, and vintage rock, the guitarist performs cunning covers and combative originals with a raggedy growl that never conforms to mainstream expectations of how women should sing.

Nevertheless, former Casablanca Records owner Neil Bogart rereleased as *Bad Reputation* on his own Boardwalk Records in 1981, shortly before he died of lymphoma.

Mixing the Ramones' guitars with Gary Glitter's tom-toms, "Bad Reputation" is a queer woman's fight song. Rebelling against outdated mores, its first verse strips feminism to its essence: "A girl can do what she wants to do." The second verse prioritizes pleasure over social advancement, and the third rejects conformity. "Never been afraid of any deviation," Jett admits while claiming her place outside society with a brusqueness that was then considered abrasive but today registers as contemporary. In 2003, bisexual Toronto musician Peaches sampled it on "I Don't Give A . . ." to caustic, spine-tingling effect.

Although her fondness for covers could have been a hindrance, Jett sealed her longevity with one so definitive many don't realize she didn't write it. While visiting England with the Runaways, Jett heard an overlooked 1975 glam B-side by the Arrows. She first covered it with two Sex Pistols on the B-side of her 1979 rendition of pop's original patriarchy-defying anthem, 1963's "You Don't Own Me" by Leslie Gore, a Quincy Jones–produced '60s teen star who later came out. With lines like "Don't try to change me in any way," Gore's hit was an apt match for Jett. But when Jett rerecorded the Arrows' cut with her new band, the Blackhearts, something unexpected took place: Jett's rendition topped *Billboard*'s singles chart for seven weeks and became the number three song of 1982.

In her "I Love Rock 'n' Roll," it's the woman who's the cocky seducer. Blustering like a dude—"And I could tell it wouldn't be long/Till he was with *me*, yeah, *me*!"—Jett wields the butch swagger that Gladys Bentley and other queer blues women brought to their records. Nowhere to be found is Janis Joplin's pain—this is pleasure personified. Jett is not only saying that she loves rock 'n' roll. With every clanging guitar riff and bravado-laced bellow, Joan vaunts that she *is* rock 'n' roll. There'd never been a Number One record this joyously dykey yet utterly universal, and there still never has.

One of early MTV's most-played clips, its black-and-white video is set in Private's, a Manhattan club, which Jett enters in full leather like spaghetti-western-era Clint Eastwood. Only once does she acknowledge the Blackhearts' teen bassist, Gary Ryan, dancing at the jukebox like the guy in the song. Her stare is fixed on us, and her desire is directed at the record machine. She and the band then appear onstage, and when the camera shows her viewpoint, Jett invites us to see the world from her empowering perspective: Girls like her are front and center. Already she's strutting atop the bar as a champion, much like Freddie Mercury, but without the royalty trappings. Instead, Jett emphasizes that being a tough rock gal who might be gay is noble yet perfectly normal.

On subsequent remakes, Joan didn't always change pronouns. For her high-volume update of Tommy James and the Shondells' psychedelic "Crimson and Clover," a US Top Ten hit for her in 1982, she dares to sing the song as written—to a woman, like Meg Christian would have. Her sapphic statement isn't subtle. It's there in the opening lines, "I don't hardly know her/But I think I could love her." This may be purely pragmatic: "Him" doesn't rhyme with "clover" like "her" does.

But Jett doesn't shy away from the resulting drift. The video starts like *The Rocky Horror Picture Show,* with an extreme closeup on Jett's lips. She's as butch as Frank-N-Furter was femme. This is bookended with shots of Jett's spitting tulips, as if literally deflowering her conquest. Jett leaps, tears the surrounding screens with her guitar, and bangs the instrument against the floor—standard rock behavior, but not for a woman of her era. In her next video, *Bad Reputation*'s remake of Gary Glitter's "Do You Wanna Touch Me (Oh Yeah)," she boxes a male challenger *and* the camera. These videos gave the mainstream its first glimpse of a woman this athletic and aggressive who wasn't an Olympic competitor.

Sometimes Jett sang about sexual urges for men, like in "Handyman," but even there she's not exactly gender normative. "I'm sick and tired of masturbatin'," she gripes. Elsewhere on 1983's *Album,* Jett suggests she wants more than one-on-one arrangements. "Secret Love" describes what at first seems to be a heterosexual love triangle, but it makes more sense if you hear the "you" in "I'm with him and you're with her" as female, especially when Jett gets to lines like "Society won't let me be the way I want it to." "The French Song" features an *en français* chorus that confesses she likes threesomes. Aiming to coax her consort into trying one, she chants, "I know what I am/I am what I am." It was likely a coincidence that Gloria Gaynor simultaneously returned to LGBTQ clubs in 1983 with a dance version of *La Cage aux Folles*'s gay-pride anthem, "I Am What I Am," but still.

Updating the pansexual freedom of *Cabaret*, the video for "The French Song" makes an analogous proclamation as it pays tribute to Jett's favorite film while acknowledging the breadth of her interests. The first shot is of Jett as a dominatrix looking down on the viewer—we look up at her like a lover she's mounting. The *Rocky Horror* lips return between similarly hazy shots of Jett's rocking out onstage, always on top. When the chorus hits, she, the band, and other outsiders stride as if in a spontaneous Pride parade. The scene shifts to the Blackhearts' playing at a bordello for an audience of lesbian tarts, drag queens, punks, hookers, johns, sailors, gay boys, and even a Doberman as the song builds to its Sex Pistol-ian crescendo. Her mischievous expression as she strides a three-pillowed bed in shiny rubber while resembling horror hostess Elvira helps rank "The French Song" among the sexiest, most jaw-droppingly queer benchmarks of MTV's glory days.

Like most of her generation's LGBTQ musical peers, Jett refrained from formal wording of her sexuality while letting her art do the talking. "Anyone who wants to know who I am can just read my lyrics," Jett once said. "I've always written about who I am." Returning Jett to Top Forty airplay, as well as her earlier Glitter-inspired sound, 1988's "I Hate Myself for Loving You" can be heard as the song of a good girl who falls for the bad boy, or as the cry of a closeted LGBTQ person. Co-written with gay songsmith Desmond Child, it captures a tumultuous love that generates gossip and stability-shaking challenges—much like coming out.

When alternative rock exploded in the early '90s, Jett turned away from the mainstream she had just reconnected with. Bikini Kill frontwoman Kathleen Hanna appears on 1994's self-descriptive *Pure and Simple*, where their "Spinster" reclaims derogatory lesbian code as a badge of pride. Returning with 2006's *Sinner*, Jett answers those who've long wanted her to define herself.

"Five" asks, "Do you want me to come out, ready or not/Do you want big proof, is that what you need?" On "Androgynous," her cover of the 1984 Replacements song about a gender-fluid couple, Jett trades piano for campfire guitars and harmonies, rendering the original's progressive prediction as nostalgia—a switch that emphasizes how commonplace gayness and gender noncompliance had become. In 2015, Miley Cyrus, Jett, and Laura Jane Grace—the trans leader of Against Me!—further countrified Jett's arrangement to benefit Cyrus's homeless LGBTQ youth foundation.

Written by Suzi Quatro's former hitmakers Nicky Chinn and Mike Chapman and first released in 1974 by Jett's glam heroes in Sweet, "A.C.D.C." was in its original incarnation a saucy commentary on female bisexuality from a straight guy who shares his girlfriend with many women. Slurring "let's be in it together" so it sounds like "lesbian it together," Sweet's "A.C.D.C." trailblazes because its singer is bemused and awed by his switch-hitting gal, not critical of her. Jett clearly appreciated this. "She got some other fella as well as me!" she bawls in her version with unmissable enthusiasm. Jett included her renditions of "A.C.D.C." and "Androgynous" on 2010's *Greatest Hits*. In a just world, they'd have become actual hits. For us, they already were.

Because the US record industry had excluded most female musicians who weren't solitary singers, only a surefire hit could've introduced the mainstream to what became the first big-selling all-woman band, the Go-Go's. Co-produced by Richard Gottehrer—the 1960s vet who oversaw Blondie's first two albums—1981's "Our Lips Are Sealed" draws from the bubblegum that made Kenny Laguna's work with Jett so impactful. But like its video featuring the fivesome cruising L.A. and jumping into a fountain, "Lips" is so irresistible that its hooks mask the oppositional depth of a lyric that speaks to queer experience.

"Can you hear them?/They talk about us," Belinda Carlisle sings. Is "us" lovers or a community of outcasts? Is "them" merely onlookers or an oppressive regime? Either way, the singer suggests that the proper response to misinformation is to stare down one's enemies with withering silence. Confront your foes righteously, and you'll turn the tables. Midway through, the song's pulse gives way to a bridge featuring intertwined guitar and bass, both ethereal. Guitarist Jane Wiedlin steps in, singing softly, as if consoling a fallen comrade. Her interlude feels weightless and transformative, the way a private moment between shunned companions or fugitives can be.

After the Go-Go's heyday, Wiedlin spoke about her bisexuality, and Carlisle became a public ally when her activist son, James Duke Mason, came out. Although rumors linked her with Sara Gilbert and Jodie Foster, drummer Gina Schock remained mum until 2020's documentary *The Go-Go's*. In it, Schock divulged she and Wiedlin were a couple in the band's early days. You can interpret "Our Lips Are Sealed" as a manifesto for reprobates in a strait-laced suburb or nerds beaten down by bullying jocks. But when you think of it as a vow of silence shared between LGBTQ lovers like Wiedlin and Schock, then forced to stay secret, this seemingly lightweight song takes on deeper meaning.

One staple of the band's early live sets couldn't have focused on homosexuality more directly. Based on Fear's antigay "Fetch Me One More Beer" and rewritten for the Go-Go's by their managers, "Johnny Are You Queer?" plays with the irrational assumption that if a guy doesn't reciprocate a gal's advances, he must be one of us. In 1981, the song went to Josie Cotton, who sings it over a '60s girl-group arrangement that suggests she's living in the past; therefore, the joke's on her. Walking a line between camp and criticism, the song inveigled (or offended) homophiles and homophobes on new wave radio stations like L.A.'s KROQ, especially after Cotton performed it in 1983's similarly satiric *Valley Girl*.

The difference between the Go-Go's and their starry-eyed girl-group predecessors is that these women know the score, convey that knowledge through their own songs, and further articulate their positions instrumentally on

1981's *Beauty and the Beat.* "We rule the streets tonight/Until the morning light," they profess in "Tonite." "Bet you'd live here if you could/And be one of us," Carlisle sings sarcastically in "This Town," an L.A. counterpart to Blondie's Big Apple anthems. Trailing "I Love Rock 'n' Roll" up the charts, the band's dance declaration "We Got the Beat" helped *Beauty* conquer *Billboard*'s Top 200 for six weeks. On April 10, 1982, the Go-Go's and Jett made history by simultaneously occupying the top two positions on both the album *and* single charts.

This inspired many who'd never heard themselves reflected so directly to start a band, or at least find friends who could give us the invincibility that roars throughout *Beauty.* Even when its lyrics reveal uncertainties and fantasies unfulfilled, the album's music gives a thirty-five-minute crash course in cooperative female empowerment. Like punk, *Beauty* suggests that if the Go-Go's could change the course of popular music, so can you.

Although Jett still rarely strays from her bad-girl persona, the Go-Go's soon toyed with their MTV-tailored wholesomeness. Co-directed by Madonna collaborator Mary Lambert, the video for 1984's "Turn to You" morphed the party-hearty quintet into a prim '60s prom band. With four-fifths of them dressing as guys, while Schock is presented super-femme, the group also appear as bouffant-wearing girly girls who pair off with Rob Lowe and each other in male apparel. That's a much queerer scenario than what's in Queen's "I Want to Break Free." But because it was enacted by gender-compliant women presumed to be straight, it didn't spook the industry.

Although Carlisle (and briefly Wiedlin) would achieve solo success, this became the band's final US hit before the exhausted quintet combusted. Society stamps women with an early expiration date, so the suits aim to get as much money out of them as quickly as possible, leaving many female artists battling financial conflicts and drug addictions. After years of hard work, the Go-Go's resolved both. Their reunions never fail to restore the group's LGBTQ-affirming, girl-gang glory.

⏭

Chapter Twenty-Five

Diana Ross and Luther Vandross

Although nearly all her Supremes hits were released before those fateful riotous nights in June 1969, Diana Ross became the first major LGBTQ-sanctioned diva after Stonewall. Some of this came down to timing and collaborators. Her solo career began at the dawn of the '70s with Ashford & Simpson, who shifted Ross away from Detroit's teen R&B to their own symphonic and adult New York soul. While her Supremes catalog often pitted gangbuster grooves against pained sentiment, early solo Ross specialized in a positivity that broke from the tormented princess venerated by pre-Stonewall gay fans. Ross incarnated the female optimism of the '70s by rarely being tragic.

Making the best of fond departures, 1970's Ashford-&-Simpson-written-and-produced "Ain't No Mountain High Enough" and "Remember Me" don't wallow in the man-inflicted sadness of Supremes hits like 1965's "My World Is Empty Without You." When Ross embraced disco with 1976's "Love Hangover," she did so with a full-throttle sensuality enabled by civic progress. "If there's a cure for this, I don't want it," she sings of desire in ways that speak to us. Only her portrayal of Billie Holiday in 1972's *Lady Sings the Blues* draws from the doomed narrative that defined our lives before civil rights, women's lib, and Stonewall. Yet implicit in the acclaim for her Oscar-nominated performance was our marvel that this paragon of empowered Black professionalism could convincingly portray its antithesis.

Since *Dreamgirls*, the 1981 Broadway musical loosely based on the Supremes, Ross has often been deemed a lightweight. But right before that, she released two artistically ample discs. Reuniting her with Ashford & Simpson, 1979's *The Boss* delivers the psychological complexity that boilerplate disco denies. In "No One Gets the Prize," a favorite at Manhattan's largely Black and LGBTQ club the Paradise Garage, Ross sings of acrimonious competition with a female pal for the same man—a tournament that destroys their bond as well as both relationships. Concise poetry such as "So we scandalized and criticized/And then we learned how to despise" captures the lacerating drama we've lived. If you're LGBTQ, you're part of a small fraction of the population, and if you're a racial minority within that, you occupy an even tinier pie slice. Like "Prize," "The Boss" deals with getting wise to how foolish Cupid can turn even those who think they're smart. "Love taught me who was the boss," Ross sings with prominent vocal backing from Ashford & Simpson. Songs like these fed our hunger to learn, even on the dancefloor, about love and ourselves. "I Ain't Been Licked," she trumpets for women, people of color, and us.

"The churches had turned them out," Valerie Simpson told me of disco's LGBTQ audience. "They were reviled by so many, so those clubs meant a lot. The messages in these songs were something that they could hold on to and take home."

At the 1980s' dawn, the chant that disco was dead became so insistent in mainstream media that many Black musicians faced obsolescence. Chic's Nile Rodgers and Bernard Edwards knew they were on the chopping block. Their band's "Le Freak" sold seven million copies worldwide in 1978 while name-checking Studio 54, and their 1979 hits for Sister Sledge—"He's the Greatest Dancer" and "We Are Family"—were Chic records in all but name. Motown executive Suzanne de Passe paired Rodgers and Edwards with Ross to boost the label's biggest superstar, but that went from surefire concept to possible career suicide nearly overnight as Chic's follow-ups to their chart-topping "Good Times" fizzled in the wake of pop radio's disco backlash, which began in the second half of 1979.

When the pair met with Ross, she told them her life story, aiming to turn her whole career upside down. Rodgers and Edwards wrote songs based on those conversations to nudge Ross away from her usual amenities and give her something personal she could reside in rather than simply sing. Chic had already been adventurous and angular. Its 1979 hit "I Want Your Love" employed female musicians—including saxophonist Jean Fineberg, formerly of the all-woman, lesbian-led band Isis—to execute disco's most uncustomary riff: a rapid, Philip Glass–like riot of notes that feels like a roller coaster off its rails. For Ross, they brought that Manhattan buzz of a twenty-four-hour amusement park where fun and danger unite, and it set her free to give her rawest performances.

When Motown heard the results, it freaked. So did Ross. The consensus was that such a radical record would ruin her. Motown engineer Russ Terrana stepped in to trim out some of the Chic-est instrumental passages, downplay the clubby bottom, and boost the volume on silkier alternate vocals. Rodgers and Edwards hated these changes, and Motown was still uncertain, so the label issued the album without a single in the hope that airplay and public reaction would help them figure out what to do with it.

Packaged with a Francesco Scavullo portrait on its cover of a casual Ross looking like she'd just walked off the Paradise Garage's sweaty dancefloor, 1980's *diana* became her best-selling and most critically acclaimed album. The eventual first single, "Upside Down," spreads disco's pulse across several instruments while proving dance music wasn't over, not even on the US pop chart, which it topped for four weeks. The verses stay on one chord, building anticipation for the chorus, where Ross sings of being turned "inside out and round and round." LGBTQ people in Stonewall's wake knew this askew feeling well. When marriage, a family, or even regular employment wasn't an option, we had no choice but to embrace life's twists.

With "Upside Down" still in the pop Top Ten, "I'm Coming Out" joined it. In recent years, Rodgers revealed this indispensable hit's inspiration. "One particular night I went to a club, the Gilded Grape, and I happened to notice at least six or seven Diana Ross impersonators. So I went outside to call Bernard and said, "You know, Diana Ross is revered by the gay community. If we wrote a song called 'I'm Coming Out' for Diana Ross, it would have the same power as James Brown's 'Say It Loud—I'm Black and I'm Proud.'"

Opening in 1974 and situated just outside Times Square, the Gilded Grape was described in *Drag: The International Transvestite Quarterly* as Manhattan's "sole and only drag hangout." Much of the staff and clientele subsequently moved to a nearby disco at the former site of the Peppermint Lounge. That club was called Hollywood and then changed its name to GG's Barnum Room, the disco that Rodgers almost certainly visited. At Studio 54, transfeminine dancers, like Salvador Dalí's alluring companion Dominican pal Potassa de la Fayette, comprised a small but essential element. GG's Barnum Room, however, focused on transwomen of color and their fans. Not only strutting and lip-syncing, as in an ordinary drag show, trans "discobats" at GG's also performed on circus trapezes that flew over the dancefloor. Nightlife photographer Bill Bernstein, who covered the scene, attests, "They were happy to be working and actually getting paid for something they liked to do." In the photographs Bernstein took there, you can see the rupture between GG's fastidiously painted entertainers of color and their drab, white male admirers. This scene inspired Rodgers, a Black bohemian, for its social hierarchy was reversed. Those on the bottom of society's totem pole led the way, just as they did at Stonewall and the early discos, which prioritized Black women, gay DJs, and a rainbow coalition of dancers over rock's straight-white-male center.

Ross reportedly had no idea she was singing anything queer. To her, "I'm Coming Out" was about busting free from Motown's formulaic confines. Miss Ross's concert opener for the next several decades, it features a commanding yet funky horn fanfare befitting a Black queen. The song also functions as a women's lib anthem. Even its unconventional vocal curves and melodic curls suggest bold yet nuanced feminine assertion. Because Rodgers understood that Ross had always disclosed emotions in her music that LGBTQ people couldn't speak in the mainstream, he knew the singer could once again be a conduit for her audience's aspirations. If they couldn't come out in real life, they could get a taste of that emancipation on the dancefloor.

WBLS's powerful Frankie Crocker once again got behind a gay record. Because the station and its disco competitor, WKTU, played on boomboxes and car radios throughout New York, the song rang through its streets like a clarion call. "The time has come for me to break out of this shell," Ross sings for herself *and* for us. "I'm spreading love, there is no need to fear," she continues, acknowledging apprehension from mutual adversaries. Implicitly pro-trans, pro-female, pro-gay, and pro-Black, "I'm Coming Out" inspired an oncoming wave of queer performers who sang their own truths in the '80s mainstream.

And it played out just as Ross and Rodgers intended. Fresh off the success of *diana* and her big 1981 ballad with Lionel Ritchie, "Endless Love," the superstar secured a twenty-million-dollar contract—among the largest of its day—with RCA Records. There she'd score other LGBTQ-surrogate hits like 1982's "Muscles," which was written and produced by Michael Jackson and promoted with an utterly insane video overflowing with beefcake. Her Ritchie duet eventually underscored *Trevor*, a 1994 Oscar-winning short in which a gay boy lip-syncs the ballad as he attempts to kill himself—a scene that inspired the Trevor Project, a suicide prevention hotline for LGBTQ youth that led to other services for our young people. For these reasons and so many more, we'll forever remember Diana Ross as a good thing.

Not long after *diana*, a Black, gay, soon-to-be superstar scored a decisive hit with the first single he released as a soloist, 1981's "Never Too Much." Well before that, Luther Vandross had already made his mark as a jingle singer, songwriter, and vocal-session arranger. He crafted and helped sing the background vocal hook that drives the chorus of David Bowie's 1975 hit "Young Americans." On that same-titled album, Bowie turned Vandross's "Funky Music (Is a Part of Me)" into "Fascination." Vandross then released his original song in 1976 with Luther, his R&B harmony group, and wrote *The Wiz*'s liberation anthem "Everybody Rejoice" (aka "A Brand New Day"). Many disco cameos followed. Former Jobriath drummer Gregg Diamond featured him superbly on Bionic Boogie's "Hot Butterfly," a 1978 favorite in late-night/early morning "sleaze" sets pioneered by gay DJs who brought dancers down from their drugs through downtempo R&B. But Vandross's breakthrough came with Change, a majestic disco act signed to "homo promo" man Ray Caviano's RFC label.

Change covered similar stylistic ground to Chic—another group for which Vandross and other New York–based session singers like Jocelyn Brown sang prominent backgrounds. On Change's 1980 debut *The Glow of Love*, Vandross and Brown swap center stage. "It's a Girl's Affair" shifts disco's liberation theme away from privileging gay men to give queer women their own club anthem. "Ladies only if you please," Brown sings of a lesbian event where "you can even mate."

Change's Italian masterminds, Mauro Malavasi and Jacques Fred Petrus, had already delighted gay dancers with Macho's *I'm a Man* and Revanche's *Music Man*. So when Vandross sang "It's a pleasure when you treasure all that's new and true and gay" on Change's "The Glow of Love," he set off disco gaydar. Airy yet intricate in the Chic tradition—interweaving a funk bassline, clipped guitar figures, Debussy-like piano chords, and billowing orchestration—it reportedly made Vandross exclaim, "This is the most beautiful song I've ever sung in my life!" Riding its waves of melody and then leaping around them like a breaching dolphin, he executes vocal flips that aren't mere filigree—they're flights of ecstasy. Decades later, Janet Jackson sampled its groove on 2001's "All for You."

Change enabled Vandross to go solo with 1981's *Never Too Much*. Its title track erupts with an onslaught of words and feelings crammed into its verses, as if the singer had held them all back for this moment. "I still remember in the days when I was scared to touch you/How I spent my day dreaming, planning how to say I love you," Vandross sings. If you're LGBTQ and set on someone who may or may not be playing on your team, these insecurities consume you. We're told we're predators, or "too much." Having waited so long, he finally finds a willing accomplice. When the contrastingly concise chorus arrives, strings ascend, and Vandross—at last supported by a partner who soothes and smooths out his anxieties—glides with them. The video intercuts footage of pedestrians listening to the singer on boom boxes and Walkmans with shots of him bathed in pink studio light. When he gets to the part where he finds his sweetheart, Vandross quivers in a way straight men never do.

For the next twenty-four years, Vandross shone a light on the vulnerabilities that complimented his virtuosic vocal confidence. Drawing upon his all-female influences, he flexed vast musical muscle while channeling an intimately wounded spirit to become R&B's LGBTQ forerunner—playful on the outside, pained on the inside.

Like its title track, much of *Never Too Much* offers Manhattan variants on Change's transatlantic exultation. Because Vandross sang and arranged vocal beds for years, a background choir flutters and swoops around him with exceptional grace throughout, even when cheer turns to anguish on an epic rearrangement of Burt Bacharach and Hal David's "A House Is Not a Home," a minor hit for Dionne Warwick in 1964. Managing to improve upon a melody from pop's most cultivated songsmith, Vandross removes the original's instrumental padding, decelerates its tempo to a grief-stricken crawl, and reinvents its phrasing so drastically over seven mournful minutes that the result exhibits both the harmonic skills of a conservatory-trained composer and the sad swing of a bluesman. When he gets to the midway lyric "when it ends, it ends in tears," the track's already faint pulse comes to a near stop and an additional, bittersweet chord change underplays this emotional cataclysm, as if Vandross had to fortify himself with a cherished memory—evinced by piano and harp glissandos heading in different directions—before continuing.

Trying to reverse the inevitable, he pleads, wandering further from the melody, further from reality, and closer to madness. Whereas many singers who favor vocal melisma seem as though they're simply showing off, Vandross gives purpose to every additional note, like a lonely songbird making one last try to woo a mate. The effort is doomed, but he cannot do otherwise; Vandross must sing this way because he must love this way. His "A House Is Not a Home" is a profound analogy for LGBTQ experience, particularly for Black people, for whom it was even more difficult to cohabitate, much less marry, than it was for their white counterparts. It's love against the odds, come what may—the cry of gay domesticity denied.

With this, Vandross shifted into overdrive. By 1983, he'd produced, written, arranged, and sung on albums for Cheryl Lynn, Aretha Franklin, and Warwick. The first of two for Aretha, 1982's *Jump to It,* gave the Queen of Soul her biggest hit since the mid-'70s and her most LGBTQ-specific one ever. "*Girl*, I got to *go*," she speaks during the intro of its title track, between choral yeah-yeahs led by Vandross. She's dishing out the Black female banter that RuPaul would turn into something even cishet white people appropriate. Then, it spoke in code: "Hey gays! Aretha's back, and she's got a record for *you*." It's timeless R&B, yet with the funky-chic groove of the early '80s' gay dancefloor. The same background choir heard on Vandross's records gives it that I've-got-all-my-sisters-with-me feel as Aretha scats and serves lip. Unlike more crossover-conscious hits to come, this is a Black and gay one—the kind its creator could no longer sing himself and maintain his mainstream trajectory.

Vandross often wrote about a split between his public and private selves while implying how a sequestered life forged this chasm. On "I Wanted Your Love" from 1983's *Busy Body*, he confesses, "We had told the world that we were gonna ring the wedding bell/But when I really thought about it, I was lying to myself." The context is hetero, but that's a strikingly transparent line for a closeted person to sing. As confirmed by 1985's gay-hinting "My Sensitivity (Gets in the Way)," devotion to someone who might not reciprocate his affections became Vandross's leitmotif. On that year's rendition of Brenda Russell's "If Only for One Night," he switches roles to become the fleeting seductor. Delicately proposing, "No one has to know/If you want to be totally discreet," he makes a cursory clandestine tryst seem paradisial. This is what LGBTQ people do when society gives us few options.

Eventually, Vandross attracted a crossover audience with his most conventional material, like 1989's "Here and Now," a wedding standard. But he never stopped singing about LGBTQ experience from within the closet—he just didn't name it as such.

Gently devastating, 1988's "Any Love" portrays an outcast looking in at love. This loner isn't holding out for something particular—just hoping for *any* kind of intimacy while combating depression and repression: "In my heart, there's a need to shout/Dying, screaming, crying let me out." The song's video contrasts the public Vandross, who is surrounded by fans, with the private Vandross, who is audibly more solitary than ever. Whereas he ordinarily presented himself in a largely female framework of steady background singers who imply lasting friendship through their near-constant presence, here only his own overdubs swirl around him, like internal howls of thwarted devotion. Vandross must now sing even his stellar backgrounds himself because here he is truly alone. What starts out subdued and harmonically sophisticated in the Bacharach tradition reaches a climax that's for Vandross uncharacteristically forceful, as if he's aching to escape the smoothness that suits his tender songs so well. The professionalism that allowed him to reach millions of fans yet required constant discretion meant secret suffocation. He said that this was his favorite and most autobiographical song.

Maintaining his serenading foundation while updating his grooves, Vandross periodically reached out to his original audience. On 1996's "Your Secret Love," Vandross gives up on a paramour who concealed another lover and intends to keep him confidential as well. The lyric uses gender-neutral pronouns that allow straight listeners to hear the song one way and us another. "Why can't we tell somebody?/'Cause secret loves never last as long," it laments. The *Rear Window*–referencing video further suggests an LGBTQ context by ending with two women grasping hands and Vandross turning off a light.

In 1987, I wrote for *Spin* what might have been Vandross's most candid profile. "I sing about the things that are not happening in my own life," he confessed. "I'm still in search of that one partner to share the rest of my life with. I'm afraid of turning 80 and still being alone. In my position, it's very hard to find someone." Our exchange was friendly yet mutually meticulous, as if we were both cautiously writing lines that one must read between to get the full story.

Years later, his management asked me to write his official biography. The one condition was that I couldn't discuss his sexual orientation. Given what Vandross had sung in his songs, I passed. Behind the scenes, Vandross's sexuality hadn't been hidden, either. After watching him film 1986's "Stop to Love" video, I rode with his background singer Lisa Fischer, who exclaimed, "Oooh, Luther would love him!" and pointed to a billboard featuring a blond hunk. Patti LaBelle, who'd known Vandross since he started her first fan club as a teen, broke the silence in 2017. She confided to gay talk show host Andy Cohen that Vandross never fully came out because he feared rejection from both his mother and his largely female audience. "He told me that he just didn't want to upset the world," she said. "It was hard for him."

During the peak of his popularity, Vandross's weight fluctuated drastically. Reporters and talk show hosts harped on his size, so he dieted severely to silence them. Yet food remained his escape from the closet's loneliness, and therefore the cycle repeated, even as he fought diabetes and hypertension. Collectively, these factors likely caused his 2003 stroke. He never regained his vocal ability and died two years later at fifty-four.

In 1998, I interviewed the singer one last time for a bio mailed out with promo copies of that year's *I Know*. Luther Vandross is one of my lifetime's greatest musicians of any sort, any genre. But he was cast in a supporting role as a troubadour whom amorous couples cue up when they want to express what's hard to say while making love and maybe even babies. As such, he was the successor to an earlier gay Black balladeer, Johnny Mathis. During our conversation, I used a seemingly harmless phrase like "love doctor" that others had spoken and written many times. I used it to state how he was perceived and to juxtapose that against his formidable talents. I was trying to help him get past the pigeonholing that held him back.

Instead, he cut me off and started screaming at me, as if in a panic attack. I calmed him down, and we went on with the interview, but it wasn't until writing this chapter that I realized what had happened. The man who enabled the love lives of so many couldn't find happiness in his own because he was forever typecast as the Black Cyrano de Bergerac—a role that demanded he deny his true self.

Chapter Twenty-Six

Grace Jones

One night in 1977, Grace Jones perched on a ledge above the dancefloor of New York's gay disco 12 West. The club's DJ, Jimmy Stuard, had been pumping an instrumental version of a song soon to be released by Jones, but no one had heard her vocal until that night. Tom Moulton, father of the dance mix, whose first productions were Jones's earliest hits, described the scene: "All of a sudden, the spotlight hits her. She starts singing 'I Need a Man,' and the place goes crazy. After she finishes, she goes, 'I don't know about you, honey, but *I need a fucking man*!'"

Tough and lusty, Jones sang "I Need a Man" so much like a man that she was not just singing *to* gay clubgoers but also *for* us, *as* us, at a time when we could rarely be so upfront in commercially aspirational music. Celebrating Blackness while subverting gender norms, Jones had just started presenting something we'd never seen before: a woman who was lithe and hyperfeminine but also exuded ribald butchness. This puissance remains so potent that even today, she's still *outré*. In her personal life, Jones might gravitate to bodybuilding dudes, but as a cultural force, she's as queer as a hetero person can get. Back in 1979, *Ebony* nailed her: "Grace Jones is a question mark followed by an exclamation point."

In 1960, the twelve-year-old Grace Beverly Jones moved from Spanish Town, Jamaica, to Syracuse, New York, with her family. She didn't have many friends; a report card described her as "socially sick." Soon she followed her brother to gay clubs. "The man in me—as well as the girl—loved men!" she exclaimed in her autobiography *I'll Never Write My Memoirs.* "I felt I was among my own even as I was so far removed." After impulsively leaving college for theater in Philadelphia, this Pentecostal preacher's daughter realized there was no going home. So she moved to New York City in 1975, modeled for the Wilhelmina agency, and doubled as "Grace Mendoza," a go-go dancer. "Even though the agency kept me pretty busy, I auditioned for every play and film I could find," she told the *Baltimore Afro-American* in 1985. "But they all wanted a Black American sound, and I just didn't have it. Finally, I got tired of trotting around, and took myself to Paris."

There, her dark skin set her apart from other models, and Jones landed covers of *Stern*, *Elle*, and *Vogue.* She recorded some European singles, and sent one to Simon and Eileen Berlin, an enterprising husband-and-wife team who later managed Tom Cruise. Jones flew back to NYC with her friend Jessica Lange and met the Berlins. Impressed by her exuberance, they signed Jones. "I thought of her as family," said Eileen Berlin. "My son had gone to college, and so I gave her his room."

At the time, Moulton's pioneering disco mixes were blowing up both clubs and R&B radio, so the Berlins begged him to produce their new client. The partnership between Jones and Moulton began with the double-sided 1976 single "Sorry"/"That's the Trouble" and 1977's bigger "I Need a Man," both on the Berlins' Beam Junction label with near-identical artwork by *Interview*'s Richard Bernstein. Hoping to capitalize on Jones's burgeoning success, the Berlins approached Island Records founder Chris Blackwell. Given the singer's Jamaican roots and Blackwell's status as a reggae ambassador, Simon anticipated a good fit. He didn't know how right he'd be.

Although Moulton and Jones made three albums for Island in three years, the two often clashed. "I teased her about sounding like Bela Lugosi," said the disco godfather. "I stood next to her while she was singing because I got so sick of hitting the talkback button. The moment she'd go off, I'd stop her. I was hard on her, I really was, but she had that determination. No matter how much I pushed her, she would take it and push herself."

Fashioned after the medleys he mixed for Gloria Gaynor, the continuous first side of 1977's *Portfolio* features Broadway tunes like "What I Did for Love" set to strings arranged by the Salsoul Orchestra's Vince Montana and performed by members of MFSB. Against their plushness, Jones sounds strained. However, the LP's second side delivers a chef d'oeuvre in its reinvention of Édith Piaf's signature song "La Vie en Rose." Jones had gotten her hands on an earlier acetate pressing sung by Teresa Wiater that was wowing 12 West, and she lobbied Moulton to cover it, not knowing he produced it. Wiater's managers had blocked the release of her version, so Jones simply sang over her tracks. Jones's deft, bilingual progression from whisper to full-bodied belt relates the transformative powers of romance. LGBTQ people must sometimes see love through rose-colored glasses to tolerate its cost.

On 1978's *Fame,* Moulton once again contrasted Philly soul's lushness—this time via arranger John Davis, another top disco hit-maker—with Jones's acerbic vocals. The combination gels because everything builds on her assurance. "I can sell an Eskimo snow," she sings in "Do or Die." Jones dedicated the disc to Jean-Paul Goude, a Parisian multimedia artist whose provocation melded with her own in much of her subsequent output and who soon fathered her only child. Laced with sadistic intent, "On Your Knees" from 1979's *Muse* points toward her pugnacious future. Moulton's symphonic production still oozes luxury, but Jones's belligerence suggests rock 'n' roll dissent waiting to be unleashed.

I grew up near Syracuse in Rochester, New York. I'd been a fan of the city's punk band New Math, whose singer, Kevin Patrick, an Island promo man, gave me *Fame*—the first piece in a disco collection that's long dominated my apartment. Then I saw Jones on *The Midnight Special,* where she sang *Fame*'s "Below the Belt" as a boxer, her hands taped for a fight. She strolled into the audience, throttled guys by their lapels, pretended to knock out a bodybuilder, and then stomped on him. At school, my drama teacher mentioned that his brother had met Jones at a Manhattan roller rink. Rather than proffering a business card, she'd handed him a plastic whip with her name on it. I knew then that I belonged in Jones's New York. A few months later, I arrived.

"On Your Knees" was the last record I bought back home and one of the first I heard on New York's disco radio stations when I got to college. Subway cars plastered with graffiti carried codes I had to crack, for danger preyed upon the ignorant. Student bar crawls regularly meant muggings. A former transit officer went on an antigay shooting spree through Greenwich Village, killing two men and wounding six. Even in this anything-goes, pre-AIDS era, pleasure and danger were already bedfellows.

Studio 54 and the symphonic sounds heard there had already peaked. Ascendant was the unwonted soul of the Paradise Garage. There, Jones held her September 1979 "baby shower" decked out in a severely triangular, utterly unflexible cardboard costume designed by illustrator Antonio Lopez; this was her maternity dress. Close-cropped clones ruled the white gay discos, which I later explored, but I didn't escape suburbia to conform in the city. I sought out the unconstrained spaces, like Mudd Club, where dub reggae and post-punk alternated with chilly synthpop and radical funk. All these genres would mingle and mutate in Jones's next incarnation.

"I wanted to treat her not as a model but to involve her as a musician," explained Chris Blackwell, who'd overseen both Bob Marley and the B-52s. "Tom had been recording the instrumentation and then having Grace come in later. I wanted her to feel as though she were a member of a band and record her the way bands used to make albums, with the singer and the players doing their thing all at once."

Blackwell's approach united British bravado and Caribbean syncopation. "I wanted a rhythmic, reggae bottom, aggressive rock guitar, and atmospheric keyboards in the middle, and Grace on top," Blackwell said of the unconventional sextet he assembled: reggae's Sly Dunbar on drums, Robbie Shakespeare on bass, Mikey Chung on guitar, and Uziah "Sticky" Thompson on percussion; Marianne Faithfull's English guitarist Barry Reynolds, and Afro French keyboardist Wally Badarou. These Compass Point All Stars went on to actuate or augment hits by Tom Tom Club, Mick Jagger, Gwen Guthrie, and others.

The sessions began with a recommendation from Talking Heads' Tina Weymouth and Chris Frantz: the Normal's severe synth-punk distillation of J. G. Ballard's symphorophilia-fueled novel *Crash,* "Warm Leatherette." Jones preserves the original's deadpan delivery and minimal melody, but the band drops its tempo to a saunter, twists its rhythm into sassy funk, and suggests that sex while dying from a car crash couldn't be hotter.

Badarou attested to Jones's active role. "Grace was there most of the time," he told me, "even during most instrumental overdubbing sessions. She was a part of the sound and the spirit that came out almost from nowhere. We all knew we were in for something unheard before, something quite experimental."

Upon its release, 1980's covers-heavy *Warm Leatherette* was too glossy for many new wave DJs, yet too reggae and weird for disco. But by the following year, both R&B radio and clubs had grown multifarious. Primed by kindred punk funk like Yoko Ono's "Walking on Thin Ice," as well as simmering Paradise Garage anthems like Taana Gardner's "Heartbeat," dance music welcomed the new Jones.

Nightclubbing from 1981 gave her newfound popularity on both sides of the Atlantic. Europeans went for a song suggested by Goude, "I've Seen That Face Before (Libertango)," a vocal reimagining of Argentine tango master Astor Piazzolla's 1974 instrumental "Libertango." In America, her R&B radio breakthrough came via what was initially an instrumental Dunbar side project recorded during the *Warm Leatherette* sessions. Equating cars with carnality, "Pull Up to the Bumper" pushes its driving metaphor to raunchy ends. "Grease it, spray it/Let me lubricate it," Jones drawls, suggesting backdoor love right before the new virus threw a wrench into that kind of fun. "Feeling like a woman/Looking like a man" goes the album opener, her version of Flash and the Pan's "Walking in the Rain." Her reggae-rock rendition of the Police's "Demolition Man," which predated theirs, similarly violates gender. Jones remains adored by just about everyone on the lesbian, gay, bisexual, trans, or otherwise-queer/questioning spectrum not merely because she sings songs like these: Jones also embodies them.

By 1982, AIDS and Reaganomics had started to strike Jones's audience, and the freedoms of the previous decade shifted to contractions. MTV had also arrived, and Jones's meticulously crafted presentation made her a music video natural, especially in the artform's early experimental days, as proven by her 1982 VHS release, *A One Man Show.* Directed by Goude and nominated in 1984 for the first Long Form Music Video Grammy, *A One Man Show* combines photography, concert footage, and video clips to distill the pair's sensational collaborations into an unbroken montage. Goude's savagely sleek visual compositions come alive through Jones, who glares in pointedly geometric designs. Imposing, alien, and almighty, she'd soon be stealing scenes in *Conan the Destroyer* and *A View to a Kill.*

What came after had to top it all. Co-writer of the Buggles' "Video Killed the Radio Star," Bruce Woolley composed 1985's "Slave to the Rhythm" for Frankie Goes to Hollywood, a band produced by his former Buggles bandmate Trevor Horn, but redrafted it for Jones with Horn and his associates. A nine-month studio odyssey ensued, allegedly costing Island $385,000—a fortune for a singer who never scaled the US pop charts. Those costs were recouped by compiling an entire LP out of this one song's many incarnations.

"I remember a huge amount of experimentation with early digital techniques, the Synclavier, Sony digital tape spliced with sticky tape, and the Fairlight," Woolley said. "We recorded eight different versions, about one every four weeks, with Horn and Blackwell in search of the perfect track."

Between acting gigs, Jones returned month after month to update her vocals to the latest arrangements. Suggesting *Star Wars* meets *The Ten Commandments,* "Slave to the Rhythm" justified all its studio work and expenditures with ornate opulence as Jones sings on multiple levels about slavery. Just as UK rock bible *NME* had certified *Nightclubbing* as 1981's greatest album, *The Face*—then England's hipness authority—declared "Slave" 1985's best single. To celebrate, Jones appeared on the magazine's cover in whiteface. Her top international hit, "Slave" underscores how Jones's incandescence makes her a far more consequential star than her sales indicate. MTV barely played the clip. Even framed by Horn's lurid brilliance, Jones was, for them, too Black and too strong. Nevertheless, with Hollywood's help and some crazy commercials for Citroën, Honda scooters, and Sun Country wine coolers, her once-underground gender transgressions penetrated the entire decade.

By 1989's "Love on Top of Love," a bossy club coup from David Cole and Robert Clivillés, the house duo who'd soon go pop with C+C Music Factory, I'd moved to San Francisco, where AIDS took away friends and lovers soon after I met them. But one night in 1993, at a local gay nightclub, I finally saw Jones perform. I took my pal Brian, whose partner, Mark, was too sick to join us. As was typical, Jones didn't take the stage until after midnight and lacked the embellishments of her Goude years. The special effect was her smile; it wouldn't stop and soon became contagious. Acknowledging the elephant in the room, she sang a dedication to the late gay artist Keith Haring, who'd painted Jones's near-naked body like a canvas for a legendary 1985 Paradise Garage show.

She kept going, granting one encore after another, patiently pausing while the soundman scoured her backing tapes to find her fans' requests, like *Fame*'s "Am I Ever Gonna Fall in Love in New York City," as if knowing many there wouldn't live long enough to see her again. Soon, I inherited Mark's cherished copy of Goude and Jones's art book *Jungle Fever*.

Bearing witness to what presidents Reagan and Bush Sr. and most of the country willfully ignored, Jones led the way while we nursed our fallen and couldn't proceed, for she knew its toll. Her lust for life represented not just resilience to repression but also a way of fighting back that still sends a message: We, who are thought less-than, shall burn brighter than our oppressors. That's why we consider this iconoclast sacred.

In 2008, Jones finally reemerged with *Hurricane*. "Prince has a presence and everybody in the room goes, 'Woah,'" said Wendy Melvoin, who, with Lisa Coleman, worked on the album's "Williams' Blood" in their home. "When Grace walks into the room, it's more subtle but has the same effect. You just go, 'My God, she's taken up all of the space with that personality.'"

Jones's belief in her own eroticism helped many find their own. With her face painted like a mask and body transformed through daredevil costuming, Jones still shape-shifts like a living sculpture while remaining undeterred. Her example reminds us that no matter how trapped we may feel by the smallness of our everyday existence, life constantly brings change, and with it there's always hope. A warrior of individuality and pleasure, Grace Jones is liberation itself.

⏭

Chapter Twenty-Seven

Michael Jackson

Part of me will always relate to Michael Jackson as I did when he and I were kids. Only eleven when the Jackson 5 became an international sensation in Stonewall's wake, he was the first juvenile star to reflect the rise of not just civil rights but also the redefinition of masculinity that came with feminism and gay pride. Dressed in purple and pink on *The Ed Sullivan Show*, he performed the group's 1969 Motown debut "I Want You Back" with the vigor of a man and the acuity of a woman. Innocent yet skilled, Jackson dazzled bright magic like my favorite cartoons; fittingly, the quintet soon had its own animated TV show. I saw possibilities in Jackson—who I could become, what I could achieve—that helped me be what I thought was the best of myself.

I started wearing psychedelic colors like Jackson. In the suburban shadow of Kodak, where nearly everyone's dad in my town worked but mine, this became a problem. People started mistaking me for a girl. Miserable at sports, I took dance, drum, and vocal lessons instead. I loved my friends, but they didn't know what Jackson understood. They didn't hold the answers to who I was or how I could transcend the limitations mounting around me. They couldn't help me with the taunting classmates who saw things in me I didn't. Everything the world told me about myself confirmed I wasn't like most boys, but I was too scared to contemplate what that meant. I wasn't sexual in any direction, even in my thoughts. I just wanted to be myself and not be hated.

Over eleven months, the Jackson 5 released their first four albums. Through their ubiquity, I learned resolve and how to polish my atypicality like Michael. Sometimes Motown emphasized his youth, like in 1970's "ABC." Mostly, he articulated adult emotions with uncanny rigor and sometimes prodigious sadness, like on that year's "I'll Be There." All too soon, I was forced to grapple with the discord articulated by "The Love You Save." I couldn't figure out why liquor bottles were hidden around the house, why my longer hair and hipper clothes and better grades created conflict, or why my family constantly argued. I kept getting messages that all this made me different. Why was that both good and bad?

One of the earliest records to help me understand myself was "Ben," the Jackson-sung, Oscar-nominated theme for the 1972 sequel to *Willard*, the 1971 horror blockbuster in which a meek young man trains rats to get back at his disparaging boss. In *Ben*, an artistic boy like me befriends the title rat. Ben first attacks the child's bully, then the men who aim to destroy his colony. Although the song's opening verse situates Ben as the singer's pal, the tenderness of Jackson's delivery and the sweetness of the music suggest something deeper. "I used to say 'I' and 'me'/Now it's 'us,' now it's 'we,'" Jackson croons, as if delivering a love song from one rebel lad to another. This scared and fascinated me.

Remarkably, "Ben" became the biggest of Jackson's early solo hits, but the last before his voice changed. While starring in 1978's *The Wiz* with Diana Ross and singing for Quincy Jones on its soundtrack, Jackson rubbed shoulders with Andy Warhol, Halston, and other queer celebrities at Studio 54. Although mainstream media still focus on Studio's ruthless exclusivity, it should also be remembered that the club's gay co-owner, Steve Rubell, barred the kind of straight clubgoers who threaten LGBTQ people. This policy ensured that the nocturnal playground he staffed with hunks was gay-inclusive without being gay-defined. Closeted moguls could safely mingle in full paparazzi view without their secrets being detected. Having been raised a

Jehovah's Witness, Jackson finally tasted freedom away from his family's watchful eye.

This liberty suffused all that came next. When an initially rejected twelve-inch remix by DJ John Luongo of the post-Motown Jacksons' first self-composed single, "Shake Your Body (Down to the Ground)," was accidentally released in Canada, the group's most disco cut grew into an international smash that laid the stylistic foundation for Michael's adult career. Inspired by the brazenness of Studio 54 and the impunity he gained there, Jackson begat dance music so fortified by exemplary pop compositions, nitroglycerine-infused R&B, jazz-informed instrumentation, and immaculate studio engineering that it rose above the disco backlash. Attaining state-of-the-art entertainment through aural audacity, 1979's Quincy Jones–produced *Off the Wall* channels the precociousness central to Jackson's appeal while presaging the insanity that would later define and eventually consume him.

Opening with a mumble, then exploding with an uninhibited "Ooooooooh!" that demarcates his newly adult solo career from his J-5 past, the self-written opener, "Don't Stop 'Til You Get Enough," intertwines themes of sexuality, *Star Wars*, empowerment, and deliverance from rationality. "Just love me 'til you don't know how," he pleads. Love power—"the force"—arrives in resolute bass, ricocheting percussion, and involute rhythm guitar that swirls around the singer like a cosmic tornado. On this decisively soulful disco song about freedom, Jackson calls on the twin spirits of the civil rights and LGBTQ movements, even if he doesn't name them. Don't stop; get enough.

Regardless of its credits, the entire album seems to spring directly from Jackson, particularly its title track. Like the other smash, "Rock with You," "Off the Wall" was written by the English keyboardist Rod Temperton. His band Heatwave had already combined simple nightlife vocabulary with melodic sophistication on hits like "Boogie Nights," but here he adds abolitionist messaging akin to Jackson's. Ballyhooing Studio 54's personal hedonism to achieve collective emancipation, the song calls for casting aside routine restrictions. Within disco, one can find and raise one's voice free from rejection: "If you take the chance and do it/Then there ain't no one who's gonna put you down." By escaping society's nine-to-five binds and uniting, we can be our true selves. As the bridge's melody ascends, Jackson sails above conventionality's storm clouds. Just as Studio 54 exposed Jackson to gay life without announcing it as such, Temperton gave him what can be read as a paean to Black LGBTQ liberation.

Throughout *Off the Wall*, dancing is a metaphor for life, but life sometimes becomes a metaphor for dancing. Jackson's "Workin' Day and Night" alludes to the singer's perfectionism. Ever since Michael was little, his father drove him abusively hard. If Jackson made a misstep in his choreography, he sometimes got a belt-whipping. Here he's tap dancing with his mouth. There's anger in it—particularly when he mimics the intro's cowbell through gasps and sighs—but also gratification as Jackson transforms workaholism's pain into positivity. Nearly every lyric is linked by exhalations that make his vocal as unrelenting as his drive to please and escape.

This momentum continues through "Get on the Floor." When Jackson reaches the first line in the final chorus, as music waves crest to a crescendo, he lets out a laugh that captures the 1970s at its culmination. Later in his career, such interjections would sound scripted, but here it comes across as spontaneous, as if the singer captured the decade's exuberance in a hiccup. "Ha-ha, hu-WAH," he squeals. He'd never sound happier.

To introduce Jackson's next solo endeavor in 1982, Epic went in the other direction with "The Girl Is Mine," an emollient, Jackson-penned ballad in which he duets and squabbles with Paul McCartney over the same dame. This tameness suggested his album would be a sell-out to middle-aged Middle America just when new wave's stylistic cross-pollination, courageous dance music, and modish synths all prodded youthful pop closer to the avant-garde.

Instead, *Thriller*, another quintessential Quincy Jones production, elsewhere rebels against what's ordinary. An immediate club hit, the opening Jackson-penned track, "Wanna Be Startin' Somethin'," heralds the album's more off-the-wall than *Off the Wall* unorthodoxy. It's an attack against busybodies who spread rumors that Jackson's "baby" has had a breakdown. But by the song's bridge, Jackson's own mental health declines. As his inner voices spew negativity, the singer introduces one of his meddlers, Billie Jean, and guitarist David Williams caricatures her with a manic funk riff. Unlike the typical rock solo, Williams's lick doesn't give release—instead, its nagging increases the tension. Then Jackson's "baby" transmogrifies into the actual baby of Billie Jean, who Jackson condemns for having a child she can't support. Changing course once again by paraphrasing "I Am—Somebody," a civil rights poem adopted by Reverend Jesse Jackson, the superstar instructs listeners to lift themselves up and profess their own authenticity: "No one can hurt you now because you know what's true/Yes I believe in me, so you believe in you." If this weren't enough of a twist, the six-minute cut closes with a generous quote from Manu Dibango's "Soul Makossa."

Having grown up in stardom's spotlight, Jackson was, at twenty-four, already rumor-sensitive, particularly about his sexuality and gender. When he was only nineteen, *Jet* printed that he was planning gender-reassignment surgery to marry actor Clifton Davis, songwriter of the Jackson 5's "Never Can Say Goodbye." In 1979, Jackson's future biographer J. Randy Taraborrelli asked Jackson if he was gay. "I am not a homo," the singer lashed back. But it's one thing to be testy about meddling media and another to fight them with a bugged-out opus. Virtually no one did this before hip-hop commodified beef. The vehemence of "Wanna" suggests more than the usual celebrity anxiety. Tabloid lies don't ordinarily turn a luminary seemingly loony.

"Wanna" has a hetero narrative: Jackson's "baby" is a "she," and there's also the suggestion that he and Billie Jean are somehow linked. But what if this fictional framework was a safe way for the singer to lash out at those who scrutinized his private life and, therefore, his sexual identity? For closeted LGBTQ VIPs, there's no difference. What if Jackson wanted Black and queer listeners to raise their voices and tell their own stories? By claiming our sexual identities, we take power away from our adversaries. They can't blackmail us when we proclaim what's true and magnificent. Just as African Americans in the civil rights era stressed that "Black Is Beautiful," LGBTQ people in Stonewall's wake insisted that "Gay Is Good." In 1982, the world wasn't ready for the gay equivalent of Jessie Jackson, even if we were. But by ending with "Soul Makossa"—an African hit popularized in the queer club underground—Jackson encoded a message within his massive mainstream statement for those who needed it most. Speak your own truth, have faith in yourself, and let the two dance.

"Wanna" dovetails with what became one of the most popular songs of all time, "Billie Jean." A composite of stories about female fans who claimed his elder brothers impregnated them, Jackson's greatest hit plays with reality like "Wanna" but even more so, for much of its magnetism lies in its ambiguity.

This tale of heterosexual intimacy's consequences begins with an argument in progress. A head-turning woman had said something to Jackson that he repeats back to her because he doesn't comprehend it: He's "the one who will dance on the floor in the round." This mysterious phrase shifts meaning as the title character, whose name echoes that of lesbian tennis champ Billie Jean King, lobs accusations against the singer. The more he feebly defends his behavior, the further he implicates himself. This would soon become Jackson's real-life modus operandi.

Almost instantly, "Billie Jean" accompanied everything. When you walked down a city street, you heard it on a boombox or a taxi radio. In a corner bodega, at the park, and in every kind of nightclub, "Billie Jean" brought accusations, denials, and a shuffling beat that synced your steps whether you knew it or not. After a showdown between MTV—which had rarely played videos by Black singers—and Jackson's record company, which threatened to pull its acts off the channel, "Billie Jean" arrived on television, too. The ambitious star flinched at gay accusations, but—in his Jheri curl, red bow tie, pink shirt, black leather suit, white socks, and two-toned spectators—he doesn't seem desperate to look straight, either. While emphasizing the song's ambiguity, video director Steve Barron stresses Jackson's own. He represents Billie Jean as a featureless body in a bed the singer climbs into—a lump that might not be female, or even alive.

The only thing certain is the star's sensational dancing that certifies Jackson's fandom of Bob Fosse. It's acknowledged that Jackson's famous "Billie

Jean" dance resembles Fosse doing "A Snake in the Grass" in Stanley Donen's otherwise forgotten 1974 film of Antoine de Saint-Exupéry's classic children's novella *The Little Prince*, but the significance of the connection is rarely discussed. Dressed in black, Fosse swivels his hips and shifts his center of gravity so he seems to slither, while speaking with exaggerated sibilance. He's essentially a gay snake. Offering to relieve the title character of life's pain through a poisonous bite, this viper isn't sexual in the book, but Fosse's song and dance sure is. "Sit right down upon/A snake in the grass," Fosse sings, punctuating his predatory invite with a pelvic thrust. The major problem here is that the Little Prince is a prepubescent child.

When Jackson performed "Billie Jean" on *Motown 25: Yesterday, Today, Forever*, a widely watched 1983 TV special, his outfit and choreography resembled Fosse's snake. With his knees out and toes pointed, Jackson replicated the viper's tilt. But this was not mere imitation. While executing Fosse's *Little Prince* moves, such as raising his knee and shaking his foot from side to side, the singer replaced the snake's swirly seductiveness with his own angularity and anger. Whereas Fosse had briefly performed a backslide in his hoofing, Jackson extended it into what became known as the moonwalk, a move that had been executed by everyone from mimes to B-boys without anyone owning it until that moment. Something truly unnerving—the shimmy of a snake aiming to seduce and kill a child—became an internationally inviting dance routine. Suddenly, both kids and adults everywhere tried to move backward while stepping forward.

Barely more than a week before "Wanna Be Startin' Somethin'" was released as a single, Jackson topped the charts with another *Thriller* cut, "Beat It." Having been routinely beaten by his dad, Jackson had reason to fear bloodshed. A 2020 UCLA study assessed that LGBT people in the US are nearly four times more likely to experience violent victimization. As the UN has noted, hate crimes against us can be particularly brutal. We're mutilated, burned, castrated, and sexually assaulted. This threat isn't limited to LGBT people. According to the University of Arizona's studies of bullying and mental health, straight, gender-nonconforming teens are bullied because they're assumed to be LGBT—they're the Q not often acknowledged in LGBTQ. If you're perceived to be gay—as Jackson was by many, and gender-nonconforming by more—you're often unsafe, just like us.

Jackson fought back by artistically asserting aggression while critiquing it. "Beat It" illustrates this paradox. An angry group tells a sole male to leave, yet if he backs down, he'll be attacked. Although Jackson recommends escape, he also reasons, "You have to show them that you're really not scared." Following Black and LGBTQ examples of insubordination through style, this pacifist does so with the '80s' angriest R&B, which introduced Jackson to album-rock radio, while the song's grimy gang video further swayed MTV.

Beginning with an acted segment and ending with an extended dance sequence executed by funky zombies, the thirteen-minute "Thriller" video builds on horror tropes that director John Landis updated from his 1981 film *An American Werewolf in London*. Notable for us is the dialogue before Jackson's character turns into a hairy beast. "I'm not like other guys," he warns his sweetheart in a dread-choked mumble. "I mean, I'm different." Even now, these words resonate with LGBTQ people, because we all utter variations on this speech when we come out. Here, it doesn't end well: Jackson reveals his true self, and his date screams in panic. As with similarly campy dialogue from gay-canonized movies like *All About Eve* or *Valley of the Dolls*, LGBTQ viewers quoted these lines in the video's wake. We'd say them at a party, and everyone would shriek. The pathos of this moment is undercut when we learn this is but a film-within-a-film that Jackson watches in a crowded movie theater while maniacally munching popcorn in a meme-inspiring shot.

The clip's crucial dance routine came courtesy of Michael Peters, the gay dancer who played the Black, mustachioed gang leader in "Beat It," and choreographed it, too. With influences from Fosse and breakdancers, Peters updated Broadway. Shortly after working on *What's Love Got to Do with It* and *Sister Act 2*, he died of AIDS, but his imprint remains. Whenever flash mobs or boybands dance in mass formation, Peters's moves return.

The video extended *Thriller*'s shelf life through 1984, when the album won eight Grammys and eight American Music Awards on its way to becoming the best-selling album of all time. That summer, Jackson reunited with his brothers, but the resulting Victory Tour, incriminatingly, omitted all songs from 1984's six-brother *Victory*, even its hit Mick Jagger duet "State of Shock," which Jackson first recorded with Freddie Mercury. The superstar's relationship with his brothers soured as the superstar encountered his first wave of negative publicity over ticket prices and availability. Making matters worse, his manager, Frank DiLeo, held a press conference to read Jackson's statement that, no, the singer had never taken hormones to maintain his high voice, or had his cheekbones and eyes altered. In contrast, he vowed, via DiLeo, "Yes, one day in the future, I plan to get married and have a family."

Following sister Janet's breakthrough with 1986's *Control*, Jackson returned the next year with his final Quincy Jones production. *Bad* spawned more pop chart-toppers than *Off the Wall* and *Thriller* combined, but none impacted LGBTQ clubs as much as the hits by Janet or the era's other ascendant female stars. Its self-conscious pugnacity didn't click with many of us. With AIDS once again turning gay men into pariahs, we had to prove more than ever we're not evil. In his autobiography, *Moonwalk*, Jackson wrote, "when you're strong and good, *then* you're bad." He'd been all those things since childhood, so why did he now make them an issue? Asserting his masculinity worked on "Beat It" because that was multifaceted. Here, simplified, it seems forced, as if he were singing, "I'm straight, I'm straight/Really, really straight!"

Aiming to sell one hundred million copies, Jackson introduced 1991's *Dangerous* with a powder keg. The John Landis–directed video for "Black or White" opens with *Home Alone*'s Macaulay Culkin engaging in a volume war with his dad, who's blown all the way to Africa, where Jackson launches into a globe-hopping expedition of folk dancing and costuming akin to Disneyland's "It's a Small World." Despite this corny setup, Jackson throws shade while walking through fire. Wailing "I ain't scared of no sheets," he slyly references both tabloids and the Ku Klux Klan. Then he sits on a stoop with members of Motown's preteen R&B group Another Bad Creation, future choreographer Wade Robson, and other kids. Culkin lip-syncs a rap that ends, "I'm not going to spend my life being a color"—a strong statement diluted by a white child actor. This theme is better illustrated when male, female, Asian, Black, white, and Latino faces morph into one another with the mutability of Jackson's own racial and gender markers.

What made the clip controversial was its music-free coda. A black panther slinks past the video's crew and onto another slum-resembling set. The panther transforms into Jackson, again dressed and posed like Fosse in *The Little Prince*. Like his model, he thrusts his crotch, but here Jackson also grabs it—a lot, which, for its time, was a big deal. He smashes windows with a crowbar and draws further attention to his groin by zipping up his fly before growling, howling, ripping his shirt, and generally flipping out. This was interpreted by savvy commentators as a symbolic manifestation of Black rage. But because the star—here more androgynous than ever—flips between masculine and feminine stances with ferocious eroticism, Jackson also embodies something no media outlet at the time could openly acknowledge: queer fury. After the video's widely hyped multinational premiere, MTV and other outlets cut this finale. Lashing out at those who aimed to confine him within binary racial, gender, and sexual categories, Jackson made his morphing exterior match his expansive interior world. For many, that was too much.

This now-overt sexuality wouldn't have been truly problematic had he not been targeting children both professionally and personally. Beginning with child actors—like Emmanuel Lewis, whom he took to the 1984 Grammys along with Brooke Shields—and then with ordinary fans, the superstar surrounded himself with minors, particularly boys. This didn't alarm his young followers; they loved him as I had. But for LGBTQ adults long accused of harming children, the mounting footage of Jackson's cavorting with little shavers was ominous, for we knew what it might mean and how it could reflect on us.

The tipping point took place in 1988, when Jackson moved into a sprawling property dubbed Neverland Ranch, an allusion to Peter Pan's island where boys can't grow into men. His film that year, *Moonwalker*, features Looney Tunes–like animation for "Speed Demon," a "Badder" re-creation of his Martin Scorsese–directed "Bad" clip featuring pint-sized hoofers mimicking his badassery, and tykes who here bookend his "Smooth Criminal" video. This child-targeting streak continued with the Simpsons' 1990 hit "Do the Bartman," which Jackson conceptualized and sang backup on without credit. In the 1991 *Simpsons*' episode "Stark Raving Dad," the singer voiced Leon Kompowsky, a mental institution patient pretending to be him. The creative team behind that episode came to believe that Jackson had been grooming boys and pulled his episode from circulation in 2019. Had "the King of Pop" become Fosse's predatory snake?

The singer embedded 1991's *Dangerous* with abundant damage control. Conceived as a Madonna duet, "In the Closet" is music's most egregious example of "queerbaiting"—luring an audience with LGBTQ content that's never fully delivered. Madonna had previewed in *The Advocate* that she and Jackson were "supposed to be writing" a song together with "an astonishing title." She spoke at length about wanting to introduce her collaborator to the House of Xtravaganza, the legendary ballroom family featured in *Paris Is Burning*. "They could give him a new style," she enthused, hoping to hook him up with the gay dancers from her Blond Ambition tour, Luis Camacho and Jose Gutierez. "Anybody who's in a shoe box in the closet cannot be in one after hanging around with Luis and Jose," she insinuated. But when she got back to Jackson with these ideas and some lyrics, the two parted ways. "I think all he wanted was a provocative title," the savvy star tactfully recalled, "and ultimately he didn't want the content of the song to . . . live up to the title."

Jackson replaced Madonna with a "Mystery Girl," later revealed to be Princess Stéphanie of Monaco, whose androgyny helped "Irresistible" become France's second-biggest hit of 1986. Here, she's merely a prop for the singer to again assert his heterosexuality, much like Naomi Campbell in Herb Ritts's disingenuous but sublime video. Although Jackson no longer resembles the man who made *Thriller*, the clip's flattering sepia cinematography ferments the Black and white and male and female elements of his presentation to fleetingly represent the best of all possible worlds—Jackson looks fabulous. But both the song and its video exploit the public's curiosity about a closet we're led to believe was packed. Jackson vocally conveys fragilities lyrically denied. His fear cuts through all contrivance when he sings, "There's something about you baby/That makes me want to give it to you." Yet the star thereafter vows to keep it in the closet and punctuates this resignation with a door slam that hits like a self-denying exclamation point. Boom!

Jackson co-wrote and co-produced this and other *Dangerous* tracks with Teddy Riley, New York's top practitioner of new jack swing, a late-'80s R&B reinvention that combines the thundercrack of Janet's *Control* snares with hip-hop's digitalization of funk backbeats. While its rigid rhythms conquered the radio mainstream via emphatically straight guys like Bobby Brown, the bottom-heavy fluidity of house music ruled the LGBTQ club underground. To bridge this discrepancy, *Dangerous*'s dance singles underwent drastic revisions by gay remixers and DJs like David Cole, who, with his C+C Music Factory associate Robert Clivillés, refashioned "Black or White" into a gospely pop-house cut. The greatest of these are Frankie Knuckles's remixes of "In the Closet," done so deftly that he irons its jagged angst into sultry sleekness. To hear his billowing remixes is to be teleported back to voguing's peak, when queens and trans women dance-battled with righteous lusciousness.

"Gone Too Soon" salutes Ryan White, a teenager with hemophilia who contracted HIV through a tainted blood-product infusion and was diagnosed with AIDS in 1984. Prompted by a parent petition, the school board prevented White from returning to school. When an Indiana Department of Education officer ruled in his favor and he did return, he was homophobically bullied. Someone even fired a bullet into his family's living room. Jackson befriended White, gave him a Ford Mustang, and posthumously dedicated this song to him. Demystifying the disease, White died in 1990 as AIDS's acceptable martyr. He was young and straight and therefore deemed innocent—even Donald Trump attended his funeral—while LGBTQ adults and HIV drug users remained guilty in the mob consciousness.

Released as the album's final single on World AIDS Day, December 1, 1993, "Gone Too Soon" flopped in North America. The child-abuse accusations against the singer earlier that year almost certainly limited the popularity of the song's video, which features Jackson with White. In the wake of those allegations, most of the dates on Jackson's overseas tour were rescheduled and/or canceled, and his painkiller addiction, which began in the mid-'80s, escalated. Near the end of the year, he proposed to Lisa Marie Presley—Elvis's daughter—over the phone. Fearful that her friend might die like her dad, she said yes. In early 1994, Jackson's insurance carrier settled a lawsuit—which alleged seduction, willful misconduct, sexual battery, intentional infliction of emotional distress, fraud, and negligence—with an approximate $23 million payment to the plaintiff, his parents, and their lawyers. In exchange, the accuser and his parents agreed not to pursue civil claims. Jackson's marriage to Presley ended after two years.

By then he'd packaged 1995's retrospective *HIStory: Past, Present and Future, Book 1* with newly recorded up-tempo material that's largely livid. On "Scream," he teams with Janet to tackle propaganda pushers, while "Tabloid Junkie" drops bombs like "they say he's homosexual" and "she's blond and she's bisexual" to parody how hyperbolic media generate controversy to divert our attention from larger concerns. Yet with those very phrases, Jackson blew similar smoke around himself. And when he resorted to "Jew me, sue me, everybody do me/Kick me, kike me, don't you black or white me" in "They Don't Care About Us," he lowered himself to their unacceptable level. When I said so in a review, I received hate mail so antigay and anti-Semitic my bosses feared for my safety. I'm not even Jewish.

For the album's biggest messianic ballad, Jackson teamed with fellow R&B superstar R. Kelly, who'd already illegally married his protégée Aaliyah when she was fifteen. The ceremony took place soon after the release of her Kelly-overseen 1994 debut *Age Ain't Nothing but a Number*. Written by Kelly, who co-produced with Jackson, "You Are Not Alone" prompted another video positioning Jackson as paparazzi prey. Framed by columns, he and Presley are nearly naked. There's little that doesn't feel scrupulously staged, yet the public went for it: "Alone" became the first single to debut atop *Billboard*'s Hot 100.

At that point, Kelly and Aaliyah's marriage had already been secretly annulled. In 2020, Kelly was sentenced to thirty years in prison following a conviction on federal racketeering and sex trafficking charges. In 2023, he was additionally sentenced to twenty years for child pornography and enticement of a minor. "You left in your wake a trail of broken lives," US District Court Judge Ann Donnelly told Kelly. "It all happened while everybody watched and nobody did anything," said Jim DeRogatis, the *Chicago Sun-Times*'s silence-breaking reporter.

Some LGBTQ listeners take comfort in "You Are Not Alone," just as I found solace in "Ben." But *HIStory*'s autobiographical "Childhood" features the only post-*Thriller* performance I'd rank with Jackson's best. My mind reasons that its lyric is maudlin, but my heart gets yanked in another direction—backward.

Like Jackson, I'd been maltreated; not in identical ways, but close enough to give me perspective. My mother nearly bled to death during my birth, and later held me accountable for her weight, her inability to get a steady job, her staying with my alcoholic dad—my blame was endless. My father sometimes drove so drunkenly that he would swerve the car out of its lane. My response was to grow up as quickly as possible; my sister insists I started reading at age two. By fifth grade, I wrote and performed puppet shows for the school. By sixth, I read faster than my teacher, who taught me to pen short stories on my own, rather than sit in his English class. Despite this independence, my mother still treated me as a burden. Asthma kept me awake, but she denied me treatment because she didn't want her son seen with an inhaler—she feared it would make her look bad. This is why I couldn't confront my sexuality until I left home: I couldn't be more of a problem than I already was. When Jackson sings "have you seen my childhood?," I understand. He's also telling my story, and maybe yours, too.

But the release of "Childhood" followed one of the several times that young men stepped forward to attest that Jackson had done more than taken them under his wing when they were boys. They said he'd molested them. I wouldn't say that scenario happened to me; I dodged it. A high school teacher who gave me the guidance I couldn't get at home fostered a connection that turned intimate, then retreated when I let him know that a sexual relationship wasn't what I wanted, which made me feel as though I'd been at fault. But I never stopped loving him, which made the situation worse, for he was as charismatic as I and others were vulnerable. After graduation, one of my classmates lived with him until that friend had sex with a woman and realized he was straight.

A couple of years later, one of my college professors invited me to his nearby apartment. I'd been tutored by proper gents, so I suspected nothing until he drew attention to his tenting trousers. "This is what you do to me, Barry," he said, as if I were responsible for his offense. I escaped, then got a lower-than-justified grade. His boss admitted my complaint wasn't the first. My grade was raised, but the predator kept his job. Maybe this all made me gun-shy during what we now know was a deadly time for a gay kid coming of age in New York. Maybe that's why I'm still alive. Maybe I'm just lucky, or not.

Throughout my career, I've written about Jackson with a mix of awe, mounting disappointment, anger, qualified forgiveness, and now trepidation. I put off watching *Leaving Neverland*—the 2019 documentary in which Wade Robson and James Safechuck testify that they were sexually abused by Jackson when they were boys—because I feared my misused inner child would be overwhelmed. Instead, it just felt familiar.

Unless there's overwhelming evidence to the contrary, I believe victims. I believe those who'd been too enchanted to tell what they then had no words to describe, just as I believe the late star's own statement that his father abused him. From "I Want You Back" to *Thriller*, I'll cherish what Jackson did to enfranchise me and so many others. Yet I condemn the songs and videos of his Neverland-era output that manipulate listeners the way authority manipulated me. I know for some this is either not enough or too much. To them, I'm sorry, but this is the only way I know to reconcile what's emancipating with its opposite.

⏭

Chapter Twenty-Eight

Wendy Carlos and Kraftwerk

Preserving old-school parlance, some of us still call ourselves "friends of Dorothy," after Judy Garland's character in *The Wizard of Oz*. We cling to the future's promise, which forever lies over the rainbow. That's why so many LGBTQ people create or adore sci-fi: The past wasn't great for us. We're drawn to space—both figurative and literal—that we can call our own. Electronic music and the Other have been connected since the theremin's spooky warble became a cinematic convention that announced ripely metaphoric aliens in 1950s sci-fi films like *The Day the Earth Stood Still*. Those ghostly ululations were pop culture's earliest electronic music—a genre we've more than proportionately cultivated for more than half a century.

Electronic music is innately queer and, therefore, limitless. Synthesizers and software allow musicians nearly infinite control over their work, which makes those tools especially attractive to those denied dominion over their own gender. As evidenced by twenty-first-century composers such as Arca, Terre Thaemlitz, and the late Sophie, electronica provides a haven for trans people. Yet the mainstream has forgotten that one trans pioneer was there at synth music's birth; she's arguably its midwife.

While beginning her transition, New York's Wendy Carlos released 1968's million-selling *Switched-On Bach*, a three-time Grammy-winning set of pieces by Baroque composer Johann Sebastian Bach played on the Moog synthesizer, which Carlos helped develop with its creator, Robert Moog. Before Carlos, these switchboard-like machines were confined to universities or the richest rock stars. Just to get one chord from her monophonic Moog, Carlos had to overdub herself multiple times, so *Switched-On* demanded a thousand hours of home-studio tinkering—a perfect pastime for a trans person doing what then had to be concealed. Her soundtrack to Stanley Kubrick's 1971 dystopian milestone *A Clockwork Orange* similarly brought classical symphonic themes into synthetic posterity. Portending his own electronic work several years later, David Bowie aptly made *Ziggy*-era stage entrances to Carlos's *Clockwork* adaptation of Beethoven's Ninth Symphony; its fabricated futurism suited his antihero's prophetic androgyny.

Despite this, Carlos rarely intersects with pop. Even her compositions and performances for Disney's 1982 computer drama *Tron* betrays her classical background. *Switched-On* remains her only hit. Yet Carlos remains an LGBTQ trailblazer for the simple fact that she was the first successful trans musician to let the world know who she was. Her 1979 *Playboy* interview with gay *Village Voice* columnist Arthur Bell still ranks among the most personal and extensive documents of what it means to be trans and how to embrace it. As a coming-out, it's way up there with David Bowie's.

Kraftwerk broke from the invisibility of electronic music that allowed Wendy Carlos to transition clandestinely. The Düsseldorf quartet did this with visuals and concepts likely inspired when its leaders, Ralf Hütter and Florian Schneider, viewed an exhibition by Gilbert & George, a gay British couple who dressed, performed, and created conceptual art as conservatively dapper yet subversive "living sculptures." Gilbert & George would dress in suits, wear metallic makeup, move like robots, lip-sync, and entrance their audience at art galleries, not theaters. By the time Kraftwerk's *Autobahn*—a hypnotic

1974 paean to Germany's famed high-speed highways—became an international hit the next year, its members had cut their hair, donned suits, and stripped away most remnants of Anglo American hippiedom. On 1975's *Radio-Activity*, the band salutes science while resembling well-groomed professors. As it would with their studio technique, these boffins would further polish their appearance to serve an anomalous persona of squareness so exacting it's hip. In the shaggy, mid-'70s rock world, that made Kraftwerk queer.

Released right before the dawn of purely synthetic disco, 1977's *Trans-Europe Express* takes its melodic cues from classical music—particularly the Viennese composer Franz Schubert, whom some scholars deem gay or bi—while drawing from the rhythms of American funk. In "Showroom Dummies," Gilbert & George's living-sculpture concept gets a nightlife update as department store mannequins come to life, break a shop window, walk through the city, and dance at a disco. Housed in a Russian Constructivist cover, on which the four members are identically posed, costumed, and painted like the mannequins they emulate, 1978's *The Man-Machine* further blurs distinctions between humanity and androids. Seizing the same ideals of Friedrich Nietzsche's Übermensch that impressed Bowie, Kraftwerk became avatars of tomorrow. What initially looked fuddy-duddy turned contemporary when new wave nerds followed their close-cropped lead.

By 1981's *Computer World*, disco's declining profits meant that dance music was growing less symphonic as Reaganomics started to affect music-making in non-white and artistic communities. Kraftwerk's minimalism on tracks like "Numbers"—an R&B radio hit and breakdancing anthem that's little besides multilingual counting over electronic drums—hastened this process, even in gay clubs, which had for years favored the lushest sounds but began throbbing to hi-NRG's synth-driven starkness. In England, radio DJs flipped the album's "Computer Love" single in favor of its B-side, "The Model," a *Man-Machine* cut that had accumulated years of underground club play. "It only takes a camera to change her mind," the resulting UK Number One declared with a feminine flash.

Kraftwerk's next new song couldn't have been more manly. "Tour de

France" from 1983 pays tribute to the annual Gallic race for fit male cyclists. Back then, sports were one of the few arenas in which popular culture celebrated men's bodies—Calvin Klein had only just begun stripping buff hunks to their briefs in his ads. Kraftwerk here breaks from disco records that faked female orgasms to present unequivocally male cycling sounds. Looped gasps for breath simulate a drummer's high-hat rhythm; an extended moan punctuates downbeats. Regardless of context or intention, the hugely homoerotic result evokes two guys fucking. The melody's grace and the arrangement's synthetic harp glissandos offset the masculinity of these sighs, as if to suggest men can be concurrently pretty and virile, that manhood isn't one extreme or the other. Returning in 1986, after Hütter recovered from a serious cycling accident, the foursome made a related gesture in *Electric Café*'s "Sex Object." Setting up the cut's carnal tension, the track begins and later persists with alternating yeses and noes. These words might be electronically generated, but their pitch is masculine, which situates this song about sexual objectification and mistreatment as between men.

For its legendary 1981 show at downtown Manhattan's Ritz, Kraftwerk brought its studio onstage: computers, custom electronic drum sets, projectors, screens, and even robots that resembled each member. The audience was racially mixed yet uniformly freaking out, because no one had seen a concert set that suggested an intergalactic science lab. When the members held out miniature keyboards for the audience to play during "Pocket Calculator," it was like a magic trick at a kid's birthday party—even hip-hop guys giggled. I touched Hütter's instrument and brushed against the zeitgeist.

When I interviewed Hütter following *Electric Café*'s release, it was like sitting down with a sexy Spock. The few journalists who've profiled the band cast Hütter as guarded. To me, he was warm. When I asked my most personal question, he smiled and sighed, "Like Greta Garbo, I want to be aloooone." I thought, "Would a straight man—even a German—say this?" I didn't press the question; to probe further would've ruined everything.

⏭

Chapter Twenty-Nine

Iggy Pop and David Bowie in Berlin

Perpetually shirtless, savagely handsome, and famously well equipped, Iggy Pop models a nearly pornographic manliness that makes him LGBTQ-magnetizing despite his heterosexuality. Revering all this, David Bowie paid back his forebear by being, as he also was to Lou Reed, his champion. Having channeled into *Ziggy Stardust* the primitive genius Iggy brought to the proto-punk Stooges, Bowie helped Pop mix that raucous band's third album, 1973's *Raw Power*. Largely employing his own musicians, Bowie then produced and co-wrote Pop's caliginous 1977 solo debut *The Idiot*. Featuring caustic yet *Cabaret*-like material eventually revived by Grace Jones ("Nightclubbing"), Boy George and R.E.M. ("Funtime"), and Bowie himself ("China Girl"), *The Idiot* invented the post-punk that powered the earliest alternative and queer dance clubs on both sides of the Atlantic, despite being made just as punk began.

Instead of promoting 1977's *Low*, the first installment in what he retrospectively named his Berlin Trilogy, Bowie toured as Pop's keyboardist and backing vocalist. The star maintained this role on *Dinah!*, a long-running daytime talk show hosted by jazz vocalist Dinah Shore, on which Shore interviewed Pop and his famous collaborator like the domestic couple they nearly were. "I love nihilism!" Bowie exclaimed. "I look for things to tear apart," Pop elaborated. Shore responded kindly, even when Pop talked about cutting himself onstage in self-punishment and when Bowie called himself a cyborg. Between wildly writhing performances, the muscled-yet-articulate cult artist accurately told her, "I think I helped wipe out the Sixties." Years before LGBTQ people became chat-show/freak-show fixtures, this pair showed middle America how natural it could be to venture beyond gender and artistic norms. In 1998, gay filmmaker extraordinaire Todd Haynes fictionalized and sexualized their friendship in his queer glam fantasia *Velvet Goldmine.*

Fresh from Pop's tour, Bowie channeled his cohort's guilelessness on 1977's "Heroes." Rough homoeroticism runs through rowdy tracks like "Joe the Lion," critiquing masculinity even as Bowie revels in it. "Heroes" is known mostly for its uncustomarily rapturous title track, which became a gay cult classic in its 1983 Italo disco rendition by Big Ben Tribe. Like so many LGBTQ favorites, "Heroes" lauds a secret love. At the time, Bowie claimed it was about a West Berliner clandestinely meeting at the Berlin Wall with an East Berliner, but he knew this would've been impossible—he recorded the album at Hansa, a studio so close to the Wall Bowie could see the armed guards. Dramatizing a rendezvous between his married producer Tony Visconti and backing singer Antonia Maass, Bowie spins their undercover affair into a six-minute epic of doomed yet glorious devotion.

With help from Brian Eno and guitarist Robert Fripp, Bowie updated Phil Spector's Wall of Sound productions as a metaphor for the walls that divide us. Visconti recorded Bowie's vocals with a complex multi-microphone system, capturing rising amounts of room ambience that make the singer seem increasingly distant. By the end, Bowie's howling as if uncontrollable forces are pulling him away from us. This heightens his lyric, which begins with fairy-tale courtship. Yet Bowie's self-proclaimed monarch drinks heavily, his "queen" is mean, and the protagonist acknowledges their affair's unsustainability. At first dreaming it'll last, he concludes that they can only be themselves together for merely a day. He doesn't view that goal as modest—it's immense. In 1977, when Anita Bryant fomented intolerance to retract freedoms we were just beginning to taste, LGBTQ listeners understood that Bowie's confluence of hope and despair wasn't contradictory. Back then, just reconciling the two made us heroes.

But there's more, and it comes when Bowie's voice reaches Visconti's most distant microphone. The singer's mind slips into a reverie of a time when he and his queen shared an invincible kiss beside the wall as guns shot above their heads like fireworks. "And the *shame* was on the other side!" he yawps with an intensity that goes above and beyond his already high bar. It's this flash when Bowie casts aside futility and beats sorrow by achieving shamelessness. Right before the fade, he downplays his drama; simply being "safer" would be nice.

We get all of this. Some critics condemned Bowie in his early glam days with the vocabulary homophobes still use against us more than fifty years later. They said he was inauthentic, contrived, unnatural, and, of course, flamboyant—straight code for gay and flaming. The sheer physicality demanded by Visconti's methods ensured Bowie is none of those things here. Nevertheless, he captures truths about LGBTQ experience. We're all victims of the shame that silences and separates us. Coming out is about coming together, and that's what "Heroes" most fundamentally honors. Its lovers transcend humiliation to be two truly as one.

During a break in a 1978 tour that brought back much of *Ziggy Stardust*, Bowie decamped to Montreux, Switzerland, to record 1979's *Lodger*. His trilogy's final installment abandoned its predecessors' split between fast art-pop and slow synth instrumentals for a fully vocal presentation of antsy rock epitomized by a punky variation on Village People's male-bonding paeans, "Boys Keep Swinging." "You can wear a uniform!" Bowie recommends like the VPs. When he sang it on *Saturday Night Live,* flanked by gay New York performance artists Joey Arias and Klaus Nomi in dresses, NBC censors silenced the next line, "other boys check you out," no doubt for its homoerotic connotations. Maybe they didn't notice the phallus that popped out of Bowie's puppet costume.

For the song's even cockier video, the singer debuted the look and stance that would define his biggest US hit streak: suited and sharp. But when the chorus comes, quick shots pop up of him in drag as a trio of female backing singers. When Bowie returns as a man, it becomes more apparent that he's not quite himself. He's burlesquing masculinity as a drag king might—not just staring down the camera as if seducing his TV viewers, but also dominating it. When an amelodic guitar solo epitomizes hysteria, a full-on drag show featuring the three background madams commences. As a 1950s jezebel, Bowie sashays, rips off his bouffant, and smears his lipstick. Then he does a similar move as a Lorelei who resembles his then-recent lover Romy Haag, a Berlin-based trans entertainer. Last, he reemerges with a cane as an elderly grand dame. No other superstar in 1979 could've made this video. But RCA refused to release "Boys Keep Swinging" as a US single, which squashed the video's North American dissemination. This was how scared the music industry was of us.

On 1980's *Scary Monsters (And Super Creeps)*, Bowie presents autobiography through the personas of his back catalog, particularly on its self-lacerating single "Ashes to Ashes." While aiming to kick his coke habit in Berlin, a heroin hotbed, Bowie had traded one addiction for another. Back then, rock superstars almost always avoided acknowledging drug dependence, but the rule-breaking star owned up on his biggest UK single and US rock radio hit in years. It recasts his "Space Oddity" astronaut as a has-been who can't shake the simian off his back: "Ashes to ashes, funk to funky/We know Major Tom's a junkie." Twisting the trippiness of late '60s pop to show how dope sent him down a spiritual black hole, Bowie outlines where drugs lead many LGBTQ people: Society still abuses us, and, therefore, our substance-abuse rates are nearly twice as high as those of straights. David Mallet—director of "Boys Keep Swinging" and future queer clips for Queen, Joan Jett, and others—cast the superstar in the song's video as the sad clown Pierrot, a listless cosmonaut, and Bowie's relatively regular self in a padded cell. Periodically, the singer is joined by various figures mouthing his lyrics, including futurist trendsetter Steve Strange, his costumer Judith Frankland, and others who were then building on Bowie's legend. They follow him while a bulldozer brings up the rear, as if to further excavate his past.

Until 2016's farewell *Blackstar*, much of what followed *Scary Monsters* failed to consistently hit the same aesthetic heights as the work Bowie made when he radiated revolutionary queer insolence. In a 1983 *Rolling Stone* interview, the superstar—then achieving his commercial zenith with that year's Nile Rodgers–assisted but only half-fierce *Let's Dance*—declared that coming out was "the biggest mistake I ever made." Many fans felt betrayed by this statement, which Bowie substantially qualified in a 2002 *Blender* article. There he explained that being bisexual, not an artist, had long been his identity in puritanical America. With this we could sympathize. As those of us who followed Bowie's lead learned, our sexual orientation and/or gender presentation was for decades the primary prisms through which straight people looked at us once we came out. Even today, not enough has changed; narrow viewpoints still spark political and physical violence against us.

⏭

Chapter Thirty

Gary Numan

Immediately following Bowie's *Lodger*, one of the superstar's most unabashed students, Gary Numan, went Number One in the UK. In the mode of his model's Berlin abstractions, "Are 'Friends' Electric"—Numan's 1979 smash with his soon-to-be dissolved trio, Tubeway Army—confirmed synthpop as rooted in LGBTQ culture yet potentially huge. Resembling a *Star Trek* crew member but with heavy eyeliner and a gold loop hanging from his right ear, then a gay male signifier, Numan smoldered with a sci-fi detachment that wasn't merely affectation. He has Asperger's syndrome, an autism-spectrum disorder. It can make socializing difficult, particularly when it comes to nonverbal communication and understanding others' feelings. It meant, like many of us, Numan grew up alone and misunderstood.

As an allegory, "Are 'Friends' Electric" speaks not only to the songwriter's struggles but also our own. Numan alternates descriptions of his isolation with flashbacks to interactions with an intimate that failed because he didn't know how to read them. The one physical presence in the song is his "friend" outside. Numan invites him in, but he's broken, so Numan is left with "no one to love," which forces him to examine his ineffectual interactions. What meant nothing to the other person meant everything to him.

Like William S. Burroughs's cut-ups, Numan's narrative is jumbled because he combined two songs for this one. Decades later, the songwriter revealed that his "friend" is a robot hustler. Even without this context, it sounds like he's using "friend" like we often must—as code for our lovers, as in the Kinks' "See My Friend." Numan's autistic confusion is a lot like what LGBTQ people still experience when we sense frisson with a potential mate who may or may not be playing on our team. Was that white lie the song mentions an attempt to reveal the truth? What's the meaning of that "sly touch"? In the 1970s, LGBTQ life was even more like Asperger's. How could we fully connect with one another, or even straight people, when revealing a key part of our identity might mean social rejection, job loss, or violence?

Largely based on the musician's never-finished sci-fi novel, 1979's *Replicas* features another "friend" song, "Down in the Park." Further blurring the distinctions between humanity and technology, it describes a nightmarish hereafter where "machmen" and machines play killing games in the park; a "rape machine" attacks, and mortals scatter. Yet its tender melody tells a different story. Like Kraftwerk's, Numan's synths might be cool, but his tune transmits the warmth of clandestine LGBTQ unions. In New York, some gay men of the era congregated in the Ramble, Central Park's secluded thatch of dense trees and serpentine walkways. There, one could meet similarly inclined fellows and relish furtive sex. Back then, when much of pre-gentrified New York was like the Wild West, you also might have encountered muggers, homophobes, or punishing cops. Numan sings nasally as a pleasure-giving "friend," accurately capturing anonymous gay relations.

All this could have been considered accidental if it wasn't for the presence of the most overtly LGBTQ song on a '70s UK album-chart topper: "Praying to the Aliens," on which Numan posits a Burroughs-eque tomorrow populated by "only boys that love only boys." Numan's "friend" returns, but this time, he's grilled about his sexual orientation and punished. The dystopian paranoia that permeates Numan's oeuvre once again zeroes in on gay identity—a sideways glance might reveal secret attractions. Yet by Numan's standards, the accompanying music is nearly bouncy, and in the closing verse's final line, the songwriter professes, "I can't imagine living any other way." Timed to his

US breakthrough, "Cars," Numan's 1980 *Saturday Night Live* performance of this track was subtitled, as if to emphasize its homophilia—perhaps in compensation for censoring Bowie's "Boys Keep Swinging" lyric just a few episodes prior. In Numan's autobiography, named after "Aliens," he writes about retreating to gay clubs because that was where glam boys like him found shelter.

⏭

Chapter Thirty-One

Duran Duran and the New Romantics

There'd long been crossover between LGBTQ clubs and some of rock's most antiauthoritarian heroes. The Sex Pistols and Siouxsie Sioux, for example, regularly hung out at Club Louise, a London lesbian nightspot, where they'd be safe from the thugs who preyed upon punks like gay-bashers. Co-owned and -operated by courageous gay men, Manhattan's first new wave dance club, Hurrah, hired DJs—like Bill Bahlman, a Gay Activists Alliance vet and former Firehouse spinner—who favored the post-punk genres straighter discos avoided. Bahlman also worked at 99 Records, his brother's hip Greenwich Village record store, which gave him access to imports and indie obscurities he soon brought to the next in-crowd club, Danceteria. Bahlman's vanguard selections even landed on MTV, which in its innovative early days drew from Danceteria's sexually mixed, everything-goes bohemia. Queer discos throughout the US hosted new wave events akin to Bahlman's Tuesdays at the Anvil. Even Jim's—a gay joint in my hometown—had nights when instead of Donna Summer's "Last Dance" signaling closing time, you'd hear Flipper's festively repellent "Sexbomb." All this meant that artists who otherwise would've been isolated now had platforms on which to counter the far right that would soon become energized by Ronald Reagan and Margaret Thatcher.

As David Bowie–inspired synthpop geysered from the underground, a nightlife scene bearing his influence began in late-1970s London and Birmingham. What became known as the New Romantic movement wasn't a reaction against punk, as many have deemed it. Instead, like punk, it followed Bowie's lead to present identity as a theatrical construct with which to express oneself, shock others, overcome shyness, escape reality, and redefine gender.

Before New Romantics had a name, they were simply LGBTQ people and pals who primped to Bowie, Kraftwerk, and other futurists. "A seedy gay club frequented by prostitutes, rough lesbians and even rougher trannies" is how former *The Face* writer Chris Sullivan described Billy's, New Romanticism's home before its DJ, Rusty Egan, and its gay fashionista, Steve Strange, moved their disco to another London venue and renamed it Blitz. Like Studio 54's Steve Rubell, Strange appointed himself gatekeeper. Would-be film noir stars, stylish butches, and other peacocks were granted entry. Those sightseeing—even Mick Jagger—were turned away.

Strange became the first of many New Romantics to transition from club-goer to club-filler when he and Egan, on drums, formed Visage, a London-based supergroup built on queer futurism. In the video to 1980's electronic psalm "Fade to Grey," Strange becomes a canvas for more makeup than even his glam predecessors. On 1982's "The Anvil," he commemorates the gay Manhattan disco with torsos pumping iron, bodies shoulder-to-shirtless-shoulder, and sticky palms. Although Visage never cracked the US mainstream, what followed often did bigger business than Bowie at his artistic peak.

Comprised of Blitz regulars, Spandau Ballet launched its own emphatically European disco-rock. Like Visage, the quintet proffered dandyism as provocation. Its 1980 single "To Cut a Long Story Short" references the Velvet Underground while aggrandizing its homoeroticism: "Standing in the dark/Oh, I was waiting for a man to come." Singing as a soldier so traumatized by war that he must hustle himself to survive, Tony Hadley brays of his own beauty, a quintessential New Romantic move that breaks heterosexuality's rule that males mustn't self-objectify.

All the Spandaus resembled models. Their songwriter, Gary Kemp, and his bassist brother, Martin, had been child actors and later had film careers—Gary appears in *The Bodyguard.* The "Cut" video dresses the band as dashing Highland infantry and situates it in an LGBTQ context with a female couple touch-dancing. "Tough is the leather that's strapped to my skin," Hadley brags in 1981's "Muscle Bound." On that year's club hit "Chant No. 1 (I Don't Need This Pressure On)," he puns, "I feel the gaze against my skin." With its 1983 US pop breakthrough, "True," the band smoothed out its subversion but still brought out the bullies.

Duran Duran sprang from an analogous Birmingham scene. At the Rum Runner nightclub, its keyboardist Nick Rhodes DJed Bowie and associated acts, while other members staffed the venue. Crossing Chic's disco-funk, Kraftwerk's synths, and the Sex Pistols' guitars, all filtered through Roxy Music's warped grandeur, Duran Duran's 1981 debut "Planet Earth" set a template that defined a decade. Just as the deluxe UK edition of Spandau Ballet's 1982 album, *Diamond,* came as a box set of twelve-inch singles, North American rereleases of Duran Duran's watershed *Rio,* all from the same year, feature remixes that emphasize danceability. Two years earlier, US labels had distanced themselves from disco. Now they promoted its latest permutation.

With its remixes, *Rio* grew into a stateside smash as MTV spread through the country. Within a year, the videogenic group morphed into idols screamed at by teen girls and secretly pined after by gay boys. There had never been heartthrobs this splendidly fey before. In their glossy makeup, precisely tousled hairstyles, and billowing costumes, the quintet boosted both androgyny and abstruseness; "The Chauffeur" remains the most convolutedly erotic track bought by millions of teenyboppers. "Save a Prayer," conversely, delivers singer Simon Le Bon's most direct couplet, one that LGBTQ listeners—still forced to limit love to fleeting doses—take to heart: "Some people call it a one-night stand/But we can call it paradise."

DD's most seditious aspect was that the world viewed this band of superior cheekbones largely through the queer eye of its video director, Australian ex-pat Russell Mulcahy. His "Planet Earth" clip opens with a shot of drummer Roger Taylor, shirtless and tipping his head back in orgasmic elation like De-Veren Bookwalter in Andy Warhol's *Blow Job.* Later, singer Simon Le Bon lies presumably naked, as if posing for gay erotica. Under a cloud of cotton candy hair, Rhodes floats beyond gender. In "Rio," Mulcahy highlights tanned babes, but subverts the straight-guy gaze with male crotch shots. Pumping out queer clips for Kim Carnes ("Bette Davis Eyes"), Elton John ("I'm Still Standing"), Bonnie Tyler ("Total Eclipse of the Heart"), and other gay faves, Mulcahy systemized music video with surrealistic kitsch. He even stuck naked male factory workers into his 1982 "Allentown" video for the straightest-ever pop star, Billy Joel. Madonna would soon blow minds with LGBTQ content, but Mulcahy's fabulously fetishy video for Duran Duran's "The Chauffeur"—in which he visualizes the queerness of this nominally hetero track with an abstracted yet eye-popping lesbian three-way—set the precedent. Nothing says "1980s" like a Mulcahy-made DD clip, the unrivaled convergence of gay-male sensibility and teen-girl taste.

That's Duran Duran's throughline. For the 1984 single version of "The Reflex," the band insisted on a stuttering remix by Chic's Nile Rodgers. The US record company considered it "too Black sounding," but it became the band's first *Billboard* chart-topper and biggest US hit. Rodgers then produced that year's "The Wild Boys," which dramatizes the William S. Burroughs novel. In it gay male gangs aim to bring down civilization at the end of the twentieth century through free love and anarchy. "Boys" doesn't mention homosexuality, but does imply it: "Wild boys never lose it/Wild boys never chose this way." Mulcahy didn't direct a feature film of the novel as intended, yet his video serves as a trailer for what might've been. Whereas his S&M imagery in "The Reflex" flashes so quickly it's nearly subliminal, here it takes center-stage. Buff punks somersault amid flaming destruction as Le Bon, clad in leather and bulging jeans, is strapped to a windmill while bassist, John Taylor, also bound, writhes on a car's roof. All this chaos dramatizes the record's collision of tribal drums, jarring rock guitar, and raffish production. Bringing gay nightlife's ostentatiousness onto daytime radio, its fussy fury forced listeners to take sides. Straight male adults were against it; boppers and queers nodded yes, yes, *yes.*

In his autobiography *Stand & Deliver*, Adam Ant suggests that the aspirational positivity central to his catalog masked the trauma of being bipolar. Much as some gay men create drag façades to fight back at a world that's branded them feminine and therefore faulty, Stuart Leslie Goddard created a persona with which to bounce back from an early suicide attempt. This was how he could hold a lifeline to queers like me.

Despite having acted in 1978's *Jubilee* by England's top gay avant-garde filmmaker, Derek Jarman, Ant struggled to be taken seriously in the crowded London punk scene. When he hired the Sex Pistols' manager, Malcolm McLaren, the Svengali molded his musicians into a new band, Bow Wow Wow, and left Ant behind. The singer then found replacement Ants and adopted swashbuckling costuming to illustrate a self-made mythology that espouses upstart idiosyncrasy over media-made conformity. This gentleman pirate privileges masculinity but puts it in quotations, like Bowie would. In doing so, Ant metamorphosed from derided misfit to dashing Robin Hood.

Adam and the Ants emerged around the time I lost my virginity to the kind of guy you can only pick when you have no experience and take chances that wary adults avoid. Like many attending Fordham University at Lincoln Center, Mike was older than most college students. A Broadway stagehand, he'd left his Long Island marriage for East Village bohemia and tearoom sex. Yet his scripts in the playwriting class we took together revealed he preferred emotional connections with women. So overwhelmed with love, I ignored all this while remodeling myself, like Ant, into someone I couldn't be back home—my true self. Ant sang sincerely to the fans he was only beginning to attract, as if he, too, were in love, with us, even while acting the showbiz rogue. "It makes me proud, so proud of you/I see innocence shining through," he howls while riding his bandmates' Burundi rhythms at the rousing end of 1980's "Dog Eat Dog." This captured so many like me at our weakest yet most empowered.

Ant attracted the mainstream while identifying with the margins. In Steve Barron's 1980 video for "Antmusic," Adam and the band make a sneak attack on a disco, unplug the jukebox, and instruct patrons to "try another flavor." Part Romani, Ant aligns himself with Native Americans on 1980's "Kings of the Wild Frontier" while warning his audience, "Down below those dandy clothes/You're just a shade too white." The Ants replicate the twanging guitars of spaghetti westerns but side with the indigenous, not their cowboy oppressors. Unlike most punks, Ant extols sex, especially when it's deviant, like on 1981's B-side "Beat My Guest," rock's merriest ode to masochism. "There's so much happiness behind these tears/Beat me, beat me!" he exclaims, inverting Smokey Robinson's trademark sentiments. Even at his most flippant, Ant encourages us to embrace nature and repudiate societal roles. Messianic commitment gives his bumptious sloganeering dimension, particularly in videos that draw from British musical hall institutions like *Carry On*, a comedic film and TV series built on bawdy drag and LGBTQ characters.

In his breathtakingly gay video for 1981's "Prince Charming," Ant plays a male Cinderella who serves evil drag stepsisters. "Don't you ever stop being dandy/Showing me you're handsome," natty bandmates console. Played by camp goddess Diana Dors, a UK counterpart to Marilyn Monroe, his fairy godmother descends from heaven flanked by a chorus line of muscled Black dancers, then transforms him into foppish royalty and sends him to the ball, where attendees do the Prince Charming, a posing dance akin to voguing. All this takes place while Ant preaches affirmations that *Queer Eye* would soon franchise.

Colliding jittery rockabilly guitar and tooting soul horns, Ant's 1982 solo debut and biggest US hit, "Goody Two Shoes," reads as an interrogation of a closeted celebrity: "You don't drink, don't smoke/What do you do?" Ant never takes the bait, nor answers the question. Flanking him with lady Ants and pitting him against an initially skeptic female journalist, the video nevertheless re-creates elements of Elvis Presley's homoerotic *Jailhouse Rock* dance sequence. Like so many Bowie-schooled peers, this natural exhibitionist nearly always leaves his sexuality and gender up for grabs. He's a beautiful butch; a male drag king.

The utmost New Romantic was also its queerest. Formerly Blitz's cloakroom attendant and briefly a singer with Bow Wow Wow, Boy George pushed androgyny even further than the futurists. With plucked eyebrows, glaring makeup, brightly braided hair, big hats, and baggy smocks, George O'Dowd of Culture Club ventured beyond both drag and gender while suggesting Hasidim. This distinctive result stood on the outside of everything conventional, even ordinary gays. And he wasn't putting on a costume: George dressed this way offstage and on.

"Give me time to realize my crime/Let me love and steal" starts the almost a cappella opening of 1982's "Do You Really Want to Hurt Me" that heralded the '80s' most unlikely star. With only one member of West Indian descent, bassist Mikey Craig, Culture Club nevertheless avoid the hokeyness that usually happens when rockers attempt reggae. Although the quartet set off a tabloid fury when it debuted the song on England's *Top of the Pops*, the composition's sadness, the arrangement's exactitude, and George's downhearted delivery make this pop's most deeply felt non-Jamaican version of the balladic reggae style known as "lovers' rock." While it depicts an affair gone wrong, it is also the testimony of LGBTQ people begging for mercy in a world that considers us criminals. George renders so much sorrow that it feels as though he's being cast out of heaven. That's why this record clicks as reggae when so many others fail—it's secular gospel.

Director Julien Temple got all of this. "Do You" was, according to him, "about being gay and being victimized for your sexuality, which George was kind of emblematic of. It seemed appropriate to me that in the video he would be judged by jurors in blackface, to send up bigotry and point out the hypocrisy of the many gay judges and politicians in the UK who'd enacted anti-gay legislation." Temple's video for the song situates George as a pan-historical figure who is ejected from a *Cabaret*-like nightclub and a 1950s health club, where he's menaced by musclemen. At the courthouse, a minstrel jury mouths his lyrics while Jamaican female backing singers release George from jail. It's their accord that sets him free.

Within a year, this video and those that followed made Culture Club more mainstream than any androgynous act since the mop-top era Beatles. On US adult contemporary radio—the favored format of white-collar softies seeking easy-listening solace—this and nearly all the band's subsequent hits achieved ubiquity. Many of us then understood that those songs dealt with being gay. But George's 1995 autobiography, *Take It Like a Man*, revealed more painful magic: George couldn't come all the way out because that would've drawn attention to his clandestine relationship with closeted Culture Club drummer Jon Moss. Their tensions and failures fed the band's art while tearing it apart. "This could be the best place yet/But you must overcome your fear," he sings with Philly soul's wistfulness in 1982's "Time (Clock of the Heart)." These are universal love lyrics: Everyone can see themselves in their plight. But when you read them as the words of a gay man trying to soothe a skittish, newly bisexual partner, they take on cogent meaning.

What isn't about their conflicts on 1982's *Kissing to Be Clever* grapples with white appropriation of Black culture or digs away at LGBTQ identity angst. If the singer submits to conformist pressure through "cut and discretion," on "I'm Afraid of Me," he may "leave no impression"—the worst New Romantic crime. "I'll Tumble 4 Ya" condenses cultural and sexual concerns into one Princely title. "Who's got the new boy gender?" George asks rhetorically. By accentuating masculinity in his stage name while rupturing what it ordinarily means to be a lad in his presentation and private life, the singer invented a new gender: his own.

Bolstered by prominent supporting vocals from Helen Terry, a fellow androgyne whose fiery hollo counterpoints George's sentimental croon, 1983's *Colour by Numbers* concentrates almost solely on the frontman's apprehension of impending loss. "Church of the Poison Mind" nails classic Motown riffs as well as the soul institution's happy/sad dichotomy. Few '80s hits were as musically elated, but George struggles to reconcile love's illusions with reality as he hints that his drummer is the source of his stress: "Watch me clinging to the beat/I had to fight to make it mine."

Similarly anticipating a relationship's end, "Miss Me Blind" further implies that George's come-and-go lover is male. "Bet you got a good gun," it flirts. The band's funkiest yet most rocking track puts ache in a pulse that intensifies with every chorus, then eases off during verses that draw from Chic's breezy disco. "Karma Chameleon" captures the contradictions of a star-crossed connection. While the band puts on a happy face, George pours his dejected heart out: "Every day is like survival/You're my lover, not my rival." The song's status as a benchmark of perky '80s pop obscures its thematic and musical desegregation. Sprightly but mellow, it's one of few new wave classics with a country feel, even as it alludes to the red, gold, and green flag of Ethiopia, the spiritual home of Jamaica's Rastafarian religion. When the tempo drops in half near the end, and the snare drum rattles out a combat rhythm, the band and its beleaguered dreamer seemingly march off to a queer promised land where loving is easy because all the hues of humanity's rainbow are welcome.

The popularity of *Colour by Numbers*—more than four million sold in the US, and ten million worldwide—stirred Moe & Joe's "Where's the Dress." In this 1984 novelty single, country and western stars Moe Bandy and Joe Stampley quote the "Karma Chameleon" guitar riff, and pose as in-debt truckers volunteering to wear women's clothes like "some old boy from England" so they can make a million as "country queens." The parody vulgarizes gay art by making it artless. Moe & Joe's act isn't blackface, but gayface, as done from the outside as a joke. Winner of Best Country Video at the American Video Awards, the clip ends with a symbolic gay bashing from fiddler Roy Acuff, who strikes the drag incarnation of Moe & Joe with his bow, forcing them off the Grand Ole Opry stage.

"The songs, however jolly they seemed, were a testament to my pain," George confesses in his memoir. "Singing about it was my only release, other than screaming or putting a gun to Jon's head. No song said it better than 'Victims.'" The solemn and personal nature of this symphonic cut stylistically aligns it with Elton John's *Captain Fantastic and the Brown Dirt Cowboy*, the 1975 concept album about John and lyricist Bernie Taupin's early partnership that relates their love story as platonic but full of emotional intimacy. Its smash, "Someone Saved My Life Tonight," recounts when Elton's gay friend Long John Baldry rescued him after a failed suicide attempt and convinced him to end his engagement to a woman he didn't love.

"Victims" doesn't follow a narrative, but it does illustrate how adept George had grown at writing in codes that simultaneously captured a quixotic struggle with his lover and a broader LGBTQ battle against bigotry. "And I keep on telling you/Please don't do the things you do," George sings both to his bandmate and our oppressors. Never does he kiss and tell, yet his turbulent love for Moss—represented by the song's Elton-y piano chords—is as palpable as John's for Taupin on *Captain Fantastic*. Melodramatic pauses and thundering drum fills further signify Moss's own struggle in a world threatened by bisexuality. Ending *Colour by Numbers* ominously, they stop and restart the song, echoing how the pair's on-again, off-again relationship put the band in perpetual peril.

I saw Culture Club twice at its peak. With "Do You" still climbing the charts, its first New York show and US debut attracted clubgoers and tastemakers, including *Record World*'s former disco columnist, Vince Aletti, who'd soon be my Tower Records boss. George's gayness was even more obvious in person yet grounded, despite its celestial appeal. Right before *Colour*'s release, the group's second NYC gig drew fans costumed as the frontman; Girl Georges outnumbered the Boys. All of us screamed throughout in a way that wasn't merely teenybopper-ish. Our queer team was winning, at least for a couple of hours. George's dauntlessness enabled a temporary coming out for fans at a time when it was not safe for the youngest to do so elsewhere. We were acknowledging *our* mascots of civilizing strength. This went far deeper than the outfits, far more internal. Culture Club proved we no longer needed to fear those parts of ourselves we had been taught to camouflage.

⏭

Chapter Thirty-Two

Kate Bush

While punk and New Romanticism challenged outdated ideas about masculinity during the late 1970s and early '80s, adjacent female musicians eclipsed their era's constrictions and opened a space for lesbian, queer, and gender-nonconformant women. Calling oneself a feminist back then was almost as mainstream-prohibitive as coming out. Yet these anomalous talents defied gatekeepers to call the shots in their sound and presentation. In doing so, they illuminated female concerns and broke ground for women ordinarily prohibited success by what was, beyond disco and punk, still an overwhelmingly male industry. Outliers like suburban London's Kate Bush let others in.

"Oooh let me have it!/Let me grab your soul!" cries the upstart more out-there than any hit act outside punk. With 1978's "Wuthering Heights," Bush became at nineteen the first woman to solely self-compose a UK chart-topper. As the ghost of Catherine, who died while giving birth in Emily Brontë's Gothic novel, after which this song is named, Bush sweeps far beyond the easy-listening mellowness expected of symphonic pop singers. Her soprano pierces to project ardors forbidden in the tellurian realm—an analogy for not only LGBTQ desire but also Bush's own trailblazing. Possessing prom-queen beauty and valedictorian esprit, she signed to EMI at sixteen and spent her advance on mime lessons with choreographer Adam Darius and dance classes with Lindsay Kemp, David Bowie's former teacher and lover. The resulting silent-film-star stance positioned Bush visually left of center—not the usual place for a pianist whose early songwriting already achieved rare adult refinement. The zeal that tilts nearly all her art, but especially her most precocious output, makes it queer like us.

The aural finery of her 1978 debut, *The Kick Inside,* both masks and adds to its insurgence. Bush had written her gay-beloved ballad "The Man with the Child in His Eyes" when she was thirteen and recorded it with Pink Floyd's David Gilmour at sixteen. Both its melody and lyric, about loving a much older guy, shift between comfort and fear, revealing the turmoil of cherishing someone who feels right when society says otherwise. Surrendering to erogenous exaltation, "Feel It" strips off the album's ornate orchestration like her stockings that fall to the floor. While its lyrics express lovemaking's emotional charge, its uncustomary chords capture sex's physical alterations, as if each harmonic progression represents rousing changes coursing through her, pushing her closer to the inevitable. "Room for the Life" consecrates her womb with a directness that only women's music typically dares. On the title track, a suicide note, Bush confesses transgressive love for a brother whose child she carries before offering herself to the gods.

This concupiscence makes her follow-up, 1978's *Lionheart,* more dissident, particularly on "Wow." Its actor is too hammy for Hollywood; he'll never "be that movie queen," for "he's too busy hitting the Vaseline." In her BBC-rejected video, she pats her butt while mouthing that lyric to confirm she's singing about a gay guy consumed with anal sex. Yet while poking fun at her thespian, Bush chews up the scenery. The overacting central to early MTV starts here: She *is* this stagy queen.

"Kashka from Baghdad" goes even further in LGBTQ alliance. Its title character "lives in sin, they say/with another man." Admiring their laughter and lovemaking, Bush watches nightly, longingly, from a nearby window, yet leaves unclear if she's singing as another gay dude, a straight woman turned on by their coupling, or a fellow boho seeking kin. Bush lets listeners read between the lines as to why Kashka and his partner never take an evening stroll.

She contrasts the surrounding darkness with their own inner light, only implying that nighttime might be unsafe for a gay Middle Easterner and his beloved. But there's no ambiguity when it comes to the song's stance on LGBTQ people. They understand what it takes to be happy, and so, she implies, the listener should understand them, too.

Bush's own confidence grew. The cover of 1980's *Never for Ever*—the first album by a woman to top the UK charts that wasn't a hits collection—resembles a child's book, except for the fact that animals fly out from under Bush's dress, as if she just birthed them. "My pussy queen knows all my secrets," she sings in "Egypt."

Bush takes full control on 1982's *The Dreaming* with the help of the Fairlight CMI, an early computerized synth that samples and alters sounds. Unlike her contemporaries, who typically emphasized the Fairlight's futurism through its digital harshness, Bush combines it with folk and classical instrumentation to blur the distinctions between past and present, music and sound effects, and what's real or imaginary—as if she'd dreamt it all. Bush grapples with dilemmas far removed from female domesticity, like pursuing knowledge and advancement as a man would on "Sat in Your Lap." Making no concessions to the expectations that women must mask their ambitions and sing smoothly, an army of overdubbed Bushes shriek "*I want it all!*" throughout "Suspended in Gaffa." Beyond Joni Mitchell and Teena Marie, Bush was nearly alone as a best-selling female musician who solely produced her own records. With her bassist/partner Del Palmer, she built her recording studio in the family barn when even male superstars rarely did that. This gave her the freedom to manifest what she'd only heard in her head.

Achieving her 1985 US breakthrough with *Hounds of Love*, Bush asserts on "Running Up That Hill" that if a woman had a man's perspective and opportunities, she'd excel just like him. Although clement, she poses pointed questions to her partner: "Is there so much hate for the ones we love?/Tell me, we both matter, don't we?" Yet weaving in and out of perception are Fairlight-manipulated screams that contrast with the instrumentation's measured locomotion, as if the singer has escaped her body, sex, and consciousness. For the final chorus, her soprano is joined by a down-pitched Fairlight treatment of her own voice to suggest technology has made her transgender dream come true.

On the surface, Bush was a mega-femme star with the highest chirp and most-flowing locks of her gender-bending generation. Not even Madonna implements ballet's leaps and dips as delicately as Bush in the video for "Running." Yet in the rigor of her art and her ability to control every aspect of it, Bush achieves a masculine autonomy only akin to her fan Prince. Throughout this bravura album, Bush proves there weren't compositional mountains she couldn't climb. Her MTV hit "Cloudbusting" lauds Wilhelm Reich, a psychoanalyst remembered for crackpot inventions like the "orgone accumulator," a box in which he claimed to harness sexual energy for curing cancer. Yet in earlier books, like *The Mass Psychology of Fascism* and *The Sexual Revolution,* Reich argued far more logically against homosexual persecution, criminalizing abortion, and sexual repression. These notions clashed with McCarthy-era America; the video in which Bush plays Reich's young son dramatizes the moment of Reich's arrest. Whenever it rains, the boy imagines his father, played by Donald Sutherland, inside his head "like the sun coming out." As the song grows from helplessness to optimism, this line also shifts. "Your son's coming out," Bush sings as him.

⏭

Chapter Thirty-Three

Dolly Parton

In 1992, I interviewed the bodacious bigwig adored by LGBTQ people, Dolly Parton, for her film *Straight Talk*. Her famous bosom was like armor; even for a gay guy, it's difficult to get past it. There was no point in asking about her sexuality, because no woman on her dizzying level of celebrity would have dared come out at the time. While her longtime friend and rumored lover Judy Ogle worked in the background, Parton replied as if dutifully adhering to a script, until I asked her to advise drag queens who want to do Dolly, which was itself a bold query. Her recommendations didn't get more specific than a big wig and some sturdy heels, but she loved the question, and for a moment dropped her façade. Signing her *Best of Dolly Parton* poster, which suggests *Lil Abner*'s backwoods bombshell Daisy Mae Yokum, she chuckled, "I kinda look like a drag queen here, don't I?"

Parton has always favored this ultra-femme image. The record jacket of 1970's *The Fairest of Them All* presents her as a fairy-tale princess, likely to deflect the quotidian seriousness within. We can only see her through a high collar's pink gauze and in the reflection of a gilded mirror. The illusion that stares back at us is akin to what butch lesbians see when they're forced to dress "ladylike"—a staged exhibition designed to appease. "I look one way and am another," she told *Ladies' Home Journal* in 1982. "It makes for a good combination. I always think of 'her,' the Dolly image, like a ventriloquist does his dummy."

One of the many reasons we're drawn to Parton is that her best work grapples with identities some thought inferior: female, alien, poor, rural. Her first hit, 1966's "Dumb Blonde," reclaims its titular putdown much like gays and lesbians take back "queer" from our oppressors. On *The Fairest*'s harrowing "Down from Dover," a pregnant teenager is rejected by her parents, much like we were then, for bringing them shame. "And even though you may not understand me/I hope that you'll accept me like I am," Parton sings on that album's "Just the Way I Am" in defense of her unorthodox self, her recognizable characters, and, by extension, us.

Her ability to see what's good in everyone and present feminist ideas in direct yet nonthreatening terms makes this small-town Tennessee-born singer-songwriter one of few universally beloved public figures, yet it's forgotten that Parton took ages to cross over beyond country. Until 1977, she got no higher on *Billboard*'s pop album chart than number 198. Even her often-covered standard "Jolene" only received scattered US pop radio play in 1973.

On that song, rather than confronting her man, Parton faces down her competition. The first verse focuses on how hot this Jolene is, and the chorus repeats her name so pleadingly that if you didn't understand English, you'd assume it was a love song to her. While acknowledging her challenger's power over her man, Parton establishes how far she'll go to keep what's hers. She flatters her opponent while asserting authority incarnated by the tune's catchiness. Anyone armed with a guitar riff as insistent as the one that motors this song isn't submissive. This guy is the only one for Parton, but these women will determine their fray's outcome, not him. Why involve men at all when girl talk gets this riveting?

Her next single, 1974's "I Will Always Love You," waves goodbye to her domineering duet partner and TV host, Porter Wagoner. It claims her affection will remain long after she leaves, but its structure anticipates the freedom she'll feel flying solo. While its verses represent her farewell's heaviness, the sustained note that comprises most of its chorus soars. Its weightlessness implies that she's already flying away to brighter prospects. That's why, unlike so many other so-long songs, "I Will Always Love You" broadcasts determination. It keeps coming back to that note, suggesting both the persistence of her love as well as how steadfastly she'll pursue her dreams. Elvis wanted to cover it and take half of the royalties, but Parton turned the titan down. This refusal earned her millions when Whitney Houston's 1992 remake turned it into one of the biggest love songs of all time. Read between its lines and it's a declaration of independence. The 1976 deep cut "Shattered Image" fights back far more directly. "Stay out of my closet if your own's full of trash," she warns tabloids.

On 1977's pop breakthrough "Here You Come Again," Parton confronts suppressed desires for a not-quite-ex who's "looking better than a body has a right to." But what if this body was female? What if she's trying to maintain her "defenses" and live a straight life? If we hear the song our way, its lyric about love messing up her mind takes greater dimension. Maintaining her country cred, the same album's "It's All Wrong, but It's All Right" becomes far more interesting if you hear it as a summation of LGBTQ lives back then: amiss in society's eyes, but appropriate for us. On its pop-hit flipside, "Two Doors Down," Parton stops crying when she crashes a nearby shindig represented by the chorus's Cajun funk, and offers to take a new acquaintance home. That's how we triumphed over adversity in the '70s: another party, another partner.

Parton boosted her LGBTQ profile even higher with the 1980 slapstick feminist blockbuster *9 to 5*. Its director and co-writer Colin Higgins specialized in uncommon screwball comedy. Pairing a suicidal nineteen-year-old coded as queer with a seventy-nine-year-old Holocaust survivor, his script for 1971's cult classic *Harold and Maude* is absurdly funny but poignant for LGBTQ people who are told their love is aberrant. "We're all Harold, and we all want to be Maude," Higgins once said. "We're all repressed and trying to be free, to be ourselves, to be vitally interested in living, to be everything we want."

This liberation theme permeates *9 to 5*. Tying up their chauvinist boss and hoisting him into the air like a sex slave, its avenging secretaries played by Parton, Jane Fonda, and Lily Tomlin prove what women can accomplish when they unite. Fonda was then Hollywood's most outspoken feminist. Tomlin's sexuality was, to us, an open secret. Co-screenwriter Patricia Resnik is also lesbian. Higgins was gay. Once you know this, the sass they gave sweet, disarming Parton gets even more subversive—particularly when she threatens to castrate the chief. Saying through her what society would not accept directly from us, Resnik and Higgins transformed Parton from homeland star to Warhol-level pop deity.

Parton seized her moment musically. An LGBTQ club hit and multiformat Number One, the movie's theme song, "9 to 5," critiqued capitalism and patriarchy right when Ronald Reagan's election augured a seismic conservative shift. Entirely about labor, often from a female perspective, its album, *9 to 5 and Odd Jobs,* leans further liberal. Parton soon reunited with Higgins for 1982's film adaptation of Broadway's *The Best Little Whorehouse in Texas,* which made "I Will Always Love You" a Number One country and western hit for the second time. Her oldies album from 1984, *The Great Pretender,* takes its name from the 1955 Platters' hit Freddie Mercury would also remake. "Just laughing and gay like a clown," Parton describes herself on it. "I seem to be what I'm not, you see." Dolled up, painted, and posed so rigidly she barely looks real, the superstar smiles on its sleeve atop a big pink triangle. To straight people, this combination is textbook 1980s, like the artwork for Duran Duran's *Rio.* To LGBTQ people who've revived the pink triangle, the Nazi symbol for the homosexuals Germany criminalized and slaughtered, it could hardly be gayer.

Higgins died of AIDS four years later.

⏭

Chapter Thirty-Four

Soft Cell and Eurythmics

Synthpop duos have long been a standard configuration, but before Soft Cell from Leeds, England, there was little precedent besides Suicide, a New York pair who may have been the earliest act to claim "punk" as a musical descriptor, and Sparks, two ingenious Los Angeles brothers who traded giddy glam rock for burnished electronic disco collaborations with Giorgio Moroder. Both acts contrasted an extroverted but not masculine singer with a scowling counterpart confined to his keyboard. Yet it was Soft Cell's singer, Marc Almond, and synth player, Dave Ball, who codified these roles in the early 1980s. Unlike Kraftwerk's rock-referencing quartet configuration, Soft Cell imply gay coupledom by virtue of being a twosome.

Originally a Motown-style 1964 B-side favored on England's Northern Soul scene, the original version of "Tainted Love" was sung by Gloria Jones, who would later be Marc Bolan's backing singer, keyboardist, and girlfriend until she drove into a tree, killing the T. Rex legend and imbuing her oldie with more doom. In Soft Cell's severe yet even-catchier 1981 cover, Ball plays the central riff on a synth that suggests a spooky church organ, while electronic zaps punctuate the track like a whip. Having been a punk producer, Mike Thorne leaves the arrangement barren to spotlight Almond's decrying the stench of a dalliance well past its expiration date. "Don't touch me, *please*/I cannot stand the way you *teeeeeease*!" he exclaims with musical theater's staginess but also punk's arch ire. In England, it was deemed 1981's biggest single until a recalculation ruled in favor of the Human League's "Don't You Want Me." Its US Sire Records release charted for forty-three weeks, then a record.

In 1985, Coil—the industrial music duo of life partners John Balance and Peter Christopherson—further emphasized the mercilessness of Soft Cell's version by slowing it into a dirge that illustrated how AIDS literally tainted love. In Christopherson's blindsiding video, a sickly young man played by Balance is hospitalized. Right before he dies, he's visited by an angel of death represented by Almond. It's now thought that Coil's remake was the very first AIDS charity record. The clip, the earliest to depict the epidemic's terrors, appeared in the Museum of Modern Art's inaugural music video retrospective. Once you see it, you'll associate "Tainted Love" with HIV, even if your own life hadn't forced you to hear it that way.

Soft Cell's cover got so big that its success dwarfed the duo's own material in the US. In the UK, where other hits from the pair meant regular TV gigs, Almond showed up in BDSM leather, eyeliner, and a winking acknowledgment of being a mad queen who managed to infiltrate the international mainstream. The very things that made Almond identifiably gay made him rebellious, which paradoxically broadened his appeal. When his UK record company tried to mute his gay identity, Almond camped it up even more. Every flick of his limp wrist was like an extended middle finger.

This nelly toughness works because Soft Cell's songs are often so recklessly tender. "Bedsitter" from 1981 picks up where the Velvet Underground's "Sunday Morning" thematically leaves off. Almond plays the role so many of us lived: a solitary youth who divides his weekends between clubland and a studio apartment. Still sounding like the evening before, "Bedsitter" nails the repetitiveness of living for the nightlife and the way in which it sucks the vitality out of one's days. It's the synthpop equivalent of English "kitchen sink" dramas, like 1961's pioneeringly gay-sympathetic *A Taste of Honey*, yet it's globally relatable. When the duo appeared on *Top of the Pops*, Almond dressed as an S&M twink and gesticulated like Liza Minnelli, letting viewers know that he was telling our tale. Years later, the singer revealed that he'd aimed to do for queer kids what David Bowie did for him with "Starman": send out a signal that they, too, could be themselves.

Mostly recorded in New York, the 1981 debut containing these hits, *Non-Stop Erotic Cabaret*, chronicles post-lib LGBTQ life right before AIDS changed everything. Deftly leading listeners down a queer path without announcing it as such, the duo begin by sketching an ordinary guy so overwhelmed with "Frustration" that he wants to either diverge or die. By "Seedy Films," the protagonist finds himself "Feeling sleazy in seedy sin city." Vicious Pink singer Josephine Warden supplies feminine giggles, but in a real porn theater, where Almond enjoys the "hands of a stranger," his accomplice would almost certainly be male or demand cash up front. The album features another pricey new synth, the Synclavier, but the track sounds cheap and claustrophobic, as if it were made in an actual Times Square peep-show booth, a setting further suggested by the cover's lurid neon glow.

A politically incorrect parody of glamour, in which the decadent wealthy wallow in a depravity proven all too real with every Republican sex scandal, "Sex Dwarf" presents a John Waters–esque scenario in which Almond walks his title character on a leash. "You know what they say about small boys," the singer insinuates. Epitomizing pansexual nightlife at its early '80s freaky peak, they procure "disco dollies for a life of vice." Set to a jaunty Motown riff that evokes a time when the Profumo affair rocked UK politics, "Secret Life" confronts an extortionist who blackmails celebrities, some secretly queer, like the narrator, who considers changing his hair *and* gender to escape discovery.

Ending the album's nocturnal narrative, "Say Hello, Wave Goodbye" presents a heterosexual parting, but queer elements abound. Almond infers parallels between his soon-to-be-ex, a promiscuous femme, and LGBTQ people deemed similarly distasteful. His lyrics are cruel, but the music's pathos tells another story. Like a gay person forced into conversion therapy, the more Almond downplays verboten desires through his words, the more his delivery concretizes them. He even misses several notes, as if he can no longer control himself. In *Soft Cell's Non-Stop Exotic Video Show*, Ball plays the song's protagonist, not Almond, who's a singer at the song's Pink Flamingo nightclub.

The clip resembles James Bidgood's literally homemade 1971 fantasia of gay male prostitution, *Pink Narcissus.* This was Soft Cell at its straightest—i.e., not very.

The 1982 single "Torch" examines the relationship gay men have with divas. Singing "I'm lost again and I'm on the run/Looking for love in a sad song," Almond conveys the distress of being estranged and how that makes us crave more meaning from art. As he yields to tears, the melody builds, growing potent as the glow from his diva's eyes illuminates a path to salvation. In the song and video, she's played by Cindy Ecstasy, a New York drug dealer. Years before the drug from which she took her name fueled the UK rave scene and eventually the pop mainstream, Ecstasy supplied pills to the duo. That's why, despite its sober themes, *Erotic Cabaret* still packs the punch of a party record. It's also why the album birthed a remixed 1982 sequel called *Non Stop Ecstatic Dancing.* In the "Torch" video, Ecstasy is expressionless, like a religious icon, while Almond bats false eyelashes and emotes diva authority. He's the ecstatic one.

Rather than maturing into a conventional dance act, Soft Cell manifested nightlife's seamiest side. Suggesting the molly had worn off along with fame's buzz, 1983's *The Art of Falling Apart* imparts the pair's anxieties through characters verging on nervous breakdowns. The album's gayest song, "Numbers," is based on John Rechy's 1967 novel of the same name. Not long after Allen Ginsberg won a 1957 obscenity trial over his homoerotic poem "Howl," Rechy wrote of unapologetic gay promiscuity in 1963's autobiographical *City of Night,* which was notably name-checked by the Doors' "L.A. Woman." By the early '80s, Rechy's tale of a stud who measures his self-worth by the frequency of his conquests had become a way of life for some gay men. Shifting between first- and second-person perspectives, Almond queries his queer Don Juan while Ball's accompaniment lurches, as if their antihero has had so much sex he can't even walk straight. "Throw 'em away like Kleenex" is what he does with tricks.

Almond draws from Jacques Brel—the Belgian-born singer-songwriter who covered unseemly subject matter (like us) even before Lou Reed—and Scott

Walker, a US expat whose UK success with crepuscular Brel songs prepped England for David Bowie. On "L'Esqualita," from 1984's *This Last Night . . . in Sodom*, Almond restages those influences at NYC's reigning drag bar, Escuelita. "Oh I would believe that she's a real diva/As she tugs at the reins of a hundred chihuahuas," he marvels, pitting daggerlike descriptions of the club's queer demimonde against Ball's woozy undulations.

Before *Sodom* hit stores, Soft Cell split. After Almond achieved European success solo and Ball did the same with his techno duo the Grid, the pair repeatedly reunited, even collaborating with Pet Shop Boys on 2022's "Purple Zone." Of all the 1980s' synthpop stars, Almond remains the most rock 'n' roll, because he still emanates defiance.

Another synthpop duo—a heterosexual but maybe even more queer-beloved one—began when it severed romantically. Formerly members of an unremarkable rock band, the Tourists, Annie Lennox and Dave Stewart launched London's Eurythmics as a vehicle for electronic experimentation akin to David Bowie's Berlin work. Lennox subsequently discovered startling star power at the base of her vocal register, and the pair's songwriting similarly became so much more decisive that, like Soft Cell with "Tainted Love," Eurythmics went from obscurity to MTV-powered notoriety, doing so with pop's most philosophical smash, 1983's "Sweet Dreams (Are Made of This)."

From a perspective so worldly it's nearly omnipotent, Lennox asserts that everybody's on a quest. Some aim to use others or to be used; some wish to abuse others or to be abused. Given these grim goals, one must hold one's head high and keep moving. That's it. There's not one extraneous word or note. Catchiness can sometimes trivialize pop messages, but the unrelenting hooks here reinforce Lennox's clout, particularly when she riffs wordlessly, as if language alone can't encompass her existential ache. In the video, she's a

Mad Men–like figure giving a sales pitch as a similarly suited Stewart sits at his computer. Surrounded by the gold records they'd soon be awarded, the pair parrot Kraftwerk's sternness. But because Lennox is commanding and not poker-faced, like Stewart, they become something nearly unprecedented in pop: an assertive woman supported by a passive man.

Despite their relationship past, Eurythmics maintained synthpop's queerness because in the mechanics of their presentation, Lennox is a top and Stewart a bottom. As he wrote in his memoir, they, too, are Gilbert & George fans and based not just their business attire on the gay artists but also their personal and professional philosophy. "They had a lasting influence on us in every way," Stewart confessed, "the understanding that art is work and work is art." From production to management, the duo took near-complete control. The entire package became musical theater.

The "Love Is a Stranger" video fabricates their performance-art personas even further. Lennox first appears as a high-class hooker chauffeured by Stewart. Regarding her compact and the camera with drag's chichi affect, she rips off her wig exactly like Bowie in his "Boys Keep Swinging" video. The shock here is that without the wig, Lennox is even more stunning. She transforms into a leather-clad dominatrix, and, back in the limo, the kind of pugnacious yuppie soon fictionalized by *American Psycho*. Again, their lyric is philosophical: Love is a fantasy amplifying reality while distorting it; an obsession that only seemingly liberates. Without marriage equality or other social support to nourish LGBTQ relationships, and with only bars, bathhouses, and discos to facilitate fleeting hookups, love for us, then, was often a stranger.

The media would soon pigeonhole Lennox as the female counterpart to Boy George and other epicene '80s males, but she was doing more than symbolically wearing the pants. After years of women singer-songwriters aiming to cut through the artifice of their girly, male-groomed predecessors with their own autobiography and naturalism, Lennox's abrupt shifts between masculine and feminine role-playing thwarted the expectations foisted on female musicians. A visual correlation of her vocal strength, her suits wouldn't have been so impactful if she hadn't been writing and singing so forcefully.

Her satiric femininity likewise scintillated because she was deconstructing prefab sexuality, not catering to it. That's why she presages the current state of drag as a heady theatrical presentation rather than its prior goal of undetectable gender illusion. Like LGBTQ people, Lennox took on the costuming and combative stances of her straight male oppressors, as well as the feminine clichés they imposed on all of us. She fought against being relegated to second-class status because she is a woman, and she did it the same way and for the same reasons that we refuse to accept being unsatisfactory simply because we're LGBTQ.

Although their public personas positioned her as the vocalist and Stewart the instrumentalist, Lennox studied classical flute, harpsichord, and piano at London's prestigious Royal Academy of Music. Just as her wigs and costumes emphasized her mutability, Lennox hit some of her lowest and highest notes within moments of each other throughout 1983's *Sweet Dreams (Are Made of This),* proving she is as nonbinary vocally as she is physically. There are conventional instruments on the record, but rarely do Lennox, Stewart, and their side musicians play them traditionally. Like Bowie in Berlin, Stewart through his production estranges nearly everything here. Nothing is ordinary.

While the arrangements grew grander and more resolute on 1983's *Touch,* insecurity marks its lyrics, particularly during "Here Comes the Rain Again," another early morning gay club cut. Lennox airs turmoil enlarged by the track's stormy symphonics. "Talk to me like lovers do," she sings as the melody drifts between faith and dread. This instability sprang from the duo's own struggles. After their domestic split and the formation of their new group, Stewart nearly died during lung surgery; Lennox fought agoraphobia. We heard their musical reflections of these troubles as analogues of our own.

The video for "Who's That Girl?" downplays their personal tensions by spoofing them. Lennox performs in a nightclub as an early 1960s singer resembling the feminine lesbian nonpareil Dusty Springfield. Stewart and most of his many dates to the club sport huge '80s hairdos. Nearly all are pop stars, and they change with every quick edit. Among them is Boy George's male chum Marilyn, an ultra-androgynous Blitz regular. Midway through, the Eurythmics singer sits in the audience as a hypermasculine '50s Elvis type. At the end, Lennox's femme and butch personas exchange a kiss. Unlike Queen's crossdressing "I Want to Break Free" video, "Who's That Girl?" fueled Eurythmics as an unstoppable force. The single's picture sleeve featured Lennox in the same drag, and MTV championed the clip, although the channel allegedly asked to see her birth certificate to verify her gender. Undaunted, she performed as her Elvis-y rocker at the 1984 Grammys, where Boy George gave his immortal acceptance speech: "Thank you, America. You've got taste, style, and you know a good drag queen when you see one."

Back in the '70s, Bowie aimed to turn George Orwell's futuristic novel *1984* into a televised musical, but the writer's widow turned him down. A decade later, the dystopian classic became a film, and Eurythmics released *1984 (For the Love of Big Brother)*, a largely wordless electronic soundtrack even more reminiscent of Bowie's Berlin canon. Among the exceptions is "Sexcrime (Nineteen Eighty-Four)," which draws from hammering hi-NRG. New wave stations aside, US radio wasn't ready for a title that suggests rape. In the novel's fictional language, a "sexcrime" is any intimacy not for governmentally approved procreation, which includes homosexuality.

Lennox sings the film's Bach-derived ballad, "Julia," from its male protagonist's perspective. In Orwell's novel, Winston Smith's liaison with the song's subject is criminal, and both are tortured. "My darling, will we still be there?" the singer asks of their legacy. Then, as today, fascism rewrites history with lies. We've long been written out of history, our LGBTQ identities rendered invisible. Lennox sings what, out of context, becomes a lesbian love song, which magnifies its transgression and further emphasizes Orwell's totalitarian-flouting themes. In a spare, face-focused video sung to Julia, the defiance in Lennox's eyes lets our truths be seen.

Be Yourself Tonight from 1985 buttresses synths with rock-guitar blasts and R&B horn squawks that Lennox wears as limitation-flouting aural attire. Its broader stylistic palate emphasizes that Eurythmics refused to be reduced to gender or genre. They can do anything, and that's what they say of women on

"Sisters Are Doin' It for Themselves." Few asserted female force like Lennox's duet partner here, Aretha Franklin, who ascended in the '60s by taking a guy's song, Otis Redding's "Respect," and making it not only one of the decade's most female-affirming records but also one that demands dignity for all Black people. Uniting the biggest female star of the British synthpop wave with America's eternal soul queen meant more than marketing. It signified solidarity across nationality, generation, and race.

Yet like many demonstrations of feminine strength back then, "Sisters" distances itself from LGBTQ interpretation. "Cause a man still loves a woman/ And a woman still loves a man," it reassures. Maybe Lennox wrote that line because many thought she was lesbian. During the recording, Stewart had to persuade Aretha that their song's bell-ringing lyric didn't allude to sapphic sex and that Lennox wasn't gay. Yet Aretha's first big hit, 1967's "I Never Loved a Man (The Way I Love You)," ranks as the greatest unintentional lesbian anthem. If you don't already know this, think about its title from a queer woman's viewpoint. At the very least, "Sisters" proved a straight guy could stand by his ex while she's standing up for women. But its hetero specificity means "Sisters" never attained top-drawer LGBTQ anthem status.

By 1986's *Revenge*, Stewart had started producing, writing songs, and/or making videos for guitar-based Americans from the Ramones to Bob Dylan. Showcasing Lennox in a growl so low she suggests the song's subject, the album's "Missionary Man" took on religious colonizers while appropriating enough bluster to snag a rock Grammy. On 1987's *Savage*, the pair returned to European modes of prominent synths and gender provocation. Instead of touring, Lennox shot a video album that begins with "Beethoven (I Love to Listen To)." In it, she plays a prim housewife so preoccupied with chores that she doesn't notice the arrival of a mischievous girl and a moping drag queen—projections of her own repression. Gazing into her boudoir mirror, she morphs into a rampaging amalgamation of both figures, then trashes her home and strides away with an imperious gait. In "I Need a Man," that same sparkly vamp staggers onto a stage and mimes the song with such two-fisted posturing that Lennox suggests not a white Tina Turner but a female Mick Jagger.

Resembling a drag queen yet performing as a drag king, she's an emancipated woman imitating a cock-rocking guy impersonating a tart. This is Lennox's most meta, LGBTQ-relevant ceremony.

The duo next collaborated with big shot US rock producer Jimmy Iovine on the ornate pop of 1989's *We Too Are One*, but the subsequent tour's high point came when the pair stripped its newly busy arrangements to simple acoustic elements that emphasized their seemingly unbreakable musical telepathy. They had long thought of each other the way many same-sex couples see themselves, as twins from different mothers. That's the other reason they emulated Gilbert & George in near-identical dress.

Yet soon they separated. While Stewart continued to collaborate with rock and pop luminaries, Lennox released her defining 1992 solo debut, *Diva*. The gay male compliment of female skill and status, *diva* had become a media buzzword, and Lennox embodies one throughout this glacial album that pits Scottish soul warmth against icily elegant synths and grandly low-key orchestration. Lennox sighingly protracts the title of "Why" as an inquiry against all injustice, between spilling forth, with stymied anguish, "the words I've never said." In my 1995 interview with Stewart, he asserted that they're all about him. In the video, a smash on MTV's adult sister station VH1 and the foundation of another VHS album, director Sophie Muller reprises Lennox's transformation in the mirror from "Beethoven," but here the singer is putting on a public persona. Donning a feathered headpiece from the James Bond film *Octopussy*, she transforms into the ultimate female spectacle, the Vegas showgirl, even while pouring her introspective heart out. Despite not having sex with thoroughly straight guys, LGBTQ people are often forced to accommodate their gaze, avoid its detection, or risk violence. In the "Why" clip, Lennox plays dress-up for that scrutiny, but her stoic demeanor suggests she's donning armor with which to wage war, even as her countenance teeters on defeat's brink.

Forced to conceal our thoughts and temper our actions, LGBTQ listeners often gravitate to confessional lyrics or music that releases pent-up emotions via gospel-derived styles, like those secularized here. Lennox's first child was stillborn in 1988, but she'd since successfully had another, so profound emotions fuel *Diva*, like the fear of abandonment in "Walking on Broken Glass," which sounds prim and happy but isn't. She sings "Little Bird" from the perspective of an outsider who's grounded by fear but longs to fly. These songs resonate for her LGBTQ fans, for she addresses self-determination and reinvention on an operatic scale.

Lennox released other albums, Eurythmics briefly reunited, and the singer now devotes herself to AIDS and women's empowerment philanthropy. Yet she peaked with *Diva* because she needed to—just like we needed her during the plague's worst. Her transcendental will buoys every sink-or-swim note.

⏭

Chapter Thirty-Five

Frankie Goes to Hollywood and Bronski Beat

Shaping perception while stimulating sales, hype feeds popular culture. But with Frankie Goes to Hollywood, promotion and provocation intertwined to such an extent that the band's publicity became art. Even *Rolling Stone*, then resistant to trendy upstarts, deemed the Liverpool quintet "the biggest pop phenomenon since the Sex Pistols." Unlike David Bowie, who said he was gay while married and newly a father, or Boy George, who emphasized his queerness while talking around it for years, Frankie's Holly Johnson and Paul Rutherford espoused their sexuality so valiantly that it defined the group. In most groups, supporting singers aren't full-time members. In Frankie's case, dapper Johnson sang lead while fetching Rutherford functioned as background-singing go-go boy, giving physical proof of their gayness like two gents at a prom. "We used the gay bit as a publicity stunt," Johnson admitted, but it was as essential to the group's ballyhoo as gayness (or its suggestion) was to glam. Frankie Goes to Hollywood was the next evolutionary step: the first million-selling group whose frontmen were gay and out from the get-go.

Frankie was the flagship act of ZTT, a UK label masterminded by producer Trevor Horn—ex-Yes singer and bassist and former half of the Buggles, whose 1979 hit "Video Killed the Radio Star" launched MTV—managing director Jill Sinclair, Horn's wife; and Paul Morley, an intellectual *New Music Express* journalist who parlayed Frankie's forbidden passions into marketable myths. The entire band and then only its singers backed by Ian Dury's Blockheads recorded early versions of 1983's "Relax," but eventually Johnson and Rutherford sang over instrumentation supplied solely by Horn and studio helpers like future Annie Lennox producer Stephen Lipson. The song's release was preceded by an ad showcasing Johnson in rubber with the slogan FRANKIE GOES TO HOLLYWOOD ARE COMING. Another featured Rutherford in clone wear and a sailor cap, captioned ALL THE NICE BOYS LOVE SEA MEN.

When the original "Relax" twelve-inch arrived as an import, months before the single's US release, its fetishy illustration and nipple-ring-pulling photo marked it as a record of LGBTQ interest. But despite being sixteen minutes long, Horn's "Sex Mix" was nothing but an impeccably engineered throb festooned with samples dripping erotic tension while withholding melody and climax. Months later, word of "Relax" being banned by the BBC and subsequently topping the UK chart for weeks seemed inexplicable. How could such an extravagant but meandering mix be a smash?

After a video set to the single version arrived on US shores, it all made sense. Brought to a gay S&M club on a rickshaw driven by Morley, Johnson undergoes a queer initiation. After being jostled by rough-and-ready patrons, he's thrown onstage to wrestle a real tiger for the amusement of a corpulent emperor. Tied to a wheel, Johnson and Rutherford are doused—an unsubtle allusion to water sports—then play horsey atop a leather-clad barmaid as the scene culminates in an orgy/riot.

All this wouldn't have mattered if the single wasn't more meaningful than its surface message. Although some of its lyrical sauciness defies easy comprehension, the song's central chant couldn't be less ambiguous about postponing ejaculation. Yet "Relax" is also about queer love of one's self and others, maybe as many as possible. "Make making it your redemption!" Johnson recommends. That's how the pre-epidemic gay man quashed the diffidence we're taught: He compensated with success and sex. When Johnson belts "hit me with those laser beams," there's more going on than exhibitionism. With the world's eyes upon him, the singer follows his own advice and does what society forbids of LGBTQ people when it denies us full equality and, therefore, safety: He relaxes.

While producing Foreigner in New York, Horn visited the Paradise Garage, which had staggeringly loud but clear sound and a famously responsive Black gay crowd. "It was only when I went to this club and heard the sort of things they were playing that I really understood about 12" mixes," Horn later admitted. Now structuring the record with protracted instrumental foreplay that builds pressure that its vocal second half releases, Horn remixed Frankie's debut into a proper orgasmic experience that justified its gushing sound effects. This restructuring paid off: "Relax" sold two million copies in the UK, where it remained in the Top Forty for thirty-seven consecutive weeks—an achievement that ranks it among England's biggest-ever hits. After a year of club and new wave radio play, alternate videos, and a visual remix of the original clip in Brian De Palma's erotic thriller *Body Double* on a film-within-a-film porn set with Johnson and Rutherford, it finally became a Top Ten US hit in 1985.

By then Frankie had tallied other overseas smashes. We tend to think of protest music as peaceful folk tunes performed by earnest singers with acoustic guitars, but 1984's "Two Tribes" argues for accord by satirizing the agitprop and automation of President Reagan's Strategic Defense Initiative, the so-called "Star Wars" program designed to destroy airborne Russian missiles. High-tech and hi-NRG, its over-the-top bombast exemplifies Cold War life in the shadow of an escalating peril that threatened to culminate in worldwide nuclear annihilation.

As Johnson explained to *Smash Hits* writer and future Pet Shop Boy Neil Tennant, the song's two tribes are delineated by an American funk bassline played on a keyboard that samples and exaggerates the slapping attack of thumbed bass popping, and an ominous Russian melody that opens the record. In the verse, Johnson depicts Reagan through a cheeky collage of biographical fragments, such as "I modeled shirts by Van Heusen." In the bridge, he represents Soviet leader Konstantin Chernenko. "Tell the world that you're winning," Johnson sings with propagandistic cheer, trailed by orchestral fanfare in the Romantic style of Pyotr Ilyich Tchaikovsky, the gay Russian composer. The promotion and packaging of "Relax" may have drawn from hypersexualized notions of LGBTQ life, but "Two Tribes" throws a spanner in gay stereotyping by tackling serious subject matter that has nothing to do with fucking, and by modernizing Tchaikovsky's tumult with nearly heavy metal guitar riffage.

Yet everything in "Two Tribes" is set to the gallop of gay discoland, allowing DJs to mix its twelve-inch incarnations in and out of typical dance fare. That meant that the grandiloquence of Horn's production—which again didn't feature the band's players—filled large public spaces, where protest music is best experienced. Immersive club systems amplified the enormity of the song's air raid sirens and godlike narration, which mimic public service films about nuclear attacks. Championed by MTV, the video, directed by former 10cc members Kevin Godley and Lol Creme, features Reagan and Chernenko lookalikes who wrestle each other with crotch-squeezing and ear-biting moves until the planet explodes. Such vehement antiwar commentary proved too much for many US Top Forty markets, but on L.A. alt-rock station KROQ listeners voted "Two Tribes" their sixth most beloved song of 1984. "Relax" was Number One.

Frankie's purposefully sprawling *Welcome to the Pleasuredome* exudes the excess of its era and then some. Occupying most of the 1984 double album's opening side, its towering title track builds even higher on ZTT's exorbitance by combining Horn's prog-rock acumen with the group's club foundation. Horn replicates a DJ's guiding hand throughout the track as it undergoes byzantine compositional and tonal changes akin to the opulent output of Eurodisco visionaries like Boris Midney while mixing in birdcalls, harmonica honks, tribal chanting, female R&B vocals, and even acoustic guitar from Yes's Steve Howe. This meticulously incandescent cut served as a signature of the Saint, New York's enormous gay disco, which was outfitted with a domed ceiling and planetarium lighting. It also inspired San Francisco's own gay mega-club, Pleasuredome.

But prog-disco fusion wouldn't be everyone's cup of tea, especially when joined by the Queen-y eclecticism of both "Krisco Kisses," a funky punk ode to fisting, and the album's symphonic "The Power of Love," another UK Number One. Some straight listeners surely felt encroached upon by a gay guy belting Bruce Springsteen's "Born to Run," as Johnson does on *Welcome.* It was the reverse of rockers going disco, yet to them likely just as threatening. The lyric remains apt: Homophobia keeps us all on the run.

As they did with Queen, critics attacked Frankie. The *Voice*'s Robert Christgau—who'd just started publishing me—designated *Pleasuredome* his December 1984 Consumer Guide's "Must to Avoid." Decrying "the appalling quality of the band's music," he deemed Frankie "a marginally competent arena-rock band who don't know how to distinguish between effeminacy and pretention." That comment suggests male homosexuality is inherently feminine—an equivalency particularly false on an album this manly. Frankie contended that the glory of gayness deserved extravagance. That made us pretentious to those blind to its virtues. *Rolling Stone*'s David Fricke considered the album "dedicated to the elevation of hip agitprop and homoerotic self-absorption."

These critiques infuriated me, for they felt aimed at not just Frankie but all LGBTQ culture. Just as it was at the so-called death of disco, the gatekeepers now growing weary of Boy George and other queers infiltrating the charts were once again distorting and devaluing us. They weren't hearing what we heard. Having experienced on the dancefloor what records like these meant to those like me and how they elevated us, I made it my mission to write about them so their LGBTQ relevance would be celebrated, not psychoanalyzed so gracelessly by otherwise intelligent fellows.

Demoralized, Frankie lasted no longer than the promotion of 1986's follow-up, *Liverpool.* When Johnson sued ZTT to be freed from his contract, he did something few musicians have ever accomplished: He won in court. That's how bad the band had it. Meanwhile, Horn produced widely imitated widescreen pop for Pet Shop Boys, Cher, t.A.T.u., and other gay-fancied acts, often with effulgent results. Yet copycats rarely approached the glory of ZTT's original shooting stars, and not even a remix of "Love Train" by house master Frankie Knuckles could help Johnson repeat his European solo success in the US.

Soon after, the singer received an AIDS diagnosis, published his memoir, *A Bone in My Flute*, and released his 1994 gay history lesson "Legendary Children (All of Them Queer)," with Helen Terry singing backup. Rutherford advanced with astute house tracks like 1989's "Oh World," but the circumstance that gave his songs weight—his lover was dying—also made it impossible to continue a solo career.

Yet the ostentation of the band's gay glory lingers far beyond the "Frankie Say Relax" T-shirts that became emblematic of its era. Whenever an act emphasizes rather than downplays its LGBTQ status, Frankie goes right back to Hollywood.

The week of June 10, 1984, was the gayest seven-day stretch in pop history. Every single then in the UK Top Fifteen had some LGBTQ connection. Dethroning Wham!, "Two Tribes" entered at Number One. Blitz alumni Spandau Ballet and Ultravox shared space with the Smiths and "Relax." Deniece Williams's gay-adopted *Footloose* smash, "Let's Hear It for the Boy," dropped, but on the upswing were vintage tracks by Michael Jackson and Sister Sledge, a new one from Elton, and the unofficial gay club theme song from prolific gay producer Ian Levine, Evelyn Thomas's "High Energy," which mimics the "Relax" rhythm. The chart even included year-old gay-crafted hi-NRG, "Searchin' (I Gotta Find a Man)," sung by a lesbian, Hazell Dean. You can't tell me that the Style Council doesn't look and cavort like gay preppies in the video for its earlier hit "Long Hot Summer." The straightest act in the Top Fifteen, synthpop's Howard Jones, eventually became the proud papa of two gay sons. But the most passionate yet political single of this gay period was the one that still speaks to LGBTQ listeners of every age and persuasion, Bronski Beat's debut, "Smalltown Boy."

The song captures one of life's most complex transitions: turning from a dependent child into an autonomous adult. Everyone undergoes this metamorphosis, but ours necessitates shedding the straight norms and binary notions inherent nearly everywhere to become someone our parents don't always expect and sometimes don't want. Always involving an inner journey of discovery, this realignment often necessitates a geographic one, especially for those of us from places where any breach of the local standard means trouble. We gamble on getting lost in the big city so we may find ourselves. For LGBTQ people, the emotional, spiritual, and physical stakes are greater, as revealed by our higher percentages of homelessness, suicide, substance addiction, and violent victimization. The nouns in "Smalltown Boy" are masculine, but its story remains the same for lesbians and bisexuals, as well as trans, intersex, and other noncompliant folk. It's one of the few songs that unites us all.

Laconic lyrics set the scene with a lone, suitcase-clutching figure on a platform as wind and rain externalize hidden tears. Mom can't comprehend why her child is moving out, but we know the reason: "The love that you need will never be found at home." The far more dramatic twelve-inch version withholds the chorus—and even the rhythm track—until all subsequent verses are sung. They suggest why he's leaving: "You were the one that they'd talk about." Bullies punish him for his divergence, but he withholds anguish, which comes out in the chorus and in its autobiographical portrayal by Glasgow-born singer Jimmy Somerville.

Possessed of a particularly pure falsetto, Somerville brings a tone akin to a preadolescent choirboy filtered through gay young-adult experience. He plays a teen on the threshold of manhood yet sings in a female register, which broadens his plight beyond gender while positioning it as a queer one. Although it's synthpop, "Smalltown Boy" bespeaks gospel's solemnity as it stages an exorcism. Shifting emphasis and syncopation as the protagonist he both represents and consoles progresses from suffering to solace, the singer knows the devil of self-doubt instilled in us for being born LGBTQ must be expelled through crying, so he soars with a shiver-inducing sob. The video, by "Relax" director Bernard Rose, further situates the song in a gay context: After Somerville approaches a young man in a locker room, he's chased and beaten, then a policeman returns him to his saddened mom and angered father. He again leaves home, but this time is joined by his family of choice, his bandmates.

The summer this record came out, I responded to it the way others have for decades: This was how I felt, and who I'd been. From the pained persistence of those synths to the pang of Somerville's angelic howl, "Smalltown Boy" found musical analogies for the hurt I'd held inside.

Unlike every other best-selling group, Bronski Beat was *all* gay—Somerville as well as his keyboard pals Steve Bronski and Larry Steinbachek. A pink triangle adorns the artwork of "Smalltown Boy" and its 1984 album, *The Age of Consent*. This title alludes to the fact that boys under twenty-one in Britain then risked arrest for having sex with other boys, but consensual heterosexual sex was legal for anyone sixteen and up. The inner sleeve of the album's European and Canadian pressings further enumerated country-by-country discrepancies.

Recalling Steinbachek getting gay bashed after a show, *Age*'s opening track, "Why?," tackles antigay savagery in ways suitably unsubtle. While Somerville protests antigay violence, racing hi-NRG rhythms conjure both the anxiety of being chased down an alleyway and our own oppositional anger: "Name me an illness, call me a sin/Never feel guilty, never give in!" The chorus confronts the fearmongers who call us sick, but the bridge reaches out to unite queer listeners against our adversaries as a string-synth countermelody ascends. In Rose's video, seldom seen in the US, Somerville takes flight as a godlike figure nods his approval.

Queer pop routinely revisits old songs, but Bronski's covers are cannier than most. Homophobes often quote Scripture to justify their hatred, so it's pushback for a gay group to revisit *Porgy and Bess*'s "It Ain't Necessarily So," the only standard that questions "the things that you're liable to read in the Bible." The group's 1985 medley with Marc Almond covers Donna Summer's

"Love to Love You Baby," accelerates to her "I Feel Love," and segues into John Leyton's "Johnny Remember Me," a BBC-banned 1961 teen-tragedy lament originally produced by Joe Meek, the gay English studio wiz behind the Tornados' 1962 smash "Telstar." His mental health compromised by having been arrested in a restroom and consequently blackmailed, as well as by poverty—his royalties had been withheld by a bogus lawsuit—Meek killed his landlady and then himself when he was unable to pay the rent. By adding Leyton's hit, Bronski and Almond acknowledge the conflicts of our past while taking back the music our disco queen tried to reframe as specifically heterosexual with her then-recent "Adam and Eve, not Adam and Steve" comment.

Bronski Beat was picked to be the opening act on Madonna's star-making Virgin Tour, but, feeling pressured, Somerville quit instead, which meant Bronski Beat never played in the US at its peak. Replacing him with singer John Foster, the trio bounced back with 1985's "Hit That Perfect Beat" while adding new slants on disco's secular salvation. Foster lets us know that his dance partner is male and, as their heat rises, addresses AIDS. Whereas Patrick Cowley's 1981 single "Menergy" celebrated what went down in disco's orgy dens with its lines "The boys in the back room laughin' it up/Shootin' off menergy," "Perfect Beat" admits that what had briefly been carefree has turned catastrophic: "Boys in the back room, their hearts destroy." Foster finishes the final verse not through club music's usual progression from sensuality to spirituality but via the sanctuary of pragmatic compromise: Hug and kiss, but protect your fellow man from hell-sent danger. Bronski Beat here confronts what most club acts ignored: The same rituals that fanned our disco inferno's flames were now engulfing us.

Named after a short-lived group of nineteenth-century French socialists, the Communards, Somerville's next project was also overtly political. "For a Friend" mourns the AIDS death of Mark Ashton, the gay communist who united LGBTQ Brits and miners, while "There's More to Love" refutes heteronormativity, arguing that nothing as genuine as affection could be unnatural. The duo's instrumental half, Richard Coles, brought woodwind, piano, and theater skills that broadened the pair beyond dance music into cabaret and other queer traditions. Yet 1986's *Communards* and 1987's *Red* went platinum in the UK, sold well across Europe, and charted in the US largely thanks to clubby remakes. "Our aim was to bring down Margaret Thatcher by doing covers of '70s disco classics," Coles remembers only half-jokingly. Like the Bronski bunch, Communards reshaped gay-patronized pop in their own queer image as a protest against being denied participation in other fields.

"Don't Leave Me This Way" first appeared in 1975 from Philly soul's Harold Melvin and the Blue Notes, who brought Pentecostal church to disco. Thelma Houston's chart-topping and even more dancefloor-friendly 1976 interpretation shifts from vulnerability to staggering strength, as if the vehemence of her desire and the bump of the track's majestic bassline could bring her wayward man back. A decade later, the Communards' faster, more forceful cover became the biggest UK single of 1986.

As AIDS fatalities mounted, "Don't Leave Me This Way" lived on as a means of mourning. In Mark Christopher's 1992 short *The Dead Boys' Club*, a young man steps into the shoes of a relative's newly deceased lover and sees visions of pre-plague gay life: hazy, glistening images of men dancing to Houston's hit that are simultaneously erotic and ghostlike. In 1994, the American Foundation for AIDS Research commissioned twenty-two artists to respond to the epidemic, and queer mixed-media specialist Nayland Blake submitted a bouquet draped by the song's title. AIDS disproportionately afflicted those already feared by many—gay men, intravenous drug users, and people of color—and because there was so little education about the disease, the epidemic triggered nightmarish cruelty against them. Even some healthcare workers neglected patients for fear of contagion, abandoning them in soiled hospital beds. No one wanted friends and intimates to leave us that way.

When Gloria Gaynor sang the Jackson 5 ballad "Never Can Say Goodbye" in a galloping 1974 rearrangement so popular in gay clubs that it snowballed into one of the first hits to define disco, she switched its pronouns. But the Communards' 1987 cover doesn't change them back. With every "boy" in the chorus, Somerville reminds us that he's singing to a guy while verifying dancefloor culture's centrality in LGBTQ liberation. He never can say goodbye to disco, or to the memories of his fallen fellow dancers.

Soon after, the Communards also split. Coles became a priest, British TV personality, and BBC radio host. Somerville released his savviest solo statement, 1990's "Read My Lips (Enough Is Enough)." It pays tribute to Gran Fury, ACT UP's art collective, which often repurposed pop culture slogans like President George Bush's bogus election promise, "Read my lips: no new taxes." ACT UP filled city streets with Gran Fury posters and placards featuring same-sex sailor couples, as well as women of color, all kissing each other with the caption READ MY LIPS. Somerville paired that phrase with the "enough is enough" chant from Donna Summer and Barbra Streisand's "No More Tears" to make his own AIDS-battling statement. Despite this gay forthrightness, Somerville isn't a separatist: Both solo and as a Communard, he has toured with female musicians. Showcasing Sinéad O'Connor and house music's Adeva both wearing ACT UP shirts in his "Lips" video, he emphasized that AIDS isn't merely a gay white man's concern. With them and so many others, he created a disco coalition.

⏭

Chapter Thirty-Six

Boy George

After Culture Club's early 1980s peak, Boy George survived numerous plummets. Rush-recorded after a lengthy *Colour by Numbers* globetrot, 1984's paltry *Waking Up with the House on Fire* announced the beginning of the band's descent. George and his drummer/lover Jon Moss split up yet kept working together acrimoniously, which sent the former into a secret drug spiral that further blunted his emotions, bittered his sweetness, and compromised his rule-breaking charisma on 1986's *From Luxury to Heartache.* Right after its release, stories broke that George, who'd been as famously antidrug as Adam Ant, had become a heroin addict. First, he was arrested, then several friends overdosed. Kicking dope but messed up from corrective pharmaceuticals, solo George lost direction on 1987's instantly dated *Sold* and 1989's also stilted *High Hat,* while the gulf between US and UK music trends widened along with his drug-damaged vibrato.

When his vocal cords healed, George found his solo artistic voice. Under the name Jesus Loves You, he redirected the wounded spirituality of his Culture Club hits into wizened balladry bolstered by house and hip-hop beats. Co-written and co-produced by Moss, 1989's "After the Love" examines family dysfunction, poverty, and consumer culture, but once again with real-life subtext: George and his ex-lover grapple to heal their connection. Even more eerie, 1990's "Generations of Love" frames gay, Black, Jewish, and Asian struggles as parallel battles. For its cinema verité video, George, Leigh Bowery, and Tallulah—all legends on the UK gay club scene—cavort as hustlers and johns in London's then-seedy Soho district. A grimy theater's grainy porn reveals itself as fake when an actor comically lip-syncs the song's "Feel it! Feel it!" refrain, but his cock is real, and the other johns seem genuine, too. George doubles as a voyeur in the seats—shortly before Paul Reubens, the actor who played Pee-wee Herman, was arrested for allegedly masturbating in a similar theater. This, too, was a reality of LGBTQ life before Pornhub and Grindr.

Collecting those club cuts, 1990's *The Martyr Mantras* pairs George with a transatlantic crew of DJs including Bruce Forest from New York's Black LGBTQ club Better Days. A remix of 1988's "No Clause 28" rallies against several Thatcher-era laws that prohibited "promoting homosexuality by teaching or by publishing material" between 1988 and 2003. The vagueness of what that meant affected UK media, schools, libraries, LGBTQ organizations, and even arts and AIDS funding as the law argued against "the acceptability of homosexuality as a pretended family relationship." Lines like "But tell me iron lady/Are we moving to the right?" magnified the political perspective that Culture Club's civility had mitigated. Now clearheaded, George regains his eloquence, especially when articulating intimacy's strife or absence. On "I Specialize in Loneliness," he swaps out the bravado of a gay-approved 1982 disco hit, Sharon Brown's "I Specialize in Love." "I know these are dangerous times for love/Shouldn't we stick together?" he sings, alluding to the epidemic's rising devastation. "You can't change the structure of society, so the best thing you can do is show people that you're intelligent and reasonable and compassionate," George told me in 1991. "If we don't learn from our own suffering, how are we doing to educate anybody else?"

The next year, Boy George's queer melancholy got its final US Top Forty platform through *The Crying Game*, an Oscar-winning film about the love between a straight man and a Black woman he discovers is trans. The role was played by a cis performer, as was the custom then, and there's a patently awful scene in which the guy sees his girlfriend naked for the first time and, surprised, pukes. But gay actor Jaye Davidson gives a nuanced performance of a fully dimensional role, and the success of this mostly sympathetic film meant qualified progress for trans representation that had been so much worse. Produced by Pet Shop Boys, 1992's "The Crying Game" updates the mistiness of Dave Berry's 1964 original with synthetic strings that float like storm clouds around twangy '60s guitar in a bereaved serenade about how love comes but often goes. Given the film's trans context, the androgynous sweep of George's croon, and the recognizable presence of the Pets' Neil Tennant on backing vocals, the song signified gay grief to LGBTQ listeners while still satisfying radio's hunger for anguished ballads tied to hit movies. Deep below, it seethes, but its calm surface reflects who we are and love. That's Boy George's superpower: facing the hardest truths with the softest cry.

⏭

Chapter Thirty-Seven

R.E.M.

In 1986, *Spin* flew me to Athens, Georgia, for its first cover story on R.E.M. The scoop came when singer Michael Stipe's mid-conversation attention shifted to a passing blond. "That guy always takes his shirt off downtown," the singer said admiringly. I suddenly understood something hugely pertinent about this famously cryptic band. Like Stipe's elliptical lyrics, which zoom in on particulars while omitting the usual stuff that makes songs coherent but ordinary, I simply repeated his comment in my article. Maybe everything he presented to the public at the time—inscrutable poetry, slurry delivery, undemonstrative stage presence—merged foreground with background to camouflage one central fact: Stipe isn't straight. Unlike the synthpoppers, he didn't speak of his queerness through recognizable codes until he reached stardom. He fronted a slow-rising cult band that had all the hetero critics creaming their jeans. Stipe never pretended to be someone he wasn't, however. Rather than fully hiding, he turned the closet into impressionistic art.

As they typically did with artists not yet publicly out, straight scribes amplified Stipe's secrecy. They nurtured the band's Southern Gothic mythology until it grew as thick as the kudzu that adorns the hazy cover of R.E.M.'s 1983 debut album *Murmur*. That tangle extended not only to Stipe's lyrics but also to the music, particularly Peter Buck's lateral guitar and Mike Mills's melodious bass. Balancing psychedelia's mysticism with proto-punk's corporality, the quartet turned Stipe's shyness into an expressivity that eventually ignited alt-rock multitudes. Decades of clarifying remasters and internet-enabled collective decoding have since given us a better handle on this slippery foursome. After Cocteau Twins, Sigur Rós, and other willfully obtuse acts, we've learned to accept what we can't discern. But forty years ago, when digitalization started making music sound crisper and cleaner, it was refreshing for a band to command attention by circumventing comprehension with every labyrinthian twist. "Pay attention but stay back!" R.E.M. seemed to warn. It's the message given off by every one of us conditioned to think we'll be abandoned if the truth seeps out.

This fuck me/fuck off quality makes R.E.M. an innately queer band. Like a black hole, these non-stereotypical Southerners sucked us in with a near-void that only gradually signified more than the longing of Stipe's prematurely matured mewl. In 2008, the singer revealed that "7 Chinese Bros." and "So. Central Rain (I'm Sorry)" from 1984's *Reckoning* were "about me breaking up a couple—and then dating both of them, a man and a woman." The first song relates to the theme of deception in the children's book *The Five Chinese Brothers.* Come-hither guitar alternates with arpeggiated chords on the chorus as a circuitous bassline snakes like the cover's artwork, filling in Buck's chords rather than reinforcing them. The second tune examines miscommunication and disillusionment in diffuse, low-pitched verses that set up the refrain's two-word keen—"I'm so*rry.*" When Stipe is this direct, he cuts that kudzu to the quick. How he reclines on the second vowel, stretching it into a howl of pain, is as articulate as his esotericism and mumble are not.

Stipe and Mills sing most of that album's "Pretty Persuasion" enmeshed—sometimes in harmony but otherwise not completely in unison. Their timing is so often off that Stipe's lyrics blur more than ever until the chorus, in which they conspicuously cry that a man and a woman each possesses what the title advertises. True bisexuals are no more confused than heterosexuals or homosexuals; we all like what we like because we like it. But few of us can avoid societal reinforcement to be as straight as possible. No one insists that teachers mustn't talk about heteros of history or families that pair a mommy with a daddy. Kids already aware they're queer rarely know how to be that safely, because a place free from flak, even now, rarely exists. When Stipe and Mills bray, "goddamn your confusion," they're ruining the conditioning that prevents us from being and seeing what and who we truly are. Ostensibly, the song is about consumerism. "Hurry and buy," they (probably) sing. Before same-sex couples in advertising signaled inclusivity, heterosexuality was capitalism's greatest product, but Stipe denounces the wrongness of it all. As on the previous tracks, he's drawn to both men and women.

With 1986's *Lifes Rich Pageant*, which initiated incremental clarity in every direction, R.E.M. grew political, although still open to interpretation. Drummer Bill Berry told me that "Fall on Me" is about acid rain, but Stipe later countered that it addresses oppression. The singer uses gravity as a metaphor for the crushing force of those in power. That's why he sounds so resolved: He's begun fighting back.

Ronald Reagan's right-wing policies topically dominate 1987's *Document*, but the band's breakthrough came via personal paradox. "The One I Love" subverts its amatory dedication by revealing Stipe has not only abandoned the ungendered object of his affection but now also coldly characterizes them as "A simple prop to occupy my time." Gay men aren't the only ones who use each other sexually, but the expedience with which we offer ourselves to one another wasn't matched in the straight world until the arrival of hook-up apps. The fact that R.E.M. has never sounded sexier illustrates Stipe's betrayal. There's no love—just illusion.

Having completed its contract with I.R.S., the indie label the Go-Go's helped grow, R.E.M. switched to Warner Bros. in 1988 with its leaner, nearly linear *Green*. Drawing from the band's brooding past while pointing toward its reflective and often orchestrated peak, its knotty standout, "World Leader Pretend," wages war not with Stipe's pure self but with the defenses he'd built around it. "I raised the wall/And I will be the one to knock it down," he growls, vowing with battle metaphors to dismantle his own closet. During his indie years, Stipe hid behind a curtain of curls. In the wake of the band's label change, he shaved the sides of his head and painted his eye sockets with mascara that also accentuated his skull, as if he'd assassinated his angelic public self and replaced it with a zombie skeleton. This was not the look of a man ready to play nice, and Stipe spun variations on it until the band's end.

What happened next likewise defied success's usual path. For a few years, R.E.M. stopped touring to focus on studio work in which its members switched instruments, learned new ones, and added players. The career-shifting hit from 1991's *Out of Time*, "Losing My Religion" marries mandolin to distinct diction. Each phrase easily scans, yet still provokes personal interpretations, because this time even the title misleads. It's a Southern expression for frustration, but few listeners elsewhere knew that. Crestfallen, Stipe seems to be singing about losing his faith—not simply in God or his relationship, but in everything. And because the composition lacks conventional contrasts between verse and chorus, it all feels stuck like its narrator. Combining folk's timelessness with contemporary dread, "Religion" remains a rare sort of arresting record that like "Bohemian Rhapsody" interrupts radio's typical flow with uncommon feeling.

Most every LGBTQ person I knew took notice. With no effective treatment a decade into the epidemic, AIDS fatalities were then a common occurrence in my age group and for the preceding Stonewall generation. In 1989, AIDS was the second-leading cause of death among men twenty-five to forty-four years old and an increasing killer among women—particularly those of color. By the release of "Religion," the number of US men, women, and children who had died of the disease had surpassed one hundred thousand. Safe-sex rules were now nearly clearcut, but risks remained: Condoms broke; alcohol, drugs, and depression impaired judgment. One of my friends seroconverted, despite being a psychiatrist and AIDS educator, because he had briefly dropped his guard as one does when grief-stricken. The straight world characterized us as irresponsible, but I'll always remember when both pals and tricks put an abrupt halt on even safe sex because they feared passing along the unknown.

When I met Bill Sherwood—writer-director of 1986's *Parting Glances*, which gave Steve Buscemi his first starring role as a punky gay musician battling AIDS—he confessed he'd stopped having sex entirely. I knew from the warmth he showed me that this was his way of saying we couldn't have a physical relationship. We became best buddies and even agreed to get our harrowing first HIV tests together in 1987. He told me his results were negative like mine. I later learned he lied. Back then no filmmaker could make another movie if word got out that they were HIV positive. A few years later, I learned he'd been hospitalized, and immediately flew across the country to see him. His parents said he looked calmer when I held his hand, but he'd already slipped into a coma from which he'd never recover. My robust and wickedly funny friend was now emaciated and nearly lifeless. Bill had wanted me to be the music supervisor on his next movie, but that was just a dream. He never got the chance to make it, and we never got to exchange goodbyes. All I could do was write his *Village Voice* obit.

When "Losing My Religion" arrived a year after Bill's death, it was for me about losing Bill. "I thought that I heard you laughing," Stipe sings. If you've grieved, you understand. The rest deals with disclosure—fretting over saying too much, or not enough. Bill made one of the first films to show life with AIDS, yet he couldn't tell me he had it, too. "Consider this the hint of the century," Stipe continues. Like the singer, Bill said more through *Parting Glances* than he could in real life. Guys like him could come out as gay but not as someone cheating death.

The song's LGBTQ connection went even deeper in its video. Its director, Tarsem, the Punjab-born future filmmaker of *The Cell* and other movies that blur corporality and fantasy, takes his cues here from Pierre et Gilles, the hyper-gay French photographers who shot pop stars as Indian gods, and Caravaggio, the painter now thought by many scholars to have been queer. When Stipe sings of being cornered, Tarsem cuts to an androgynous Black man rendered as an angel in Pierre et Gilles's style. After Stipe sings of being spotlighted, there's a P&G–esque image of Saint Sebastian pierced by arrows. This homoerotic iconography has long been associated with gay martyrdom; Derek Jarman's 1976 film *Sebastiane* is solely devoted to it. I can't explain what straight viewers get out of this clip, but it won six MTV awards, when that meant a lot, and has since racked up more than a billion YouTube views. What I can say is that when *we* saw this clip, we knew Stipe was revealing something about himself: His struggle was ours. R.E.M. not only became far more popular in its wake but also a band of widespread LGBTQ interest.

Having released dozens of moody minor-keyed songs, R.E.M. rebelled against itself with "Shiny Happy People," a radiant tune that remains de rigueur for straight critics to slam. Beginning with a waltzing string section, the song segues into Buck's dulcet guitar. Yet the beat is so bouncy and its mood so cheerful that some miss the mischievousness of a grave band being gay in both of the word's senses. "Throw your love around," Stipe recommends. "Take it into town!" Like Parachute Club on "Rise Up," he's suggesting we spread transformative mirth.

Maybe that's why "Shiny" topped AOL's 2006 list of the "111 Wussiest Songs of All Time" despite its not being the least bit timid. The harmonies and solos from Mills and guesting B-52 Kate Pierson beam out the positivity that those condescending critics aim to crush. The haters thought it embarrassingly ebullient—the same way they see boa-clad queens prancing on Pride. But when our friends were dying, its guilelessness gave us life.

Instead of celebrating the resulting sales of *Out of Time* with an elated victory lap, R.E.M. came back with its downbeat death album, 1992's *Automatic for the People.* When earlier that year the group accepted three Grammys, Stipe wore a cap that read WHITE HOUSE FIGHT AIDS, and rumors started circulating that he had the disease. He didn't, but like many of us, he feared he'd long since been infected. "I thought that I was going to die before I made it to thirty," Stipe later said. That fear, combined with the rising death toll and governmental indifference, shaped R.E.M.'s most cohesive work. Critics understood that the album confronted mortality from a nostalgic angle, but its queer vantage point went overlooked by the now-adoring mainstream.

Yet it's there in the ominous opening "Drive," on which R.E.M. repurpose the menace and near-nonsense lyrics of David Essex's 1973 glam hit "Rock On" into an anthem about resisting adult strictures. "Nobody tells you what to do, baby," Stipe advises kids being "bushwhacked" by the first Bush administration. He encourages them to steer their own path, as LGBTQ people endangered by AIDS and hatred must do, to affirm life while confronting oblivion.

On "Try Not to Breathe," Stipe writes about his grandmother's aiming to end her long life, but we recognized that resolve in our ailing peers. My friends Mark and Brian decided, when they simultaneously got sick, that they weren't going to seek treatment because their pals' medication had made them worse. As a result, their own health rapidly ebbed. Once Mark died, his lover, Brian, followed within weeks. Was this intentional, or did Brian's body and spirit shut down? I don't know any survivors I could ask. "I had watched, intimately, an entire community decimated by AIDS," Stipe revealed in 2017 about what shaped *Automatic*. "I have seen things that you will never see," he sings.

Elsewhere, Stipe eulogizes queer notables. "Monty Got a Raw Deal" honors Montgomery Clift, the actor whose scorching sensitivity helped Hollywood present a new masculinity in the early 1950s. In *Suddenly, Last Summer*, he was as gay as the industry allowed. Clift's own life was later depicted as tragic, like that Tennessee Williams story, but Stipe suggests that the myth that LGBTQ people are inherently unhappy only comforts the fearful. "Nonsense has a welcome ring," he sings, connecting Clift's lore to his own life before dismissing it entirely. In the 2018 documentary *Making Montgomery Clift*, co-director Robert Anderson Clift clarifies that his uncle wasn't conflicted about his sexuality. The turmoil came from his exploitative biographers.

In "Man on the Moon," Stipe praises Andy Kaufman, the performance artist who played peculiar roles with such comic conviction that he blurred fact and fiction. Many believed Kaufman's wrestling matches with women weren't staged. Kaufman's weirdness spoke to teenage Stipe just like the punk pioneers did. The singer later characterized them all as "my island of broken toys." Most of our generation knows this reference. In the classic TV special *Rudolph the Red-Nosed Reindeer*, the Island of Misfit Toys offers sanctuary to defective and unwanted dolls who gladly welcome Hermey, the nerdy blond elf who was the closest pre-Stonewall TV got to a gay children's character.

Seen through Stipe's eyes, Kaufman is much like Hermey: scorned but endearing. Did Stipe see things in Kaufman that the actor hid? In the 2014 biography *Andy Kaufman: The Truth, Finally*, his final girlfriend, Lynne Margulies, reveals that Kaufman insisted on living in the Castro and told her he was gay. The book even speculates that Kaufman's lung cancer may've been caused by AIDS. Sauntering through the desert in the video like Clift in *Red River*, Stipe similarly occupies the American Dream's fringes. Featuring an R.E.M. soundtrack, Miloš Forman's Kaufman biopic takes its title from this cut.

Stipe grapples with what's forbidden throughout *Automatic*. On "Star Me Kitten," the mumble and vocal-burying mix of R.E.M.'s primitive days return, allowing Stipe to thrice sing "fuck me kitten." On "Nightswimming," he draws from childhood memories of skinny-dipping under the stars. "The fear of getting caught," he brays, as Mills's circular piano figure captures anxieties we grasp. The singer pines for the impossible, represented by the moon. But not even Earth's watchful satellite could apprehend the glory of swimming in the dark beside a special someone like two astral bodies locked in orbit. Stipe thought he knew this ungendered person, and thought they knew him, but much goes unsaid between these children of the night. "You I cannot judge," Stipe sings, as if to his secret love. Under his breath, laughter escapes, voicing the unmentionable—a marvel that infuses R.E.M.'s greatest ballad. Even its oboe whispers what the singer holds back.

Another one, "Everybody Hurts," features Buck picking triplets akin to those in David Bowie's "Rock 'n' Roll Suicide." Like the Starman, Stipe advises listeners not to give up. He even quotes the culminating "Suicide" line, "you're not alone." While bluesy verses empathize with those battling depression, Stipe belts the chorus and bridge as if extending a hand to his community in the soul tradition. He has said the song was intended for young people, yet we heard it as directed to us—the sick, or those caretaking the fallen. The video restages the traffic-jam opening of Federico Fellini's *8½*, but for San Franciscans, it evoked when AIDS activists shut down the Golden Gate Bridge during one morning rush hour in 1989. "Are you wondering, 'Why me?'" their leaflet asked. "So are we."

Designed to facilitate R.E.M.'s return to touring, 1994's *Monster* is a "rock" album with air quotes. On "What's the Frequency, Kenneth?," Buck finally takes a grandstanding solo, but backward, which accentuates its camp. Rebelling against their own gentility, Buck and Mills trade detail for distortion, while Stipe, once again buried beneath them, renounces niceness. "Half the population saw me, unfairly, as the face of AIDS, or activist liberalism, or both," he told *Newsweek* twenty years later. Stipe portrays monsters throughout but also wrangles them.

The singer did this knowing that during *Monster*'s promotion, he would address the ultimate monstrosity: his sexuality. "I'm an equal opportunity lech," he told England's style bible *The Face*. "I'm trying to challenge people's ideas of what is regular and what is right and what is normal and what is not." Having had relationships with both genders until settling down with a guy in the late '90s, Stipe grappled to define himself at a time when words like *pansexual* weren't often used. "On a sliding scale of sexuality I'd place myself around 80–20, but I definitely prefer men to women," he clarified in 2011. But on "King of Comedy," a song about media manipulation, he opens the closet door with a meta flourish. "Make it charged with controversy/I'm straight, I'm queer, I'm bi," he sings over a Kraftwerk sample.

With that R.E.M.'s final inhibitions vanish. Stipe turns up his swagger, particularly on "Crush with Eyeliner." Taking tips in overstatement from the New York Dolls, Stipe comes on with a flirtatious con. "She's a *reeeal* woman child," he winks, as if "she" weren't completely female. Illusions and realities mingle to construct an ambiguous subject while warping his relationship to it like the warble on Buck's woozy guitar. Fakeness makes her sexy, stimulating Stipe to simulate seduction. If she isn't a drag queen pursued in heterosexuality's pantomime, my name is Courtney Love. (You bet she thought this song was about her.)

Though R.E.M. lost much of its Southern solidarity when Berry left after 1996's *New Adventures in Hi-Fi*, that concord returns to inform the band's own parting glances on 2011's fond farewell, *Collapse into Now*. Male friendship is rarely a rock subject, but this is what Stipe celebrates in "That Someone Is You." The band began when Stipe met Buck in an Athens record store, where the singer waited for the guitarist to "make the first move" and rescue him "up and out of me." This is what bonhomie does for us.

For more than thirty years, R.E.M. honored a bond bigger than any one member. Most groups come down to chemistry, but this one more so. Without soloists, rank, or designated songwriters, its cohesion spurred everything. Even Stipe—especially during those self-effacing early years—was a team player. That's the band's contribution to what we've since called indie rock. Each member made it not about impressing girls and boys or becoming famous. R.E.M. made it about all kinds of love, and sometimes especially ours.

⏭

Chapter Thirty-Eight

The Smiths and Morrissey

Let's get this out of the way: Morrissey can be an asshole. Emboldened by outspoken LGBTQ artists like Oscar Wilde, the Manchester-born blatherskite has always said or sung something to offend, as he freely acknowledged in 1986's "Bigmouth Strikes Again." Back then his controversy came with an eloquence rarely eclipsed in indie rock. Introducing himself as "a prophet for the fourth gender," Moz began as an angry young man giving voice to the voiceless while advocating for change. When in 2018 he supported For Britain, a far-right party that aimed to reduce Muslim immigration to the UK, this son of Irish immigrants fully stepped into his role of angry old man aiming to keep England the same as it was more than a half century earlier. But you must understand that for decades, Morrissey was *our* asshole.

Starting with the Smiths, the band he founded in 1982 with guitarist and co-songwriter Johnny Marr, Steven Patrick Morrissey became rock's most idiosyncratically queer post-Stonewall figure. In the wake of his 2013 memoir, *Autobiography*, in which he acknowledged cohabitational male relationships, he's continued dodging conventional categories lobbed at him. "Unfortunately, I am not homosexual," he chides. "In technical fact, I am humasexual. I am attracted to humans. But, of course, not many." Way back in 1984, *Rolling Stone* announced that he was gay—a declaration the singer long denied—but he's never been so in the old-fashioned sense. Literally no one would accuse Morrissey of putting a merry face on homosexuality. He may be pop's most self-pitying figure, but he also ranks among its most hilarious, particularly when whinging. If rolling your eyes at life's tedium made a sound, it would surely be the Smiths' 1984 UK hit "Heaven Knows I'm Miserable Now."

More than even David Bowie and Lou Reed, Morrissey nailed the pains of being something other than heterosexual at the twentieth century's end, especially in the Smiths' early years, when he wrote almost exclusively about life and love on the margins. With the quartet's debut 1983 single, "Hand in Glove," he forced indie rock's mostly male fans to contemplate other guys' butts. The first of many Morrissey-designed duotone sleeves, the single features a photo by Colt Studio's Jim French, the gay-porn pioneer whom Vivienne Westwood pillaged for her gay-cowboys T-shirt. Its nude male model leans against a wall, his back to the camera and his face tipped downward as light emphasizes his statuesque bottom. It's a pose of vulnerability and sorrow, even as the camera captures him as an object of sensual pleasure—an unstable combination that echoes Morrissey's irresolute lyric and the singer himself.

"Hand in glove/The sun shines out of our behinds," this song opens. His lovers fit each other so well that even their darkest places glow. Homophobia aimed at gay men zeroes in on anal sex; it's the thought of a dick going up another dude's ass that terrifies. Morrissey spins that blight into beatitude while accentuating anomaly. Bourgeois onlookers laugh, but Morrissey isn't concerned, for he and his partner, both destitute, possess what those who judge them do not. All this implies impending violence, yet that utopia promised by "Over the Rainbow" and "Somewhere" looms tantalizingly on the horizon, so the singer vows to protect his ungendered beloved. But as the composition crowns, Morrissey's faith crumbles, and he concludes they'll likely not meet again, singing this dénouement three different ways, as if contemplating alternate scenarios, all doomed. The single version fades just like it gradually entered: with a harmonica melody so piercingly poignant it feels as though it always existed.

For the follow-up, the Smiths released 1983's "This Charming Man," which captures the elation of a young male cyclist rescued in a desolate countryside by an older gent. Morrissey soon became rock's most militant vegetarian, but here he's entranced by the motorist's leather upholstery. He sings of it so vivaciously that the purpleness of his posey becomes an asset, for it reveals in a nonthreatening way that the biker might do anything this chap proposes.

"I would go out tonight, but I haven't got a stitch to wear"—no hetero bloke would ever say this; not even a Brit. The driver has probably asked Morrissey on a date, and when the singer thusly responds, this player replies with fruity flirtation, "It's gruesome that someone so handsome would care." Noticing a ring on his rider that likely signifies previous engagements, the automobilist tells him to return it, clearing a path for more liaisons. A mere gamin basking in the glow of an upper-crust roué, much like Shirley MacLaine meeting Ricardo Montalbán in Bob Fosse's *Sweet Charity*, lowly but love-stricken Moz will likely go along with even this. Having relayed so much wooing, he repeats his best bits, twisting the title into eight swoony syllables. Packaged in a Moz-designed sleeve featuring a still from Jean Cocteau's *Orpheus,* in which the gay artist's lover Jean Marais lies beside a puddle as if entranced by his comely reflection, or dead, this single lives on as indie rock's most abiding and adored same-sex love song.

Released with a Morrissey-designed sleeve featuring Joe Dallesandro in the 1968 Andy Warhol–produced hustler film *Flesh*, 1984's *The Smiths* excels at what rock would otherwise not brave, especially on its opener, "Reel Around the Fountain." There's likely an age and certainly an experiential difference between the song's subject and its protagonist, once again played by Moz. Verbs shift between past and present tenses, so it's unclear if the narrator is drawing from distant or recent memory. Singing "slap me on the patio/I'll take it now," Morrissey signals consent, yet it's strongly suggested his adoration isn't reciprocated. His delivery is disarmingly fond, yet our fragile man-child adores what's likely just a hooligan. While organ-led accompaniment reaches an ecclesiastic peak, Moz nevertheless affirms him, as if at an altar no man then could reach with another guy in matrimony. During "What Difference Does It Make?," Moz sings of a secret that remains tantalizingly unspecified. While admitting criminality, he never names his transgression. Instead, he suggests the familiar LGBTQ scenario of revealing to a longtime friend who we are and the feelings we've been forced to conceal. Here, it ends badly. "But now you know the truth about me/You won't see me anymore," Moz bemoans, yet he's still willing to take a bullet for his buddy.

While accentuating Moz's anomalies, Johnny Marr's gift for playing and arranging preternatural guitar orchestrations spurred an anti-macho "twee pop" movement that remained underground until Scotland's Belle and Sebastian in the mid-1990s. Some Smiths songs follow a standard structure built on proven harmonic progressions, but many don't—even some of the catchiest. In keeping with this atypicality, the Smiths often delegated its greatest material to non-LP singles and even B-sides. As announced by "Hand in Glove," the Smiths honored backsides—a gay-male orientation in the most literal sense—and so did its gay-led US label, Sire, which often improved its North American releases of overseas albums by adding UK singles, such as "This Charming Man" to *The Smiths*. As with its labelmates Yaz, the Smiths scored their eternal US hit with what began as a European twelve-inch B-side.

The A-side, "William, It Was Really Nothing," dismisses traditional marriage's necessity for those not physically or emotionally inclined. As the band kicks out a 130-second rampage of ringing guitars, the pressure to conform and conjugate falls like rain. But Morrissey urges a friend (or possible lover) to resist chaining himself to a woman who is likely no more than a beard. It was rumored that Morrissey wrote the song for the Associates' Billy Mackenzie, so the gay Scottish singer answered with "Stephen, You're Really Something," a pert riposte packed with homoerotic puns.

The even shorter flipside "Please, Please, Please Let Me Get What I Want" offers optimism otherwise denied, but the singer's hunger takes prominence. Back then Morrissey sidestepped sexual orientation questions with his self-announced abstinence. While LGBTQ advocates taught cishet people that sexual orientation and gender identity aren't choices, Morrissey argued that celibacy for him was "an involuntary decision," which magnified his unavailability and, therefore, his sexiness. On the other "William" B-side, "How Soon Is Now?," he spins a long and droning grind of perpetually deferred desire.

There's a class element in nearly every Smiths song. In "How," Morrissey proclaims himself the son and heir not of wealth or social standing but of mere shyness. The proletariat are taught that work solves everything, so the singer must toil to overcome insecurity as well as something else implied by the song's quotable line, "I am human and I need to be loved/Just like everybody else does." Morrissey fights LGBTQ battles even while distancing himself from contemporary gay culture, and with those fourteen words, he summed up our entire movement. A hetero person could've written that line, but we *had* to.

Like much of the music in this book, "How Soon Is Now?" captures a universal condition while signaling to us that it might be specifically about ours. What makes its quest even more impactful is that Moz sets it at the nightclubs that provide refuge, if one can mute the demons of internalized homophobia that Marr dramatizes with danceable but stuck-in-a-rut drones. Marr's howling doppler guitar effect sounds like a locomotive passing us by—one we can rarely catch.

"How Soon Is Now?" wasn't the US smash it should've been, even when rereleased as an A-side and added to North American pressings of 1985's *Meat Is Murder*. Instead, it topped alternative radio playlists for years; in 1990, San Francisco's Live 105 listeners voted it the station's Number One track. The song's lack of mainstream recognition meant it belonged to us—not solely, but enough to make some uneasy. While dissing an "art fag," the Dead Milkmen's "Instant Club Hit" sneered, "You'll dance to anything by the Smiths."

For three more years, the Smiths put out a dizzying quantity of music while maintaining its quality. Though the queer specificity of other B-sides like "Handsome Devil" momentarily faded, it came back in broader form throughout 1986's *The Queen Is Dead*. Packaged in a Morrissey-designed sleeve on which Truman Capote leaps with gay abandon, its introductory single, "The

Boy with the Thorn in His Side," voices the Smiths' ongoing frustration. "How can they see the love in our eyes/And still they don't believe us," Moz sings, blurring distinctions between his group and LGBTQ brethren. We're seen as illegitimate, like the band; our devotion means little. "Love is natural and real/But not for such as you and I," he aches in "I Know It's Over." "I've got no right to take my place in the human race," "Bigmouth Strikes Again" bawls.

Camp is the coping mechanism to counter all this. On the title track, Moz breaks into the Palace to confront "Her Very Lowness" after learning he's "the eighteenth pale descendant of some old queen or other." But there's little romp or release; much of the song doesn't deviate from one chord Marr stretches with progressively wilder wah-wah to emphasize that England can't escape royalty's strictures. For the closer, "Some Girls Are Bigger Than Others," Moz laments that mankind's foremost fascination is breasts and their size—a conclusion that in others' hands would be slapstick. Wrapped around one of Marr's most melancholic guitar parts, it haunts instead. Morrissey gives countrified props to a cross-dresser of the cloth in "Vicar in a Tutu." And on "Cemetry Gates," he admonishes optimistic straight listeners while affirming his acerbic queer alliance: "Keats and Yeats are on your side/While Wilde is on mine."

All this levity offsets the Smiths' matchless "There Is a Light That Never Goes Out." Once again, Morrissey sets the scene in someone else's auto, and once again he stresses its liminal and therefore magical status. He begins, "Take me out, tonight." He's entreating the driver to steer him beyond his drab existence; "out" can only be better than "in." He's singing from the perspective of a teen rejected—as so many of us were and still are—by his birth family. But this evening, he's enchanted by nightlife's possibilities, not simply because, like the Shangri-Las, he can never go home anymore, but also because he's no longer profoundly alone. Moz is so bonded to the automobilist that he cares nothing about their destination. Happy to die en route, he sees heaven as a ten-ton truck crashing their car and killing them on impact. This admission is funny because it hits you with its bluntness: Pop usually avoids such morbidity. But it's also unsettlingly sad, because Morrissey implies that he can't imagine a regular life with his flame, only a spectacular annihilation.

The clincher is when they drive through a "darkened underpass." Akin to a train entering a tunnel in an Alfred Hitchcock film, this is shorthand for the promise of physical intimacy. But rather than seizing the moment, Morrissey finds himself unable to do or say anything. Every lesbian, gay, bisexual, trans, and queer person knows this angst when we consider releasing what's held inside. We face not only possible rejection but also that part of ourselves that much of the world still hates. Getting smashed into bits with this ungendered but presumably male treasure by his side means the singer can enter the afterlife loving this guy, not being shunned or succumbing to suicide's final solitude. Instead of being tragic in the Greek or Shakespearean sense, this wished-for conclusion is limitless, eternal—as happy an ending as LGBTQ people could hope for in the bad old days.

That's why "There Is a Light That Never Goes Out" is for us a mindfuck. Morrissey swaps despair for shimmeringly amorous but stymied allegiance—just as Marr's bouncy arrangement builds into symphonic splendor through artificial strings and flutes. Moz's blaze will never diminish, because he cannot fully share it with another person. It will remain pure, like Marr's melody, at no time risking reciprocation. It's the light of an otherwise dark closet but also what holds him within—the dreams we daren't make real.

Not all Smiths songs are about men, nor are they always informed by them. Even in his teens, Morrissey read the feminist writers who fueled women's music—Germaine Greer, Susan Brownmiller, Nancy Friday—as well as dissenters like Joan Didion and *A Taste of Honey* playwright Shelagh Delaney, who adorns the cover of 1987's *Louder Than Bombs*, a B-side-heavy compilation that rivals the band's best albums. These writers' insights shaped Morrissey's questioning worldview and show up in *Bomb* cuts about women pop ordinarily ignores. Tipping a hat to Delaney, "Sheila Take a Bow" presents its female empowerment theme so blithely that the casual straight listener might miss that this glam-flavored rocker is likely directed to a budding lesbian. "Come out and find the one that you love and who loves you," it implores.

Underlining the lyric's flux between male and female, its single sleeve shows Candy Darling on the set of 1971's Warhol-produced film *Women in Revolt*.

Morrissey's lesbian-feminist connection goes beyond his words, which invariably view hetero relations from a critical distance, and even the Smiths' music, which upends rock's mannishness without compromising its saunter. Just as David Bowie's Ziggy mullet showed up on a generation of gay gals, Morrissey's towering James Dean quiff has for decades been the go-to hairstyle of butches everywhere. Same goes for his horn-rims. When I'm checking out what across the street looks like a lad on a Vespa, she's almost always a dyke in a Moz 'do and specs.

By the release of 1987's *Strangeways, Here We Come*, the Smiths had severed. Marr was already recording with other acts, which is likely the context of its rueful goodbye, "I Won't Share You." The guitarist's collaborations grew into a who's who of LGBTQ favorites, including Bryan Ferry, Talking Heads, the Pretenders, Pet Shop Boys, and Everything but the Girl.

Meanwhile, Morrissey plunged himself into solo work that initially recalled the Smiths. Barbers often bear the brunt of antigay jokes, but 1988's "Hairdresser on Fire" depicts Moz's as a superhero psychologist. In 1990's "Piccadilly Palare," which highlights Polari lyrics, he presents himself as a hustler plying his wares in Earl's Court, a hub of London LGBTQ life. Both reappeared on 1990's *Bona Drag*, a Polari phrase for "nice outfit." Same-sex attractions persist in that decade's "Billy Budd," "The Boy Racer," "Roy's Keen," and beyond.

Morrissey's mounting alt-rock radio presence made him a considerable US concert attraction until the conflicted star earned a bad twenty-first-century rep for canceling concerts and even entire tours. When he does show up, swarming queer kids regularly storm his stages, grab him, and cry while he keeps crooning. In these moments, as well as on 2004's *You Are the Quarry* and 2006's *Ringleader of the Tormentors*, Morrissey lives up to his legend.

Outside music is where Our Beloved Bigmouth crosses a line. Hyperbole has always been his mother tongue, but while discussing animal rights in 2009, he railed, "You can't help but feel the Chinese are a subspecies." Then he supported anti-Islam activist Anne Marie Waters, the unfortunately lesbian leader of her now-defunct nationalist party For Britain.

On the 1985 Smiths B-side "Rubber Ring," Morrissey sent a message to us, his fans' future selves. While we outgrow what once kept us steady, like we do with training wheels on a bike, vinyl records—the Smiths' rubber rings—never change. "Hear my voice in your head and think of me kindly," he sings. Another section epitomizes Marr's compositional ingenuity with striking chords as Moz asks his matured listeners, "Do you love me like you used to?"

No, Morrissey, I don't. I can't. You did both us and your music a disservice by siding with our oppressors. You were once society's victim, but you've since joined its bullies. You've become what you long despised.

This means that to rationally process Morrissey's music today, I must split myself in two. I must first remember the man I was in my twenties. While lovers and pals came and went, the Smiths healed my wounds. I could surrender myself completely to Morrissey, for his wit and wisdom were trustworthy.

Yet my older, present self must acknowledge that much of what has come out of Morrissey's mouth since then is not trustworthy, and that throws everything he's recorded under an incriminating light. LGBTQ people already have so little we can call our own, and it hurts that the same music that once saved our lives can retroactively be thought poisonous. We're expected to make apologies for it, like we once did for our attractions or appearance. As evidenced by how the media turned on Boy George, LGBTQ acts are punished if they don't maintain a higher moral standard than straight artists.

But here's the thing: No other record can take the place of "This Charming Man" on the soundtrack of my life—and maybe yours, too. Remember when so-called Christians would say of us, "Love the sinner but hate the sin"? We can similarly renounce musicians who forsake us but still relish their songs that offer support. Those old rubber rings did us no wrong.

⏭

Chapter Thirty-Nine

Hüsker Dü and Bob Mould

I don't remember how I learned that Bob Mould and Grant Hart of Hüsker Dü—the St. Paul, Minnesota, hardcore trio that birthed alt-rock—were both queer. Handlebar-mustachioed bassist Greg Norton was the band's only gay-looking member, yet he was its sole straight. Maybe some insider explained this, but more likely I decoded it from their lyrics. Gay guitarist Mould has always directed his love songs to a gender-neutral "you"—a technique he learned from the Buzzcocks' Pete Shelley. The late bisexual drummer Hart sang to women until he, too, preferred "you," a shift that may have been imperceptible to the band's hetero fans and even the media. In four years, Hüsker Dü placed five consecutive albums in the top twelve of *The Village Voice*'s annual music-critic poll. This was all the more unlikely coming from a punk trio mixing pop songcraft with a delivery that accommodated balladry but more often brought the musical equivalent of *The Texas Chainsaw Massacre.*

Nevertheless, Hart's small pronoun adjustment welcomed *us.* He and Mould were never more than platonic. When their musical partnership took a competitive turn as they shifted from sociological to personal concerns, however, their songs and how they were sequenced changed. On their final albums, the drummer and guitarist seemingly address each other in a public lover's quarrel akin to the infamous infighting that ignited Fleetwood Mac's *Rumours*, but here it's man to man.

On 1986's *Candy Apple Grey*, Hart sings, "Don't Want to Know If You Are Lonely." Mould responds, "I Don't Know for Sure." Bringing the battle to a boil, Hart's "Sorry Somehow" refuses to ask forgiveness, then Mould wallows so low on "Too Far Down" and "Hardly Getting Over It" that his depression seems lethal. *Candy* continues this way, alternating self-scrutiny with volcanic freakouts, until Mould concludes with "All This I've Done for You" the way a contentious but committed partner might summarize to another. Their interaction was so visceral it condensed queer love and hate into one inseparable thing.

From the start, Hüsker Dü went further than even its hardcore brethren. Immediately before recording 1984's double-disc concept album, *Zen Arcade*, the trio covered the Byrds' psychedelic "Eight Miles High" as a drug-induced panic attack. Mould screams so forcibly that he loses intelligibility, as if he can never come back down. This is not how sensible bands warm up.

Not surprising, speed, booze, heroin, and festering resentment ripped Hüsker Dü apart in early 1988. At the end of the group's 1987 tour, which began with its manager jumping off a bridge onto a frozen river, Hart's methadone leaked, and fearing his bandmate's withdrawal, Mould canceled what would've been the trio's last gig on its tour, as well as its appearance at an AIDS benefit Hart helped organize. The latter was a subject of personal importance to the drummer: Before recording the band's culminating 1987 album, *Warehouse: Songs and Stories*, he was told he had HIV. Hart kept his diagnosis private. It wasn't until months after Hüsker Dü's collapse that he learned his test result was wrong. In hindsight, Mould realizes this mistake likely exacerbated Hart's drug use, which in turn hastened the band's dissolution.

That's a severe amount of sorrow for one threesome, and it's all there in the music. Just as Joe Strummer led the Clash despite Mick Jones having a more radio-friendly voice and scoring most of its US hits, Mould fronted Hüsker Dü, even though Hart initially outshone him on a smaller number of often more-tuneful songs. This discrepancy fueled their power struggle but also fostered creative competition. *Zen Arcade* tells the tale of a teen who escapes abusive parents only to find the outside world even more uncaring. That isn't only our story, but LGBTQ runaway rates remain disproportionally steep. Sung from the perspective of an outcast kid giving up on his elders, Hart's folky yet furious "Never Talking to You Again" throws down the gauntlet. Toward the end of the album, Mould's "Whatever" elaborates on it. Leaving a goodbye note, the guitarist sings, "I'm not the son you wanted, but what could you expect/I've made my world of happiness to combat your neglect."

I asked Mould if there were times when he tried to suggest his sexuality in his music before he was ready to directly discuss it. Before I finished the question, he answered, "Side Two, *Zen Arcade*." Its uninterrupted string of Mould songs zeroes in on the disassociation that came with growing up gay when the subject was cumbersome for all involved. "Told you everything I knew about me/Didn't listen to a word I say," he grunts in "I'll Never Forget You." But because *Zen*'s sound was as harsh as the reality it illustrates, few fathomed the queerness that fed it. Even we are taught to believe that LGBTQ composers never make music this bloodthirsty.

By 1985's *Flip Your Wig*, Mould melodically caught up with Hart, which bolstered their scrappy soulmate rapport. "Makes No Sense at All" might be a dig at some vindictive queen, but the impishness of Mould's melody gives his usually punitive guitars the punchiness of a pillow fight. On the single's B-side, he sings "Love Is All Around," the theme from the LGBTQ-beloved *Mary Tyler Moore Show*, a nod to the band's Twin Cities base. Again, he's gruff, but Mould still captures the effervescence of the star and the city where her hit TV series took place. A straight hardcore band would never do this.

Generating more diverse and complex chords, Mould joined Hart in steering Hüsker Dü toward fellow midwestern power pop bands like Cheap Trick, while continued despondence and distortion kept the band anchored in murkier waters. Still not slick enough to win much commercial airplay, *Candy Apple Grey* nevertheless intensified fan scrutiny, much like Olivia Records' sonically improved product with pro engineer Sandy Stone. Did higher recording standards mean selling out? Did the band's contract with Warner Bros.—the US label formerly behind the Sex Pistols—flush away all that punk credibility? While Grant's and Mould's tunes grew richer, their lyrics became darker. "When I look back at the really painful songs," Mould now reflects, "some of them I can say, 'Oh yeah, it's that guy who broke my heart.' But the deepening of the well that happened at the end of Hüsker Dü, I think that was from year after year of watching things get worse and not being out. By 1985, the death toll was high, and there was still nothing happening."

Inflamed by Hart's erroneous HIV test, *Warehouse* sustains *Grey*'s argumentative sequencing across twenty cross-talking tracks. The culmination of the band's maturation, Mould's "Could You Be the One?," addresses a seemingly closeted partner who is the subject of gossip. To bridge their breach, the singer must bring his own love into view. This, given his gayness, proves difficult: "And I don't even know what I'm hiding for/I don't even know what I'm crying for." But his harmonies with Hart imply accord. And the way all three members land on the same note after the title's iterations similarly signals congruence, as does the guitar solo's Buzzcock-ian embellishment of the vocal melody.

Yet Mould never solves the title's riddle, and that's telling. It's often said that lesbians don't hesitate to settle down: Every lesbian comic spins her own variation on a joke in which one gal or the other brings a U-Haul to the second date. Many gay men have the opposite tendency, because we're taught to conceal intentions that may trigger dangerous reprisals. As "Could You" concludes, Mould reiterates that he hasn't stopped hiding or crying. Mainstream radio still balked, but the band played *The Late Show Starring Joan Rivers*. After the song's performance, possibly the loudest of its era on talk-show TV, Hart hugged the gay-deified host—another so-unpunk-it's-punk gesture that's natural for us.

Despite critical and major-label approval, Hüsker Dü never entered the mainstream. This wasn't by choice. For us, success is sexy, because it's often denied by not just the gatekeepers but also by our own justified fear of failure. In the twentieth century, most of us couldn't be our authentic selves *and* ambitious; we had to choose between the two. Consequently, we don't share straight people's rules about what's cool and not, because for them we'll always be the misfit toys. I was once reminded of this by the *Voice*'s Robert Christgau at Mould's prestigious Bottom Line gig during his first solo tour in 1989. I told Christgau how much I enjoyed the guitarist's then-new solo debut, *Workbook.* "I've *never* cared for your taste in music!" he snapped back. I'd dared to embrace the interior Mould that he deemed inferior. The patriarchy has a long history of disregarding LGBTQ art, and sometimes it does this without even recognizing that art as queer. When straight white men are not marginalizing it, as they also do with works by women and people of color, they can grasp and occasionally revere its difference, but they often want it to reinforce their own experience, not ours.

Workbook bares intricacies Hüsker's hardcore foundation denied. Just as many of us resent sexual orientation labels, Mould fights against being defined by punk outrage, although some persists. "I see you swing by your neck on a vine," he sings of his former bandmate in "Poison Years." Elsewhere, Mould abandons the pack mentality of his band-enabled extended adolescence in search of a discrete adult self. In "See a Little Light," he discovers hope in his beloved's eyes. He has learned that language of glances we teach one another for our solidarity and survival—not just gaydar but also how to read and write with looks when words remain incriminating.

I read these guarded confessions as a tentative coming-out. When I interviewed Mould in 1989 for the *San Francisco Examiner*, I built my questions to the biggest one: Are you gay? Pointing out how challenging the music biz can be for anyone attempting anything interesting, let alone those who are gay, he replied that he couldn't answer. I shifted to another subject. Interrupting me with a shy smile, he added, "I'm sure you can guess from the way I've avoided answering that question what the truth is." I sensed his desire to do the right thing, as well as his unease that it could diminish a career already afflicted by more than its share of setbacks. So I left that remark unpublished until a song on 1992's *Copper Blue* by Mould's next trio, Sugar, made his sexuality more relevant for readers of *The Advocate*, where I also contributed a column. Back then there was so little crossover between LGBTQ and mainstream media that his coming-out-by-not-coming-out statement stayed within our community.

Mould's official disclosure was orchestrated two years later by *Spin*, which presented Mould with a choice: Either spill the tea to the gay novelist Dennis Cooper, or the magazine would out him. Rightfully feeling pressured, Mould blurted during the interview, "I'm not going to be paraded around like a freak." Anyone sensitive about their own unorthodoxy should've been sympathetic to what he meant. But by emphasizing that quote and positioning it under a warped, wide-angle photo, *Spin* did what Mould most feared.

Hüsker Dü's heavy alt-rock template had become big business, so Sugar went Top Ten in the UK while conquering US alternative radio and MTV with melodic punk that would've remained uncommercial had it appeared earlier. This was especially true of my *Advocate* column's subject, "The Slim."

Its first verse obliquely addresses how each of us have a sexual history dictated by chance and perception. Even if we remember every pleasure, most of us will never know who our partners have been with and what they've done when drugs, lust, and lies have clouded their decision-making. The chorus alludes to condoms, but it's unclear if one is used or not, or if it breaks. The narrator then reports his partner "rushing in," as if anal intercourse and ejaculation have hastily taken place. Subsequent verses confirm that he's now dead, leaving the narrator with anger, a possible HIV infection that would then likely lead to his own death, and memories of what they shared. "The chances seemed so slim," he sings—a rationalization for what they gambled and lost. The song ends with this survivor alone and repeating marriage vows as piledriving guitars and drums persist like a fate that cannot be escaped. Punctuated with swaying triplets that accentuate the narrator's instability, "The Slim" is rock's most harrowing AIDS song and Mould's underacknowledged masterpiece, one that no peer dared to write, much less inhabit with bellowing agony. The rage that fed Mould's art but had hindered its accessibility finally found the right subject and time.

Grant Hart never achieved such synchronicity. His greatest post-Hüsker release remains his first, 1988's "2541," which Mould thinks might've been intended for *New Day Rising*. It's about an apartment where Hart and a boyfriend briefly lived, one that happened to share a street number with the band's eventual office. Mould vetoed this sweet song, a decision he now regrets. After Sugar split in 1995, the guitarist became a professional wrestling scriptwriter, and a move to New York City prompted his immersion into gay life and club music. Reconciling his alt-rock past with his LGBTQ present netted mixed results until he formed the duo Blowoff with Richard Morel, a gay electronic musician who'd honed that blend on his 1999 single "True (The Faggot Is You)." Mould then returned to his punk beginnings through a politically queer consciousness that remembered when silence equaled death, the ACT UP mantra that closed his video for 1990's "It's Too Late."

This headstrong homesteader is still making brusque, breakneck pop better than anyone of his generation, while maintaining the magic of three men playing like one with his latest trio. Unlike Morrissey, Mould grew up. That brought him back here with us, *as* us.

⏭

Chapter Forty

Grease and Olivia Newton-John

When Olivia Newton-John died in 2023, my Facebook feed was awash with sorrow from gay and lesbian fans alike. But throughout much of the 1970s, she wasn't anyone's idea of LGBTQ quintessence: The country-pop singer-actor joined that era's top sellers by virtue of her ordinariness. While her post-hippie contemporaries got their freak on, Newton-John filled the mid-'70s middle-of-the-road void with a middling Anglo-Aussie slant on Middle Americana.

As you may've guessed, I wasn't an early fan. All her hits until the late '70s drove me up the fucking wall, especially 1974's treacly "I Honestly Love You." It was co-written by Peter Allen, another Aussie expat, who, as an ex-husband of Liza Minnelli and straight-as-a-rainbow solo act, had impeccable LGBTQ credentials. Still, I can't relate to country Olivia. I have never been mellow.

Then *Grease* happened. The highest-grossing film of 1978, *Grease* is for my LGBTQ generation what *Funny Girl* was for the previous one. And unlike most musicals that galvanize gay men, it also resonates with lesbians and trans folk. In its own daffy way, *Grease* is pop's post-Stonewall pan-queer urtext.

As its popularity with high school drama clubs attests, *Grease* does this without ever being explicitly lesbian, gay, bisexual, or trans, although you can't call its queerness accidental, either. Its LGBTQ creators included co-writer/songwriter Warren Casey, screenwriter Bronté Woodard, director Randal Kleiser, producers Robert Stigwood and Allan Carr, Paramount Pictures CEO Barry Diller, actors Dennis C. Stewart and Fannie Flagg, and singer Cidny Bullens. *Grease*'s boffo box office allowed Carr to swim with the other big entertainment kahunas while being screamingly gay—right down to his signature muumuus—yet never formally identified as such.

That aesthetic is the film's. Packed with old-timey stars like Eve Arden and Joan Blondell, *Grease* revisits late 1950s repression via late '70s camp that registers as nostalgia to straight boomers while speaking in queer tongues to us. Central to this duality is the film's unstated but omnipresent theme: The peer pressure of the McCarthy era meant men and women alike couldn't be themselves because they were forced to uphold opposing gender roles.

The greasers at Rydell High, the T-Birds, are only into cars and sexual conquests. The corresponding girl gang, the Pink Ladies, are likewise defined by their interest in boys. Portrayed by John Travolta at his post–*Saturday Night Fever* peak, T-Bird leader Danny Zuko had secretly stepped out of his Italian stallion guise the previous summer when he fell for virtuous Australian Sandy Olsson, acted by Newton-John. Now a Rydell senior, Danny can't be both a he-man to his buddies and the sweet guy he'd been to Sandy. In public, he must keep up his bruiser front and hide his affection, because showing it would make him seem effeminate by gang standards. Sandy, meanwhile, has the inverse problem. Regarded by the Pink Ladies as a hopeless goody-goody, she reflexively resists Danny's advances because that's the expectation foisted onto nice girls. These dilemmas force them both into the closet—even as heterosexuals.

Performed with less satire and more seriousness by Stockard Channing, the Pink Ladies leader, Betty Rizzo, also struggles to be her true self. Even while consenting to sex with Danny's best T-Bird friend, Kenickie (Jeff Conway), and despite his torn condom, she's aloof. What she hides keeps her distant from everyone except the pinkest lady, Frenchie Facciano (Didi Conn), who idolizes Rizzo just like the T-Birds' Kenickie looks up to Danny. For the LGBTQ viewer, Rizzo's dark clothes, short hair, cutting remarks, and other manifestations of bad-girl otherness broadcast lesbian identity akin to independent women in gender-defying '50s films like *Calamity Jane* and *Johnny Guitar*. Even by 1978, we couldn't have an overtly lesbian character in a mass-market musical, but Rizzo comes close.

She and Frenchie are coded as a pre-Stonewall butch/femme lesbian couple far more connected to each other than to any guy. The encrypting between Danny and Kenickie isn't as explicit until a telling moment when the latter asks the former if they can be like cowboys in a western. They punch each other affectionately, hug, and then, realizing they're being watched, fumble for their combs to resume their greaser roles. That's the front *everyone* in the '50s—and many in the '70s—had to maintain lest they be perceived as one of us.

All this leads up to the last day of school's big reveal: Repressed Sandy is reborn as randy. A shame-free fusion of manly severity and feminine duende, her makeover—red high heels, black Spandex pants, black leather jacket, blaring makeup, and huge teased hair—is so fashion-forward she seems to have time-traveled into the 1980s. "You better shape up!" this minx instructs Danny in *Grease*'s nearly worldwide Number One, "You're the One That I Want." There's no country crooning. Instead, Sandy belts R&B-infused rock 'n' roll, and Danny responds in kind. Ascending in their bitchin' roadster, they reach for that sanctuary unobtainable to those who can't be their integrated selves. As emphasized by the film's reprise of its Frankie Valli–sung theme, with Barry Gibb–written lines like "conventionality belongs to yesterday" and "we got to be what we feel," Sandy and Danny achieve emotional and sexual liberation. They transition and in essence come out.

Newton-John's transformation themes didn't stop with the elephantine camp of 1980's *Xanadu*. Originally envisioned as a guy's song, 1981's "Physical" gets its saucy power from the way it vacillates between suggestive-yet-controlled verses and a corporeal, demonstrative chorus—a shift Newton-John mirrors with vocal restraint and release. Everything in it switches from Sandy One to Sandy Two. This assertion, from an ex-ingenue who'd epitomized mild countrified pop, made "Physical" daring for its day.

Despite "Y.M.C.A." and the gay male muscling-up it captured, the Jane

Fonda–fueled fitness craze was still building steam. Released in MTV's launch year, "Physical" stirred up the perfect carb-burning storm. In her new boyish haircut, sweatband, and bright tights, Newton-John pioneered in its video a look that permeated the '80s even beyond the gym. Opening with Newton-John amid musclemen pumping iron, the clip replaces its hunks with flabby fellows flailing about. But while she showers in her gym clothes, they exercise themselves into Speedo-clad beefcake. Returning in tennis whites, Newton-John eyes them as if she's just hit the hetero jackpot. But two by two, these studs stroll off in each other's hands and arms.

For the first time, a music video illustrated that super-buff dudes can also be gay, which bucked the old propaganda that all homos are limp-wristed wimps. Although it's played as comedy, the seductiveness with which these studs regard the camera sent out an invitation and challenge to the viewer, especially us: If we resembled these men, we'd score; straight gals would also find us hot, and jocks wouldn't beat us up because we'd look like them and be able to kick their asses. This may seem delusional now, but you must remember, "Physical" went Number One for ten weeks. According to *Billboard*, the '80s' biggest US hit wasn't a Michael Jackson, Madonna, or Prince song, it was this—the crux of 1981's *Physical,* its Grammy-winning video album, and its Nielsen-busting prime time TV special. This plucky public display of LGBTQ affection went mega-mainstream via an Aussie Trojan horse we helped make more popular than ever.

This landslide couldn't last. Not even Elton John co-writing, co-producing, playing piano, and singing on 1988's "The Rumour" or Shep Pettibone's NRGetic remix of it could give her another US pop hit after 1985's sleazy "Soul Kiss." "Love and Let Live" argues for AIDS education, but few US fans saw its cautionary 1988 video. For some, she'd grown passé. For others, she'd become too Sandy Two.

Nevertheless, Newton-John's transformation launched a lasting paradigm. It modeled how to remake ourselves, even beyond the gym. To not be hated by their family and community, LGBTQ children often strive to be, like Olivia/Sandy One, as honorable as possible. That's why so many of us still become priests or nuns. This impulse toward innocuity also remains why some of us dash off in the opposite direction when we come out.

A Sandy-type switcheroo is now expected of all young stars aiming to take ownership of their adult careers. Sexual provocation is almost always involved, but this adjustment is foremost about artistic autonomy, which is now often played as a figurative, if not literal, coming out. Several artists in the next few chapters underwent one, and in the twenty-first century, so did every former Disney-child-actor-turned-pop-showgirl or -twink. Even today, Newton-John's about-face serves as a lesson: Sometimes the figures you first dismiss as hopelessly dull can become the most subversive of all.

⏭

Chapter Forty-One

ABBA

Somewhere, right now, ABBA's 1976 chart-topper "Dancing Queen" is playing at an LGBTQ club, bar, or house party. We and our lucky straight friends are waving our arms, striking stagy poses, and shamelessly singing along to the sugary pop standard that's become synonymous with queer nightlife. It's our variation on what fans do at ballgames when their team is winning, but with a camp exuberance ignited by the song's brassy harmonies and handy references to feminine royalty. Trump and his followers can't take this one from us.

Thanks to stage and screen incarnations of *Mamma Mia!*, garish costumes from gay designer Owe Sandström, and consummately crafted songs thar are now even more omnipresent than in their '70s and early '80s heyday, ABBA has for decades been the bull's-eye of the LGBTQ pop universe. Outwardly cheerful but packed with drama and peppered with Scandinavian melancholy, the Stockholm mixed-gender quartet is to many gay fans what the Rolling Stones are to straight listeners: archetypes whose appeal transcends time, place, and age. While pathfinders like Madonna polarize opinion, every color of the gay rainbow agrees on ABBA.

This wasn't always the case. Back when Donna Summer reigned as our indisputable dancing queen, ABBA didn't get much gay club play. Disco's top mixer, Tom Moulton, considered "Dancing Queen" perfect as is, so he turned down the chance to remix it. (He has since regretted this.) From the earliest subterranean clubs to Studio 54, the original discos were powered by Afro Latin grooves and, usually, Black singers. Most exceptions—like Barry Manilow's "Copacabana (At the Copa)" from 1978—have LGBTQ ties. But as a rule, gay DJs and their audiences then favored underground divas and obscure orchestral maestros they discovered and popularized, not pop acts plucked from AM radio.

Things changed in the early 1980s when the US mainstream media declared disco dead, and major record labels purged it from their rosters. This challenged club DJs who since *Saturday Night Fever* had a rhythmic deluge from which to draw. Straight clubs shifted to slower funk, but the well of speedy, gay dancefloor arias nearly ran dry. Raul Rodriguez—DJ at the nightclub New York, New York—came up with a solution when he extended ABBA's 1980 album track "Lay All Your Love on Me" in his home studio with tape and razor blades. The edits created a percussive BAM, BAM, BAM. "The first time he did that, it was a mistake," recalls Robbie Leslie, DJ veteran of the Saint, the maximum '80s gay disco. Rodriguez turned his splicing flub into a thunderous attention-grabber that packed the air with pumping fists and poppers.

Like Leslie's similarly beloved 1980 mix of Jimmy Ruffin's "Hold on (To My Love)," Rodriguez's ABBA transformation only appeared on Disconet, a gay-owned subscription remix service. The ordinary consumer couldn't walk into a store and buy it; you could only hear it at gay clubs like the Saint, where it remained in weekly rotation for years. This forced a twelve-inch release in the UK of the unchanged 1980 LP cut, which preserved the exclusivity of Rodriguez's revision. ABBA's North American label issued "The Visitors" as a 1982 single, but again, another gay remix service, Hot Tracks, supplied the superior club version. Soon the Latin Rascals replicated Rodriguez's machine-gun edits on records like Diana Ross's 1984 smash "Swept Away."

As ABBA recorded what would be for decades its final sessions, others filled the gay demand for lusty hi-NRG. San Francisco synth wizard Patrick Cowley's 1982 reunion with Sylvester, "Do Ya Wanna Funk" broadened the genre's international appeal, while Montréal's Lime maximized the gender gap between married couple Denis LePage's gravelly growl and Denyse LePage's squeaky chirp on chipper cuts like 1982's "Babe, We're Gonna Love Tonight." After transitioning, the former released music in the twenty-first century as Nini Nobless.

When hi-NRG ran its course, Erasure released 1992's *Abba-esque*, a love letter of cover versions. The originals then appeared on 1992's *ABBA Gold: Greatest Hits*—one of the best-selling albums of all-time—as well as in '94's *Muriel's Wedding* and that same year's drag/trans road comedy *The Adventures of Priscilla, Queen of the Desert*. At AIDS's apex, ABBA was reborn into paragons of gloom-relieving kitsch.

But if bombastic outfits and bubblegum hooks had been ABBA's sole gifts to LGBTQ culture, its gay appeal would've plummeted after the lifesaving arrival of antiviral cocktails shortly after those films left theaters. Beneath its satin and sequins, ABBA has often favored conflicts and counterintuitive contrasts: lovey-dovey surrender fortified by vigorous instrumentation in 1974's "Waterloo," stout choral harmonies capturing moments of solitary weakness on 1975's "SOS," and crestfallen lyrics combined with a bouncy melody in 1976's "Mamma Mia." Few US critics appreciated this pop maximalism that masqueraded as simplicity; *The Village Voice*'s Robert Christgau wrote of the group in 1979, "We have met the enemy and they are them." However, what might seem like contradictions to straight people sound like reconciliations to us. Our strategy has always been to counter hate with love. We manifest gayness to abide its antonym.

Reflecting its rare gender parity as well as Scandinavia's early embrace of feminism, ABBA often defies traditional male/female roles, and its songs sometimes hint at queerness. Take 1976's "Fernando." Initially about departed love as sung in Swedish on ABBA vocalist Anni-Frid Lyngstad's 1975 solo album *Frida ensam*, the song's lyrics, rewritten in English by the group's Björn Ulvaeus, find Lyngstad singing as a man to another man, both Mexican freedom fighters, now old, looking back on battles fought together. Every musical element exudes romance that implies the pair share innermost affection, as on the brazenly gay but oft-covered 1920s wartime standard "My Buddy." Straight listeners don't catch this, because they hear a woman crooning tenderly to a guy.

Yet on the most fundamental level, ABBA's heterosexuality is more overt than that of the straightest all-male rock bands. Even before the group's 1974 Eurovision breakthrough, the foursome's other main singer, Agnetha Fältskog, and Ulvaeus were amative partners; so were Lyngstad and principal composer, Benny Andersson. As represented by 1975's schlocky "I Do, I Do, I Do, I Do, I Do," both couples married. Subsequently, far more nuanced relationship themes, often about doomed partnerships, crept into their increasingly adult material, starting with 1976's "Knowing Me, Knowing You" and climaxing on 1980's "The Winner Takes It All" just as Fältskog and Ulvaeus finalized their split. The next year, Lyngstad and Andersson divorced as well. For "Winner," Ulvaeus wrote an anguished lyric about their marriage's conclusion, but his ex belts it like a champion, even while voicing defeat. Its distress was an omen of an end that came quietly in 1982 and soon seemed final. "We will never re-form," Ulvaeus said when I interviewed him in 1994. "Why would we?"

As its first-name acronym implies, ABBA was from its beginning a supergroup. The guys had been in flourishing rock bands—guitarist Ulvaeus in the Hootenanny Singers, keyboardist Andersson in the Hep Stars. Both gals had solo careers; even as a teen, Fältskog penned some of her hits. Ulvaeus and Andersson wrote, produced, and played on ABBA's records just as they'd previously done for both Fältskog and Lyngstad.

When all four got together, the women's vocal synchronicity drove the men's songs so strongly that sex-lib anthems like 1979's "Gimme! Gimme! Gimme! (A Man After Midnight)" seem queer-tailor-made. Effectively sampled by Madonna for 2005's "Hung Up," a synth piccolo suggests Fältskog atop the Scandes like Julie Andrews twirling through the Salzburg hills in *The Sound of Music*. Instead, she's alone in her flat, bracing herself against autumnal chill. She walks from the TV, throws open the window, gazes into the night, and prays for a sensual savior. "Take me through the darkness to the break of the day," Fältskog blasts in a disco mating call we've since claimed as our own. Being strong women and sensitive men who respect each other is central to the group's alchemy as well as its LGBTQ appeal. This is who we are and how we want the world to be.

And it nourished their reconciliation. Even after divorces and decades apart, ABBA reunited with such dignity on 2021's *Voyage* that it reaches a *smultronställe*—literally a wild strawberry patch, a Swedish concept that film director Ingmar Bergman illustrated with 1957's *Wild Strawberries*; a secret place where fruits of the heart grow freely. It's ABBA's gift to LGBTQ culture—an oasis within the mega-mainstream that gay pioneers helped landscape.

⏭

Chapter Forty-Two

Cher

Like all kids my age, I grew up on TV variety shows. Designed as family entertainment, yet peaking as the generation gap widened, they presented establishment and counterculture entertainment side by side in a prime-time circus of music, fashion, and claptrap. On a good night, you'd get the Doors' Jim Morrison in full leather. A bad one got no better than *Ed Sullivan Show* regular Topo Gigio, the mouse puppet. Through Carol Burnett, Johnny Cash, Flip Wilson, Glen Campbell, the Smothers Brothers, and other TV hosts, boredom-relieving showbiz blessed our living rooms every few days. Quantity mattered more than quality when we were too young or too stuck in the suburbs to experience it firsthand.

Debuting in 1971, the variety show that most served as LGBTQ special ed was *The Sonny & Cher Comedy Hour*. When 1965's "I Got You Babe" led to a string of Sonny-penned hits that introduced the duo as a convention-defying couple, I was too young to decipher their us-versus-them subtext: Cher was still a teen, Sonny was thirty. The arrival of psychedelic rebels like Jimi Hendrix meant their assembly-line pop was soon considered squaresville. Even the Vegas crowd heckled them. Cher would sass back. Sonny would reprimand his wife, and she'd counter with a snappy retort. Maybe this all was scripted. Or maybe Cher spontaneously defied her husband and audience.

Either way, this schtick subsequently made for great TV. Cher bust her little butt to duet, dance, joke, and flirt with her guests, yet made it all seem easy. When Sonny stopped producing her, she became a more powerful singer. But even when partnering with superior singers, Cher projected her true self. She wasn't overpowered by Linda Ronstadt. She danced alongside the Jackson 5 without embarrassing herself. She'd pronounce certain words peculiarly, yet could accommodate anybody from David Bowie to Jimmy Durante. For those coming to terms with an identity deemed subpar, this idiomatic versatility remains instructional. Even in the most mismatched situations, Cher was and always will be herself. That's our goal, too.

Cher's individualism grew more potent when paired with blatant pop that paradoxically emphasized her outsider essence. Launching her *Comedy Hour*–era hit streak, 1971's "Gypsys, Tramps & Thieves" plays on both her ethnicity (Armenian, white, plus a little Cherokee) and her unstable childhood (actor mom struggled with poverty while dads came and went; at sixteen, Cher left school and home). Like what was to come, "Gypsys" wasn't written, produced, or played by in-crowd rockers, yet it's awash with tricky syncopations and unexpected harmonic shifts. A contributor to the soundtrack for Russ Meyers's queer exploitation milestone *Beyond the Valley of the Dolls*, songwriter Bob Stone packs his pulpy lyric with underage sex, prostitution, and other lewdness that rubs against the music's carny gaiety, much like Smokey Robinson's sadness does in "Tears of a Clown." "I was sixteen, he was twenty-one," Cher sings from experience. "Papa woulda shot him if he'd knew what he'd done." What others condemn, Cher personifies. She's no Sandy One.

Taking its melody from a French tune that also sired Perry Como's schmaltzy "It's Impossible," 1972's "The Way of Love" opens with an innocuous line: "When you meet a boy that you like a lot." Then Cher prophesies that her former partner will one day be rejected by this fellow "just the way that you said goodbye to me." If you aren't following the pronouns, nothing seems unusual, but the song only makes sense if her ex is bisexual. Either they are a guy who gets dumped by another dude, or a lesbian who has a heterosexual fling only to find herself abandoned like the singer. Its lesson is that passion not only brings pain but also ironic twists: The way of love is not always straight.

It's valid to complain that 1973's "Half-Breed" is bogus, because Cherokee heritage is matrilineal. If a Cherokee woman was impregnated by a European American dad, her daughter would still be Cherokee, not white as the lyric claims. Popular entertainment is full of dumb mistakes like this one, because white people tell most of the stories and often don't do the research. Yet what "Half-Breed" gets remarkably right is the resentment engendered by racism. I'm not Native American, so it's not for me to say whether Cher's bloodline gives her enough authenticity to sing this song without appropriation. The "tribal" chanting and drums are based on a false generalization of indigenous music, but they do give this ditty a rebellious rock spirit that Cher rides into battle. "Half-Breed" is one of the angriest Number Ones to address bigotry head-on.

Cher's performance releases the fury all outcasts must repress. When this record was new, I was crushing on David Bowie like only a twelve-year-old can when his secret self finds a musical soulmate. Made within L.A.'s pop establishment, "Half-Breed" nevertheless made that frightened kid feel heard, even today. As it builds, Cher's rage rises, particularly on the third verse, where she admits her shame, leaves home, and roars its culminating rhyme: "My life since then has been from man to man/But I can't run away from *WHAT I AM*!" Her gay costumer, Bob Mackie, may've glamorized what Hollywood already caricatured of Native American dress for her accompanying outfits, but nothing about Cher's delivery is fake. She's metaphorically relating her own story, which is also ours. We live in a binary, black-and-white world aiming to rid itself of the gray areas in which we live. LGBTQ people know what it means to have both sides against us since the day we were born.

The noir drama kept coming with "Carousel Man," "Dixie Girl," and "Dark Lady." In the latter 1974 hit, Cher consults a fortune teller whom she catches with her guy, then murders them both. This time, she's not cast as the swarthy stereotype, but this emphatic brunette still evokes one. In the song's animated video, the narrator is blond, while the "dark lady" resembles Cher.

LGBTQ audiences root for women like her because that's how society sees us. We treasure their sordid stories because our love is also thought tawdry.

During this time, Cher's marriage to Sonny collapsed. She partnered with David Geffen, both personally and professionally, then followed suit with Gregg Allman. But with every step into credibility, her results grew blander, until she signed with the flashy disco label Casablanca. Then writing, producing, and/or arranging for LGBTQ royalty like Dusty Springfield, Donna Summer, and soon Barbra Streisand, her gay collaborator, Bob Esty, capitalized on her husky contralto androgyny throughout 1979's "Take Me Home." He positions Cher in that sweet spot between seduction and surrender, archer and target. While its assertive lyrics anticipate a swift bedroom retreat, Esty's supple yet steely orchestrations luxuriate in the dancefloor present. Cher's certain she's gonna get this ungendered somebody, so she lags behind the beat, relishing every sugared second. "Just a one-night affair would be *so fine*," her come-hither sighs bargain. Resplendent with arousing builds and polyrhythmic release, the twelve-inch version is a towering monument of sybaritic desire—the purest disco by a pop superstar. Even at the Paradise Garage, where DJ Larry Levan served fierce underground funkiness for a chiefly gay Black crowd, "Take Me Home" ignited the dancefloor cognoscenti.

But Cher soon traded club music for rightfully unpopular rock, until acting took over. Robert Altman cast her in 1982's *Come Back to the Five and Dime, Jimmy Dean, Jimmy Dean*, one of the earliest films with a complex, valid trans character. Cher's portrayal of a blue-collar lesbian in 1983's *Silkwood* further confirmed her talent, as did her Oscar-winning performance in 1987's *Moonstruck*.

Now signed to Geffen Records, Cher's music profile attained another plateau via heavy MTV and VH1 rotation. "If I Could Turn Back Time" particularly delighted LGBTQ fans through its preposterously queer 1989 video. Straddling one of many absurdly phallic USS *Missouri* cannons and strutting about in a sheer leotard, revealing tattoos on both butt cheeks while fresh-faced sailors go apoplectic with lust, Cher never looked happier. Like the song, it's corny, but colossally so.

Subsequently stricken with Epstein–Barr, the superstar convalesced between infomercial gigs and shilling for her Gothic mail-order biz. Her largely London-made *It's a Man's World* in 1995 should've restored her artistic reputation, but its most significant US success came in LGBTQ clubs through remixes.

Cher's UK label head Rob Dickins then suggested that the star record an entire album of dance music from scratch for her gay fans. Back then US majors would never have wanted this. By the late '90s, only Madonna, Janet Jackson, and the occasional upstart could still crack North American Top Forty radio with up-tempo club tunes. The period's gayest dancefloor genres—clattering tribal house and trippy instrumental trance—often lacked substantial verses and distinctive choruses, while radio-friendly pop trended toward similarly melody-minimal R&B and hip-hop. None would flatter a living legend in need of contemporary material she could wrap her still-substantial pipes around to wring out the pathos of being an unconventional fifty-two-year-old woman in the compromising center of a risk-averse, youth-obsessed entertainment industry. What Cher required was old-fashioned disco with newfangled sounds.

To appreciate what became known as "the Cher effect" on 1998's clubby "Believe," one needs to understand the musical term *portamento* and how it interacts with Auto-Tune software, which was originally designed solely to shift flat or sharp notes to their proper pitch. Portamento is when a vocalist slides between notes continuously, rather than hitting them squarely with pauses between. Implying a roller-coaster continuity between life's ups and downs, Cher favors this technique. On "Believe," the producers applied Auto-Tune at its highest setting to Cher's swoops, pioneeringly accentuating the program's pitch-correcting qualities to such an extent that she sounds like an android short-circuiting from the pressure of the emotions that make us human. "I c-a-a-an't break through," she trills, as if malfunctioning. Rather than wallowing, "Believe" seesaws between resignation and resolve. "Do you believe in life after love?" Cher asks the listener—and herself—first doubting, then declaring. This was a battle embedded in the record's very creation. As the song amassed revisions, Dickins was fired. Others felt the Auto-Tuning was overdone, but Cher shrewdly insisted it remain. With sales exceeding eleven million copies, "Believe" became one of the biggest, most innovative singles ever. Sonic grandchildren of those 1950s sci-fi theremin howls that signified the Other, its queer quavers still signify not just the alienation of gay Black singers who employ Auto-Tune creatively like our Frank Ocean, but also Black America in general.

Mainstream gatekeepers almost always reject women over forty, but LGBTQ audiences don't. Nearly every female entertainer who maintains a career beyond her thirties does so with the help of queer fans, because we're uncommonly loyal. We love our mothers and grandmothers, symbolic or otherwise. Having occupied our living rooms for decades, Cher's like family—the ideal kind. Ours don't always stand by us like she did soon after her first child, Chaz Bono, came out as lesbian and later transitioned. Beneath her svelte frame and ever-morphing face, she's as solid as all those scoundrels she fell for were wayward, yet remains divergent—the dusky outlander perfectly fine with never fully fitting in, the bad girl we all know is far better than simply good. For all of us sexual and cultural orphans, Cher represents the individuated maternal spirit in a Mackie gown.

⏭

Chapter Forty-Three

Cyndi Lauper

When I first saw Cyndi Lauper, she got booed. Opening for the Human League at the height of its synth-chilled coolness, her momentarily hot band Blue Angel was retro, guitar-driven new wave, and by spring 1982 already lukewarm. Like pre-Eurythmics Annie Lennox in the Tourists, this Queens-raised shooting star fronted an earthbound ensemble. Compensating for its ordinariness, she grated, and the crowd turned on her. I've never seen someone who could sing so well bomb so badly.

The next year, Lauper released *She's So Unusual*, which transformed her into a 1980s superstar and an enduring LGBTQ treasure thanks to a man's song she made hers and every woman's. In songwriter Robert Hazard's original demo of "Girls Just Want to Have Fun," his honey only wants to have "fun" with him—she loves another guy. But by dropping its forgettable bridge, cutting the relationship angle, singing from an independent woman's perspective, and changing the rhythm from locomotive punk to reggae-fied Motown, Lauper reworked "Girls" into a festive feminist proclamation. Hazard served her a cease-and-desist order when she said she wrote part of it, but he acknowledged a revision. His version: "All my girls are tryin' to walk in the sun." Hers: "I want to be the one to walk in the sun."

This alteration makes a massive difference, for it tells Lauper's own story. At the height of *Unusual*'s popularity, she spoke of her identification with Janis

Joplin. "I was so totally alienated from everybody else that I felt like I was always out of step and I would never catch up," she said, as if describing queer experience. "The doors were always closing on me. I got harassed all the time because I was so different."

Lauper attains ascension and transcension with "Girls." Atypical of female newcomers, her creative control extended even to its video, which she recounted making when I interviewed her in 2014.

"I was working at Screaming Mimis," Lauper said of NYC's vintage clothing store, which supplied some of her early outfits. She asked, "'Can some of the girls come to the shoot that day? We need a Black girl. We need an Asian girl.' That wasn't being done on television at the time. It was segregated. The only time you saw a Spanish girl in a video with white people, she was taking her clothes off.

"I went under the radar of every sexist mofo because we were laughing all the time. But what I was really doing was bringing the races and generations of women together. Every little girl was able to see herself. And every little girl could feel joy and know that she could be free-spirited. That's highly political, but we did it in such a way that nobody was threatened."

Lauper did something similar with Prince's "When You Were Mine," but this time without changing a word. "I know that you're going with another guy," she sings throughout to a male lover who'd brought the fellow home to sleep with them. Lauper outclasses even Prince here, bringing out more melancholy with her melodic and contextual improvements. She's okay with her ex's wearing her clothes and being bisexual. Although her interpretation deals with a man leaving her for a dude, it's about emotional loss, not sexual orientation or gender. On a best-selling bonanza, this too was newsworthy.

Lauper ups the taboo ante in "She Bop," another song on the Parents Music Resource Center's "Filthy Fifteen," by getting her rocks off with gay beefcake: "Well I see him every night in tight blue jeans/In the pages of a *Blueboy* magazine." This might've sailed over straight heads, but most queer guys knew *Blueboy*—it was gay *Playboy* with twinks in its centerfold.

In 1985, Lauper fought endometriosis while one of her closest friends,

Gregory Natal, succumbed to AIDS, which together shaped the earnestness of 1986's *True Colors.* On its title track, she honors her pal, as intended, with the dignity of "That's What Friends Are For," 1985's worldwide smash ballad from Dionne Warwick, Elton John, Gladys Knight, and Stevie Wonder that raised more than three million dollars for AIDS research and prevention. "I wanted to sing it softly to Carl [Natal's partner] and all the folks who loved Gregory," her 2012 memoir says of the title track's deviation from Tom Kelly and Billy Steinberg's country-gospel demo. "I wanted us to heal a little." Rather than wailing, she sings its bulk with a whisper, as if she were an angel sitting on the shoulders of those who've lost. "Your true colors . . . are beautiful like a rainbow," she croons.

Enkindled by rock's inclusivity and LSD's vividness, artist Gilbert Baker devised the rainbow flag as an answer to the Stars and Stripes that the Bicentennial made omnipresent. The original rainbow flags flew in 1978's San Francisco Gay Freedom Day Parade months before Supervisor Harvey Milk was assassinated. In 1987, ACT UP adopted the Silence=Death Project's political poster that revived the pink triangle to convey the consequences of not speaking up about AIDS. Rainbows subsequently grew in popularity as a brighter alternative that captured the synergy of varied, racially diverse LGBTQ experience.

Lauper's "True Colors" video hints at this. After the first chorus, a little girl stares at a rowboat in which a white woman and a Black woman regard each other fondly before stroking sand that turns to water. Lauper appears smiling, as if their bond created her—a reflection of their love. Childlike and surreal, the open-endedness of the song and video allowed all of us to see ourselves in it.

Just as the rainbow became a queer signifier, "True Colors" grew into an LGBTQ anthem that many have sung, yet few master. Although Lauper approaches the verses with a youngster's innocence, they're full of tricky syncopations. For the final chorus, she hits crucial words hard, then adroitly backs off, singing "*don't be afraid* to let it show." These irregularities are intrinsic to the song's message: What makes you complicated and aberrant is also what makes you beautiful. That's why "True Colors" talks to us. Lauper's rendering is a multihued oil painting rendered with the candor of kindergarten watercolors.

Lauper slipped from the Top Forty as her music grew more courageous. Combining *Unusual*'s rock musicians with the gay DJ Junior Vasquez and the lesbian songsmith Allee Willis, 1993's *Hat Full of Stars* augments socially conscious folk-rock with hip-hop. A co-write with country's Mary Chapin Carpenter, "Sally's Pigeons" tells the true story of a childhood pal who gets pregnant, has a back-alley abortion, and dies, yet Lauper sings it so lovingly that it becomes a universal testimony of friendship. After *Roe v. Wade* was overturned in 2022, she released an even sadder version.

The more Lauper sided with queers, the less music biz support she received. Packed with drag queens, the video to her 1994 "Girls" update, "Hey Now," helped sell the single and her hits collection overseas, but according to her, the label quashed the clip in the US. Her 1997 single "Ballad of Cleo and Joe" chronicles Little Joe's nightly transformation into Little Cleo, dancing queen. Pummeling techno suggests the drudgery of Joe's minimum-wage world, while accordion pyrotechnics evoke Cleo's vibrant escape. Growling and howling like a bluesman, Lauper transfigures, too. Long gone is the Betty Boop-y character who squeaked out the *Pee-wee's Playhouse* theme song. In the video to Soul Solution's house remix of "Cleo," Lauper accentuates her baby bump with a mirrored disco ball—a metaphor for her reborn status as LGBTQ mama. But per Lauper, Epic's dance-music department head thought "Cleo" was "too gay."

Having appeared at AIDS benefits since 1985, as well as Pride parades, Lauper delved deeper into advocacy and fundraising. Battling LGBTQ youth homelessness, her True Colors United organization grew from what she knows: Her gay friend Gregory's parents threw him out when he was twelve, and her sister is lesbian.

Yet Lauper's crowning post-'80s achievement remains *Kinky Boots*, the 2012 Billy Porter–starring, Harvey Fierstein–scripted musical for which she wrote the songs. It tells the story of a Black drag entertainer—not coincidentally named Lola—and the son of an old-fashioned crispin who team up to create footwear built for queens. A tale as quintessentially rock 'n' roll as the Kinks' hit, *Boots* illustrates how people who are male, female, white, Black, straight, gay, cis, trans, and all-possible-combinations-thereof can transcend oppositional traditions by uniting to enable harmony and liberation for everybody.

Lauper followed a similar narrative. An initially retro singer, she turned into an ever-contemporary songwriter while outwitting rock's boys' club. By queering her work, she's brought it closer to her core—that bullied, irregular child she never renounced. She's still blessedly unusual.

⏭

Chapter Forty-Four

Madonna

I'll likely never write about anyone more than Madonna. We have similar origin stories featuring industrial suburbs, parental loss, dance classes, gay mentors, and much more. When I moved to Fourth Street and Avenue C right before she released 1983's *Madonna,* I learned she'd lived literally around the corner. When I later saw pre-stardom photos of her, I realized from her jacket—graffitied "WEBO," an early '80s dance that inspired her publishing company's name, Webo Girl—that I'd Skanked, Smurfed, and Wopped alongside her. Like the DJs and artists she dated, Madonna personified the downtown scene that was so good to us.

When I wrote my first Madonna piece, a *Village Voice* essay that encompassed her Radio City Music Hall appearance on 1985's Virgin Tour, I was still an NYU cinema studies grad student, back when semiotics ruled pop scholarship. The first male rock critic in a high-profile publication to call out the misogyny and hypocrisy of how my peers treated Madonna, I also identified her as a postmodern signifier who put sexuality in quotes, which meant I was among the earliest to situate her in an intellectual context—a future cottage industry. I'd been on track to get my master's degree but couldn't quite complete it when *Voice* deadlines took precedence over my final papers. My professors had mixed feelings about their youngest student's being published more than they were. One docked me for "inappropriate humor"—the kind for which the singer would soon be famous. So when Madonna told Keith Haring, who told his friend, who told my friend, who told me she loved my review, I put academia on permanent hold. My new career allowed me to write about everything I loved, and all of it came together in Madonna.

Produced by her Danceteria DJ boyfriend Mark Kamins, her 1982 Sire debut single, "Everybody," aped the sound of Prelude, West End, and other NYC dance labels that pumped out twelve-inch singles flaunting funk hooks, tough vocals, and slithery studio tricks that propelled disco into the '80s. Madonna wasn't yet at the level of Prelude peers like former Harlette Sharon Redd, who died of AIDS in 1992, or France Joli, who sang so stirringly that nobody cared she was a white Canuck teen. But neither was Madonna as coarse as Loose Joints' WBLS-approved "Is It All Over My Face?," an eruditely crude 1980 West End jam by Arthur Russell, who became an indie demigod decades after he, too, died of AIDS in 1992. The way Madonna careens into "Everybody" lines like "find a groove and *let yourself go*!" sells her self-written liberation song. Nothing inflames haters and stans like the subject of her voice, but rhythm reigns here, and she already rides it like a pro.

Thanks to Miles Davis's former guitarist Reggie Lucas, most of *Madonna* sits between Prelude's polish and West End's enthusiasm. Its producer, Lucas, had been creating R&B-flavored club music so graceful and gay-adored—like Stephanie Mills's 1980 hit "Never Knew Love Like This Before"—that it circumvented radio's disco backlash. But when Lucas digressed from Madonna's demos, the singer asked Funhouse DJ John "Jellybean" Benitez to remix several Lucas cuts and to produce from scratch her first pop hit, "Holiday."

Penned by Curtis Hudson and Lisa Stevens of Pure Energy, a Paradise Garage–favored act, "Holiday" announced that its singer—whose racial identity was initially concealed by Sire—could maximize her presence via R&B work ethics. She didn't have half the lung power of Loleatta Holloway or other big Garage gals, but the way Madonna accentuates key bits in lines like "we're gonna have a celebr*aaaa*tion!" echoes how church-trained singers summon the Holy Spirit. Even in this escape-seeking song about release and togetherness, Madonna externalizes her haunted inner life. That process is soul music's essence. Racism and every other form of bigotry denies humanity, but soul at its most fundamental level embodies it. An ordinary white girl without inner demons could not sing about salvation so instinctively. Those demons give "Holiday" its depth, and they're why we relate to it; Madonna, too, had to propel herself over the rainbow.

That prayerfulness also permeates "Lucky Star." She's wishing on a star, her lover, but also on herself. Unlike most pop acts then, she was a trained dancer, which means she could kneel and bare her midriff while declaring dominion in a flatteringly minimal, maximum-impact video. Although her stance suggests an oral bottom—a role introduced by the earlier single "Burning Up"—her attitude is that of a top. We know that's not a contradiction. Others wanted to learn more, or were repelled by something nearly unprecedented. Joan Jett displayed a guy's impenetrability and dressed like a dude. Madonna similarly perfects male authority's hard gaze here but looks soft and yielding. Born with the face of her namesake, she's the sort ordinarily placed on pedestals. Seeing her in black mesh and lace crawl through the dimensionless, limitless white space of her "Lucky Star" video made some queasy. Madonna's button-pushing began early.

This refusal to be confined is further played out in Lucas's "Borderline," which maximizes her pop appeal through R&B smoothness. Its video similarly straddles Latino street dancing and upwardly mobile modeling, yet Madonna won't be contained by either. Defying her onscreen Puerto Rican suitor, she poses for a suited white photographer, then graffities his set and returns to her sweetheart. A mirror of Jellybean, then also her real-life romantic partner, he coaches Madonna on how to hold a pool cue—a pointed euphemism for not just sex but also playing the showbiz game. In the shadow of *Thriller* and the second British Invasion, this quintessentially NYC dance act, originally thought to be niche, crossed over in 1984—pop's most impactful year since the Beatles' US arrival two decades earlier—to become MTV's biggest breakout ever.

Since *Madonna*'s release in the summer of 1983, I'd been working in Tower Records' dance-music department, where I'd recommend her album to shoppers who couldn't afford multiple twelve-inch singles, because that's what it basically was. Tower sat between the West and East Village, the perfect vantage to observe her look spreading through Manhattan and the boroughs via fan replicas known as "wannabes."

With 1984's *Like a Virgin*, Madonna attracted an army of wannabes larger than the audiences of every one of her punk and new wave labelmates on Sire combined. That meant her bangles, bows, and bare midriff grew more ubiquitous than Michael Jackson's red leather. I wore the rubber bracelets she popularized, doing so as a badge of local pride, for they accentuated that I'd become a genuine New Yorker who couldn't speak without waving my hands. But it wasn't merely Madonna's sound and look that signified. It was the life-force she manifested. She represented everyone I'd left home to go to school with, dance with, dream with, fall in love with, and eventually mourn in NYC. I will always love Madonna for that.

Penned by future "True Colors" writers Tom Kelly and Billy Steinberg, "Like a Virgin" demarks Madonna's transition from everywoman clubber to singular pop sensation. Fresh from David Bowie's *Let's Dance*, producer Nile Rodgers and his Chic compatriots give her a similar invincibility. As light as their beats are heavy, Madonna squeals out a peep akin to when Donna Summer impersonated Marilyn Monroe for "Love to Love You Baby." But even while labeling herself a "boy toy" in the video with her epochal belt buckle, the fire in her eyes announces she's anything but. Chauvinists can't tell when women are playacting. They think every guise and faked orgasm that feeds their inflated egos is real.

The song's most satisfying passage comes when its melody pulls helium-high Madonna back to earth, down to her regular vocal register. "Yeah, you made me feel/I've nothing to hide," she sings. At the heart of a song my generation has heard so many times we've almost lost the ability to truly take it in, lyricist Steinberg embeds in this line something akin to Sylvester's "Mighty Real." Although we've been around a well-traveled block and might have a time bomb ticking inside us that no doctor could then defuse, "you" make us feel virginal. Your love takes us out of our closets. We can be ourselves.

Similar twists propel "Material Girl." Co-writer Peter Brown had queer-relevant dance hits of his own, such as 1984's "They Only Come Out at Night," a Jellybean-mixed clubbing ode coded as an LGBTQ parable. "Material Girl" spoofs the lingering notion that women can only advance through the mating game. Madonna's nasal vocal references stealthy flibbertigibbets portrayed by Judy Holliday, while Mary Lambert, who also directed "Borderline" and "Like a Virgin," situates its video in heterosexual satire by re-creating Marilyn Monroe's "Diamonds Are a Girl's Best Friend" from *Gentlemen Prefer Blondes.* Just as Monroe's luminosity blinded many to her smarts, Madonna bamboozled those who took her green-grabbing parody literally. She'd paid her dues, like Keith Haring, yet the media typecast the singer as her hit's namesake—an embodiment of 1980s greed.

Her radio and MTV profile exploding with several singles charting simultaneously, Madonna confirmed her dancefloor artistry with a worldwide smash relegated in the US to a twelve-inch B-side. Originally intended as a demo for Cheyne, a Danceteria elevator operator who instead scored with 1985's Kamins-produced club hit "Call Me Mr. Telephone," "Into the Groove" soundtracks the Danceteria scene in Susan Seidelman's *Desperately Seeking Susan,* a Madonna-starring feminist update of classic Hollywood's comedic capers. Co-written and co-produced by the singer with her Black ex and former bandmate Stephen Bray, it's the rare song about dancing that shows insight into its liberating force—likely because it illustrates a turning point in Madonna's own life. In 2010, she spoke in *Interview* about her gay ballet teacher, Christopher Flynn, who mentored her throughout high school and college and drove her to her first gay disco. "I always felt like I was a freak when I was growing up and that there was something wrong with me because I couldn't fit in anywhere," she told *Milk* director Gus Van Sant. "But when he took me to that club, he brought me to a place where I finally felt at home."

That simultaneous sense of abandon and arrival connects clubbing to coming out on "Into the Groove." Over an electronic track so streamlined and impactive that it's the post-disco equivalent of the early Beatles sound, Madonna sings of the freedom dancing provides her within her unseen, locked-up secrecy. Like so many of us initially trapped in our childhood bedrooms, she longs to share her discovery with a special someone. That's why she begins by inviting the listener to dance, not simply for release but "for inspiration." What follows is as catchy in its verses as it is in its chorus, yet the liberation-themed bridge lifts her excitement even higher. When she repeats "now I know you're mine" at the end of its second iteration, elevating it in conquest, she attains ecstasy. For me, this is one of pop's greatest passages. When I think about my time in New York, when everything fell into place and I finally felt as though I belonged, I remember "Into the Groove" coursing through the summer of 1985. Music like Madonna's had taken me out of my shell, onto the street, and made every step down the sidewalk feel like I was dancing with all of Manhattan.

By 1986, her wannabes were sweeping the clubs and airwaves. Bray produced and co-wrote Regina's "Baby Love," whereas Alisha's "Baby Talk" just had me dancing in its video (I'm the extra wearing a bright blue Keith Haring sweatshirt, naturally). That year's *True Blue* further eclipsed them. A secret Madonna sings of but never reveals gives an existential weight to *True*'s "Live to Tell." I covered her 1987 AIDS charity concert at Madison Square Garden for the *Voice*, fixated on the song's line "Would I grow old?," and pondered if her contemporaries would. Many didn't, like her gay former roommate Martin Burgoyne, who designed her "Burning Up" sleeve and died in 1986. The concert was in his memory.

Madonna became a lightning rod for all kinds of controversy. Did "Papa Don't Preach" fight the patriarchy or advocate a pro-life position? Was her peepshow dance in Jean-Baptiste Mondino's video for "Open Your Heart" feminist or anti-feminist? Its audience includes gay sailors, a lesbian of color, and a pre-teen boy who mimics her moves. Does he desire her or want to be her? When I was his age, I didn't know the difference. I'm not sure I do even now.

As her marriage to actor Sean Penn unraveled, Madonna's friendship with Sandra Bernhard blossomed. The bisexual comedian wouldn't label herself as such then. I once interviewed Bernhard right after a journalist who chastised her for this very thing fled in tears. There wouldn't be an out star in her field until Ellen DeGeneres spectacularly left the closet in 1997. The few out people on TV were expected to smile like queer Uncle Toms while submitting themselves to condescending talk-show hosts and insulting audience members.

Bernhard didn't play that game. She appeared on *Late Night with David Letterman* during the 1988 run of her Off-Broadway show *Without You I'm Nothing*, which closed with her lusciously lezzie take on Prince's "Little Red Corvette." After showing off insinuating news clippings about her and Madonna, she invited the identically dressed singer to join her. The pair did nearly every provocative thing they could to confirm that the rumors alleging they were lovers were true. Clearly they were messing with Letterman, his viewers, and the media. Yet their chemistry was just as obvious. That combination made for something queerer than any conventional coming-out and set a precedent for Madonna. Not only would there be women whose presence in her highly public private life invited speculation. They'd also appear in her increasingly libidinous, definition-dodging art and help situate it beyond heteronormativity.

With 1989's drastically more personal *Like a Prayer*, Madonna further complicated her persona with the title track and its incendiary video. Addressing religion's separation of sexuality from spirituality as her lyrics, sound, and imagery reunite them, she and the Andraé Crouch Choir sing, "I'm down on my knees/I wanna take you there." That line rattled many, but not us; the same positions some find demeaning give us salvation. Her most seditious move was launching the single with a sappy, two-minute Pepsi commercial that premiered on *The Cosby Show*—the introduction of a five-million-dollar sponsorship deal—then debuting Mary Lambert's not-at-all sentimental video the next day on MTV.

Racially and sexually charged, the video mixes imagery considered sacred—including a statue of a Black saint, who comes to life and is arrested—with what's thought profane. While many TV stations banned the video, MTV pumped it. Pepsi withdrew its sponsorship, yet Madonna kept its money. Cynics deemed this a publicity stunt, but in *Billboard*'s 2011 poll, Lambert's video was voted second only to "Thriller."

For us, "Like a Prayer" packs a punch because of the discrimination we're still fighting. In the old days, the patriarchy criminalized sharing queer moments of heaven among ourselves, which continues today with the outlawing of drag. Thanks to those who'd rather make our lives hell than reveal their true nature, even our saints are thought sinners.

Created between two petitions for divorce as well as an assault report against Penn, *Like a Prayer* comprehensively concentrates on Madonna's emotional fallout. Alternatingly pensive and exuberant, she honors perseverance as well as the persistence of family ties that aren't always traditional. She yells out, "Come on, girls!" at the start of "Express Yourself" as a signal that her Sly and the Family Stone–inspired anthem addresses women *and* gay men. Having weathered a marriage in which she craved yet feared candid communication, she advises those with male partners to speak openly, demand that these guys also share their feelings, and treat us properly. "Make you feel like a queen on a throne," she winks.

This welcoming gesture extends to the video by future film maestro David Fincher. Set to Shep Pettibone's heavier house remix, which replaced the album's instrumentation and became the single, it examines racial, gender, and economic structures by way of Fritz Lang's sci-fi classic *Metropolis*. Retreating from the pressures of enslaving a rain-soaked workforce rich in gay beefcake, a pampered and possibly queer autocrat takes pleasure in Black jazz musicians he seemingly triggers by remote control. A monocled Madonna spoofs his authority, but she also appears shackled on a bed, then laps up milk from a bowl like a cat. Some considered Madonna's role-playing as feminist; others, the opposite. We hadn't seen a female superstar draw so extravagantly from gay culture. Costing five million dollars, this was then pop's priciest video. Our Pedro Almodóvar didn't spend that much on an entire movie back then.

Madonna strengthened her LGBTQ bond with "Cherish," the debut video from Herb Ritts. Like his also-gay predecessor Richard Avedon, this photographer presented women at their most exemplary; those are his similar shots adorning the covers of *True Blue* and Olivia Newton-John's *Physical*. Ritts catches Madonna's gift for looking at the camera the way we all want to be seen—like we're as special as she is. Rendering her straightforwardly at the beach in classic black and white, he nevertheless queers the situation by pairing her with mermen whose tails are so realistically dolphin-like that they make us think about flesh—theirs, hers, and our own.

Because AIDS peppered its victims with Kaposi's sarcoma lesions that were often the first indication that someone was sick, gay men's skin then was under attack and constant surveillance. Benign morning moments in the bathroom mirror could without warning turn into horror. Seen through Ritts's lens, Madonna's water-stroked skin is a simple thing of wonder. The mermen—a metaphor for LGBTQ existence: so graceful, yet so fraught—play with each other the same mirthful way her tune tickles our ears. Like the video's merchild, they represent our innocence before homophobia and other bigotries corrupt it. In 2002, Ritts died of pneumonia, not the pneumocystis kind common to AIDS patients but because his HIV-weakened system couldn't fight anymore. AIDS isn't over—even for those who can afford the best healthcare.

Although few knew of his gayness in the early 1980s, Pettibone became a local NYC celebrity via his exclusive edits for the dance-music station KISS. Studio remixes followed, first for dance indies like Prelude and Salsoul, and eventually for pop titans like Pet Shop Boys and George Michael. Pettibone's Madonna mixes led to his working with the star for what was first intended as a B-side but wisely held back for 1990's *I'm Breathless: Music from and Inspired by the Film Dick Tracy*, which proved she could ably sing tailormade material from gay Broadway giant Stephen Sondheim. Nevertheless, what sold the album was its Pettibone assist, "Vogue."

Before it, few beyond New York's Black/Latinx gay and trans circles knew about voguing, a queer dance with which participants dispute their opponents through stylized gender performance. A product of Harlem's drag ball competitions, its hieroglyphic movements—like poses for a *Vogue* photo spread—trickled downtown when DJ David DePino, from the House of Xtravaganza, brought voguing to the club Tracks in 1988. Junior Vasquez followed suit at the Sound Factory, but only gay dancers—usually of color—took notice.

Lifting the curtain on this secreted scene, "Vogue" outlines how the dance reconfigures the social order by elevating those who are rich in spirit but low in finance. Instructing listeners to take stock of the heartaches that encircle us, Madonna alludes to urban life as it was lived by those Reagan disenfranchised, and advocates dancing as a portal into reinvention. Once again, she reveals that her mind's eye is on the spiritual prize as she reminds us that what we hold inside can also set us free; race and gender aren't of consequence. Like Sylvester sang in his Patrick Cowley–written 1979 disco hit "Stars," the dancer becomes a source of light, a beacon of transcendence. "Beauty's where you find it/Not just where you bump and grind it," Madonna sings. House music doesn't get more bluntly poetic than that.

Despite flukes like David Cole and Robert Clivillés's hit 1988 remix of Natalie Cole's "Pink Cadillac," a Bruce Springsteen cover, house hadn't become mainstream in the US the way it was in Europe. Radio—even R&B stations—feared its proximity to disco, a closeness that "Vogue" confirms through horn blasts that Pettibone based off his remix of the Salsoul Orchestra's "Chicago Bus Stop." Had Madonna not recorded the greatest dance-craze song since Chic's "Le Freak," this wouldn't have changed.

Re-creating the surrealistic lighting, framing, and subjects of *Vogue* photographer Horst P. Horst, who was gay, as well as the Art Deco paintings of Tamara de Lempicka, who was lesbian, Fincher's black-and-white video buffs voguing's upwardly mobile motions to irrefutable sleekness. Stardom shoots out of Madonna, but in nonhierarchical dancefloor fashion, it also proliferates from every white, Black, Latin, and Asian participant who cross-examines Fincher's camera with a severity and specificity not ordinarily allowed of supporting players. Here, they veer from clownish mainstream LGBTQ representations with godlike nobility. Their screentime is substantial; their composure sublime. Everything is of an elegant piece—a rare accomplishment considering that these were then unknowns and Madonna ranked among living women only second in fame to Princess Diana and maybe Di's mum-in-law.

Being venturesomely aspirational broadened the appeal of "Vogue" and its video. Like Nile Rodgers and Diana Ross with "I'm Coming Out," Pettibone and Madonna took a scene rooted in Black trans experience and rendered its ambitions universally. Some still accuse the pair of appropriation, but "Vogue" gave a voice to those denied one at the height of a gay, Black, and Latino holocaust. Then as now, those in charge wanted us dead, and all they had to do was nothing, which is exactly what they did. Watching something so multiculturally queer become so successful brightened our darkest hours.

Topping the charts in thirty countries, "Vogue" set a defiant stage for 1990's Blond Ambition World Tour. For this fifty-seven-show spectacle, Madonna approached what's known in theater as the *Gesamtkunstwerk*—the "total work of art." It's what the nineteenth-century German composer Richard Wagner aimed for by designing his operas as a unified package, and it has since become the unspoken goal of most interdisciplinary artists. Reliant on different co-songwriters and drawing from several albums, videos, and her boyfriend Warren Beatty's film *Dick Tracy,* in which she appeared, Madonna couldn't achieve complete cohesion. But through comprehensive multimedia, Blond Ambition advanced pop concerts by presenting unapologetic female sexuality through queer culture's confrontational prism.

Many of the tour's main collaborators are gay—co-director and choreographer Vincent Paterson, costumer Jean Paul Gaultier, Madonna's brother and art director, Christopher Ciccone, and nearly all of her dancers, including her voguing experts Luis Camacho and Jose Gutierez, both Xtravaganzas. With them, Madonna violated gender and sexuality mores in a kaleidoscopic cavalcade clearly not intended solely for the straight male gaze. Her female singer-dancers groped her. The star threw them around. Madonna made Gaultier's cone bra infamous, yet Camacho and Gutierez donned bigger, pointier ones. No doubt offended by her reframing "Oh Father" and "Papa Don't Preach" as a critique of Catholicism, Pope John Paul II deemed Blond Ambition "one of the most satanic shows in the history of humanity." Even I can't beat that superlative.

Like in vaudeville, Madonna linked her songs with banter customized for each performance. At the beginning of "Into the Groove," she remarked, "These days, you never really get to know a guy until you ask him to wear a rubber." During the second Oakland Coliseum show I reviewed, she added, "I wonder if Barry Walters has this problem." Naturally, I jumped up as if I'd been crowned Miss America, which prompted some jerk behind me to call me a faggot. That was LGBTQ life circa 1990.

The tour's 1991 documentary, *Madonna: Truth or Dare*, served behind-the-scenes dish but also functioned as a then-rare gay chronicle. Decades after 1973's *An American Family*, reality TV hadn't yet made a comeback, and although *Paris Is Burning* validated Harlem's voguing underground, that landmark film didn't reach beyond the indie circuit until doing so via the internet. The biggest doc of its day, *Truth or Dare* played everywhere. Many young viewers hadn't seen two people of the same sex kissing before or experienced unfiltered gay humor or even queer community. And although it has since sparked accusations that Madonna exploited her minority cast, it often caught her flaws while showing them sympathetically. In San Francisco screenings, fans cheered their kisses. Before it, we had little opportunity to see ourselves in a mainstream setting beyond what was provided by the musicians in this book.

Madonna further tested what was permissible when she launched 1990's *The Immaculate Collection* with "Justify My Love." Whereas its cleverest lyric—"Poor is the man whose pleasures depend on the permission of another"—warns that those who only enjoy what society sanctions are bankrupt, Jean-Baptiste Mondino's instigative video illustrates the wealth of those who do otherwise. In it, Madonna cavorts with butches, queens, and then-boyfriend Tony Ward, a Joe Dallesandro–esque hunk. Reminiscent of Jack Smith's 1963 queer-movie milestone *Flaming Creatures*, the video demands repeated viewings to follow who's doing what to whom. Ward climbs atop Madonna, but through the magic of editing, he's replaced by a close-cropped woman who kisses Madonna while Ward watches as if nearly combusting with lust. That gal gets a pencil mustache from an identical butch while a dominatrix re-creates Charlotte Rampling's S&M look in *The Night Porter* alongside trans women, gay boys, and Gutierez, whose sweeping arm gestures suggest he's a supernatural orgy conductor orchestrating every ambiguously gendered body.

Naturally, network TV banned it aside from a sole *Nightline* airing, which was followed by an interview. Madonna asked, "Why is it that people are willing to go and watch a movie about someone getting blown to bits for no reason at all, and nobody wants to see two girls kissing and two men snuggling?" *We* did: Its video single sold a million copies and became an LGBTQ bar fixture.

To promote her acting in 1992's *A League of Their Own*, Madonna did a stylistic about-face with "This Used to Be My Playground." Recorded at the end of the sessions for her next album but released before it, this elegiac ballad belies her childhood love of Simon and Garfunkel. It's steeped in bygone New York as well as ghosts conjured but never named. Having shifted to writing about photography, *Voice* critic Vince Aletti framed his review by confessing he rarely went clubbing anymore. By then most of the quintessential queer Manhattan venues had shuttered. Many of their DJs and dancers were long gone or nursing those who'd follow. Before the year was up, Larry Levan would die of heart failure at age thirty-eight. Gay kids didn't stop partying: Sound Factory, Limelight, and other dance palaces thrived. Yet Madonna's nighttime playground—and that of so many LGBTQ people of our generation—would never be the same. "I was thinking of the East Village, Danceteria, the Roxy, my friends that died of AIDS, the good old days, and a million other nostalgic thoughts," she told Aletti.

Beneath its bellicose surface, 1992's *Erotica* covered corresponding turf. It was the maiden album from Maverick, her Time Warner–backed entertainment company, which would soon prosper with Alanis Morissette. Madonna's gay fans love *Erotica*: It remains her queerest record, one that gained overdue accolades decades after its release, after women and LGBTQ folk made media inroads. Yet what nearly everyone else focused on was *Sex*, Madonna's photobook that followed a day later.

Sex is many things, not all of them good. The author's comments about prostitution and abusive relationships are uncharacteristically naive, and many of its visuals are derivative of Robert Mapplethorpe, Guy Bourdin, Helmut Newton, and other dissident photographers. But even what doesn't work is pugnaciously queer—not simply in stance but also in its abettors and subjects, including photographer Steven Meisel, actor Udo Kier, Bernhard's ex Ingrid Casares, gay porn star Joey Stefano, the Chelsea Hotel, Times Square's male burlesque house Gaiety Theatre, and those S&M dykes Madonna cavorts with in its first few pages. The last reappear in the book's greatest gender-defying accomplishment: a grimy shot in which one androgynous woman fondles another's butt by a row of urinals also occupied by two also nearly identical skinhead guys with their asses exposed. The pink presence of Madonna superimposed over them insinuates that this tableau remains on her mind and that she's one of them. When the far right weaponizes fear against trans people and makes a colossal issue out of them simply using public restrooms, they're turning a fantasy like this one into a nightmare. As for the photo itself, it's fabulous.

If you were an LGBTQ person of a certain age and sensibility, you *had* to see *Sex*. Topping the *New York Times* Best Seller list for three weeks and selling one and a half million copies, it was the first best-selling book that lifted the curtain on queer sexuality in a participatory way. We knew long ago that Madonna was steeped in our world, but *Sex* confirmed she might not be entirely straight; certainly her art no longer was. Nevertheless, her playmates' authenticity accentuated her makeup's fastidiousness and her fetish-wear's newness, which sometimes made her look like a pampered tourist slumming in Queer Pervland. Was Madonna ripping us off? Or was she us?

This ambiguity upset readers—*a lot*. Most reviews took a condemning tack, as if turning the tables on Dita, Madonna's dominatrix alter ego and *Sex*'s narrator. "Of course, some of us actually like the opposite sex; some of us believe it is possible to have great sex without whips, third parties or domestic pets," groused not some chauvinist windbag but Caryn James, a *New York Times* film critic. There had been grumblings all along that Madonna was motivated exclusively by money and fame, yet with *Sex* this became the sole media discourse about her. Unlike far more mercenary guys, she had to be punished for her acumen, which distracted from the book's true transgression. Never had a female superstar flexed such fearless pansexual power.

That might also motors *Erotica*'s BDSM-boosting title track. "Give it up, do as I say/Give it up and let me have my way," she sing-speaks as Dita over a rock-funk fusion that anticipates trip-hop. In fashion arbiter Fabien Baron's video shot on *Sex*'s sets, Madonna gets steamy with Isabella Rossellini, Vanilla Ice, and others intercut so rapidly that gender differences dissolve. Belting on "Deeper and Deeper," Madonna again leaves the closet: "But my love is alive/ And I'm *never gonna hide it again*!" This avowal is emphasized in a disco-situated video in which Kier plays a Warhol-like figure around which a coterie of Factory types—represented by Debi Mazar, Chi Chi LaRue, Seymour Stein, and others—twirl, kiss, and act as naturally rainbow-hued as her other gay nightlife representations are elsewhere stylized.

During most of what follows on the album, she struggles. Relationships fall apart as she awakens from spells cast by deceptive lovers on "Bye Bye Baby," "Waiting," and "Words." A friend steals her man in "Thief of Hearts." Booze and anonymous sex can't numb the pain of this "Bad Girl." Like many of us, Madonna sought out raunch to achieve emotional autonomy and distance herself from pain—a tactic she celebrates here but also exposes as futile. Like *Sex*, *Erotica* is her conceptual work about love and lovemaking under plague's shadow.

"Why's It So Hard" grapples with repression while seeking change. Once more she identifies as one of us: "Why can't we accept that we're different/ Before it's too late?" "In This Life" addresses in its first verse Madonna's loss of Burgoyne, and in the second her mentor Christopher Flynn. Establishing a gay context with the line "shouldn't matter who you choose to love," she acknowledges AIDS without uttering its name. Instead, the epidemic looms as "this thing"—a destructor of unknown status, paralleling how politicians and pundits deemed the disease unmentionable.

With the Beatles' 1965 milestone "In My Life," John Lennon looked back in fondness but placed faith in the present with his repeated resolution "in my life I love you more." With her nod to this autobiographical turning point for that band and pop itself, Madonna favors the past. "In this life I loved you most of all," she sings to the departed. This seemingly small switch is significant, for it says that Penn, Beatty, and all the other high-ranking hunks she has bedded can't compare with her pre-fame gay pals. They loved her when the world thought she was nobody and helped make her somebody. Madonna stands beside them like they did with her.

On *Erotica*'s jazzy and recondite closer, "Secret Garden," Madonna ponders her feminine essence as a paradise of pleasure, a genital Garden of Eden. Revealing insecurities ordinarily concealed, her positivity once again blossoms. "And I'm strong, and there's a chance/That I will grow, this I know," she sighs for all of us. The bass is immense, the piano delicate, and the chorus unlike anything else in her cannon. It wonders and wanders, twisting downward to her vocal bottom, but with an unusual melodic resolution that presages future breakthroughs. When I think of music that gives insight into what it means to be anatomically female, I think of Minnie Riperton's "Inside My Love" and this.

If you were born in the twenty-first century and grew up with porn and potential hookups always a few clicks away, it might be difficult for you to apprehend *Sex*'s and *Erotica*'s altruistic intent. By showing clandestine activities that look dangerous but are medically harmless, Madonna endorsed safe sex.

So did I. Part of why I'm still around is that my friends were under the care of the first doctors to glean what was most and least likely to spread HIV, and published the first safe-sex guidelines. Penises, vaginas, rectums, semen, saliva, blood, and antibodies became routine subjects of discussion because we wanted to keep one another alive. This came too late to save those already infected, so I felt it was morally imperative for me to write about sex whenever I could to break the silence that was still killing us. I'd been making up for lost carnal time, so I'd already had more partners than most straight people do in a lifetime. Some were willing to do plenty without any discussion. I'd ask a basic question in a bathhouse or sex club—like, "Do you know your HIV status?"—and often the response would be, "No one has ever asked me that here." During these chance encounters, it was easier to stick a dick in your mouth and shut up.

When Madonna and other artists gave me an opportunity to write something that might save someone's life, I went for it. In 1992, I became the first critic to be awarded by the National Lesbian and Gay Journalists Association, which commended me for an "everyday infusion of a queer perspective" at the *San Francisco Examiner.* Much to my editors' dismay, I did this, almost literally every day. When the antiviral cocktails arrived in the mid-'90s and AIDS fatalities dropped so low that in its August 13, 1998, issue there were no obituaries in San Francisco's LGBTQ weekly *The Bay Area Reporter* for the first time in seventeen years, I shifted my priorities. I no longer needed to be so gay so often.

After *Sex*'s backlash, Madonna took a related tack on 1994's *Bedtime Stories.* By pairing with Dallas Austin, Dave Hall, Nellee Hooper, and Babyface—the hitmakers behind R&B's TLC, Mary J. Blige, Soul II Soul, and Toni Braxton, respectively—she repurposed their creamy goodness to soften her art. What she lost in blatant otherness, she gained in subtle craft, like on "Forbidden Love," which praises "love without guilt" while basking in transgression. The disc's humongous hit ballad "Take a Bow" sounds defeated, but that's its point. Madonna sings to a lover but reprimands all who took her for granted, while Babyface's simmering, sukiyaki-flavored Orientalism goes down so smoothly that many miss the lyrical barbs that critique masculine fakeness. "The show is over, say goodbye," she croons her sugar-coated kiss off. When blunt gals get this gentle, they're sometimes saying "fuck you."

While portraying the blond ambitions of Argentina's First Lady activist Eva Perón, Madonna further tempers her own intractability in 1996's film adaptation of Broadway's *Evita.* Andrew Lloyd Webber's demanding score meant she had to learn to sing from her diaphragm—a required technique for music theater performers—to reach and hold higher notes on standards like "Don't Cry for Me Argentina." She never achieved the ease of Barbra Streisand or Patti LuPone, nor should she have; Madonna's greatest moments come when she captures existential aches through vocal strain and grain. But her fortified technical ability combined with the soul-seeking that sprang from giving birth to her daughter Lourdes in 1996 prepared Madonna to realize, soon after splitting from that child's father, the best version of herself on 1998's *Ray of Light*.

To reach it, Madonna paired with William Orbit, a gay-approved London electronic musician who had achieved scattered success via his productions and remixes but hadn't yet attained stardom. Madonna also brought back her late-'80s accomplice Patrick Leonard and added Rick Nowels, who'd co-written hits for Belinda Carlisle and would later assist Lana Del Rey. With their support, she achieved something personal yet still pop, like David Bowie and others who straddled the mainstream and avant-garde worlds and therefore spoke to our own experience of being both inside and outside society. We are affirmed by what's distinctive yet popular because it gives us hope that our own differences will be exalted, and not simply tolerated.

This duality drives *Ray of Light*'s queerness despite its lack of explicitly LGBTQ material. "Drowned World/Substitute for Love" solemnly announces Madonna's shift from measuring herself outwardly through her popularity to contemplating fame as abusive isolation from within a crowd. *Evita*'s vocal coaching shows in how relaxed she sings, as if forsaking celebrity's superficiality allowed her to finally fully exhale. Having lost her mother to cancer at age five, Madonna—like many of us who are abandoned by family who would rather cut us out of their lives than accept our sexuality or gender—sought immersive mending. Music became both means and ends.

When giving birth via cesarean meant she couldn't exercise strenuously, Madonna turned to yoga, as reflected in "Shanti/Ashtangi," as well as psychotherapy and kabbalah study. "Swim" leaves unclear whether she is drawn to water for its purifying qualities or as a means to permanently escape pain through suicidal drowning. Right before recording its vocal, Donatella Versace told Madonna that fashion designer Gianni Versace—Donatella's gay brother and the singer's close friend—had been murdered. That's why it, too, sounds like a prayer.

Ray of Light isn't all somber club ballads. The title track is so uplifting that it makes the whole album seem upbeat. It's based on the first verse of "Sepheryn," a 1971 obscurity by the English folk duo Curtiss Maldoon. Madonna's rewrite shifts the song's original subject—Zephyrus, the westwind god—from masculine to feminine. Further morphing the lyric from third-person perspective to first, Madonna both describes and embodies a fleet-winged goddess on a cosmic journey to find a safe place in the universe. LGBTQ people can relate. We hear the song not just as an empyrean "Small-town Boy" but also as a women's music narrative. Progressing from amazement to exultance, "Ray of Light" gives Madonna's ethereal abstractions corporeality. Orbit's gizmos and guitars take us on Zephyr's sky ride, which, true to Madonna form, ends in her accelerated video on a disco dancefloor. "And I *feel*," she sings again and again, angling that last word like only she can until trailing off on a culminating "AaaahhhAAAAAHHH" that is her entire career's emotional apex. More technical singers don't often let loose enough to achieve such bliss.

I had been waiting to interview Madonna since she and I started, and in January 1998 it finally happened for *Spin*. I was among the first to hear *Ray of Light*, and days later I met her in a coffee shop near her Los Feliz home. She'd just filmed the video for "Frozen," so her hands were still covered in mehndi, but everything else was so casual that the star didn't resemble her public self. She came without bodyguards, publicists, drivers, or anything else that keeps celebrities safe but also wedges distance between them and the media. "If it looks like I just got out of bed, I did," she admitted. I had to stop myself from being dumbfounded. This was the woman who'd been playing Madonna all along.

I was sitting in a booth with my longtime friend who'd driven us from San Francisco to Los Angeles. I introduced him, but he didn't leave, so she asked with some concern if he was going to remain for the interview, and I found myself in a predicament. In the early 1980s, he contracted HIV the very first time he had sex. On our road trip, he told me that one of the hardest things for him to accept was the likelihood that he'd die before seeing Madonna fully evolve. With *Ray of Light*, she did exactly that. Impulsively, I told him to tell her this. She let him stay.

Madonna's longtime publicist, Liz Rosenberg, told me, "I think you got the most realistic interview out of her." Perhaps her ordinarily always-on client wouldn't have been so personable had I not encouraged my friend to tell his sad story with the happy ending: He's still healthy.

My approach was to do what few had done: treat Madonna like the serious musician she is. We talked about how collaboration for her extends through the entire record-making process.

"When I work with people who seem uptight, I open them up," she explained. "I try to get them to go off the beaten path, to improvise and throw the rules out the window. When I work with somebody who's very chaotic and disorganized like William Orbit, then I have the opposite effect. I toe the line and become more focused."

Female singers didn't often get the chance to prove they're this clear-sighted; they're encouraged to let men take the lead. That's why women's music and girl bands had to happen. A co-producer on nearly all her albums, Madonna doesn't surrender her authority to anyone. Every cohort I've spoken to stresses how hands-on she stays. That's how she has managed to maintain via her persistent interchange of masculine and feminine elements a queer outsider throughline.

"You really have to find that place of caring but not caring what people think," she said, "where you are desirous of things and you want to be successful and you want to make music that reaches people, but you can also detach yourself from it. That's really hard to do."

Her secret?

"Well, getting the shit kicked out of me on a regular basis is a very humbling experience. From the very beginning of my career, people have been writing shit about me and saying, 'She's a one-hit-wonder; she'll disappear after a year.' Maybe that's all been a good thing, because I've never felt like my shit didn't stink."

Being deemed ungodly sets Madonna apart from straighter superstars, and the bullying she still receives feeds her continued estrangement. Like us, she remains on a quest to find the sanctity—that ray of light—within.

After all these years, she's still searching, still critiquing. "What It Feels Like for a Girl" from 2000's *Music* begins with a sampled quote from *The Cement Garden* in which Charlotte Gainsbourg's character tells her brother that girls can look like boys because the world accepts men, yet a boy looking like a girl isn't okay because men think girldom is degrading. "When you're trying hard to be your best/Could you be a little less?" Madonna sings, mimicking the patriarchy's message that women are always too much. We also get this directive. If LGBTQ people do manage to excel, we, like all minorities, are taught to leave our truths behind, turn down our flame, and stamp out the spark that ignites it. When I was a child and idiots mistook me for a girl, they not only suggested that being an actual female was considered less-than but also that I must eradicate the ambiguities that were for them offensive. Madonna speaks our language because she's told to shut up for equivalent reasons.

Even when she slips below her musical benchmark, Madonna's visuals almost always remain on-point. Performing "Hollywood" on 2003's VMAs, she donned groom drag along with Missy Elliott in a symbolic four-way marriage to Britney Spears and Christina Aguilera that culminated with her kissing both brides on the mouth. "I am the mommy pop star, and she is the baby pop star," the singer said of Spears to Lourdes, "and I am kissing her to pass my energy on to her."

Madonna endows twenty-first-century pop to such an extent that many who missed her heyday resent that every pop heiress for whom she opened a door gets compared with her, including Katy Perry, Lady Gaga, Taylor Swift, Charli XCX, Dua Lipa, Kim Petras, and Chappell Roan. Their fans couldn't know that she made us feel like we were at the center of everything because that's where she stayed for decades.

Fame isn't the only substitute for love. So is fandom, for we live out through our idols what's not always possible in our lives. Now that I have my own family, I don't need Madonna to be my surrogate sister like I did during her provocation-packed first twenty years of uninterrupted greatness—a longer, hotter streak than anyone else's. But unlike cuddlier cultural mainstays, her lovability is enmeshed in how she still inspires loathing. That's the heart of her queerness. Everything she does asserts a thoroughly unapologetic self, as if her entire output and even her existence were an elaborate, lifelong coming out.

No one hides less than Madonna.

⏭

Chapter Forty-Five

Wham! and George Michael

Even before Wham! became global teenybop gods, George Michael spoke to us in indirect but comprehensible codes. Born Georgios Kyriacos Panayiotou, Michael—like his duo partner, Andrew Ridgeley—was the UK-born son of an English mom and an immigrant dad. Michael's father hailed from Greece; Ridgeley's papa was Egyptian. Handsome and outgoing, Ridgeley took shy Michael under his wing at school and insisted they form a band. But Michael's old man didn't believe in his son and cared less for George's ambitious friend, whom he saw as a bad influence. Ridgeley's gracious 2019 memoir plays out like a star-crossed love story, right down to Michael's parents forbidding him from their home. When that didn't work, Pops gave Michael—still in his teens—an ultimatum: Find yourself a record contract or respectable employment in six months, or leave.

"Get yourself a job or get out of this house!" Michael lashes back in the original 1982 single version of "Wham Rap! (Enjoy What You Do)." He raps over disco rooted in the same Prelude singles as early Madonna, but with punk ripostes. Like the narrator in Dire Straits's "Money for Nothing," Michael's father resented pampered rock stars; he thought they were *all* gay. So with his very first record, Michael pushes back against Pa's assimilation. Rather than being ashamed of something thought unrespectable, he owns his aberration. Although the song's lyric deals with going on the dole—as Ridgeley did—and feeling no shame whatsoever, other lines suggest Michael is defending something else: "I choose to cruise" is one of several lines from 1983's rewritten album version that jumps out to LGBTQ listeners. By its roof-raising end, "Wham Rap!" feels like queer gospel, right down to its video, in which Michael and Ridgeley suggest an even gayer *Grease*. Nearly everything about the pair, from their matching clone clothes to the knowing way they regard each other, infers that they were a couple. It wasn't until they became ridiculously famous that Ridgeley's secret was exposed: He's straight.

We all feel a twang of disappointment when a buddy finds a significant other who impinges upon our friendship. In 1982's "Young Guns (Go for It)," that chagrin is played for high gay drama. In the once-again rapped verses, Michael confronts his compadre (or lover)—played in the video by Ridgeley—about the girl on his arm. When Ridgeley introduces his fiancée, Michael spews disdain in the freedom-praising chorus, which climaxes with the condemnation "death by matrimony!" followed by tooting trumpets that smack like a chivalric glove across Ridgeley's face. Michael then foresees that his pal will forsake their fun-filled life for one he suspects will be disastrously false. Then the fiancée—Wham! backing singer Shirlie Holliman, Ridgeley's actual girlfriend—steps in. "There's somethin' 'bout that boy I don't like," she insinuates. In the video's parting shot, Ridgeley yanks off his tie as if removing a noose and follows leather-clad Michael through a subway tunnel, signifying a return to subterranean ways.

While filming the "Club Tropicana" video at Pikes hotel, Michael got it on with the Ibiza getaway's otherwise-straight proprietor, Tony Pike—the clip's mustachioed bartender—and came out to Ridgeley and Holliman. To extricate itself from a lousy contract hastily signed to satisfy Michael's dad, the duo signed with Jazz Summers, who'd later look after Scissor Sisters, and Simon Napier-Bell, a gay contemporary of Beatles manager Brian Epstein. Out went the jeans and leather. In came butt-clinging hot pants, bleach-streaked mullets, and teen-targeted material. The resulting squeaky cleanliness of 1984's "Wake Me Up Before You Go-Go" felt to me like a betrayal. Where went Wham!'s outsider satire?

That year's *Make It Big* brought it back on "Everything She Wants." Michael sings as if playing the Ridgeley of "Young Guns," who now works nonstop to satisfy his newly pregnant wife/beard. He maintains a stoic front—"I'll tell you that I'm happy if you want me to"—but failure awaits. "My god, I don't even think that I love you," he admits.

Real-life Michael found himself confined to an analogous prison of his own making. He'd created a false pop persona—a mirror reflection of Ridgeley—to mask the pressures of being a pinup who hated what he'd become. The overnight success his dad demanded swelled beyond Michael's wildest dreams, but at a cost: The singer couldn't be himself. That's hard for everybody. But for LGBTQ people who lack the self-esteem that family and society fail to nurture, inauthenticity can be lethal.

Yet his talent couldn't have been more real, particularly on the Wham! singles that exude the effortlessness of exacting craft. Both "Careless Whisper" and "Last Christmas" convey love's sorrows with timeless classicism, because Michael understood pop's mechanics. Back then I thought they were crass. Yet their creator's tragic life has since tempered their blatant commercial intent. Like any closeted teen, Michael chose safety over realness in "Careless," reasoning, "We'd hurt each other with the things we want to say." Yet only a pop prodigy could compose that undeniable sax riff or sing a vocal that glides around it in a frictionless but doomed promenade. Sung by, as its lyrics hint, "a man undercover," "Last Christmas" weighs even heavier in perpetuity. Even in a seasonal song, Michael pits the hell of his ongoing misery against the heaven of his fleeting escape.

"I was supremely confident I was writing pop classics," Michael later explained. "But I was also supremely aware that if I left the imagery a little bit more to Andrew, kids loved it. Then we were massively successful, and I went from being Andrew's shadow as a sexually confident being to being the center of attention. At that level, I lost all my confidence. I suddenly felt like a fake, so the whole thing turned me into somebody who felt the camera was my enemy."

Yet to the millions of young girls who comprised the bulk of Wham!'s audience, Michael's signature stubble and all that went with it meant hetero virility, not gay macho. If Culture Club had divulged queerness at its popularity's peak, much of its diverse audience wouldn't have been devastated. Wham!, however, then sold mostly to girl tweens. "Everything She Wants" still earns spins today because the instrumentation Michael played himself is so nonchalantly funky, but hipsters didn't queue up all night in the middle of a New York winter to buy tickets for Wham!'s local debut in 1985. I can verify that its audience would've been disappointed with real-life Georgios. They came to see Michael and Ridgeley enact the Western pop equivalent of *yaoi*, or "boys' love," a homoerotic manga subgenre designed for straight women. Enchanted by what Napier-Bell identified as Michael and Ridgeley's "erotic intimacy," the duo's young female audience fell safely in love with two dashing boys who cared deeply for each other but avoided labels to satisfy their audience's demand for illusionary availability. No out gay teen idol existed back then, because neither the media nor the public would endorse one.

Not even supersized fame could strain their friendship, so these pals intentionally pulled Wham!'s plug with its parting singles. "Wanna take you, wanna make you/But they tell me it's a crime," Michael sings in 1985's Motown pastiche "I'm Your Man." The greatest Wham! non-hit, 1986's "Battlestations," waves goodbye to a lover, but one of its rhymes also serves as a farewell to fans who only saw his façade: "I never have the guts to let you look inside/I don't think you'd appreciate the things that I hide."

While launching a Sandy Two solo strategy that left behind his teenybop twink incarnation, Michael found himself at the center of a controversy about pop's role in the AIDS crisis. Largely because former matinee idol Rock Hudson died of the disease in 1985, the mainstream finally began addressing what gay people had been battling for years. But rather than recommending condoms and safe-sex education, religious leaders and politicians preached abstinence or monogamy. For some, these were workable options. But for many, these goals were unrealistic or even more dangerous. Few then had access to the earliest blood testing or knew their HIV status, a knowledge that brought complicated challenges. Yet the government, organized religion, and other institutions preferred the illusion of easy fixes because those media-friendly methods meant nobody had to discuss subjects thought unseemly. Those in power would rather let LGBTQ folks, people of color, women, and even teens drop dead than discuss jizz in buttholes.

In the satin-sheeted video for Michael's "I Want Your Sex," the lead single from Michael's 1987 solo debut *Faith*, the singer writes EXPLORE MONOGAMY in lipstick across largely naked makeup artist Kathy Jeung, who was falsely reported to be his girlfriend. The truth was that he'd written "Sex" about a guy. The singer had fallen for French playboy Tony Garcia, yet their relationship wasn't consummated. "Sex," and all the literally horny permutations of the twelve-inch single's "Monogamy Mix" suite, is driven by unreciprocated passion that's frustrated but, finally, self-aware, which reflected Michael's shift in self-definition from bisexual to all-the-way gay. With lines like "Not everybody does it/But everybody should," the song exudes sex positivity. Some stations wouldn't play it, while syndicated radio DJ Casey Kasem refused to speak its title. The fact that gay sex was by many considered more terrifying than ever meant that even this quintessentially Sandy Two hit was framed with Sandy One messaging. Having already demanded cuts, MTV introduced each early airing of the video with Michael's spoken disclaimer: "In the past, there were arguments for and against casual sex. Then, it was a question of morality. These days, it can be a question of life or death. It's as simple as that. And this song is *not* about casual sex."

Yet like many LGBTQ artists of his day, Michael stuck a limb out of his closet door for each one hiding behind it. Launched with another flurry of leather and denim, 1987's *Faith* ramps up the hardness of Michael's performative masculinity while further exposing his softer side through vulnerabilities couched in confident, universally appealing pop. Selling more than ever, Michael averred his art's queerness by integrating what the world told us was antithetical to it.

Referencing early Elvis Presley by way of Queen's own '50s pastiche, 1979's "Crazy Little Thing Called Love," "Faith" gets manly with rockabilly guitar riffing and lyrics about Michael's bulwarking himself against someone only offering physical charms. Fragmenting his body like the era's underwear ads, its video presents its star to an LGBTQ audience as a butch gay while repositioning him to his newly adult female audience as a stud. Before the song even starts, his glutes fill the screen. Whereas Michael Jackson sang "your butt is mine" in his then-current hit "Bad," George Michael intimated that his butt is ours.

Further divergence comes via the song that matured Michael into an adult singer-songwriter, "Father Figure." Like Prince, Michael intertwines racy innuendo and romantic allegiance to honor what's sacrosanct in sexuality. It's a balm to protect him and his ungendered companion, whom he woos with allaying delivery—sighing during the ballad's verses, commanding on its gospel chorus. Both approaches are necessary, for Michael knows well the complications of loving a guy like him. "Sometimes I think you'll never understand me," he moans. Renouncing illegality, he also suggests what's verboten is a matter of perception. But the song's most brazen misfeasance comes with its simplest, most unsettling command: "Put your tiny hand in mine."

There's no evidence to suggest Michael procured children, or even chicken. Instead, "Father Figure" let him play Daddy—a celebrated status for gay men, who are otherwise taught they mustn't age—despite being only twenty-four. This was an accomplishment for someone who'd been a "Go-Go" boy only three years prior. Moreover, the song allowed Michael to celebrate forbidden desires without drawing attention to his own. LGBTQ love isn't only mistaken for a crime—it still *is* a crime in much of the world. Even now, we're criminalized on our own soil. The elements that nudge the song's lyric toward off-limits territory serve as metaphors that bring Michael as close as he could get to writing honestly without alienating his audience. For although the 1980s embraced LGBTQ musicians with a fervor we've only recently seen since, the era rarely allowed gay songwriters to call our love by its proper name, let alone top the charts with it.

On "One More Try," Michael juxtaposes his once again ungendered but this time experienced lover's authority against his own subjection. Whereas on a typical power ballad the singer often blurs the melody with melisma, Michael hits nearly every note here straight on, as if hammering home a message that pushes past the funereal organ, past the tormented lyric, into raw, psychically battered territory. He might be spinning a figurative phrase of awe when he sings of an earlier time when he was just a stranger positioned at his lover's feet, but with it he also suggests that their pained connection began with an anonymous blowjob and that its aftermath's heat is now far more dangerous.

You might think I'm being rude by reading the song in light of subsequent history, but the song's second verse does something wildly metatextual: "I wrote the song/I know it's wrong!" he sings. Protesting with a vocal force outside the easy-listening mean, that simple rhyme documents Michael's personal journey as a closeted gay person pursuing monumental fame to squash the self-hatred instilled by paternal and societal shaming. By acknowledging his entrapment, he's launching a flare. That's why he's singing to his "teacher" so desperately, then angrily—especially in the video's culmination—but lastly resigning himself to an adverse fate, admitting he'll hold on and, therefore, like Morrissey, never escape his torment.

Having seen Wham! during its upswing and then Michael at Madison Square Garden when *Faith* was on its way to twenty-five million in international sales, I was knocked out by the singer's transformation from awkward upstart to confident, consummate artist. He didn't strike me as a man conflicted by mega-stardom and his sexuality. I, like the still-screaming crowd, felt the strength of both. But as we'd eventually learn, Michael wasn't comfortable with all the mandatory deceit that went with their combination.

So he shifted gears again. Whereas *Faith* was erotic and concentrated, 1990's *Listen Without Prejudice Vol. 1* is despondent and diffuse, even as its title asks Michael's audience to not be bigoted against what he dared not directly address. As with concurrent works by R.E.M. and Pet Shop Boys, AIDS provides subtext, especially on his US chart-topper "Praying for Time," which not only documents late capitalism's economic and ecological traumas but also its spiritual lacerations: Martyrs are left "Hanging on to hope/When there is no hope to speak of."

Reprising a Wham! title to further sever from his past, *Listen*'s most-remembered hit, "Freedom! '90," extols self-expression in a compositional master class of tension and rightful release. Michael goes as far as he can to confess his sexual orientation without stating it. "There's something deep inside of me/There's someone else I got to be," he sings while tracing his career's outwardly victorious but inwardly frustrating trajectory. Embodied by the gospel strokes of his "FREEDOM!" refrain, which propels the chorus forward like a defiant fist, he brings his true self here. No longer beholden to the song's "you," the straight mainstream, Michael proclaims his artistic and spiritual autonomy in a prideful hit when we most needed a boost.

As with all *Listen* clips, the superstar refused to appear in the song's video, and although director David Fincher's gloss negates the rebelliousness of Michael's message on one level, the clip's opulent femininity reinforces it on another. Repudiating *Faith*'s machismo, Michael cast the era's supermodels (and some secondary hunks) as lip-syncing stand-ins—a gesture akin to drag, yet MTV-savvy. It echoed how glam's Roxy Music had earlier showcased stunning women on its seductive album covers as an emblem of its frontman Bryan Ferry, who looked like a leading man but moved as a femme fatale. "Freedom! '90" still ranks among the 1990s' most '90s videos.

While feuding with his record label, Sony, via a protracted court case that he ultimately lost in 1994, Michael downplayed *Listen* in concert in favor of queer-friendly pop and R&B covers, including Culture Club's "Victims." Rather than releasing *Listen*'s sequel, Michael contributed three songs to the 1992 AIDS charity release *Red Hot + Dance*. Mixing more supermodels with drag stars Joey Arias and Lypsinka to flourish the fabulousness of gay designer Thierry Mugler's costumes, the video for its "Too Funky" casts co-director Michael as the cameraman, emphasizing that what we're seeing is from his queer vantage point.

The first release on DreamWorks Records, a label co-founded by David Geffen, 1996's *Older* turns *Listen*'s plague subtext into text. Michael had lost his first soulmate since Ridgeley, Brazilian fashion designer Anselmo Feleppa, to AIDS after only two years together. The singer dedicated the album to Feleppa and fellow Brazilian Antonio Carlos Jobim, the bossa nova pioneer whose elegant airiness permeates *Older*. With Jobim's stylistic presence standing in for Feleppa, Michael brought his beau back to life. Instead of acknowledging his sexuality directly to the press, he let this elegiac, plague-shaped, LGBTQ love album largely about loss do the talking.

"To my fans and the people that were really listening, I felt like I was trying to come out with them," he later told Oprah Winfrey. By "them," he meant his updated, close-cropped clone look, the album's dedication to Feleppa, and what he identified as the disc's "fairly obvious male references." In doing so, Michael went further than his less-commercial yet also-closeted queer peers. He released an out album without being out himself.

Opening *Older*, the international hit "Jesus to a Child" depicts love as a religious experience that comforts him in Feleppa's absence and bestows upon him a nestling's innocence. Given the song's Christian imagery, Michael's male-on-male context is subversive; he's likening his gay, AIDS-afflicted sweetheart to Jesus. The song is so solemn that it feels not like a conventional ballad but a Brazilian funeral. Its end reveals that his dearest is now living only in memory. "And the love we would have made/I'll make it for two," Michael resolves, as though kneeling by Feleppa's casket.

Subsequent *Older* singles fortified this AIDS ambience. "Fastlove" seeks commitment-free sex to escape the past—an impossibility underlined by its wound-licking lyrics and prominent sampling of Patrice Rushen's 1982 disco-funk classic "Forget Me Nots." Stealthy metaphors again put the track in a man-on-man context: "Stupid Cupid keeps on calling me/But I see nothing in his eyes." "Spinning the Wheel" takes a critical look at these hookups. Michael likens to roulette the probability that his current lover—here depicted as a danger-addicted gambler—will contract STDs that will also put the singer at risk. "You're gonna bring some home to me," each chorus ends. "I won't go through it again," he sings, referring not simply to his lover's incautiousness but also the possibility that these risks may result in another casualty. Despite the song's European success, US radio nixed it.

That fate also befell "You Have Been Loved," which laments a man's passing. Its initial verse focuses on his troubled mother, who feels as though she's being punished by an unjust god. "'Take care, my love,' she said," Michael sings in the first chorus. Then with one tiny pronoun change, he sings the rest of the song from his own perspective. That shift is subtle but immense, for it confirms that the singer was the late fellow's lover. Both he and his beau's mother struggle to make sense of why their mutual treasure was so cruelly taken. Though then not allowed to legally marry another man, Michael nevertheless depicts himself as a widower through his arrangement's ghostly weightlessness.

It was momentous for a superstar on a worldwide smash album to include a threnody that mourned with us. The average listener didn't grasp this because the mainstream largely still ignored our losses. We had to tell our own stories to one another on records like this because otherwise there were few opportunities to listen and learn. Years later, *Older* co-producer Jon Douglas testified that the album helped gay fans come out and got them past suicidal periods. He knew this because that's what they wrote to him.

In 1998, Michael was arrested for "engaging in a lewd act" in a restroom in Beverly Hills' Will Rogers Memorial Park. Not since the '50s, when queer celebrities like pre-Elvis crooner Johnnie Ray were regularly ambushed, had a superstar faced this kind of scandal. Finally coming out, Michael lampooned the bust in 1998's carefree "Outside." With the lines "I'd service the community/But I already have you see," he references his crime, his sentence, and his initial status as a bubblegum bimbo. The song's video intercuts swooping, helicopter-enabled shots of alfresco couplings with similar faked surveillance footage. Dressed as a policeman in the style of Village People's Victor Willis, Michael performs in a men's room disco replete with mirrored urinals. At the end, the gendarmes who had been arresting sex offenders kiss each other incautiously before the camera pans past JESUS SAVES signs. Everyone—heterosexual and homo, cop and criminal—is concupiscent.

Like many who'd since gotten used to long stretches of inactivity from Michael, I gasped while sitting down for Christmas dinner in 2016. A wave of emails asked me to write about the singer, who died that day, aged fifty-three, as if finally destroyed by the challenges that fed "Last Christmas." I focused on his accomplishments in my tribute, but beneath my brave face, I was scared. Like many LGBTQ people, I saw myself in Michael.

His demise brought me back to 1995, when my friend Mark Finch jumped off the Golden Gate Bridge. As co-director of Frameline, San Francisco's International LGBTQ+ Film Festival, Mark helped me create *Barry Walters' Fabulous World of Queer Pop Video*, a presentation that took me to London and Austin, and filled SF's majestic Castro Theatre. Mark's dry English humor and giddy dance-pop fandom masked his depression, so his suicide stunned me. Around this time, I broke up with the guy I thought I'd be settling down with for life. This being the mid-'90s, there were other endings, too, which cumulatively became too much. I couldn't call my family, because we long ago stopped talking for the usual gay reasons. After consulting my therapist, I checked myself into the mental health wing of a local hospital because I no longer felt safe alone with myself.

To my dismay, not much else happened. I was prescribed an antidepressant. My friends came to visit. But when I left a few days later, they all thought someone else would stay with me, so nobody did. That was the hardest lesson, one I've had to learn repeatedly. I've been in therapy much of my adult life. Writing this book meant going back on psych meds. But the only one who can fully heal the trauma that comes with being what much of the world still finds unsavory is me.

Michael never accepted that. He relied on sales figures and chart positions for validation. He believed the lie that pop is quantifiable only through its marketplace value. When he couldn't duplicate his 1980s success, he felt he'd failed, even with his most audacious work. He couldn't appreciate that his vulnerability gave his art dimension. He couldn't fathom that what made him flawed also made him lovable. Worst of all, he couldn't fortify himself against the homophobia floating in the atmosphere, and so he harnessed its destruction against himself. Once he gave up on music, that became his final escape.

⏭

Chapter Forty-Six

Whitney Houston

Before I write about the mercurial character who put me through my professional paces like no other interview subject before or since, I want to discuss a particular kind of female R&B singer: those who came up after Martin Luther King Jr.'s death in the late 1960s but before MTV opened its doors to some of them in the mid-1980s. I mean the categorically Black, Aretha-era women: the divas. It's common knowledge that LGBTQ people love them, yet it's not often discussed why, so I want to shed some light.

When my parents separated because of my dad's alcoholism, he bought me an album of my choice every week, mostly rock, to compensate. After he died, when I was seventeen, I started collecting more disco: singles by Cheryl Lynn, Gloria Gaynor, and other divas. I must've craved something spiritual to get me through my grief, but I wasn't yet self-aware enough to realize that. Their records simply took me where I needed to be: that heavenly body that Lynn *zoooooooms* to in "Star Love." A few months later, I left for college in New York City, where voices like theirs kept speaking to me through WKTU, WBLS, and the stereo of my sophomore year roommate, who worked at Saks Fifth Avenue and taught me the ways of big city gayness.

What sealed my lifelong diva deal was seeing the original Broadway run of *Dreamgirls*, which featured what I still consider the most intense performance

I've ever witnessed, and that includes the Clash the night *London Calling*'s bass-smashing cover photo was taken. It was by a largely unfamiliar vocalist with a song that hadn't yet hit radio, so I had no idea what was about to hit me. This was Jennifer Holliday singing "And I Am Telling You I'm Not Going."

She did it as Effie, a character amorously attached to the manager of the Supremes-like trio the Dreams in which she sang backup. As personified by pre-diet Holliday, Effie is outsized in every way. But like most women of the 1960s, she's still dependent on men. That makes her mad and monstrous. To the heel who just fired and dumped her with one blow, she walks with ambling steps, like Godzilla stomping over Tokyo. Everything she tells him is a refusal. *No*, she won't accept that their love is now one-sided. *No*, she won't let a man determine her destiny. *No*, she won't move on. "And *you*, and *you*, and *you*," she sings to this manager, the other Dreams, and every creature in the universe: "*You're gonna love meeeeeeeeeeeeeeeeeeeeeeeeeeee!*"

By fighting for her agency with this monumental act of resistance, Effie grows like a cyclone, even as what's whirling between her outstretched hands turns illusory. The sheer force of Holliday blustering through this song, as if able to move time backward, back to when things went her way, was *unfuckingforgettable*. The audience went so berserk—hooting and hollering and willing her delusions into reality—that her cataclysmic display became victorious. She doesn't get back her man, or her place in the Dreams. But through us, her only sympathetic witnesses, Effie receives the love otherwise denied her. She stands tall in her truth, as we must.

Opening on Broadway in late 1981, *Dreamgirls* set a high-water mark in the fundamental alliance of Black and gay artists. Its cast was Black, and many key production players were gay, including composer Henry Krieger, writer/lyricist Tom Eyen, director/choreographer Michael Bennett, co-choreographer Michael Peters, and producer David Geffen. This combination united overlapping Black and LGBTQ audiences much like the singers the show symbolized. As represented by their Diana Ross–like leader (played by Sheryl Lee Ralph, who was also amazing), the Dreams depict the discipline and dignity of '60s Motown, while Holliday as Effie epitomizes the far more demonstrative women that redefined R&B in the '70s and early '80s.

In the absence of role models, pre-Stonewall gays adopted singer-actors like Judy Garland and Barbra Streisand as idols because they embodied conflicts we knew well. Subverting male songwriters' fantasies of feminine passivity, they sang against the grain with anxiety, even anger. But for the generation who grew up with the Supremes and gay lib, Aretha and the Black beauties who followed were apter paragons of transformation. Long-afflicted yet ascendent, they came of age with civil rights and feminism, and reflected both in their devout vocal tone, intrepid stage presence, and sky-high Afros, which collectively accentuated difference. Having traveled from small-town churches to big-city turntables, they wouldn't kowtow to the expectation that they should suffer guys *and* whites with a smile. Our viragoes of soul broke from all that accommodation—just like gay men left behind clichéd representations of us as helpless pantywaists, and our lesbian counterparts abandoned straight characterizations of themselves as invisible spinsters.

Echoing queer estrangement, these metaphysical matriarchs soundtracked our nighttime liberation. Similarly repudiating suppression, their veracious voices exploded in a torrent of contrasting expressions, never shying away from sensuality, even when conveying what's sacred. Like them, we're told the freedom we can't achieve in this lifetime arrives on the far side of Heaven's gate—the promise of countless Negro spirituals. If someone asks you why many LGBTQ people adore Black music, remind them of this, and add that our enemies still believe we receive our final reward only if we first renounce everything we are and love.

Models of modification and transcendence, divas bring out the best of mostly male-written material by putting interpretive flesh, muscle, and spirit on the songwriting bones. Like us, they made a world that was not built by them their own. Sharing gospel-honed insight on how to deal with love, adversity, and loss, divas expose what we're forced to conceal, becoming our preachers when the church has shut us out. This truth-telling makes most of them Black Sandy Twos.

For these reasons and more, LGBTQ people feel solidarity with Black women. We empathize with their conflicts and seek kindred resilience. We, too, strive to turn what are considered multiple negatives into positives.

With Dionne Warwick as an aunt, Leontyne Price as a cousin, and Cissy Houston as her mom, Whitney Houston boasted seriously diva-dominant DNA. In her Sweet Inspirations days, Cissy backed many R&B, pop, and rock stars, including Van Morrison, Wilson Pickett, Dusty Springfield, and, most often, Elvis and Aretha. She groomed her daughter as a church soloist and backing singer—the latter on Cissy's own 1978 disco classic "Think It Over" and Chaka Khan's 1980 Paradise Garage pick "Clouds." Between modeling gigs and singing support for Cissy's cabaret shows, Whitney cameoed on projects like 1983's *Paul Jabara and Friends*, which included the Weather Girls' epochal "It's Raining Men." Despite all this, Newark, New Jersey's finest broke the mold as a Black Sandy One.

In 1983, Whitney's mentor and record label boss, Arista's Clive Davis, introduced his discovery on *The Merv Griffin Show*. We'd recognized both Davis and Griffin as our own long before they spoke up about it; Davis came out as bisexual in his 2013 memoir, whereas Griffin just joked to *The New York Times* in 2005, "I tell everybody that I'm a quarter-sexual. I will do anything with anybody for a quarter." On his program, Whitney sang "Home" from *The Wiz*. As a Black retelling of *The Wizard of Oz*, *The Wiz* brings together R&B and gay audiences like *Dreamgirls* did, particularly in this parting song, which is to *The Wiz* what "Over the Rainbow" is to *Oz*—a secular spiritual of longing for sanctuary. In it the singer must find in herself "a world full of love/ Like yours, like mine, like home"—a message understood by people of color and LGBTQ folks alike. Branded outsiders, we must look inside our hearts to find our own haven. When Whitney nailed the song on TV as an unknown, Black and gay grapevines buzzed about this girl.

But unlike so many '70s divas, Whitney didn't launch her solo career through gay-targeted dance anthems. Davis strategically snowballed her fame by first wooing R&B radio with smooth soul singles from 1985's debut *Whitney Houston*. Initially withholding the album's obvious pop smash, he finally sent his protégé sashaying to the club crowd with "How Will I Know," its Jellybean Benitez remix, and its MTV-conquering video.

In the last of those, Whitney turns the corners of a rainbow-hued maze while chorines in new wave makeup and gaydar-triggering guy dancers leap out at her with Bob Fosse–esque moves that offer their ballet-honed bodies as potential pleasure options. But how will she find the right one? The clip coyly toys with queerness. Two girls straddle one guy, as if in a threesome. Then a fellow dressed as a groom on one side and a bride on the other pirouettes. Whitney eyes this metaphorically intersex character and smiles at the camera like she's into them. Although the clip's mainstream crossover intentions are clear—white hoofers outnumber their Black counterparts eight to two—it still positions Whitney within the gay cabaret that nurtured both her and Cissy. Participating in Arlene Phillips's choreography with bemused gusto, she's a Black Barbie strutting through a labyrinth of racial and sexual possibilities. "This love is strong/Why do I feel weak?" the rising star belts with little sense of submission. She'd rarely again be this lighthearted.

That video aside, much of Whitney's early music and image-making wasn't for me. I preferred Garage goddesses—like Loleatta Holloway, Gwen Guthrie, and Jocelyn Brown—who brandished rhythms as vicious as their vocals, and could never be, as Whitney was, accessible to many straight white men. Back then this ingenue let herself be swaddled in the same showbiz chintz and airbrushed love songs as her gay labelmate Barry Manilow. Mixing gospel, jazz, R&B, rock, Broadway, and trad-pop phrasing, like Donna Summer but with flashier vocal fireworks, she became all-conquering as a sales force yet harder to fully perceive because of the persona foisted upon her: the acceptably Black girl next door. Lithe, light-skinned, and gorgeous, she became my generation's Diana Ross.

That prefab familiarity also made her a target. In 1987, *Time* scrutinized the singer's relationship to her "tall, slim, severely handsome" best friend/roommate Robyn Crawford, who lip-syncs on the far right in Whitney's "You Give Good Love" video and worked for her much like Judy Ogle did for Dolly Parton.

"Because of their easy intimacy," *Time* insinuated, "the tattle mill has ground out the story that they are lovers. Both women shrug off the rumor. Says Robyn: 'I tell my family, "You can hear anything on the streets, but if you don't hear it from me, it's not true." Houston also alludes to family: 'My mother taught me that when you stand in the truth and someone tells a lie about you, don't fight it. I'm not with any man. I'm not in love. People see Robyn with me, and they draw their own conclusions. Anyway, whose business is it if you're gay or like dogs?'"

Crawford's 2019 memoir revealed the depth of their relationship. Not long after they met, when "Nippy" or "Nip," as family and friends called Whitney, was seventeen and Crawford was nineteen, the pair became intimate on every level. Like many Black women even now, this couple had little use for labels, and their bond proved stronger than many marriages. Only Whitney's own marriage to fellow singer Bobby Brown in 1992 challenged it.

Whitney halted the sexual component of their relationship before signing her Arista contract in 1982—a switch she formalized by giving her life partner a Bible. "She said we shouldn't be physical anymore, because it would make our journey even more difficult," Crawford writes. "She also said she wanted to have children one day, and living that kind of life meant that we would go to hell." Yet in the back of that Bible, they wrote love pledges. "We knew that God understood what we felt and that we had a bond that no one could penetrate. It would be our secret, and it would hold us together."

As her career continued, Whitney sometimes alluded to the strain of occupying overlapping communities locked in conflict. "I remember the way that we touched/I wish I didn't like it so *much*!" she sang as if to Crawford in 1987's "So Emotional," another smash from the "True Colors" songwriting team. Whitney belts the bejesus out of its poppy rock, but some Black folks didn't like it so much; at the 1988 and 1989 Soul Train Music Awards, she was booed. Fighting back, 1990's *I'm Your Baby Tonight* adds R&B friends such as Luther Vandross, as well as new jack swing's L.A. Reid and Babyface, who'd scored with Brown. In the video to its title track, the ever-shrewd director Julien Temple sends Whitney through the looking glass, where she reappears as the gender-defying bisexual actor Marlene Dietrich in her *Blonde Venus* cabaret songstress persona. A Black man lays his hand on hers, but white women also look at her lustfully. On her second trip through the mirror, she becomes all three Supremes, and when she emerges from a third, she reprises Audrey Hepburn's beatnik dance in *Funny Face*. "Whatever you want from me/I'm giving you everything," she sings. These seemingly superficial showbiz representations reveal a deeper truth: Whitney's talent—and identity—was such that she could not be reduced to any one unchanging thing.

This video manifesto foreshadowed her expansion into Hollywood with 1992's blockbuster *The Bodyguard*, its all-time best-selling soundtrack, and the biggest-ever single by a female singer. Whitney's cover of Dolly Parton's "I Will Always Love You" accentuates solitude; she's utterly alone for its pensive first forty-five seconds, joined not even by instrumentation. By holding the song's already-lengthy notes for so long that her lung power seems superhuman, Whitney exponentially magnifies the power and persistence of Parton's independence declaration. In both the song's music video and the film, all that determination is directed adoringly at a white guy. Yet it's also a Black feminist statement simply because it's one of the most heroic records by an African American woman.

This mega-hit's omnipresence is such that we've long stopped thinking about its significance, so I'm challenging you to listen anew. Can we interpret Whitney's rendition of "I Will Always Love You" as not just a metaphor for but also a manifestation of her forbidden yet persistent love for Crawford? As her partner's memoir attests, their connection didn't disappear the moment Whitney got married. Surely Crawford weighed on her mind when she recorded the song in April 1992, ahead of her July wedding to Brown. Can we, therefore, hear in its herculean strength the resilience, which Whitney still possessed but couldn't sustain, to fight the forces that irreparably damaged their relationship toward her life's end and ultimately killed her? With more than twenty-four million copies of its single and an estimated forty-five million of the film's soundtrack sold internationally, "I Will Always Love You" belongs to everyone. But is there any good reason why we can't also apprehend it as a reflection of our own eternal flame, one that, despite centuries of homophobia, racism, and all their combined devastation, can never be extinguished or erased?

Whitney's next film, 1995's Black-woman-bonding-romcom *Waiting to Exhale* yielded another soundtrack that eclipses its cinematic source. Returning the singer to church, 1996's soundtrack to *The Preacher's Wife* became gospel's all-time bestseller, but it couldn't reach her high airplay bar. The film similarly failed to make as much money as expected. R&B's crossover queen had to prove herself all over again.

This she did with her first film-free album in eight years, 1998's *My Love Is Your Love.* Packing a punch with coaching from hip-hop innovators such as our Missy Elliott, Whitney infused her most consistent and unified disc with an embattled, autobiographical approach so thorough that the liner notes include the same fiction-insisting disclaimer that most movies include in their credits. By this point, the public knew Whitney's private pain. Brown's headline-grabbing arrests for violence, drunk driving, and disorderly conduct had escalated, while she endured three miscarriages.

Underproduced by her lush standards, *My Love Is Your Love* acknowledges that life in Whitneyland wasn't like her old ballads. "Heartbreak Hotel" extends *Exhale*'s theme of women's awakening from having been wronged. Whereas star-studded R&B collaborations of this era were often empty marketing exercises, this musical Dear John letter unites Whitney, Faith Evans, and Kelly Price in contemptuous coherence. In the video, the trio accost the camera as if interrogating male emotional poverty. Unlike Whitney's early work, it feels personal.

Whitney's biggest surprise of this period was an up-tempo remix of the *My Love* cut in which she tosses out her unfaithful, lying lover, "It's Not Right but It's Okay." As Thunderpuss, ex–Hot Tracks remixer Chris Cox and gay former Kon Kan frontman Barry Harris forged it into a sound that still aurally stamps the gay raves known as circuit parties: assailing percussion, epic builds, and suspenseful drops. Back then that sound was synonymous with gay clubs, so it broke from standard practice when Top Forty radio favored Thunderpuss's mix over the hushed album version. Reframed by a doubled and fortified rhythmic pulse, Whitney seems furious.

This wasn't typically allowed of Black female superstars. In her memoir, Crawford relates that many at Arista thought that Whitney looked "too Black" and "not friendly enough" because she wasn't smiling on her debut album's cover. LGBTQ listeners, however, love it when divas get angry, because they release the resentment we, too, must repress. Thunderpuss's characteristic martial drums ramp everything else up from resignation to rage, setting Whitney in full diva-attack mode. That switch made this remix the gayest pop hit since the '80s' gender-bending heyday.

To celebrate, Whitney made a surprise appearance at Heritage of Pride's annual Lesbian and Gay Pride Dance in New York in 1999. With their dignitary at long last in their midst, the crowd went nuts—and so did she. "I'd never seen her like that," Crawford writes of the singer's crowd-fed exuberance. "Hearing Nip finally say, 'I had fun' made me sad." It had been ages since Crawford had heard her ex-lover use those words.

These acknowledgments of Whitney's LGBTQ sovereignty led to my profiling her for *Out*'s May 2000 cover story, her first and last major gay interview. Remember how Madonna spoke to me in a Los Feliz coffee shop without any of fame's trappings? My Whitney meeting in Beverly Hills—where she would die exactly twelve years later—was the opposite of that even before it started. I was given airfare and instructions to wait in my hotel room for a call. When the phone rang, I was told to get into a car that was waiting for me. I still wasn't informed of my destination. When I arrived at Le Meridien, its busy lobby, where our conversation took place, was substantially cordoned off and swarming with her staff.

The previous year, I'd stumbled into a similar scene at West Hollywood's Chin Chin restaurant, where my friend and I were randomly seated a few feet from what turned out to be Whitney. Her hulking bodyguards would've escorted us out if we gawked, but occasional sideways glances revealed this: She was sometimes just a regular person laughing with her friends. So during our interview, I decided that if the celebrity circus swirling around me got any stranger—and believe me, *it did*—I would remember the superstar enjoying Chinese food.

Having come from her costume fittings and rehearsals for both the Grammys and Clive Davis's renowned pre-show bash, Whitney wore a designer T-shirt, running pants, and a smock-like jacket, all hip-hop baggy. The rock in her wedding ring was so huge it seemed to have rolled out of a gumball machine. But covering her head was a tight checkered hood that reminded me of the eccentric Beale women in *Grey Gardens*. This clash of Compton and East Hampton made her look disjointed, even before the world witnessed her waning on 2005's reality show *Being Bobby Brown*. In 2000, we hadn't met that gal. We'd only seen her meticulously modulated media ideal. I had to forget that, forget everyone surrounding us, and focus solely on this fragile person sitting beside me with the fiery stare. She knew what I'd eventually ask.

This eminence was about to release 2000's *Whitney: The Greatest Hits* with imagery by the whimsical queer photographer David LaChapelle, whose work would also accompany my *Out* feature. Compiling ballads on one disc and dance remixes on the other, it picks up where Thunderpuss's diva-maximizing "It's Not Right" redesign left off, accentuating the singer's dual status as Middle American sweetheart and LGBTQ dancefloor priestess. "From 'How Will I Know' to 'Love Will Save the Day,' that girl's gone," she told me while surveying my test pressing. "From 'I Will Always Love You' on, that's *a woman*." Whitney had so compartmentalized herself to fit everyone's expectations that even she recognized she'd become a different person once she'd placed herself on the marriage track to Brown. Her switch from Sandy One to Two went inside and out.

We started by discussing how she first encountered LGBTQ people. "My mother's best, most beautiful, brightest audience was gay men," she reminisced.

"We used to work at Reno Sweeney [a Village cabaret modeled after the gay Bon Soir where Babs Streisand got her break]. My mother used to pack that club *out.* I mean, the queens would be *around the corner*! Around the corner, waiting to see Miss Cissy."

Whitney understood how her mom's generation of Black talent helped heal what antigay abuse did to us.

"I watched the way my mother dealt with gay people," she said. "They could tell her anything and she wouldn't trip. She'd be like, 'If so-and-so and so-and-so don't treat you right, fuck 'em! Leave 'em, and move on to the next thang.' She sang from her heart about *love*, the tragedies—the ups, downs, the *all-arounds* of love—and she somehow made you feel like you'd come out triumphant, no matter what. This had a strong hold for gay people. She'd come out in her slippers and sing. They'd love that. 'Sing, Miss Cissy!' She was *real.*"

But I sensed that Whitney talked about her mom to dodge her own issues. I also felt she wasn't seeing me for who I was. So I told her I'd been more of a clubber than a cabaret-goer, then rattled off a few hotspots where I'd danced. When I mentioned Better Days—a Manhattan joint Blacker, gayer, and rougher than the Garage—everything shifted. I could tell, in her eyes, I was no longer just a polite white gay guy, but someone who also enjoys Black queer scenes and could, therefore, handle unadulterated Whitney. She then projected that howl of hers across Le Meridien's enormous lobby.

"BAHHHHHHBY! *BAHHHHHHHHHHBY*!" she called. *Everyone*'s head turned. Her husband rushed over as if an emergency had taken place. Instead, she merely told him I'd danced at Better Days. This did not impress Brown like it did Whitney.

"Is he asking you nice questions?" he menaced. "I don't have to catch him outside, do I?"

"No—he's very sweet," she replied. "He's from *Out.*" Her tone then flipped from motherly to curt. "Pick me up some miso soup. I need miso, like *now.*"

"Wait," Brown paused. "Say that again. I like the way you said 'now.'"

"Oh *baby*," she countered. "I didn't mean it like that."

"Say it, say it," Brown chanted, jumping up and down. Then he lisped like that pink cartoon puma Snagglepuss. "*Ssssay* it! It turns me on, I *sssswear*!"

I may have been mistaken for a girl when I was twelve, but I've never talked like that. Since then, I've overheard anti-LGBTQ remarks, because some now assume I'm straight. But once again, they were coming at me directly, and from a guy whose records I rarely admired. I knew that if I spoke my mind, everything would unravel, so I thought of Whitney at Chin Chin and merely shot her a look.

"Get outta here!" she told him. "Crazy man!" Brown left and she gasped, "He is so *sick*! I love him—he doesn't give a *shit* that you're gay."

He most certainly did. And if he greeted me with a verbal gay bashing in public, what did Whitney withstand in private? For the interview's sake, I moved on. But with that, I felt the heat. Now, anything could happen. Not all of it was bad—far from it. No longer code-switching, the superstar paid me the kind of compliment she didn't give to Diane Sawyer or even Oprah. She was Nippy with me—until we got to my fundamental question.

But first Beyoncé and the other members of Destiny's Child unexpectedly showed up in scene-stealing space-hooker outfits. They had just rehearsed in costume and had been ushered in to meet the singer, yet they cowered before her as if meeting the pope. Whitney jumped out of her chair. "SAY MY NAME! SAY MY NAME!" she belted, the hook of their current hit. Once again, all eyes were on us. "I listen to you! You be *saangin'*! You're the inspiration!" she told them, her arms waving in her smock like a preacher's in his robe. One asked for a hug. Whitney granted her request, even when acknowledging that the quartet was vying for the same Grammy as her (both lost to TLC).

We realigned on the moment when the glow of her religious background faded and the media started snooping for dish. "'Who is this African American kid coming in here and singing pop music like Barbra Streisand?'" Whitney lampooned. "'We have to inspect this girl. We have to pick her apart!' Barbra had her day too, you know, as an American Jew. So did Diahann Carroll, Lena Horne. They had *real* tough issues to deal with—grinning onstage with the white people and then coming home and having to deal with civil rights issues. They picked me apart 'cause I surpassed the so-called rules. I beat the Beatles *and* the Elvises."

Black superstars at that time rarely discussed racism with white journalists so forthrightly. Whitney regarded me as James Baldwin might have, as one queer person does with another. She knew I know about discrimination firsthand. But what I didn't understand then was that she couldn't be honest with me about her sexual difference and thus spoke of her racial difference so I could still feel her struggle. Almost certainly, she sensed what I was about to ask, and that she'd need to lie, and, therefore, she wanted me to sit with her in the analogously harrowing truth she *could* discuss. Maybe this was subterfuge, but maybe that's what all minorities and women must do. We're all forced to translate our pain into something else because the world isn't ready for it straight-up. Whatever was going on, it hit me hard. Part of me wanted to hug her. Part of me didn't want to go further. But I knew I was getting to the crux of who she was and that she'd likely never again trust a reporter to go this deep.

It didn't take long at the start of her career before the apparent vacuum of her personal life was filled with a persistent rumor: The diva is a dyke. How did that get started?

"Mmmmm," Whitney hesitated. "I suppose it comes from knowing people . . . who are. I don't care who you sleep with. If I'm your friend, I'm your *friend*. I have friends who are in the community. And I'm sure that in my days of bein' out, hanging with my friends, having nothing but females around me, something's gotta be wrong with that. I ain't suckin' no dick. I ain't getting' on my knees. I can't just really sing. I can't just be a really talented, gifted person. She's gotta be gay."

With every query, she grew more animated. "Listen, I took a lot of grief for shit that wasn't me, okay, 'cause I had friends, 'cause I was close to people." Her hands waved, her eyes blazed. "But that ain't me. I *know* what I am. I'm a *mother*. I'm a *woman*. I'm heterosexual. *Period*."

You can be a mother and still be gay, I heard my inner voice say. *You can be a lesbian and still be a woman*, I wanted to remind her. But what was that going to achieve? I knew—just as I did with Brown—that if I said what I was thinking, the interview might be terminated. For the bulk of her professional career, reporters had tried to expose her as gay to bring her down. Yet here she was with a fellow LGBTQ person who wanted her to leave the closet so I could help lift her up. I can't imagine her anguish in that moment.

"But I love everybody," she continued. "If I was gay, I would be proud to tell you, 'cause I ain't that kind of girl to say, 'Naw, that ain't me.' The thing that hurt me most was that they tried to pin something on me that I was not. My mother raised me to never, ever be ashamed of what I am. But I'm not a lesbian, darling. I'm not."

"I am *a mother*, thank you," Whitney repeated. "I love to hear my child call me Mommy. That's what I am—not lesbian, not gay, not all the bullshit. . . . Sometimes I swear to you, it feels like nothing is going my way. Then I look at my little girl and know that she needs me for me and not anything else. That makes me wanna live on so much harder, 'cause I can't stand to think the world would teach her something I wouldn't teach her. That makes me live, baby."

She actually said that. Three years after her mother's death, Whitney's daughter, Bobbi Kristina Brown, was found unconscious in a bathtub, much like Whitney had been. Bobbi died six months later at age twenty-two.

Maybe in her mind, Whitney wasn't lying. Maybe she thought that because she'd stopped having sex with Crawford before morphing from private Nippy to public Whitney, that the latter wasn't and never had been lesbian. I responded by suggesting that her newly official alliance with her gay audience was not simply an opportunity to hawk a hits package but also a chance for her to set the record straight about her sexual orientation and move on.

"Listen, I *always* move on," she replied. "Nothing can stop me from movin'. What didn't kill me made me stronger, sweetie." Then she laughed. I'm sure this cheered up both of us in the moment, but now it makes me shudder.

Her defensiveness made clear that she hadn't moved on at all. The media mistrusted her, so I said I believed her when she told me she's straight. Then she flew a red flag by getting even angrier. "It's not for you to believe me!" Whitney huffed. "I don't give a shit if you believe me or not."

But she did, and I'll tell you why. After I put away my recorder and she autographed my test pressing, the singer—all animosity gone—walked me over, without prompting, to meet Crawford. I knew in that unguarded moment why the tabloids said they were lovers: Robyn is clearly lesbian. But I also sensed in this brief introduction something I didn't get from Whitney's interaction with Brown. I felt the love and peace between them. The superstar wanted to be as honest as she could with me, and this was her way of doing that. I didn't want to repeat what the tabloids did to them, and so I wrote in *Out*, "This introduction suggests these longtime friends have nothing to hide." In an ideal world, they never would. But in the unwelcoming, bigoted, homophobic world we're forced to live in, the concealment that echoed through Whitney's family and business associates proved lethal.

Nippy, not Whitney, came out to me. She did it not through words but through action, through showing me the love that Whitney had to hide.

I can't tell you if she was high or not. Whitney reminded me of friends who act as though they're always doing drugs but aren't. That's why we hit it off.

When Crawford discussed my interview in her memoir, she mentioned how relaxed Whitney seemed through most of it. Yet despite our in-person meeting, she also wrote that I'm Black. I take that as another compliment.

Soon after our interview, Nippy and Robyn went their separate ways for good. According to Crawford, the final straw came when Whitney couldn't get it together to rerecord her vocal with George Michael for a proposed dance remix of "If I Told You That." When Whitney and George did unite for a video set to the cobbled-together duet version included on *Greatest Hits*, they looked as though they were yelling at each other. There's zilch chemistry.

Instead of finding a sanctuary in her heart, like she sang about in "Home," Whitney searched for it in what ended her life. Like other stars, she couldn't be rehabilitated because drugs weren't her only problem. Too many people around her made too much money from an illusion built on self-denial. Her story is our most tragic one: Whitney had everything but lost it all because she couldn't accept that part of herself that was us. Like George, she wasn't solely culpable; music's most mainstream core wasn't ready. The whole entertainment industry, as well as her entire audience, would've had to support who she truly was: Nippy.

Since then there's been progress. Hannah Montana, such a Sandy One that she's a Disney fiction, became gender-fluid Miley Cyrus, married a man, and still calls herself queer—the new normal for Sandy Twos. But not so long ago, what happened to Whitney was commonplace. We just couldn't read about it because women like her didn't get in the papers unless they possessed her talent. None did.

⏭

Chapter Forty-Seven

Depeche Mode, Yaz, and Erasure

There are many reasons why Depeche Mode belongs in this book, but let's start with its 1984 North American pop entry point, "People Are People." Unlike the bulk of this suburban London synthpop act's large catalog—which is often bleak, erotic, and so open to interpretation that white-supremacist screwball Richard Spencer declared the group "the official band of the Alt-Right"—the band's first US Top Forty radio hit frankly confronts prejudice. Agitated by clanging and clubby musique concrète, frontman Dave Gahan barks out a melody that's bright, then soft when the quartet's androgynous songwriter Martin Gore contrastingly croons, "I can't understand what makes a man hate another man." In the video, he sings this in black eyeliner and platinum blond curls.

Back then the hetero foursome was routinely thought homo. Even as the band skyrocketed, a 1990 *Rolling Stone* feature began with its most masculine, now ex-member Alan Wilder remarking, "I've been called a faggot about 20 times today." Years later, Gore explained to Atlanta's gay magazine *David* that "People Are People" was inspired by thugs chasing and beating him. We hear "now you're punching and you're kicking and you're shouting at me" as a gay bashing, but Gore's biological father was a Black American GI; Gahan's birth dad was of Malaysian descent. In 2004, an entertainer who routinely tackles homophobia, transphobia, and racism aptly covered the song: RuPaul.

From the beginning, Depeche Mode has played out these differences in gender and sexual nonconformity. In the group's video for 1981's "Just Can't Get Enough"—a new wave staple and still a fixture of the band's setlist—its members shimmy their skinny hips in brazen leather-man drag. Not even the genuine homosexuals of Bronski Beat would look this gay.

"We were living in Basildon, which is about thirty miles from London," the group's initial main songwriter Vince Clarke reminisced to me. "Going to London was a *huge* adventure. Dave Gahan was the one who would go to the Blitz club there, so he was much more exposed to that New Romantic movement. He was always trendy and very hip, so we looked up to him."

Suburban and younger than the big-city New Romantics, these impressionable Depeche kids absorbed the always implicit, yet often explicit LGBTQ ideals of that futurist scene. On the quartet's 1981 debut album *Speak & Spell*, the first of many released in North America by Sire Records, Clarke sometimes gives his precociously perky tunes homoerotic lyrics. "Take me for a ride," he recommends via Gahan in "Boys Say Go!" In "What's Your Name?," the chorus repeats "Hey you're such a pretty boy" so many times that it becomes an unabashedly enthusiastic, unquestionably queer love song. This, remarkably, wasn't his intention.

"I'd just discovered songwriting," Clarke said of those songs. "I wasn't trying to write a deep and meaningful lyric. I was just thinking, 'What rhymes with lover?'" He hadn't even known any gay people until befriending Stephen Luscombe of Depeche Mode's 1981 opening act Blancmange, a UK synthpop duo that soon scored its own hits, like 1983's "That's Love, That It Is," another Saint standby.

While "Just Can't Get Enough" was still filling dancefloors, Clarke left the band he'd led. But the implications of that video's butch clone look linger via the group's subsequent principal songwriter, Gore. In 1984's gay "black party" standard "Master and Servant," he lauds BDSM as a metaphor to represent patriarchal power struggles. "It's a lot like life!" the song's Queen-like a cappella opening choir reports. Once again, in the video Depeche doesn't look remotely straight. Leather-clad Wilder tows and twists leather-festooned Gore around on a chain as if in a Kenneth Anger flick, in time to the track's jackhammers, whips, and screams.

Between the release of "People Are People" and its belated US Top Forty breakthrough the following year, the band released 1985's "Shake the Disease." It's not about AIDS, but if the plague was on your mind, you couldn't *not* make that connection, especially with the video, in which each member of the band is shot askew, floating through domestic scenes as if in illness-induced hallucination. Gahan sings a melody of ominous beauty that once again vocally hands off to Gore. Alone in an empty room, shirtless in a leather jacket, with his face painted even heavier than before and his hair so bleached-white it glows, the songwriter repeats "understand me," taking his tune up and back down in subdued urgency while the camera slowly closes in. This shot is one of pop music video's queerest moments for it reflects LGBTQ vulnerability at a time when AIDS eroded our physical and emotional well-being. KROQ listeners voted it 1985's song of the year.

Depeche further reconciled melancholia with dance on 1986's *Black Celebration*, but the US mainstream looked the other way until 1987's *Music for the Masses*, after which this quasi-gay weirdo band sold out the Rose Bowl, playing to more than sixty thousand fans in Pasadena, California. I'd long been a Mode-fixated homo, but somehow didn't see Depeche in concert until the Madison Square Garden stop on that tour. Rather than coldly approximating those records, everything eclipsed them to generate maximum emotional heat, right down to the opening act, Voice Farm, a gay San Francisco duo replete with dapper outfits and choreography that would've upstaged any ordinary headliner. Like Stevie Nicks, Gahan twirled, but way faster, as if propelled by gyroscopic force. Gore singing "A Question of Lust" in leather shorts and a chain-festooned halter provoked squeals from girls *and* grown men. Not even New Yorkers had seen anything like it beyond Christopher Street. "Dave Gahan has become an accomplished bum wiggler," Neil Tennant once wrote before he and fellow Pet Shop Boy Chris Lowe made a thing out of standing still.

Mostly I remember the rush I got from that concert's rendition of the song that climaxes Depeche concerts even today, "Never Let Me Down Again." Since the Rose Bowl concert film *101*, "Never" has become an arm-waving rocker, even though it's not really rock despite its guitar-sampling intro and Led Zeppelin–esque drums. Like every 1960s song with the word "high," "Never" metaphorically deals with drugs—or, in this case, the dread of returning to the numbing normalcy from which self-medication temporarily respites. Yet more literally it illustrates male intimacy. "I'm taking a ride with my best friend," it begins, perhaps unconsciously echoing "Boys Say Go!" Gahan sings the verses mostly on one terrestrial note, but on the chorus, he's buoyed by higher Gore harmonies that manifest an accord that is more than chummy. As they start flying, the song levitates.

This invincible glide—further emphasized at the arrangement's peak by a sampled choir howling an operatic huzzah—conjures the refuge that LGBTQ people create in one another's arms. There, at least in private, those who hate us can't touch us. If you've experienced the song in concert, you know this is an exalted, erotic zone. In *101*, Gahan sweats through his clothes as if having the ride of his life. "He knows where he's taking me," he sings of his playmate, weighting each word to suggest what cannot be said. Like a junkie chasing an eternal fix, we never want to put our feet back down on the same soiled ground as our adversaries.

Soon after Depeche attained sweeping success with 1990's *Violator*, Gahan became one of music's most self-destructive addicts. In 1995, he slashed his wrists like the protagonist of the group's goth ballad "Blasphemous Rumours." The next year during the last of several overdoses, his heart stopped for two minutes, which prompted him to clean up. Gore struggled another decade with alcoholism.

While merging further with rock on subsequent albums like 1993's *Songs of Faith and Devotion*, Depeche Mode lost much of its visual and musical gender neutrality. Yet like others in this book, the remaining duo of Gahan and Gore still models how to maintain outsider identity within the mainstream, much like our own coming out. In doing so, we proclaim ourselves separate from the majority, which frees us to find our place and peace among it, even in opposition.

After leaving Depeche Mode, Vince Clarke partnered with local punk/blues singer Alison Moyet, and their resulting brief success surpassed Depeche's own then. Sire launched Yazoo—or Yaz, as Clarke and Moyet were known in North America for legal reasons—with "Situation," the European B-side added to domestic pressings of the duo's 1982 debut *Upstairs at Eric's*. A push-pull of desire and disgust driven by smarting keyboards and Moyet's ravenous vocal, its conflicts invite interpretive leaps. When I first heard the rhyme in which the singer soulfully fumes in a tenor rage that nations are standing against a gender-ambiguous "lover" who should be treated as a "brother," I naturally thought Moyet was a Black gay man railing against racial and sexual injustice, rather than a straight white British gal who resembled a new wave lesbian. Remixer of many Paradise Garage treasures, François Kevorkian added dubby effects on his immaculate US mix, which made "Situation" even more of a Black gay club jam.

Having departed Depeche Mode after one album, abandoned Yaz after two, and then pursued one-off projects that only produced singles, Vince Clarke in the mid-'80s seemed as though he couldn't stick with anything. What followed, Erasure, didn't seem built to last, either. At first, it was Yaz redux. Singer Andy Bell began as Moyet's vocal doppelganger, and when he came out at the duo's launch, the only surprise was that Clarke isn't gay, too—especially because both dance the cancan in drag in the video for 1985's debut single "Who Needs Love Like That."

"When our first album didn't do anything, we played every shitty venue in England, and it drew us together," Clarke recalled. "It made us strong because we're both facing the same humiliation, but it's not actually humiliating because there's someone there with you." Allyship happens this way.

And just like Depeche, Erasure soon became teen-mag pinups overseas, even as 1987's "Hideaway," about a boy's coming out, spoke to us more specifically. What's notable about the duo's 1988 North American breakthrough on Sire with *The Innocents* is that both of its US pop radio hits feature LGBTQ-relevant messaging.

"Chains of Love" tackles the dilemma queer songwriters face when trying to get our love songs past straight gatekeepers. "How can I explain/When there are few words I can choose?" Bell begins. If he picks a masculine pronoun to address his honey, doors will close. A female one would be false, so he looks back on an easier time, before AIDS and its resulting wave of renewed antigay mistreatment. Aiming to rise above our challenges, he beckons the listener to join him and his "baby"—one of the few gender-nonspecific words he *can* choose—to break the shackles that stop us from not only embracing who we want but singing about it, too.

"A Little Respect" poses a question in its second verse that relates to "Chains." "What religion or reason/Could drive a man to forsake his lover?" Bell sings. "Lover" is also among the few words LGBTQ people can chose as a synonym for a same-sex sweetheart. It isn't a deal-breaker for straight listeners because it's ambiguous, yet it signals "gay" to us. Religious and civic strictures are this song's chains of love, and why Bell's relationship falters. He and his mate struggle to respect each other because society disrespects them—even through limitations on language.

"A Little Respect" never fails to send queer dancers' arms to the sky. In concert, it's an LGBTQ hymn. Shifting the song's subject from his lover to the listener and back again through differing applications of "you," Bell reaches out to those who've oppressed us and begs them to respect him and every other LGBTQ person.

"Those songs weren't written for that reason," Clarke pointed out. "They became that. When we now do shows in the US, people will say to us, "A Little Respect" that changed my life.' Or 'That really helped me when I was a teen.' When Andy forgets the lyrics onstage, as he often does, the audience fills in the blanks." We also do this through the meaning we bring to Erasure's music.

As Bell outgrew his Moyet mimicry, he proved himself a galvanic performer in angel wings, boas, and showgirl tulle, suggesting Liberace crossed with Rudolf Nureyev. The more Bell reveled in his queerness, the brighter his charisma burned. "I'd had enough of being bullied," he explained, "so I thought I'd put myself out there, as outrageous as I could be, so there was nothing more that people could say."

A UK hit in early 1990, "Blue Savannah" became a "morning music" staple, especially via Shep Pettibone's "Out of the Blue Mix," which inexplicably remained promo-only. Like Raul Ramirez's ABBA transformation on Disconet, you could only hear its up-tempo-yet-languid lushness late at night on the gayest dancefloors. Gen X circuit queens still swoon at its memory.

Disco's women have long sung songs in which they lay into a loser they long venerated but now loathe. Riposting men who romance like Romeos while acting the rogue, Erasure's "Love to Hate You" from 1991 strips this preservation practice down to diva metatext. Every chorus segues into the recognizable violin riff from disco's greatest self-loving/you-hating anthem, Gloria Gaynor's "I Will Survive." This, too, engenders a hands-in-the-air moment on LGBTQ dancefloors. Renouncing these cads with our victory dance, we, too, have survived.

Erasure reiterated its queerness by way of 1992's *Abba-esque*, a four-song EP of ABBA covers that became a smash nearly everywhere but the US, much like Queen's "I Want to Break Free." Once again, the likely reason for this discrepancy was a cross-dressing video. Portraying Benny and Björn in male attire, Bell and Clarke re-create ABBA's already goofy "Take a Chance on

Me" clip by also donning trashy Anna-Frid and Agnetha drag. Just as Bell fought back against his bullies with tutus, their sparkles here pay tribute to the Swedes while delivering a smiley-faced fuck-you to detractors who thought Erasure too pop, too queer, too *too*. At times, Clarke serves total Agnetha realness, yet there are also moments when he can't keep a literally straight face. This proved so contagious in Europe that it kicked off a rebirth of ABBA's popularity.

US Top Forty radio went instead for one of Erasure's subtlest, 1994's "Always." Produced by early Human Leaguer Martyn Ware, it retains Erasure's trademark synthpop twinkle, but its balladry is nearly operatic, both in Bell's rhapsodic performance as well as in the song's pathos. The singer beckons his companion to present his authentic self and come out to strengthen a bond that'll warm the cold and brighten the dark. "There will be no shame," Bell promises. To illustrate this, something unusual in pop this pretty takes place: a 5/4 measure at the end of each chorus. Every time Bell sings "Oh love," an extra beat flutters, as if his heart flip-flops. But its pulse, like Bell's devotion, keeps gently beating.

This is a metaphor of LGBTQ existence. Feared by many and scolded with religion, we're prone to that emotion Bell aims to avoid: shame. Yet if we cleave together, "Always" suggests, we'll stay steady. That's why David McAlmont—a gay Black Brit I rank among our generation's greatest living vocalists—sang it via video for my wedding to my dearest.

Following this final brush with the US establishment, Erasure returned to its original cult status in America while moving in and out of the mainstream abroad. Well after Madonna's Maverick label released 1997's *Cowboy*, the duo's LGBTQ content and club hits kept coming. It's now estimated that Erasure has sold some thirty million records. Bell was out for every one of them, and in 2004 went public with his HIV-positive diagnosis. Way back in 1991, *Entertainment Weekly* criticized his "Everywimp vocal stylings," but that just goes to show how wrong some can be while bashing us.

⏭

Chapter Forty-Eight

New Order

Rendering the buzzsaw guitars of punk strange through sonic manipulation that conveys estrangement, Joy Division's small output epitomizes an alienation not specific to LGBTQ people but familiar to those of us who feel an anguish that exceeds what pop typically articulates. On sad songs like 1980's "Love Will Tear Us Apart," Ian Curtis croons in a bass tessitura as if biologically destined to manifest depression, yet he could also convey elation from those depths. After he killed himself one month before that single's release, the surviving threesome named itself New Order, added keyboardist/guitarist Gillian Gilbert, and incorporated club music into its rock.

Gigging extensively in New York nurtured New Order's dusky danceability. Watch the *Taras Shevchenko* video, filmed in 1981 at the same Ukrainian National Home where David Mancuso later resumed his Loft parties, and imagine me standing within grabbing distance of bassist Peter Hook. I've rarely had a crush on a musician, but at that show a severe one began. In his scruffy beard, a new wave anomaly, Hook looked so serious, and with his bass hanging low, barely within reach, I found him and everything he played positively magnetic. Transfixed, I feared looking elsewhere, as though my thoughts could be read across my face, all caps. *COULD HE SEE THEM?* All four members emulated Kraftwerk's performance-art sense of anti-performance, even as drummer Stephen Morris walloped his kit. Guitarist Bernard Sumner could never replace Curtis's resonant croon, but Hook's sonorous basslines made the band sing.

Drawing from the distinctive kick-drum pattern on Donna Summer's "Our Love" and the octave-jumping bass of Sylvester's "Mighty Real," 1983's "Blue Monday" captures the nascent hi-NRG sound while taking it further from its soul origins. Back then LGBTQ clubs still favored Black divas, while the exceptions aped ABBA's pop polish. Lacking both, Sumner sings bitterly of being manipulated by a partner, as so many R&B women have done. There's no chorus: only three verses of decreasing length. Circling back to his opening lines, Sumner's closing incrimination—"Tell me how does it feel/When your heart grows cold?"—could have been lifted from Diana Ross.

Yet Sumner's delivery is anti-diva, still evoking Curtis but detached, barely musical. Inspired by Ennio Morricone's soundtrack for the spaghetti western *A Few Dollars More*, Hook's six-string bassline—the track's emotional center—conjures dueling cowboys as it magnifies the lyric's tension to melodramatic dimensions. That bassline is as virile as the song's synthetic choir, sampled from Kraftwerk's "Uranium," is ghostly. Much of the rest comes from a sequencer Sumner built from a kit. But the track's synthesis of disparate elements meant New Order coalesced a punk-disco fusion that was as instrumentally perfect for gay clubs—its jet-like woosh midway through even approximates an amyl nitrite rush—as it was for new wave nightspots. Atop the most pugnacious four-on-the-floor drum programming of its day, it crests, falls, and rises again: a cathartic man-machine symphony that signified the era's metronomic gay masculinity.

Although "Blue Monday" became an instant Danceteria smash, LGBTQ clubs first preferred its instrumental B-side dub, "The Beach," much for the same reason that our DJs often favored instrumental versions of otherwise gay-friendly Italo-disco records with wonky, heavily accented singers: Sumner could not yet sing well. Those DJs eventually played the A-side as it became one of the 1980s' everlasting records partially because of its pop inaccessibility. Unlike virtually every other dance hit, there was no radio-ready single edit until "Blue Monday 1988," a US remix. And like most New Order songs, its title is never sung. At two million copies, it's still the best-selling twelve-inch single of all time.

On the same July 1983 day that New Order played the Paradise Garage—while the club's DJ, Larry Levan, toggled a joystick that made the band's performance ricochet in circular surround sound—a college friend and I sneaked into the club and spotted Sumner. The two of us improvised a story of wanting to interview him for a newsletter issued by Vinylmania, a record store specializing in Garage tracks, but mostly we just wanted to meet the band. Sumner agreed right then and there. I was still a year away from becoming a professional journalist, but I managed to hide my giddiness, even during what still ranks as the most unexpected event in my long career as a music critic and avowed homosexual.

Out of nowhere, Hook jumped onto a bench facing us, dropped his sweatpants, and waved at me the first uncut cock I'd ever seen. *WHAT WAS HAPPENING? Was he reading my mind?* Or had I somehow hypnotized him like he'd done to me at the Ukrainian National Home? When I profiled New Order for *Spin* ten years later—as they sunned themselves beside a Los Angeles hotel pool—Hook, clad only in a Speedo, admitted he didn't remember his stunt at all. "We made Mötley Crüe look like kindergarten children, but we kept quiet about it," Sumner later told me of the band's hard-partying ways.

As New Order accumulated more club and alternative-radio hits, Sumner developed his own expressive vocal style, best heard on "1963," the B-side to 1987's US pop breakthrough "True Faith." A murder ballad in synthpop clothing, it's largely sung by someone pleading for their life. The second verse shifts to an omniscient narrator who sets a heterosexual marriage context, but the perspective shifts back mid-verse to the victim. "Johnny, don't point that gun at me," Sumner sings, as though still in love with the brute even seconds before being fatally shot. This is the happy-sad simultaneity of Motown taken to its logical extreme, and it's in the context of a straight narrative that sounds like a gay love song.

For those of us who grew up with movies in which the LGBTQ character always meets an early end, this made perfect sense. It certainly did for me: Right after the release of "1963," my first boyfriend, Mike, died of AIDS.

⏭

Chapter Forty-Nine

Pet Shop Boys, Dusty Springfield, and Liza Minnelli

Before conquering the world with Chris Lowe as the synthpop duo Pet Shop Boys, Neil Tennant wrote for *Smash Hits*, a British music magazine and camp hotbed. Assigned to interview Sting in New York, Tennant also made sure that he met Bobby Orlando, who co-wrote, co-produced, and played all the instruments on 1982's "Native Love (Step by Step)" by Divine, the drag superstar of several deliciously recalcitrant and queer films that made his director John Waters a trash-cinema legend. Orlando had similarly inaugurated his production career with Jayne County when she was billed as Wayne County but already presenting as a woman. (Her 1976 debut, "Max's Kansas City," captures the moment when glam begat punk.) After that, Orlando devoted himself to DIY disco that paralleled the hi-NRG Patrick Cowley pioneered in San Francisco. Orlando's cheap synth productions achieved regional US radio success and sometimes even cracked the European mainstream. But the Bobby O sound most came alive in LGBTQ clubs, where its Spandex sheen blended with hi-NRG and new wave. While lunching with Orlando, Tennant told the producer that he and Lowe wanted to make records like his.

A few weeks later, the pair did just that. Initially issued in 1984, Orlando's original production of Pet Shop Boys' "West End Girls" didn't ignite most LGBTQ dancefloors, because our DJs rarely played tracks like it during the night's peak. Finding a new manager in Tom Watkins, a gay graphic designer whose company created artwork and ads for Frankie Goes to Hollywood, Tennant and Lowe landed at EMI, where they rerecorded the Orlando material, mixed it with ballads, and launched a three-year stretch during which they were among the world's most successful musicians.

The twenty-first century has generated hip-hop so laid back it's known as mumble rap. But in the mid-80s, hip-hop was defined by Run-D.M.C. and LL Cool J—Big Apple emcees who shouted like rock stars. So it was startling to hear a white North Englander rhyme with the insouciance that Bernard Sumner brought to New Order. Tennant rapped about class relations, commerciality, and, subtly, us, too: "Which do you choose, a hard or soft option?" One of Bette Midler's more recent Harlettes, Helena Springs, adds a dab of diva drama on the 1985 rerecording of "West End Girls." As with so much gay-favored dance music since Motown, the contrast between mood and delivery emphasizes the record's opacity. We've since heard emotionally ambivalent hip-hop interrupted by impassioned pop choruses so many times that many have forgotten that the Pets bucked convention decades before Drake.

Dodging queries about their sexuality for a decade while reveling in queer idiom, Pet Shop Boys were well served by this mutability. Whereas most Wham! videos at least gave Andrew Ridgely a guitar to substantiate that he's somewhere on the records, nearly all early PSB videos feature Lowe doing not much more than looking good and glum in hats. That prompted the question: Why is he there at all? Lowe co-writes and plays plenty of the music to which Tennant sets his lyrics, but you wouldn't know that from the clips in which Lowe does absolutely nothing. In comedy-duo terms, Lowe is the straight man. Because his visual passivity was initially so over the top it's camp, he first came across to hetero viewers as the John Oates to Tennant's Daryl Hall, but we read him as the bookish singer's miserable rough-trade boyfriend. That dynamic made the chorus to "Opportunities (Let's Make Lots of Money)"—which boasts, "I've got the brains/You've got the looks"—so convincing that many didn't understand it was meant to satirize Thatcherites.

Although the Boys weren't lovers, 1986's debut, *Please,* begins and ends with relationship songs that suggest otherwise. The opening "Two Divided by Zero" reads as a statement of intent culminated by the closer, "Why Don't We Live Together?" The latter sometimes infers gender fluidity—"The woman in me shouts out/The man in me just smiles"—but mostly it's Tennant's nudging inflections and how his tenor ascends to falsetto that certifies an identity other than straight. There's more than a little Amanda Lear in his vocal DNA.

That is only a small part of why 1987's *Actually* features hits ranking among pop's most complicatedly queer. "It's a Sin" addresses Tennant's Catholic schooling with cloak-and-dagger clashes of European art song and orchestral samples that crack like flogging. The narrator is taught to be pure but fails, for everything and everyplace he's done, will do, has been to, or will visit is sinful. Such broad strokes made this widely relatable yet relevant to us, especially when the Vatican's declination to budge on its anti-condom stance during the AIDS crisis confirmed that they thought us better off dead. Gothic hi-NRG situates the song in an LGBTQ context, and Derek Jarman oversaw the video's homoeroticism. As Lowe holds Tennant in chains, the camera lingers over Lowe's crotch—an image that adorns European twelve-inch singles of Ian Levine's remix. But the most extreme thing about "It's a Sin" is its success. Topping more European charts than even "West End Girls" and going Top Ten in North America remains an unparalleled achievement for a song that critiques religion from our queer vantage point.

The next hit, "What Have I Done to Deserve This?," marks one of pop's loveliest LGBTQ collaborations on two levels. It's co-written by Allee Willis, the lesbian songwriter who helped write Earth, Wind & Fire's "September" and "Boogie Wonderland." It also reintroduced Dusty Springfield, the British Invasion singer who in 1970 confessed to the *Evening Standard*, "I'm perfectly as capable of being swayed by a girl as by a boy." Springfield and Tennant duet about wanting different things but somehow end up together, fall apart, bemoan that they're both single again, and at the end wonder if they can work something out. There's whimsy in the song's contrast between its kvetchy title, repeated in monotone, and its melody, which takes flight during the Willis-written bridge. Logically, solitude should be better than clinging to a partner who wants what can't be delivered. But if you consider the real-life sexuality of both singers, the record gets even droller when they conclude that it's not. Their voices evince this accord by merging into one inerrant sigh of blue-eyed and blessedly queer soul.

To those tuned into the Pets' gay coding, "Rent" hints that Tennant plays a "rent boy"—British slang for hustler. Yet much of its lyric more strongly suggests he's portraying a mistress. The tune soars as she acknowledges her comfort, yet returns to earth as she laments the freedom she's lost. With every chorus, this kept woman repeats pop's most brutal line: "I love you, you pay my rent." Critiquing male-female relations with the acerbity of women's music, Tennant sings the caged bird's song.

Around this time, Tennant and Lowe started writing and producing equally enlightened hits for women. Pairing the resilience of "I'm Not Scared" to a big-voiced diva would've been ordinary. Instead, Eighth Wonder's Patsy Kensit enacts their Eurobeat melodrama with a baby-doll chirp that testifies even femmes can be tough. PSB's song for the 1989 historical drama *Scandal*, Springfield's "Nothing Has Been Proved," oozes cinematic opulence from David Lynch accomplice Angelo Badalamenti, whose mutedly tense orchestration suits the suspenseful singer. Her 1990 comeback, *Reputation,* is full of LGBTQ contributors, including Willis, Lauren Wood, Dan Hartman, and the Pets. Their gay club favorite with her, "In Private," contrasts confidential affection against public fronts. When in 2006 they rerecorded it as a duet between Tennant and Elton John, its latent LGBTQ connotation became blatant.

The grand tsunami of gayness came when Tennant and Lowe produced, played on, and wrote much of Liza Minnelli's foray into contemporary pop, 1989's *Results*. Despite having recorded several albums dating back to when she was a teenager, the daughter of Judy Garland and the secretly bisexual film director Vincente Minnelli never had a US hit single. All of her previous albums took a variety-show approach; rarely did they address her personal journey.

"I was a sensitive kid in a dysfunctional family," she told me with some understatement when *Results* was new. "I'd take what was painful, not deal with it, then use it in a song. Or, if I couldn't understand what I was feeling, I would find a song that expressed it. So, when I had a crush on a boy in school and didn't know why I was so confused, my father would put on *Ella Sings Gershwin*. I'd hear, 'I could cry salty tears/Where have I been all these years?' [from "How Long Has This Been Going On"] and think, 'YES! That's how I'm feeling!'"

Despite her Broadway background, Liza's aha moment as a young artist was catching an early US performance by Charles Aznavour, the Armenian-French singer-songwriter whose 1972 song "Comme ils Disent"—rereleased in 1973 as "What Makes a Man," which Liza would later sing live—remains the most heartrending but accurate musical depiction of that era's drag artists. Aznavour was for her what David Bowie was to so many others—the figure whose ability to lose himself in his music's characters was so absolute that his fans did the same.

Liza saw in Tennant and Lowe kindred souls. "They were speaking on their records over these heavy dance tracks that really bounce you around," she said, "but with minor-key, weird, beautiful melodies and bittersweet, almost Noël Coward-y words that were very sophisticated. I mean, 'I love you, you pay my rent'—I understood that lady." The three hit it off so well that PSB agreed to oversee her entire album, which meant that for the first and only time Liza would work with pop equivalents of Bob Fosse and Martin Scorsese—uncompromising auteurs who create thoroughly coherent worlds for their performers to occupy. She could do what she'd always done with her longtime gay collaborators, the Broadway songwriters John Kander and Fred Ebb, but with a better beat, and come closer to her teenage inspiration. With the Pets, she could be a synthpop Aznavour.

"They knew who they were writing for," she said of Tennant and Lowe.

"Onstage, they're the Pet Shop Boys. In the studio, they're massively enthusiastic and talkative and silly, yet so precise. They really made me work, and I loved it."

I asked her if she knew they were gay—she didn't. "There are, I don't know, a *lot* of straight songwriters," she replied, "but I've never met any, really—*really*!" Thinking of her bisexual ex-husband Peter Allen, I struggled not to laugh and failed.

Then I told her that the urgency she brings to the work of her gay accomplices resonates with those of us who are told we must keep a lid on our feelings. "There are so many things we're not allowed to say," she reasoned, "and maybe that's exactly what I've found in the music. I can be strong. I can be ballsy. I can be what I can't necessarily pull off in real life. All the songs Kander and Ebb write that I love so much are about 'GET OUT OF THE WAY! I'M GONNA MAKE IT! I don't care if what happened was crappy—*this* will be better. And if it's not, that will be okay, too.'"

Then she left for *The Arsenio Hall Show*, where the host disdained disco to his legendary guest who'd practically lived at Studio 54. *Results* went Top Ten in the UK, sold well throughout much of Europe, and conquered LGBTQ clubs worldwide via its clubby remake of Stephen Sondheim's "Losing My Mind." Although I served as *The Advocate*'s pop music columnist for a decade, our interview for that magazine was never published. But I still have the David LaChapelle glossy she autographed. "You were the first who understood," Liza wrote. I try to remember that when I'm feeling insecure, which is often.

At the 1980s' end, Pet Shop Boys went from what Tennant coined the duo's "imperial phase"—a phrase that's since joined the pop-criticism lexicon to describe when an entertainer can do no wrong—to a second stage, in which its output became even more expressive but less commercially successful. In

1987, their imperial phase reached its apex with PSB's hi-NRG-yet-mournful rendering of the pop standard "Always on My Mind": A 2014 BBC poll deemed it the greatest cover version of all time. That phase stopped with next year's "Domino Dancing," a side trip into Latin freestyle, the genre that birthed Exposé and other dance-pop acts usually from Miami or NYC. Like Noel's eerie 1987 freestyle apogee "Silent Morning," "Domino Dancing" could be heard at face value—a faithful lover rebuking a wayward one—or as a chilling AIDS commentary. Over Exposé kingpin Lewis A. Martineé's Cuban trumpets and guitar, Tennant sings "watch them all fall down" while his amour's tricks drop like dominoes. Set in Puerto Rico, its video is ostensibly hetero but favors hunky shirtless boys. The straight male gaze couldn't accept this, so the single became the Pets' final US pop radio hit.

The mood-establishing opener of 1988's dancefloor-directed *Introspective*, "Left to My Own Devices" juxtaposes Trevor Horn's gloriously grandiose production against Tennant's calmly rapping report of a typical day that's interrupted by childhood memories many of us find familiar. "I was a lonely boy, no strength, no joy," he recounts. While maturing, the narrator surrenders to his inner voice's accompaniment—"Che Guevara and Debussy to a disco beat." Combining all three, the track peaked circuit parties for years because it gave us hope: This once-isolated lad now leads the contented life he deserves by actualizing seemingly unobtainable ambitions.

When "Devices" stalled on US radio, *Results* underperformed in North America, and *Reputation* failed to get a domestic release, Tennant and Lowe didn't bounce back with blatant commerciality. Instead, 1990's *Behavior* added ex-Smiths guitarist Johnny Marr and more Badalamenti while dialing down the duo's danceability, despite being co-produced by Giorgio Moroder's former conspirator Harold Faltermeyer. The queer content on tracks such as "Nervously" is—like the album itself—more nuanced. But *Behavior* is mostly beloved by us because it opens with one of the era's greatest gay achievements: "Being Boring."

As suggested by the 1989 B-side "Your Funny Uncle," Tennant lost a best friend to AIDS. "When we were teenagers we would always discuss that we wouldn't settle for boring lives," the singer recounted. In the early '70s, that friend threw a party. Its invitation included a quote from Zelda Fitzgerald's feminist essay "Eulogy on the Flapper," which advocates ambition to avoid boredom.

Accordingly, Tennant positions the first verse of "Being Boring" in the liberated 1920s defined by the Fitzgeralds: Inspiration comes from those who open doors of opportunity, but the Great Depression will soon close them. Set in the similarly freewheeling 1970s, the second verse echoes the leaving-home theme of Bronski Beat's "Smalltown Boy" but with a warning: Carelessness may lead to emptiness. In the final verse, the narrator lives in the just-begun 1990s. He sums up the calamitous loss that came with AIDS in two terse lines: "All the people I was kissing/Some are here and some are missing."

Not only is he hinting he's gay, the singer strongly suggests that his friends and former partners are already dead. This small statement broke a vast silence. Even back in the 1960s, when countless US musicians lost their peers in Vietnam, few hits acknowledged catastrophic absence. Tennant follows Fitzgerald's advice and far exceeds his dreams. But his friend—the greater part of the song's "we," who grew ill just as Tennant became a star, and its beloved "you"—never got that chance. We all mourned friends like these, and others followed. Indeed, many then consoled by "Being Boring" are now long dead. Forgive me for returning to this topic, but it's crucial that you know this.

In earlier 1990, right before PSB recorded *Behavior*, Stock Aitken Waterman released one of its most effective records, Kylie Minogue's "Better the Devil You Know." Like nearly all SAW songs, "Devil" features a subtly dissonant ascendant modulation between its verses and chorus that's almost unconsciously unsettling yet edifying. PSB configured "Being Boring" the same way, but most of its vocal melody wanders beyond its chords, which further illustrates Tennant's dislocation. The narrator doesn't explode with repressed pains. Instead, he whispers as if in prayer, elevating only slightly for his chorus's higher plane while knowing others he kissed will also soon be six feet under. In doing so, he encourages the listener to feel his loss for him. That's why "Being Boring" ranks for my generation among our saddest songs despite its vivacious video by the bisexual photographer and filmmaker Bruce Weber. "Boring" pulls us in because it's so eloquently, elegantly restrained. For the longest time, I couldn't get through it without shedding the tears Tennant vocally withholds, and the same was true for my friends. Its politeness represents the open doors that will one day close in on us all.

The Boys finally toured the US in 1991. Created by opera director David Alden and theatrical designer David Fielding, their tour, simply named *Performance,* swapped out visible instrumentalists—two played in the wings, while Lowe only intermittently touched his keys—for ten dancers and three background vocalists, including Sylvia Mason-James, the voice of disco's Voyage, who sometimes sang lead. Every cut was staged, choreographed, costumed, and lit to illustrate an abstracted progression from childhood to the afterlife. An avant-garde ballet staring Gilbert & George's truest spiritual descendants, it was the queerest thing I'd ever seen besides porn. "If Madonna fulfilled the dream of her 'Justify My Love' video and became a male couple," my *Examiner* review read, "she'd be the Pet Shop Boys."

By the show's encore, I and my friend—the same guy who'd behaved himself during my Madonna interview—found ourselves at the stage's lip. Suddenly, he started pushing me upward. When I resisted, he, without warning, jumped onto the stage, climbed on top of Lowe, who was lying face down on a bed, professed his love with a kiss, and hopped off. This is described as a comic incident in *Pet Shop Boys Versus America*, a book about the tour in which the author characterizes Lowe's reaction as "quite clearly thrilled." Unless you're the president, you can end up in jail for something like this today, and that's good. I have no defense for my pal's behavior except to say that gay life was so hard then that when someone spoke our language as emphatically as PSB did, we sometimes lost our minds.

I should also mention that for most of my life, I've dealt with my dad's alcoholism by being what in punk circles is known as "straight edge"—no booze, no recreational drugs. When I now reread what I wrote then, I can tell that this show made me deliriously high. *PSBVA* quotes my review, which Tennant read with delight. "We shouldn't meet him," Lowe says of me in the book. "It's always bad to meet people who like you because they're always mega-disappointed." (We've only since met at a record signing, where I handed them my mega-rare promo twelve-inch of 1996's "The Truck Driver and His Mate," which features two identical and quite large photos of a penis. "*Oh*, we *don't* sign *those*!" Tennant said before I introduced myself. Then they did.)

A rave-influenced, extroverted counterbalance to *Behavior*'s solemnity, 1993's *Very* captures this craziness. "Can You Forgive Her?" depicts the plight of a bisexual man humiliated by a female partner for not living up to heterosexuality's demands. "She's made you some kind of laughingstock/Because you dance to disco and you don't like rock," Tennant rhymes. This woman complains of his abilities in bed and grows jealous of his distant memories with boys. Yet he loves her, even as her cutting remarks gash him like the track's orchestral blasts. Tellingly, the title's question is never answered.

By now, few could ignore the queer implications of titles like "Liberation," "To Speak Is a Sin," and "Young Offender." In "Dreaming of the Queen," Tennant depicts a nightmare in which Princess Diana—then an AIDS activist—tells Queen Elizabeth II, "There are no more lovers left alive/No one has survived." Near the song's end, its dreamer awakens alone, sweat-drenched. As Tennant later revealed, the narrator is also ill.

But *Very*'s gayest move is its Village People cover. It happened after Lowe impulsively insisted the Pets perform "Go West" at a 1992 event for Derek Jarman, who was battling AIDS. Back in 1979, we read the original version as an LGBTQ update on manifest destiny. "When the Village People sang about a gay utopia it seemed for real, but looking back in hindsight it wasn't the utopia they all thought it would be," Lowe reflected. "I knew that the way Neil would sing it would make it sound hopeless." Bombastic brass, a Broadway-style men's choir, and a newly written bridge emphasizing the song's freedom-seeking theme all rub against Tennant's melancholy, turning the track concurrently promising and lachrymose. The resulting club ubiquity helped make *Very* PSB's final US gold record. But in Europe where it joined the duo's biggest pop hits, "Go West" became of all things a football anthem. Just like the VPs themselves, this achievement goes to show that what's queer for us can be the opposite for others.

In 1994, Tennant came out in the UK LGBTQ magazine *Attitude*. "I do think that we have contributed, through our music and also through our videos and the general way we've presented things, rather a lot to what you might call 'gay culture,'" Tennant defended. "What I'm actually saying is, I am gay, and I have written songs from that point of view." That's why in 1986 I came out in *The Village Voice*—to properly discuss those very songs. I remember gasping when I saw the photo that accompanied my *Please* review. It was by Robert Mapplethorpe, which literally illustrated my point: Gay pop acts back then disclosed their sexuality through their music and its presentation, not through press statements. Still, it was huge that Tennant made it official.

For 1999's hazily electronic yet heavily orchestrated *Nightlife*, the contrary duo embraced showy tunes, costuming, and theatricality that picked up where 1997's hi-NRG cover of *West Side Story*'s "Somewhere" left off. "The 1990s has been a decade of naturalism, which is just another style," Tennant then explained. "I remember the Supremes on *Top of the Pops* when I was really young, and I just couldn't imagine those were human beings! We want to be like that."

Nothing in the lyric of *Nightlife*'s "New York City Boy" situates its protagonist as queer—instead, the music does this. With help from New York house-music DJ David Morales, it captures the rush of a suburban kid running amok in Manhattan. Disco strings and horns evoke the Salsoul Orchestra, because they're arranged and conducted by its creator, Vince Montana. Montana even quotes a riff from Donna Summer's "MacArthur Park"—a rare retro move for a largely futuristic act. The song's pinnacle arrives when the background vocals expand and rise into a celestial choir. This time, we glimpse the promised land free from plague's clouds. There's zero irony. Because we're thought to be unnatural, we're not considered capable of such sincerity. Yet here it is, the rapturous heir to pre-AIDS disco and the sunshine of Stonewall's deliverance. It deserved to be a smash.

When it wasn't, Pet Shop Boys became cult-supported synthpop standard bearers. Even today, PSB maintain the lowest shit-to-hit ratio of any still-active 1980s vets, because Tennant and Lowe remain singer-songwriters of the highest order. Subtract their synths, and you're still left with incisive lyrics, indelible melodies, intricate compositional harmonies, and an uncommon vocal confidant who makes the most formidable social commentary seem intimate. Only Morrissey approaches Tennant's humor. When it comes to heart, there's no contest.

Tennant and Lowe remain the Jedi knights of open-ended, all-encompassing pop queerness. Unlike acts of the social-media age, they reveal themselves to us almost solely through their art, not their celebrity: Pet Shop Boys are personas, not people. Yet their gay perspective tailors everything the duo creates, from the thump of its machines to the fonts on its record sleeves.

There's still nobody else like that.

⏭

Chapter Fifty

Tina Turner and Bonnie Raitt

While all these largely gay male synthpop sounds were happening, similarly alternative female aesthetics fermented in 1980s music. They didn't have a particular costume, gender approach, or even genre. "Women in Rock" stories would show up every few years, rarely doing more than noting the apparent novelty of women kicking ass. LGBTQ culture's role in nurturing these gals couldn't be mentioned—Don't frighten the straight men! Don't give anyone any reason to be further marginalized! Instead, we were forced to claim certain artists as ours in secret. Only when we attended a concert and exclaimed, "Wow, there are a lot of queers here!" would we publicly honor our participation.

Most often our fandom began at home. Like most kids my age, I first encountered Ike and Tina Turner not through Top Forty radio, which only occasionally played the pair, but on TV. My sister would sound the alarm whenever they appeared, and I'd come running. Ike's band was solid, but Tina and the Ikettes—nominally her background singers, but crucially her dancers—kept our focus. Every performance brought a rigorously synchronized riot of go-go boots, micro-mini'd thighs, and long, floppy wigs designed for maximum flailing.

Their 1971 showstopping smash cover of Creedence Clearwater Revival's "Proud Mary" taught baby gays like me to lip-sync, for Tina's spoken opening monologue was too good to merely observe. You *had* to recite with her that she and the band never did anything "nice and easy," they always did things "nice and rough." When I was nine, that phrase seemed like a contradiction, but Tina and the Ikettes proved that it wasn't. Performing a song that honors feminine resilience via its titular ship, the "riverboat queen," but also in their version its narrator, these women were smiling but also screaming, executing dance steps of extreme precision yet throwing a fit. By the song's accelerated end, I, my sister, and most of young America would be wiggling around the living room. No one needed to explain that these Black and Proud Marys learned how to permissibly step outside what was ordinarily proscribed and that I must do the same for my sanity. I just knew.

Bizarrely, few hits followed. Tina played the Acid Queen—a prostitute/witch/pusher in Ken Russell's nightmarishly camp 1975 film of the Who's rock opera *Tommy*. She and Ike divorced—few then knew why—and Tina prematurely played the oldies circuit until teaming up in 1983 with the former Human Leaguers behind Heaven 17. This UK synthpop trio rearranged an Al Green oldie for her in the image of its own "Let Me Go," a 1982 gay-sanctioned club hit that split the difference between soulful new wave and haunting electronic disco.

Featuring a nearly a cappella opening that forced DJs to play it from its first note while dancers marveled in the drama of Tina's presiding delivery, "Let's Stay Together" swiftly became an LGBTQ club must-play. WBLS jumped on an import twelve-inch, while its video echoed the single sleeve's pose. Two kneeling women flank the star—then forty-four and still enviably hot—with their hands on her thighs, their mouths at crotch level, and her hands on their heads, as if she'd pushed them down there. This was an overt reenactment of Tina and her dancers' covert lesbian eroticism. Indeed, that's ex-Ikette Edna Richardson on the right.

Because this unexpected, gay-triggered success meant Capitol Records had no time to overthink her comeback, 1984's *Private Dancer* has a sweep and spontaneity that makes it feel personal, despite only one cut, "I Might Have Been Queen," written for her. Like the star herself, its flashpoint, "What's Love

Got to Do with It," isn't just one thing; it's pop, reggae, rock, and soul that Tina made hers. Most didn't yet know what she'd withstood, but it's there in how she substantiates the lyric's lie with offhand lightness, particularly during the melody's most anxious moment. "I've been thinking 'bout my own protection," she sings. "It scares me to feel this way!"

This is a universal condition, but particularly an LGBTQ one. We're afraid to let loose and love freely, because we're told ad infinitum that we mustn't. In the video, Tina walks through mean New York streets littered with tough guys but also robust broads. The straight viewer might not notice, but she's ogled by these chicks, too—one even sticks her tongue out. Tina flirts with them all.

To the average listener, "Better Be Good to Me" was a new song. But to all-night dancers at the Saint, where Robbie Leslie, Sharon White, and other queer DJs had been playing the 1981 original by hard rock's female-fronted Spider, this grinding groover was already a late-morning sleaze special. The *Private Dancer* version retraces Spider's except for Turner's far more emboldened vocal. No way will she again allow anyone to treat her improperly; a message maligned LGBTQ people made our own. "Why can't you be good to me?" we beseech those who debase us.

But even this hit paled next to what she did with the title track. Writer Mark Knopfler was wise not to release it with his band, Dire Straits, for Turner's definitive rendition makes it one of the womanliest songs ever written by a rock dude. In it she plays a taxi dancer: a paid partner. Prevalent in the early twentieth century, these lap-dance predecessors were by the 1980s an anachronism. This meant the song was heard then as it is now as a metaphor. Knopfler's private dancer is nearly but not quite a hooker, yet that inference spreads when he follows his lyric "I'll do what you want me to do" with another doozy: "And any old music will do." As his narrator, Tina craves comfort and family but finds herself in a compromising position in which she's forced to do, and by extension sing, *anything*.

This made "Private Dancer" an unusually confidential hit that divulged harsh truths about what it means to be Black and female in a white male medium, which in turn reflects what it's like being queer in a straight world.

Mid-tempo, but with a balladic granite that makes it feel slower than it is, the melody sometimes waltzes against its foursquare rhythm, as if the singer was not only disconnected from her men, but also estranged from her music. As this long song climaxes, she leaps out of her chronicling capacity up into that higher, husky, sexily strained voice we know as Tina, as if to say that she—like her private dancer—must play a role the market demands. Director Brian Grant and choreographer Arlene Phillips, the same pair behind Whitney's "How Will I Know" clip, depict her in the video as drifting between past, present, fantasy, and reality in a textbook 1980s montage. Study the dancers, and you'll spot two women paired as if sexually partnered and at least one guy in drag. This is our song, too.

Private Dancer sold millions worldwide, transforming its singer from has-been to sensation. Subsequent discs dimmed *Private Dancer*'s unpremeditated flash with the kind of calculation that often extinguishes the vibrance of money-making women who don't write or produce. "I Don't Wanna Fight" from the 1993 biopic *What's Love Got to Do with It* stands above all that because by then we'd learned her story: Ike had routinely battered Tina. But *Private Dancer* still proves what can be won when a woman of color—or any minority—manages to kick herself out of all boxes. She can at last be free.

Radiating a youthful autonomy particularly appealing to women who like her walked their own path, Bonnie Raitt turned heads while singing clear-skies blues. Her 1972 album, *Give It Up,* grew into a word-of-mouth hit through crafty covers like "Love Me Like a Man." The original—"Love *You* Like a Man"—is a typical rock boast in which its songwriter, Chris Smither, lets a prospective partner know he can deliver in bed. In her bluesy rewrite, an answer song, Raitt repositions Smither's words to state her womanly requirement: blue-ribbon fucking. In 1972, this was shocking coming from a baby-faced girl who projected not only a dude's cocky confidence but also his instrumental chops—Raitt can rip on the butchest of blues instruments: slide guitar. Remember when I mentioned earlier that Aretha's "I Never Loved a Man (The Way I Love You)" became a lesbian anthem? This one can be similarly interpreted, for its narrator wants to be loved *like* a man. That means so many things.

Although she'd eventually pen more material, Raitt for decades primarily drew from feminist blues pioneers like Sippie Wallace, R&B mainstays, and contemporary singer-songwriters whom she vocally outdid. Her sunny candor plays against the bleakness of Randy Newman's "Guilty," turning it far more disquieting in her 1973 rendition. In the song, drunk and cocaine-high, she returns self-pitying and self-hating to a lover, likely an ex, because she's in trouble for something unstated. Strongly suggesting that she's guilty not simply for what she does but for what she is, the song summarizes this shame with its parting lines: "It takes a whole lot of medicine, darlin'/For me to pretend that I'm somebody else." Because she belts those words so bluntly, their vulnerability blindsides. LGBTQ people—particularly lesbians who couldn't come out because they were dependent on unsympathetic husbands and families—heard their desperation in hers.

Raitt became a rare female regular on '70s rock radio until addiction unraveled her. When a mid-'80s skiing accident postponed her working with Prince for a potential album on his Paisley Park label, Raitt got sober. Although her sessions with the funkateer were never released, she clicked with another unexpected collaborator: producer Don Was, whose participation meant 1989's *Nick of Time* bucked convention, much like his waggish band Was (Not Was). Rather than taking the expected rock-funk route to resurrection, as Tina had done on Capitol Records, the label they now shared, Raitt returned to her roots while modernizing her message. At age forty, she started winning Grammys, selling millions, and topping charts her way.

On *Nick*'s "Nobody's Girl," Raitt sings of a likely bisexual who does what she wants when she wants "with anyone you know." Like many folk songs, it has a third-person narrator who might also be its subject—Raitt stayed single for much of her life. Yet in the final chorus, the perspective abruptly shifts for one phrase when the singer confesses, "But I ache for her inside." Are these sympathy pains? The mere result of singing a guy-written song? Or does she also long for this unattached outsider? Echoing women's music pioneers who apprised both lesbian listeners as well as the merely curious by leaving their lyrics open-ended, Raitt remains ambiguous here—just like nobody's girl.

Luck of the Draw from 1991 gave Raitt her first pop radio hits, twenty years after her debut. Written by Canadian singer-songwriter Shirley Eikhard, "Something to Talk About" tells the tale of two friends rumored to be much more. "They think we're lovers kept under covers," Raitt sings of herself and her pal. Instead of pining clandestinely for each other, the narrator suggests they consummate and announce their connection. LGBTQ people, especially lesbians, hear "Something" as our own. Since busybodies are bound to run their mouths off on us, we might as well give these gossipmongers something to chew on. When Eikhard died in 2022, her obit revealed that the love of her life was a woman, which substantiated our reading of her song as a coming-out mantra. "Now that we know it, let's really show it darling!" Raitt sings for Eikhard and all of us told we must be discreet.

Luck's other smash, "I Can't Make You Love Me," captures the soul-crushing pain that comes when someone realizes they must forgo a partner who can never fully return their love. "You can't make your heart feel something it won't," Raitt dejectedly croons, the melody rising and falling with her resignation in a gently devastating performance.

Six years later, George Michael scored a major UK hit with his own interpretation. Although the superstar had committed relationships, he also compulsively cruised for clandestine sex with straight-seeming partners who clung to the same status quo Michael's withholding dad demanded of him. That futility sparked a dignifiedly tortured cover we can posthumously hear as a queer cry for help. Michael searched for approval precisely where he couldn't get it and never found the fortitude to walk away. In both Michael's and Raitt's renditions, we can hear our own struggle for self-respect. "Don't patronize me," they sing.

⏭

Chapter Fifty-One

Phranc and k.d. lang

As much as Tina Turner and Bonnie Raitt deserved overdue coups, 1980s music needed new female talent that wasn't Madonna or Whitney even more. A mid-decade trickle of tangentially related but all unconventional women musicians turned into a wave that crested at the '80s' end, then inundated '90s rock and pop. We didn't know it then, but the beginnings of what became a global movement began with someone who sold in the mere thousands: an often unplugged but never restrained dyke with a few of the era's funniest and most feminist songs.

The first out and emphatically butch lesbian singer on a major label, Phranc first passed through fleeting but ferociously queer L.A. punk bands including Nervous Gender and Castration Squad—you can see her playing guitar with Catholic Discipline in Penelope Spheeris's 1981 punk documentary, *The Decline of Western Civilization*. That year Warhol associate Paul Morrissey captured her acoustic guise in the feature film *Madame Wang's*. By her 1985 debut, *Folksinger*, Phranc was fully formed and at the forefront of punk folk.

Like Meg Christian's *I Know You Know* a decade before, *Folksinger* is searingly serious one moment and comical the next. The difference is that Phranc presents a persona: "the all-American Jewish lesbian folk singer." On songs like "One o' the Girls" and "Amazons," she plugs into punk's blatancy as an unmistakable lez. Even her name puns on this bluntness. My gay critic colleague Johnny Ray Houston remembers Phranc opening for the Smiths in Detroit on their *Queen Is Dead* tour. You'd think her queer defiance would have been welcomed by Moz fans. Instead, they pelted her with coins, but she did not back down. Facing such resistance, Phranc absorbs glam's performativity, which breaks from the naturalism of women's music and steers her closer to reinvention-favoring glitter boys and trans people. Despite multiple signifiers of realness, right down to her album's title, she's often winking like Warhol—critical of popular culture, yet Pop Art.

Consider 1989's *I Enjoy Being a Girl*, her first album for Island, Grace Jones's former label. Its title cut, from Rodgers and Hammerstein's corny 1958 musical *Flower Drum Song*, is so schmaltzy that it's nearly satirical in its original version. Sung by a dyke in a crewcut, the song's declaration that its singer is "a strictly female female" takes on new meaning. She delivers it straight, which, through her camp context, makes it queer. Somewhere in my keepsakes, I still have one of the tampons that she hand-stamped with the song's title and tossed out at her gigs.

In "M-A-R-T-I-N-A," Phranc sis-boom-bahs for the lesbian tennis champ Martina Navratilova. But in "Bloodbath," she wrestles with the guilt that comes with belonging to an oppressive racial majority; lesbians aimed to dismantle white privilege even back then. And in "Take Off Your Swastika," she takes to task fashionistas who mistake fascism for anarchy and neo-Nazis who endanger punk's safe outsider space. Her grievance is personal. "I'm a Jewish lesbian!" she roars. Declaring this remains radical today, but then it was revelatory.

Everything came together on 1991's *Positively Phranc*. Looking like a Beach Boy in her pj's on the cover, she praises actor Kim Novak, the transgender jazz pianist Billy Tipton, a retirement-age hot-rod mama, a fellow surfer girl, and implicitly Jonathan Richman, the proto-punk pioneer who became a queer ally with his hip-shaking 1992 performance of "I Was Dancing in the Lesbian Bar" on *Late Night with Conan O'Brien*. By remaking Richman's "Pablo Picasso" as "Gertrude Stein," she points out that modernism's highest-ranking butch was as rakish as its reigning dude.

All this positivity takes a turn in the closing cut, "Outta Here," on which she honors fashion and artworld greats who had recently died of AIDS. The straight world thinks gays and lesbians are like apples and oranges and that we don't get along. But at the epidemic's worst, lesbians were there for us. At ACT UP, I saw this every week. The fury of activists like Ann Northrop, future co-host of *Gay USA*, was like that of a mama lion fighting for her wounded cubs. Phranc is gentler, but her spirit also affirmed that we were all in this together.

Touring as Neil Diamond in her 1993 review *Hot August Phranc*, the singer combined borscht-belt comedy with drag-king showmanship, right down to her chest wig. Released by the queer-supportive indie label Kill Rock Stars, 1995's *Goofyfoot* yielded another LGBTQ classic in "Bulldagger Swagger," which stands with drag queens and trans people where it matters most. "I went to the ladies' room, I had to pee/Why was everybody starin' at me?" she sings. Phranc is the summer camp counselor we all should've had.

When in 1992 k.d. lang announced she was lesbian in *The Advocate* and the next year appeared on a haute, Herb Ritts–shot *Vanity Fair* cover with Cindy Crawford, mainstream media considered these deeds the birth of "lesbian chic." But for fans who bought her 1984 Canada-only first album, *A Truly Western Experience,* the story had already been told. That album leads with "Bopalena," a rowdy cover of the rockabilly standard in which lang sings "she's my gal" twelve times and "I love her so" six. Up north, lang paralleled what Phranc was doing in Southern California.

Although it's tempting to claim the two invented lesbian camp, Frances Faye embodied it way back in 1959 with her pansexual cabaret manifesto "Frances and Her Friends," while fellow lesbian Rusty Warren was also singing ribald female-focused numbers, such as 1960's "Knockers Up!" But the way Phranc and lang spoke complicated truths through cartoony guises made them queer in a way most lesbian predecessors weren't and relatable to those raised on Bowie and Blondie. When I was in my twenties, what I knew of women's music didn't speak to me, nor did much folk or country. Phranc and lang said plenty.

Beneath the *Hee Haw* hokum, lang boasted new wave bona fides. Sire released her international debut, 1987's *Angel with a Lariat*, which was produced by Rockpile's Dave Edmunds. Rockabilly fortified by electric fiddle, her band, the Reclines, here play almost as fast as the Ramones, while their cover of Patsy Cline's "Three Cigarettes in an Ashtray" weeps with strings arranged by Art of Noise's Anne Dudley. Possessing the unequivocal authority of androgynous grace, lang suggests Presley channeling Patsy, but with an abandon akin to Iggy Pop. "I feel emancipation!" she declares on the title track while riding liberation's spirit like a bucking bronco. Our collective gaydar went ping-ping.

Consummating the obsession implicit in her band's name, lang employed Cline's former producer Owen Bradley, who reunited her studio musicians on lang's *Shadowland* to revive bygone country and cabaret for 1988. In San Francisco, drag singer Arturo Galster was already performing as the country-and-western pioneer, but a hip newcomer hadn't approached the hoi polloi with a pre-rock retro slant since the gay ole days of *The Divine Miss M*. Similarly reveling in camp's artifice and audacity, lang reenacted the mid-century melodrama that made Douglas Sirk's "women's pictures" of the 1950s touchstones of LGBTQ taste and an inspiration to our filmmakers.

On the title cut, a previously discarded song so difficult Bradley considered it "unsingable," the narrator drifts in a post-love limbo—not dead, yet trapped behind her torch. Gliding without gaps between her mezzo-soprano and falsetto in a way ordinary singers cannot, lang occupies this sensual purgatory, making it seem delightfully deluxe, as LGBTQ artists so often do. Likewise navigating between staginess and sincerity, lang combines country, blues, rock, and jazz in the same way she unites tinsel and torment. For some this made her as impure as Freddie Mercury, and similarly polarizing. The night I first saw lang, when she opened for Chris Isaac in 1987 at NYC's Bottom Line and blew my gay mind, my straight *Voice* editors felt she was contrived. If this country Canadian lesbian with soul vocal clarity, a postmodern sense of quotation, and a cowpunk band baffled intellectual New Yorkers, Middle America was likely to condemn her to the queer margins.

A month after moving to San Francisco, I reviewed lang at the Fillmore on New Year's Eve 1988. This was my first nearly all-lesbian audience and the first time I saw an out and uproarious comedian, Marga Gomez, open for a mainstream-ascendant musician. Surrounded by her people, free to camp it up yet be authentic, lang radiated the gusto she brought to *Pee-wee's Playhouse Christmas Special*. This crowd didn't respond politely, like at the Bottom Line. They greeted her as if she were what they'd been waiting for: an exemplar of lesbian excellence—a dykon. Starting my life over in gay mecca during a gay plague soon proved problematic, but the community that night made those challenges worthwhile. So excited, I misspelled Gomez's name in my review—I called her Marlo, as in Thomas. She phoned to harangue me but soon became my friend, teacher, and, eventually, wedding officiant.

Having grown up in rural Alberta's prairie, lang grapples with who she is and where she finds her truth on 1989's *Absolute Torch and Twang*. She locates the latter in the wide-open spaces conveyed by capacious tracks such as "Trail of Broken Hearts" and "Pullin' Back the Reins," which recall Jimmy Webb's vast expanses of melody for Glen Campbell. "Big Boned Gal" salutes her bonny self in the third person with a whoop that is similarly voluminous. When lang sang it live, the elation of female fans who'd never heard themselves musically venerated made it even more festive. She was them, and they were her.

Yet Nashville barely noticed that *Twang* snagged a country Grammy. As before, lang didn't receive US airplay proportional to her artistry or sales. And when in 1990 she kissed a cow, identified as a vegetarian, and supported animal rights in a PETA ad, the meat and country music industries flipped out. "That's not what I call ladylike," said one Kansas broadcaster. Clearly his beef went beyond her beliefs.

lang's courage continued through her participation in *Red Hot + Blue*, 1990's eminent AIDS benefit album of Cole Porter covers that launched the Red Hot series of compilation albums and related media. Unlike the contributions from U2 and Neneh Cherry, lang's rendition of "So in Love" doesn't diverge from the gay songwriter's Broadway base. The update came in its video, in which at first she's merely doing laundry. When lang pulls a slip out of a sink and gives it a kiss, it's implied that the character she's playing is mourning a female lover who just passed from AIDS and that she may also have HIV. "I'm yours 'til I die!" lang belts at full throttle in the heart-wrenching final shot, in which she looks squarely at the camera as if to her departed, while the lighting grows nightmarish and then radiant, reflecting both her turmoil and allegiance. No other music video reveals more about the epidemic.

Having further asserted her masculinity in 1991's *Salmonberries*—a dreamlike film by *Bagdad Cafe* director Percy Adlon, who'd also created her *Red Hot* clip—lang explores her womanhood throughout 1992's *Ingénue*. Its femininity suggests not only her heart's permeability but also her love object's gender. "Watch over me with a mother's eyes," she sighs on its Joni Mitchell–esque opener "Save Me"—not words one sings to a guy. In "Miss Chatelaine," she ponders why a mere kiss would expose hidden muliebrity. We know why: Another mademoiselle is making her feel like the belle of the ball. Its accordion suggests Grace Jones's take on "La Vie en Rose" *and* Lawrence Welk, while its video brings that schlockmeister's trademark soap bubbles. Lit with Sirk-ian neon shades and wrapped in miles of taffeta and wig curls, lang surrenders to love but stops short of passivity. Waving her arms aloft, she instead becomes a sublime drag queen. Queer women had begun to explore hyper-girlie sides in New York's and San Francisco's underground drag scenes, but this was the mainstream's "faux queen" moment. She's doing high femme as my singer friend Leigh Crow, aka Elvis Herselvis, does—as a butch.

Elsewhere, *Ingénue* brings interiority. Like countless other queer musicians, lang had been privately out for ages, but she still masks herself reflexively: Her heart hides what "The Mind of Love" reveals. "Outside Myself" testifies that she'd been fearful so long she's nearly numb. These and other diaphanous songs linger in that same shadowland between thought and action. For an extroverted presence like lang, such restraint amplifies her allure. In real life, she'd been pining for a married woman. The entire album feels designed to will this gal out of another's arms and into hers.

All that desire coalesces on the final track, "Constant Craving," in which lang conjures yearning of galactic scale. Forbidden to marry each other or have children without a heterosexual pretext, generations of gay people had no choice but to turn away from the life force that populates the planet. lang does the opposite. She's saying that despite all her fretting on the previous nine tracks, she resolves to stand tall in perpetual thirst and never falter. "Always someone marches brave/Here beneath my skin," she blazes. Leaning into key notes and holding one after the other without the slightest wavering of pitch or power, she transmits her devotion's steadiness. Not only channeling that élan vital of which she sings, lang embodies it. Nothing will stop her from loving her likely unobtainable beloved.

We know "Constant Craving" comes from a specifically queer place, but it also captures urges so comprehensive that the song's universal appeal cut through what happened next. Three months after *Ingénue*'s release, lang came clean. "I don't want to be out like Phranc is out," she admitted in *The Advocate*. Some today might consider that cowardly, but would you be willing to be pelted with pennies while you're performing? Having already weathered the PETA backlash, she understandably feared another.

Instead, "Constant Craving" became a Grammy-winning breakthrough *after* her announcement—an achievement akin to the success of *Ziggy Stardust* two decades earlier in the wake of David Bowie's proclamation of bisexuality at its launch. Like many songs in this book, "Constant Craving" set a cultural benchmark far higher than its US pop chart position—thirty-eight, despite protracted radio play—and that helped *Ingénue* go double platinum.

"I feel this great emancipation," lang told me in a 1992 interview on the heels of her *Advocate* cover story, "a lot closer to my audience than I ever have before." This reward was profound. "*Ingénue* was about totally releasing what's inside of me and not being concerned with the industry at all." Its success exemplifies that if the right LGBTQ artist defies those who tell them they mustn't be themselves or talk about their identity, they can create artistic verities that society thinks it doesn't want but has been itching for all along.

Rather than exploiting this shift, lang continued bucking convention. Although superior to the substandard 1993 Gus Van Sant film it scored, lang's *Even Cowgirls Get the Blues* soundtrack received much of its exposure through house-remixed LGBTQ club hits. Fully eschewing country, 1995's *All You Can Eat* adds R&B flavors alongside alt-pop so suave it masquerades as easy listening. Paradoxically, not even that radio format played this or any other subsequent lang record in the US. The lyrics of *Eat*'s "Sexuality" likely didn't turn the tables, but a famously out lesbian singing, "Now how bad could it be/If you should fall in love with me?" may have. While teasing a potential partner, she's posing a rhetorical question to our gatekeepers: Will the party be ruined if you let us in? "You're OK" asks for reassurance from someone lang loves to make sure she's not making a fool of herself. But we can also read its lyric as the star fearing rejection in coming out's wake. "I am wrought with paranoia/For I have brought myself before ya," the opening lines admit.

We didn't need radio play to keep buying lang. Both *Eat* and 1997's *Drag*—a left-field cabaret concept album forged from covers of songs about smoking and addiction—went gold. With 2000's *Invincible Summer*, she trades the saturnine frost of her post-country records for sunny West Coast pop, especially on "Summerfling." Here, lang is as disencumbered by love's potential as she'd elsewhere been hobbled, and in its Bruce Weber-y video, she wakes up with a woman beside her. On "The Consequences of Falling," lang once again frets that what she feels might not be requited. She and Morrissey share more than strong jawlines and fetching quiffs: Each replay themes of concealment and exposure because LGBTQ people live in that queer space of possibility between them. Bashed or adored, we never know what awaits us when we step from darkness into light. This time, she gets the girl.

To observe her landmark's twenty-fifth anniversary, lang revisited *Ingénue* in full. At Stanford University, where I saw her, all the big-boned gals stayed in their seats. Then in her fifties, lang resembled latter-day Wayne Newton, not early Elvis, P. *or* C. Accordingly, she didn't perform the album as she did at age thirty. Instead, its liminal songs grew less physical, more spiritual. Having learned as a Buddhist to live in her uncertainties, lang greeted them with equanimity. Reconciling and amalgamating her conflicting sides, lang sang as if she were freedom itself.

This is why the ease of lang's croon remains insurgent. It reminds the world that lesbians can be sanguine *and* fulfilled. Even today, women like her are told the right man will "fix" them. Nothing about that voice suggests she is in any way broken.

⏭

Chapter Fifty-Two

Sinéad O'Connor

Sinéad O'Connor will evermore have our respect. Despite four heterosexual marriages, this singer-songwriter was more than an ally. In the August 2000 cover story of the lesbian magazine *Curve*, she surprised even her interviewer by declaring herself lesbian. She'd later qualify this, telling *Pride Source*, "If I fall in love with someone, I wouldn't give a shit if they were a man or a woman," and in the same interview, also explaining she'd long been inspired by LGBTQ people, "Because if a guy is brave enough to walk around dressed as a woman . . . any of us can fucking do anything." Her singular combination of femme upper register, butch shaved head, combat boots, and near-constant defiance wasn't merely gender-recusant: O'Connor's relationship to *everything* was queer. She stood with those on the outside because that's how she identified. When briefly selling mass quantities of records and, therefore, temporarily treated as an insider, she didn't squander stardom's spotlight or become a proper lady or product. Even as she struggled with her mental health, she never lacked the courage to be herself.

Not only giving consent, "I Want Your (Hands on Me)," a cut from her 1987 debut, *The Lion and the Cobra*, places O'Connor in the driver's seat, even when receiving pleasure. She's "a pushy bottom," as we say in the gay world. Women aren't supposed to tell guys, or anyone else, that they want to be touched and how. She tackles this taboo through repetition: In the album version, she tells her lover to place their hands on her body *103* times. The 1988 single remix adds MC Lyte, who also emphasizes feminine agency. Rockers rarely had rappers on their records back then, especially female ones. This alliance is more unusual if you hear Lyte as answering O'Connor's call to erotic action.

The singer found another comrade in performance artist Karen Finley, who appears on the twelve-inch of 1988's similarly sexual "Jump in the River." Performing one-woman shows that depict rape and misogyny through rituals of nakedness, food, and incantatory poetry, this Danceteria vet would in 1990 become notorious as one of the "NEA Four" artists whose National Endowment for the Arts grants were denied because of their queer, feminist, sexual, and political content. Finley's additions to "Jump" meant even most club DJs wouldn't touch it. "After my mother washed me, powdered me/I insisted that she masturbate me," Finley brays. We hadn't yet learned what O'Connor's mother had done to her child.

"Jump" resurfaced minus Finley on 1990's quieter but no less harrowing *I Do Not Want What I Haven't Got.* It isn't women's music per se; sympatico men including ex–Adam Ant guitarist Marco Pirroni and ex-Smiths bassist Andy Rourke play on it. But topically it's among the most female multiplatinum albums because nearly all of it deals with maternity and daughterhood through recovery's lens; that's why it opens with the Serenity Prayer. When tears rolled down O'Connor's face in gay director John Maybury's star-making video for 1990's nearly worldwide Number One cover of Prince's "Nothing Compares 2 U," viewers thought they knew her. They didn't know that Prince's use of "mama" to describe his lover made her think of her mom, who'd sent her to Catholic school for delinquent girls and died. They didn't know why she cried.

That song's success propelled O'Connor's art toward a public unprepared for the political stances that came naturally to a resolutely Irish artist born into all sorts of upheaval. In another Maybury-directed video, this one for her *Red Hot + Blue* contribution "You Do Something to Me," she sings as a Veronica Lake–styled bombshell for a queer *Cabaret*-reminiscent crowd, then sits at a candlelit AIDS vigil. Similar big-band sounds dominate 1992's *Am I Not Your Girl?,* which includes gay-beloved standards, such as "Secret Love," that belie their easy listening arrangements with autobiographical commentary.

Two weeks after that album's release, her October 3, 1992, *Saturday Night Live* appearance flipped what was originally intended to be a straightforward promotional appearance into my generation's most courageous act of political theater. Intending to draw attention to clergy abusing children while the Vatican looked the other way, she sang Bob Marley's "War" a cappella, changed some of its already incensed lyrics, and ripped up a photo of Pope John Paul II. Few knew that O'Connor had been sexually assaulted by her mother and that it was her mother's photo of the pope that she shredded. Rather than fighting, as O'Connor said at the song's end, "the real enemy," the media and public turned on the singer. Stripped of her cultural power, she was treated as a witch and virtually burned at the stake. For calling out abusers, she became the abused. We know what that's like.

Time grilled O'Connor for this, yet she wouldn't back down. "I can't be put in any category, and that freaks people out," she summarized. Years later she reflected in her memoir, "I feel that having a number-one record derailed my career and my tearing the photo put me back on the right track."

"No Man's Woman" from 2000's musically more mainstream *Faith and Courage* juxtaposes O'Connor's resistance to letting herself be physically controlled by any man against her willingness to be spiritually guided by one. Defying Catholic doctrine dictating that priests represent Christ's likeness, she'd broken the utmost gender rule when in 1999 she became ordained. Those still confused about her pope statement couldn't get behind this, or the feminist and lesbian implications of "No Man's Woman," so her comeback faltered.

Like so many in this book, O'Connor made music as therapy, but for her it could only heal so much. What she achieved for others, however, remains immeasurable. The strength she revealed while exposing her weakness still helps us strive for something better than ordinary life. That's why she's among the queerest of artists. Her survival anthems acknowledge the price she paid for living in perpetual insubordination but also testify to all she gained.

⏭

Chapter Fifty-Three

Tracy Chapman

A month after Tracy Chapman released her eponymous debut album in April 1988, I saw her at the Bitter End, a tiny Greenwich Village folk joint where Bob Dylan and many others got their start in the '60s. She was then as she'll always be: understated, unadorned. A month later, this Cleveland-born rookie performed in London's Wembley Stadium to honor the seventieth birthday of Nelson Mandela, South Africa's then-imprisoned anti-apartheid activist who would become the divided country's first president and Black head of state. When Stevie Wonder refused to perform without the missing disc that programmed his keyboard, Chapman was suddenly called upon to play a second set. Now in a headliner slot broadcast all over the world, she sang "Fast Car."

Anyone not born into wealth or opportunity can hear themselves in this song, which would become an international smash. I know I did, as both a working-class drunkard's son and as an LGBTQ person; a fast car can take us over the rainbow. Chapman plots her escape "just across the border and into the city," the promised land of so many queer-written and -favored songs, where her old story will conclude and a new one can be written. The singer-songwriter demonstrates home's stasis with a lilting guitar riff that first suggests hope but soon denotes stagnancy, verse after verse, until the assurance of her long-delayed chorus. Like Bruce Springsteen's "Born to Run," but also

Bronski Beat's "Smalltown Boy," "Fast Car" captures the potential of those moments between past and future. Just being in that car, side by side with her chosen one, gives Chapman that sanctified sense of belonging, as in the Smiths' "There Is a Light That Never Goes Out." "I had a feeling I could be someone," she sings at her hymn's repeated peak.

If you're LGBTQ, you're told in so many ways that you're nobody. Two decades after AIDS's worst, we're still considered a potential source of physical infection and emotional contamination. If that wasn't the case, LGBTQ education and drag wouldn't be banned in the places where other minorities and women aren't respected. There would be no Don't Say Gay or Trans acts; no anti-LGBTQ curriculum laws. If you're queer, female, *and* Black, that thirst to "be someone"—Chapman's otherwise-denied authentic self—is exponentially stronger. This is all audible in her cry, which many of us hear as our own. Chapman is the smalltown girl, the smalltown boy, the smalltown they/them who can't be themselves back home. She's us, longing to be free.

Some lucky gals have a Chapman story earlier than mine. Back in her short Afro days of 1986, the singer performed at the largely lesbian Michigan Womyn's Music Festival. Introducing it as "a song that's based on a true story—not about me, however," she sang another future showpiece, one that holds even more resonance for LGBTQ listeners. Throughout "For My Lover," Chapman juxtaposes her darling's glory against the price she must pay for it. "Two weeks in a Virginia jail," the first line testifies of a punishment received from those in power for merely loving someone they think she shouldn't.

By situating the song in Virginia, Chapman evokes Mildred and Richard Loving, the Black woman and white man whose union defied a Virginia state law against interracial marriage. They took their case to the Supreme Court, which in 1967 overturned their conviction and ended all race-based marriage restrictions in the US. What is no longer called miscegenation could be named, but the very fact that this song's subject is not indicates that she's singing about something far more prohibited: Chapman's protagonist is imprisoned for a queer love then still illegal throughout much of the US. Not until 2003 was same-sex intercourse decriminalized in Virginia, the so-called land for lovers. For her crime, she's psychoanalyzed, drugged up, and interrogated, but she won't confess to what she sings of here through implication. The guitar picking is bluegrass, which heightens what's forbidden. Through Chapman's scraggy soulfulness, "For My Lover" intimates that a woman can be Black *and* queer *and* rural, things thought mutually exclusive.

It was unusual to find someone who even looked like Chapman in record store bins outside of the R&B section. LGBTQ listeners know her closest forerunner, Joan Armatrading. In Europe, this West Indian Brit scored several hits in the 1970s and '80s. In the US, she has enticed critics and a cult following significantly comprised of us. But because her ever-changing folk comingles with jazz, blues, reggae, rock, and more, defying what gatekeepers expect from a woman of her complexion, she's never had a Top Forty single in the US. In 2011, Armatrading married a woman, but still dodges media inquiries about it, even though her music has long appeared in queer settings. In 1989, Two Nice Girls released "Sweet Jane (With Affection)," an ingeniously sapphic medley of the Velvet Underground's "Sweet Jane" and Armatrading's 1976 ballad "Love and Affection." Testifying its abidance among us, the latter underscores a love scene in Billy Eichner's super-gay 2022 romcom *Bros.*

As of this writing, Chapman has not officially come out. However, Alice Walker—the esteemed author of *The Color Purple*, a Black LGBTQ milestone—has long spoken of her romance with Chapman. In 2022, Walker published her journals, which discuss the relationship in enamored detail. "I've never loved anyone as much as I love Tracy," Walker admitted to herself when their three-year connection ended in 1995.

Chapman's civil rights work amplifies the schism between refusing to talk about her private life while reflecting it in hugely popular music. As I've mentioned, this dichotomy is all over 1980s pop. Think of Boy George—who was for years not officially out—singing "Do You Really Want to Hurt Me" in a dress, or George Michael, even more closeted, performing "Father Figure" in leather-daddy drag. In Chapman's case, this duality is especially striking because her debut's scene-setting song "Talkin' 'bout a Revolution" announces her spiritual alliance with the gladiatorial folk singers of the '60s.

To straight listeners, "Revolution" isn't considered in any way coded. "Poor people gonna rise up," Chapman sings, "and take what's theirs." Yet her anthem emerged when our mere existence once again became endangered. ACT UP had just emerged to fight back, fight AIDS, and to remind everyone, not just us, that silence equaled death. We could sense that "Revolution" also talks about taking an LGBTQ stand, but the singer leaves it up to us to hear it that way and manifest this interpretation amongst ourselves.

This we did. *Tracy Chapman* became a fixture of queer life like *The Freewheelin' Bob Dylan* had been a bohemian must-have. On its way to twenty million copies sold worldwide, Chapman's debut played in our cafés, bookstores, bars, and community centers. We sang it at our protests. It bridged gay male and female experiences, because we could all find ourselves in it. Even in a seemingly nonpolitical number like "Baby Can I Hold You," we could recognize our battle to communicate the love we're taught to repress, play down, and compartmentalize. Here, too, in the most confidential spaces of all, silence equals death. "Maybe if I told you the right words," Chapman fantasizes, our detrimental training will fall away. Maybe then we'll all get to be mighty and real with one another.

⏭

Chapter Fifty-Four

Indigo Girls

"Indigo Girls, a young Atlanta folk duo with a 1989 breakthrough almost as big as their voices, look as though they might be indicative of what the musical 1990s will be like." I managed to predict the future in a concert review for the *San Francisco Examiner* that December not because of Amy Ray's and Emily Saliers's singing that night, which was, of course, stellar. It was their fans who told me something special was happening—something that would make Indigo Girls institutions of LGBTQ life.

Back then, it was a major event just to see one gay musician at a time and to take in that they were accomplished and adored. That alone could change our lives. But to see two lesbians working together, vibing off the crowd in tandem, and pushing each other above their already high bar was transformational on a communal plane. It confirmed what LGBTQ people are taught—that we're loners and losers with no social skills—was wrong.

For decades, the Girls have provided an antidote to this nonsense. You can't call their rapport sisterly, because siblings are far more quarrelsome than these two. They're literally in harmony, yet neither sings nor writes nor even plays like the other, which illustrates another life lesson: We don't need to conform to create community. We can realize what's distinctive about our dissimilar selves when we build supportive nonhierarchical unions. Ray and Saliers model abiding queer friendship.

All this is substantiated by their first and eternal hit, 1989's "Closer to Fine." An English major and daughter of a theology professor, Saliers looks for simple answers to complicated philosophical questions throughout a compositionally cheery and direct but lyrically anxious and winding song. The more she realizes there's not one definitive truth in a world of apparent absolutes, the more she's at peace. But it's not only her words that proclaim this. The song's most convincing spiritual accord lies in the way she jumps up in soprano harmony whenever Ray, an alto and a religion/English major, enters to continue her melodic line. It's the pal she's known since elementary school who elevates Saliers musically and metaphorically to a higher plane. We all want to get there, but as women and queers, the Girls *need* it. These seekers lead us up the mountain, not by providing solutions but by posing quandaries with such ebullience that the result sounds like lesbian empowerment, because that's what it is.

"In Atlanta, we played at the Little Five Points Pub—we were kind of their house band," Saliers told me about where the duo honed their craft before signing to Epic. Although not a gay club, it was run by a gay man, John Blizzard, who nurtured the Girls before dying of AIDS. "It was a motley crew, but primarily the audience was lesbian. I remember being overwhelmed and overjoyed that we were able to translate what happened there to a wider audience."

Although they performed solely as an acoustic duo at the time, Ray and Saliers often play folk with punk's speedy tempos, and sometimes with its musicians, like drummer Budgie and bassist Sara Lee. Just as Cris Williamson and other women's music pioneers prompted immediate and immersive crowd participation, the Girls straightaway inspired sing-alongs when moshing was the order of the day. Their Grammy-winning, double-platinum, 1989 breakthrough, *Indigo Girls,* features many of the duo's most lyrically complicated songs, yet the San Francisco fans I witnessed that year had already memorized them. They even belted Michael Stipe's fervent cameo on "Kid Fears." Well before an LGBTQ network of PTSD therapists emerged to minimize the cumulative mental and physical damage inflicted on us for being queer, Ray tapped into recovery's redemption. "Replace the need with love," Stipe sings. That's what the duo did from the start.

The duo's audience was already living for these affirmations, and the Girls returned its ardor tenfold. You wouldn't have mistaken Ray for Guns N' Roses' Axl Rose, the era's definitive (and sometimes antigay) hard-rock star. Yet likewise tattooed and attired in ripped jeans, a T-shirt, and a vest, she was just as commanding, and with similarly swiveling hips. Her relationship to Saliers has never been carnal, but it's tangibly tight, and it fueled baby dykes to scream. Maybe a few objectified them as if at a New Lezzies on the Block show, but mostly the crowd mirrored their exhilaration through secular queer spirituality.

"I think we were scared to be fully out when we were young and had internalized homophobia," Ray reflected. "We were very self-righteous about the need to be accessible to not just women but men as well. When our career blossomed, it was eye-opening for me. What do you do with the love of all these other people when you don't even know how to appreciate who you are internally and love yourself? Suddenly, you're allowed to celebrate that part of you that's sexual, and it's okay you're attracted to women, and it's okay you don't feel binary. I was influenced by Patti Smith, who was extremely extroverted in a sexualized way with no label on anything. I felt, 'Oh! I can be that, in myself, as a lesbian.' That's kind of amazing when you've been told you're a horrible person for a long time and you've felt shame about yourself, your body, and who you're attracted to."

"You can't deny that when people gather to see queer artists, so many of those energies are intersectional," Saliers picked up the thread, "whether they're sexual or spiritual, especially when there hasn't been much of a queer scene, and all the sudden there is one and you can all be attracted to each other in one way or another."

Much like their gay male peers, the Girls first revealed this side of themselves to us just by showing up, then gradually shared more of it with everyone else. Ray sings their cover of Dire Straits's "Romeo and Juliet" on 1992's *Rites of Passage* from the perspective of both lovers, but sighs, "Ahh Juliet, when we made love you used to cry" way more libidinously than its songwriter. In that album's "Virginia Woolf," Saliers croons to the queer author, acknowledging "the place where you hold me" as if to a flame. And on "Joking," also from *Rites*, a male friend kisses Ray's first-person protagonist but doesn't connect to her romantically, or she to him. The video further explicates this. Three young pals—a queer guy, a butch gal, and a femme—act pointedly buddy-buddy as if holding their own traveling rally for Queer Nation, an ACT UP offshoot that fought antigay abuse with public demonstrations of affection in straight bars and other hetero zones. The mainstream may've read all this as merely rebellious, but we saw it as the Girls getting gayer.

At 1993's March on Washington for Lesbian, Gay, and Bi Equal Rights and Liberation, Ray and Saliers sang their a cappella rendition of "American Tune," Paul Simon's Vietnam War–era ode, recontextualized there into a commentary on US LGBTQ policy. I marched with my friends Mark and Brian, but despite the presence of a million fellow protesters, all I remember is them, because they both died soon after.

Next year, the Girls came out officially in *The Advocate* and *Out* before releasing *Swamp Ophelia*, on which their all-embracing humanitarianism blossoms in expansive arrangements that broaden the pair's scope. In Ray's "Touch Me Fall," queerness permeates the music itself and how it winds from dulcet folk to string-enabled prog-rock before further accelerating into punk frenzy. Elsewhere, Saliers contributes her most direct material. Like the duo's previous albums, *Swamp* sold well—more than a million copies in the US. But its failure to put the pair in *Tracy Chapman*'s sales category was likely due to the courageous video for its standout, "Power of Two."

Saliers's lyric sums up the paradox of queer existence: The desire that complicates our lives also makes them worthwhile. This isn't specific to homosexual connections, but her ballad encapsulates contradictions we know more than most, especially in the couplet "The closer I'm bound in love to you/The closer I am to free." Set to music similarly succinct and affirming, its video includes all kinds of couples—old, young, Black, white, Latin, straight, gay, and lesbian—which was then unusual. Same-sex partners were expected to be "discreet"—i.e., invisible. As soon as a man showed up with a man or a woman with a woman who was more than a friend, their gayness would dominate in the minds of many straight people. To them, entire situations became queer, and the same was doubly true of art with any LGBTQ content. It was cordoned off, kept from children, ghettoized—as it is now once again.

Only a few months earlier, Bruce Springsteen cracked the pop Top Ten with "Streets of Philadelphia," in which he sings about wasting away from AIDS while others abandon him—a searing summation of not only *Philadelphia*'s plotline but also of how society betrays its whipping boys. Unlike that film, Springsteen's song only implies his character is queer, and in its video, the sole gay guy is represented fleetingly by *Philadelphia*'s straight star Tom Hanks.

In the "Power of Two" clip, we're represented by our own; the everyday lesbian and gay people in it are genuine, diverse, and receive significant screentime. In the video's first few seconds, two guys hold each other in one corner while an image of prescription drugs appears in another. This juxtaposition indicates love's necessity during plague, yet it likely made the work "too political" for much MTV play. Ironically, that year the network broke reality-show ground with *The Real World: San Francisco* and its most compelling participant, Pedro Zamora, a gay, Cuban-born AIDS activist who died the day after the season's final episode aired. Gatekeepers could get behind the Boss doing anything. He and the Girls had become core acts of a radio format known as "adult album alternative," resulting in stations more folky than KROQ but hipper and more female-friendly than regular adult-oriented or classic-rock radio. San Francisco's KFOG, for example, was quintessential triple-A. Yet "Power of Two" got scant Top Forty radio support for what should've been a supernova. Even "Closer to Fine"—a triple-A staple—couldn't get higher than number fifty-two on *Billboard*'s Hot 100.

In 1995, "Power of Two" and the Girls themselves appeared in *Boys on the Side*, a Whoopi Goldberg–starring hit film featuring both lesbians and AIDS. In 2009, gay jazz crooner Michael Feinstein and gay Broadway star Cheyenne Jackson teamed for *The Power of Two*, a nightclub act and album showcasing

Saliers's song, one that has accompanied countless LGBTQ couples down the aisle both before and after we won full marriage equality in 2015.

At the Indigo Girls' 1994 show at UC Berkeley's Greek Theatre following their coming out, the audience was even more female and queer than the one I witnessed in 1989. "It's the closest a guy can get to experiencing one of those massive womyn's music festivals," I wrote during a long career stretch in which I reviewed arena-rock shows almost weekly. As my tinnitus attests, those decibels took their toll, and so did the toxic masculinity that came with it. Rather than ridiculing the Girls, which for male music critics was nearly de rigueur, my review reveled in how refreshing it was to get a reprieve from all the dude rock. The Girls' mellifluence and the collective warmth they created made it feel like a queer revival meeting.

"In the early San Francisco days of the Warfield, the Fillmore, and even the Greek, it was astounding to us what was going on," Ray remembers. "It was hard to process it, except for in a joyful way. You sure feel better about yourself when you're in that community and environment."

Yet the pair didn't soften. Also in 1994, the Girls guested on *Jesus Christ Superstar: A Resurrection.* Released by Ray's own Daemon label, this indie reenactment of Andrew Lloyd Webber's rock opera showcases Saliers as Mary Magdalene and Ray as Jesus. As LGBTQ statements go, that's a corker.

"I grew up in the church," Ray reflects. "And the way for me to deal with it is to say, 'You can't take it away from me, and you can't claim Jesus as your savior and not mine.' That's been my stance for a long time, and I think a lot of artists end up sitting in that space, because that's what's informing the powers against you."

Being good Christian gals didn't stop the Girls from making statements that some rebellious stars would never risk. "You hate me 'cause I'm gay," Saliers sings in "It's Alright." Such point-blankness was unprecedented from any longtime LGBTQ bestsellers, and it's on the pair's highest-charting album, 1997's *Shaming of the Sun.* From that year to 1999 (and again in 2010), the pair participated in Sarah McLachlan's Lilith Fair, and appeared several times at what birthed that tour of female musicians, the Michigan Womyn's Music

Festival. When tensions came to a head between Michfest and trans activists protesting founder Lisa Vogel's intention that the event be for "womyn-born-womyn," the pair interviewed each side, donated its 2013 festival earnings to trans activism, and didn't come back. Two years later, Michfest closed for good. As summarized in the Girls' official statement, "we all know who benefits from 'divide and conquer' and it's not womyn or queers."

Unlike most veteran acts, Ray and Saliers never staged a comeback, because they've rarely been away. But in 2023, their profile rebounded when "Closer to Fine" appeared throughout Hollywood's subversively feminist supernova, *Barbie.* When the doll leaves her playhouse, Saliers's existential quandary both scores and underscores Barbie's ontological odyssey. All of us who are forced by society to question our nature's existence take these trips. Indigo Girls give these journeys a voice, one mightier than the sum of its harmonic parts. That's how it is with sisterhood and the LGBTQ movement itself.

▶▶|

Chapter Fifty-Five

Melissa Etheridge

My 1992 interview with Melissa Etheridge began like many others with LGBTQ artists who weren't yet professionally out. We talked about music upfront, then gradually turned to more personal topics. It was my policy that if someone seemed uncomfortable when I edged toward asking them about their sexuality, I'd switch gears back to their work. I try to avoid making those I admire squirm.

Etheridge didn't do that. Instead, she responded unlike any other LGBTQ person I've profiled. She smiled and said, "I think I know what you want to ask. I want to answer but I'm not quite there yet. When I am, I'll tell you everything."

Etheridge kept her word. Early the next year, she attended the inaugural Triangle Ball for President Bill Clinton, the first president to outwardly court LGBTQ voters. Her friend k.d. lang proclaimed to the crowd that coming out was the best thing she'd ever done. Etheridge, however, hadn't planned to make that kind of statement. Nevertheless, out of her mouth came, "I'm proud to say right now I'm very proud to have been a lesbian all my life." Soon after, she invited me into her home for *The Advocate*.

This Kansas-born singer-songwriter ranks among rock's most singular LGBTQ figures. Most of our musicians since David Bowie have drawn from genres with roots in gay life and then set their left-of-center sounds to similarly subcultural lyrics or presentation. Although lang, for example, started with country, what she did with it was confrontational. Her punk-informed performances made clear that she set out to change the world—like many of us who are told who we are and who we love is wrong—and started by reshaping its music. Etheridge, however, has always been mainstream in approach and appeal. Although her politics are the same as those of radical rockers and pop agitators, she didn't intend to be a lesbian poster child.

Yet Etheridge became a pillar of queer success that proved LGBTQ artists could proclaim their gayness and not lose their audience. Instead, it could grow as hers did, exponentially. That's not to say that she didn't have lesbian fans from the start. Before she made a record, Etheridge played in lesbian venues throughout the US. Despite this, she received a rejection letter from Olivia Records. The financially faltering label couldn't afford to put her on the road.

Her eventual boss, Island Records founder Chris Blackwell—the guy who signed Grace Jones, Bob Marley, U2, and other titans—first saw her perform at Que Sera, a Long Beach lesbian club. Like Sire Records' Seymour Stein, Blackwell is the rare record magnate who built an empire nurturing talent that others marginalized, watered down, or excluded. He and Etheridge trashed an overproduced early version of her first album because she'd lost control of her music. "I want the girl in the T-shirt and leather jacket," Blackwell insisted. Seizing the reins, Etheridge and her band rerecorded the album in four days. This time, she gave him that gal in the lesbian bar. The result, 1988's *Melissa Etheridge*, sold two million copies in the US and went gold or platinum in six other countries.

With this debut, Etheridge announced that she was less like her lesbian contemporaries and more like John Mellencamp, the liberal but musically conservative midwestern singer-songwriter who epitomizes "heartland rock." Derived from vintage country and folk, but with louder guitars, heartland rock is rooted in late-twentieth-century straight white male, US blue-collar experience. It's based on the baby-boomer premise that if you live, love, and work hard to actualize the American Dream, you'll get the girl *and* the white picket fence. When she takes the house and you're left sleeping in your muscle car because the factory has shut down, you're entitled to sing the blues. Naturally, heartland rock is as straight as pop gets. For Etheridge to become the genre's first and only female superstar, she had to be the sole vocal virtuoso in a field of gruff and gravelly guys. She became a diva not via vanity but through superiority and emotionality.

Etheridge begat both in a song added to her rerecorded debut, "Bring Me Some Water." Written about her open relationship with Kathleen, a stagehand she'd met while playing at the West Coast Women's Music Festival, it recalls the pathos of another heartland honcho, Bob Seger. Etheridge's gill was often on the road and sleeping with other girls. Not knowing how this extracurricular activity might endanger their affair jacks up Etheridge's jealousies, which in turn feeds heartland rock's perpetual, nearly mythological thirst. Through S&M-tinged imagery, the singer strongly suggests she'll find a willing accomplice to drown out her internal voices. "Sweet devil's got my soul!" she howls. That dickens won't be a dude.

On the set of the song's video, Etheridge met its assistant director, Julie Cypher, who'd become her next partner. Back then, the aspiring filmmaker was married to *La Bamba* actor Lou Diamond Phillips. What you see in the "Water" clip is Etheridge doing everything she can to woo Cypher. While sizzling in the grease of her girlfriend's infidelities, she's trying to charm the pants off a rising Hollywood star's wife. That's a heartland-rock scenario so queer it had to succeed. As they parted, Cypher whispered in Etheridge's ear, "If I wasn't married . . ." Eventually the two canoodled. Cypher told Phillips. Divorce ensued, and in the wake of Etheridge's coming out, Cypher and the singer became pop culture's first lesbian power couple.

Etheridge excelled from the start at expressing as much as she could about herself without assigning gendered nouns to her love objects. Instead, she gives them to her competition. *Melissa Etheridge* fixates on the other women Kathleen had been seeing, which means its songs are packed with feminine imagery that fires up the erotic imaginations of both straight male and lesbian listeners. Its simmering opening cut, "Similar Features," plays this to the passive-aggressive hilt. In it the singer notes that her latest rival looks like her. Etheridge is clearly peeved, but instead of insisting on monogamy, she tells her sweetheart to think of her while fucking this chick. "Go on and close your eyes," she sings. "It shouldn't bother you."

In "Like the Way I Do," a track that has peaked Etheridge concerts in elongated form for decades, the singer presents her unfaithful flame with a questionnaire that emphasizes that this other woman can't compete. "Does she know just how to shock you?/Electrify and rock you?" Etheridge sings. Because she throws herself into these corny lyrics, especially onstage, they illustrate her point better than intellectual poesy. Etheridge's yearning is so strong it's alchemic, and it helped her infiltrate rock stations usually hostile to lesbians. No one could deny they were her birthright.

"You Can Sleep While I Drive" from 1989's *Brave and Crazy* didn't achieve as much airplay as "Way I Do" until Trisha Yearwood had a country hit with it in 1995. Like a thousand Springsteen songs, it's set in a convertable and seemingly optimistic, yet downcast. Etheridge's first autobiography reveals that she wrote it about touring cross-country with Kathleen and their pals to play more women's venues before signing with Island. As with Chapman in "Fast Car," Etheridge's idealism turns to realism. Knowing her lover is unsatisfied, she proposes this trek as a final attempt to rekindle their spark. If Kathleen won't join her, she can sleep—at home, alone—while Etheridge leaves, presumably for good. While delivering that ultimatum, the singer's voice softens as her accompaniment trails off, suggesting not togetherness but solitude. This is the sad flipside of all those U-Haul-on-the-second-date jokes. Some lesbian bonds end as suddenly as they begin.

While waving goodbye to Kathleen and welcoming Cypher, 1992's *Never Enough* reaches beyond heartland rock's nostalgia into contemporary pop. A randy ode to down-low nookie, "Meet Me in the Back" draws a line in the sand at unsafe sex. "If I don't get protection/I will just say no," Etheridge warns, punctuating that last word with silence. "Must Be Crazy for Me" can be heard as a lesbian wrapping her head around mounting evidence that a hot woman married to a famous hunk is falling for her, but its Janet Jacksonian beats didn't break the rocker on pop radio.

Fresh from coming out, Etheridge entered the studio with UK producer Hugh Padgham for the 1993 disc that did that and more, *Yes I Am*. Having invented with Phil Collins the '80s' enormous and defining drum sound, Padgham brings punchy sonic drama that helps Etheridge's voice leap from even the tiniest speakers in torrents of desire and steadfastness. The same goes for guitars that evoke the Rolling Stones without postmodernist quotation. As a result, Etheridge reached her commercial and artistic apotheosis by finding the throughline between women's music of the '70s and emphatically male heartland rock of the '80s.

Whereas gay, bi, and gender-blurring presentation typically favors theatrics, women's music and heartland rock minimize the gap between entertainer and audience. Bruce Springsteen fans don't want to see their rock-star reflection in costuming like Bowie; the Boss must sweat in the same jeans and tees as his followers to affirm their mutual strain.

Give or take a k.d. lang, things were much the same in women's music. Crippled under a twofold pay gap between themselves and their straight male equivalents, lesbians were starved for positive representation because they'd been denied and degraded in mainstream media, if acknowledged at all. They didn't need another prefab construct of feminine perfection. Like all minorities, they deserved to see themselves on big stages. They were looking to be uplifted by someone down-home.

When Etheridge affirmed herself and by extension her LGBTQ following on *Yes I Am*, audiences that rarely overlap intersected in support of a woman who satisfies parallel needs, as represented in the video for her Top Ten smash "I'm the Only One." Although the entranced stares of one lone buck represent the gaze of MTV's target audience, he's also beefy and shirtless—eye candy for straight gals and gay guys alike. As in George Michael's *Listen Without*

Prejudice–era clips, which this resembles, women crucially far outnumber the men and circle each other like lust-stricken lizards who've descended upon the same cramped island during mating season. There's beaucoup bumping and grinding in dreamlike slo-mo, mostly between chiseled babes, and some girl/guy kissing to reassure straight viewers that this isn't an entirely queer free-for-all, but for a moment there's even a guy dancing with another guy. The result is a bit like bi porn for straights. But when lesbian films were few and *The L Word* was a decade away, this meant progress. The video's fevered end affirms the star's singularity: Everyone sweats, but Etheridge solely brings the heat. "It's only fear that makes you run/The demons that you're hiding from," she reminds Cypher, herself, and us.

That's also what we heard in *Yes I Am*'s other humungous hit, "Come to My Window." Even before she reached her popularity's peak, Etheridge struggled with being away from Cypher, so they fought long-distance. Her pane is a metaphor for negotiation: If we can't see eye to eye, let's look at things from another side. Framed by a video in which Juliette Lewis plays a distraught and isolated psychiatric patient, the song became a symbol of LGBTQ people both figuratively and literally imprisoned by a society that pathologizes our passion. In the clip, Lewis yells lyrics as if to an adversary, but it's the song's invincible bridge that most matters, especially in concert. Etheridge—and by extension every fan who can be counted on to sing it with her—pays no mind to those who sit in judgment of us. "What do they know about this love anyway?" she laments.

Like "I'm the Only One," "Come to My Window," which won Etheridge a second Grammy, wouldn't go away—it charted for nearly a year. Her entreaty became pop culture's cry of lesbian frustration and affirmation. It demands that the world comes to *their* window and sees them for who they truly are.

Yes I Am sold six million copies in the US alone and helped double the sales of her previous discs. For a while, Etheridge received unprecedented media support, and her arena-packing concerts became LGBTQ rites of passage. Only Cher, Dolly, and Elton could unite Middle America with us like Etheridge. Janis Joplin cracked rock's glass ceiling, but our best-selling lesbian broke it while coming out, and she kept on living. She's nobody's casualty.

That doesn't mean Etheridge didn't pay her price. Reflecting her live band's bluster, 1995's *Your Little Secret* cracks open a door on what little homelife she had. Heartland rock themes of infidelity and authenticity persist, but everything's heavier, although the exceptions became pop hits. Combining wide relatability and queer specificity on "I Want to Come Over," Etheridge longs for a lover who might be merely unavailable, but lines like "I know you're confused" suggest this gal maintains a straight façade while repressing her truth. In the Cypher-directed video for "Nowhere to Go," the star and the filmmaker take a *Thelma & Louise*–type trek. Rather than driving off the cliff, they embrace at its edge and, therefore, rewrite as happy the woeful ending of Hollywood's famously lesbian-coded film.

Yet in this case, Etheridge's art didn't mirror her life. She and Cypher made headlines in 1996 when announcing via *20/20* and *Newsweek* that they were having a baby. This was the first time a prominent gay couple had done such a thing—back then all queers were expected to remain childless—so it triggered an uproar. Every dumb joke was told. Etheridge stayed home to help raise their daughter, and then their son. An early 2000 *Rolling Stone* cover story revealed the biological dad of both: veteran rocker David Crosby, which provoked more cringey comedy.

Those poking fun likely didn't know or remember that when he was with the Byrds, Crosby wrote and recorded one of the '60s' queerest songs. In "Triad," originally recorded in 1967, he invites a lover to join him and a mutual female friend in a ménage à trois. Like the Velvet Underground, Crosby welcomes what's ordinarily off-limits. His generation was then rejecting nearly everything traditional, even when it came to sex, so his lyric reasonably poses the question "Why can't we go on as three?" Nevertheless, Crosby's ordinarily countercultural bandmates refused to release their version of this "freak-out orgy tune," as Byrds leader Roger McGuinn reportedly called it, so Crosby offered it to his aggressively antiestablishment but also hugely successful friends in San Francisco's Jefferson Airplane. Grace Slick's gender and pronoun change on that band's *Crown of Creation* from 1968 raises the taboo of "Triad" even higher. Instead of a guy attempting to coax a woman into making love to another woman while making love with him (a turn-on for many hetero guys), Slick suggests her mate should get sexually familiar with another dude—still a far more disapproved-of proposal. By singing the song himself on Crosby, Stills, Nash & Young's live hits-packed *4 Way Street*, Crosby landed his polyamorous bisexual ode on a 1971 chart-topper. And by teaming up with Etheridge and Cypher in a poetic turn of events, Crosby completed a nonsexual yet nevertheless biological triad.

Soon after they became moms, Cypher told Etheridge she was "no longer gay." Attempting to save their relationship, the singer toured with Cypher and the kids. By September, the pair of twelve years disclosed their separation right after Ellen DeGeneres and Anne Heche—the era's other celebrity lesbian couple—split.

Etheridge foreshadowed all this on 1999's *Breakdown*, which I covered for *Rolling Stone*. "It was the first time I felt that one of my albums got a really serious review," her autobiography notes. I was struck by how the disc begins much like any by her, then turns adventurous, more about us. "Mama I'm Strange" she sings for the wounded inner child of so many who can't fit into heterosexuality and cisgender's confines. "Scarecrow" retells the murder of Matthew Shepard, the Wyoming student who in 1998 became a symbol of LGBTQ oppression when two homophobes tortured him and left him to die. Yet I was most taken with "My Lover." "No one manipulates/Like my lover," she brags, barb after lacerating barb. Its mix of irreverence, gentleness, anger, and agony reminded me of early solo John Lennon, so I likened it to his disconsolate "Mother." "I really drank that in and was grateful," Etheridge wrote of my comparison. Learning I'd helped her during a difficult time gave me a boost to finish this chapter.

I've emphasized Etheridge's tumultuous biography because she has always made it relevant through tell-all tracks that culminated in 2001's *Skin,* an anguished and largely acoustic account of her split with Cypher. Earlier queer pop celebrities often hid behind their music, but Etheridge always parts the curtains on the window of her world as far as a commercial giant can. This open-book policy is the context through which we comprehend all her art. She became the first LGBTQ rock star not to be eccentric or estranged; the first one thoroughly relatable to regular Joes and Josephines. Through her death-defying bawl, Etheridge encapsulates the agita of ordinary life.

⏭

Chapter Fifty-Six

Nirvana and Hole

Just as synthpop's rise defined the 1980s, alternative rock's cataclysmic shift shaped the 1990s. This was grunge—punk without gay men because we were busy caretaking, grieving, protesting, and dying. Its foremost act, Nirvana, rocked as hard as its manlier Seattle peers, but with candy-coated hooks and outcast insights that clicked with those of us on the outside critical of the inside. Its leader, Kurt Cobain, both masked and manifested his sensitivity through wounded fight songs like 1991's battered and battering "Smells Like Teen Spirit" that reflected alienated young America in Ronald Reagan's wake. We heard ourselves in another iteration of ambivalent music that set lugubrious lyrics to rousing pop.

Nirvana was the first huge hetero rock group that fought homophobia not nicely but through the same confrontational tactics as revolutionary queers. At the end of the 1992 *Saturday Night Liv*e episode in which it performed, the band's towering bassist Krist Novoselic locked lips with drummer Dave Grohl, then did the same with Cobain in an echo of Queer Nation's kiss-ins. In the liner notes to 1992's *Incesticide*, Cobain wrote, "If any of you in any way hate homosexuals, people of different color, or women, please do this one favor for us—leave us the fuck alone! Don't come to our shows and don't buy our records." He then sang, "What else could I say/Everyone is gay" on 1993's "All Apologies," which Sinéad O'Connor soon covered. Ordinary guys don't have the guts to chant "Rape Me" so many times and with such conviction that there's no question his empathetic wrath sprang from identification with women and other victims of sexual assault.

Nirvana's LGBTQ legacy didn't end the next year with Cobain's suicide. Novoselic formed Sweet 75 with lesbian frontwoman Yva Las Vegass, while Cobain's widow, Courtney Love, continued fronting alt-rock LGBTQ favorite Hole as a conduit for controversy. In 1991's dissonant "Teenage Whore," she squalls, "GET OUT OF MY HOUSE!," words we've heard from parents who disapprove of not simply what we do but who we are. This discord flatters a rebel who embodies feminism's defiance in everything she does, from her unsettling childlike *Lolita* look to her band's leviathan menace.

I can attest that Hole—nearly all female—and grunge quintet L7's all-woman lineup drew different crowds than the dudes. "If we were in San Francisco, half the audience were dykes," the latter's Donita Sparks recalls. Meanwhile, there were times when reviewing shows by Pearl Jam, Spin Doctors, Blind Melon, and other monsters of not-so-alternative rock that I felt once again stuck in the suburbs, back with the jocks and stoners. The moshing that spread from hardcore punk to generic grunge made even hip but chiefly male festivals like Lollapalooza feel like frat parties. The gay-club/alt-rock radio crossover that popularized Soft Cell and so many others petered out when KROQ and related stations favored grunge's bludgeoning guitars.

This changed only when woman-led bands like Stereolab, Garbage, the Cardigans, and Luscious Jackson—the last an all-girl unit with a lesbian drummer, former Beastie Boy Kate Schellenbach—brought back new wave's melodicism and danceable diversity. Schellenbach's girlfriend was the Breeders' Josephine Wiggs, whose loopy bassline in 1993's hit "Cannonball" links the three-quarters-female group to post-punks like Au Pairs and cleared space for Imperial Teen, which features two women and two gay guys. One of them, Roddy Bottum, also of alt-metal's Faith No More, now leads the even gayer duo Man on Man. Once again, queer-inclusive women moved music forward.

⏭

Chapter Fifty-Seven

C+C Music Factory, Deee-Lite, and House Music

When house music originated in 1980s Chicago at venues like the gay Music Box and the queer Warehouse as karmic payback for that city's Disco Demolition, it was much like what Paradise Garage members called garage music: the most soulful, sonically adventurous, and diva-driven side of disco favored by LGBTQ people of color.

This was no coincidence. The Black leaders of house and garage—the Warehouse's Frankie Knuckles and the Garage's Larry Levan—had long been buddies. They'd previously DJed together at the Continental Baths, and their shared sensibilities permeated New York and Chicago's parallel post-disco scenes. When in 1986 I met Windy City musicians while writing the first national article on house music for *Spin*, I felt as though I already knew them because they were much like Garage heads: mostly Black, often gay, and yanking music out of next to nothing. House at the start was little more than recycled racy disco. It was to club music what punk was to rock: cheap but exhilarating underground noise. And it reintroduced the avenging diva via Xaviera Gold, Kym Mazelle, and Liz Torres, whose collective sass culminated in "bitch tracks" by trans trash-talker Candice Jordan, aka Candy J., aka Hateful Head Helen, aka Sweet Pussy Pauline.

In early 1987, Steve "Silk" Hurley's year-old "Jack Your Body" went Number One in the UK, and house's four-on-the-floor soon shaped nearly all club music that isn't hip-hop. What first emerged from England was poppier, more polished, and less soulful than Chi-Town groups like Ten City, but sometimes even gayer, like Rick Astley's 1987 Stock Aitken Waterman–helmed "Never Gonna Give You Up." When that song became a nearly worldwide Number One, Europe spawned a slew of house upstarts yielding international dividends, much like disco did in *Saturday Night Fever*'s wake. Every odd name—M|A|R|R|S, S'Express, and on and on—was new.

This is not how the US music industry likes to do business. It would much rather sell ten million copies of one album, like Nirvana's *Nevermind,* than one hundred thousand from one hundred acts. Rhythmic superstars like Madonna and Janet Jackson did those numbers, so for the first couple of years in the 1990s, house got a chance. New York's C+C Music Factory began a brief but era-stamping run with 1990's "Gonna Make You Sweat (Everybody Dance Now)," which combines diva thunder from Two Tons o' Fun/Weather Girls vet Martha Wash with a stern rap from Freedom Williams, who serves banjee realness and the chiseled abs gay guys perfected. Yet as she did with the Italian house outfit Black Box, Wash went uncredited. In both cases, a video-friendly hottie lip-synced Wash's wail. As I'd mentioned earlier, dance music's anonymity welcomed musicians pop often shuns: big ones, dark ones, and us. When MTV achieved ubiquity, this anonymity became harder to maintain, prompting some labels to hire models as fronts for their actual artists, which became an issue with the breakout success of one such duo, Milli Vanilli.

Not so for the early '90s club act that most emphasized inclusivity: Deee-Lite. Singer/fashion designer Lady Miss Kier, Ukraine-born DJ Dmitry, and Korean Japanese DJ Towa Tei exuded hallucinatory vibrance in every direction. Kier's retro-futurist costumes reflected the queer New York "club kid" scene, which meant every Deee-Lite video, photo shoot, and sleeve was as cartoon-bright as the times were funereally dark.

Embracing multiple genres and generations, the trio's international hit "Groove Is in the Heart" adroitly juggles more than a dozen funk, jazz, disco, Latin, and TV sit-com samples while Kier's neo-beatnik wordplay sparks with A Tribe Called Quest rapper Q-Tip and funk luminary Bootsy Collins. On that and other exhilarated cuts from 1990's *World Clique*, which features lettering from East Village drag pioneer Tabboo!, Deee-Lite asserts that anything is achievable through individual determination and collective emancipation.

Yet behind the scenes all was not well. Deee-Lite and its gay Black manager Bill Coleman—a former *Billboard* dance-music columnist—acrimoniously severed. Tei went solo, while Kier and Dmitri's romantic relationship ended. Despite its far-reaching creativity, Deee-Lite failed to impress those in power and in 1994 dissolved. "The president of the label had never been a fan of our music regardless of our success," Kier later reflected. "He told us it was too Black and too gay." Meanwhile, C+C Music Factory's sales plummeted during the illness and death of its gay Black center, David Cole, in early 1995. The official cause was spinal meningitis, one of many opportunistic diseases afflicting those battling HIV.

Dance music of the 1990s produced substantial entities, such as Moby and Daft Punk, while it mutated into a myriad of sub-sub-genres. But as gay men in the record biz disappeared as a result of backlash, exclusion, and death, it became impossible to miss that most of these new styles were dominated by European, male, and heteronormative participants hellbent on credibility within their micro-niches and therefore lacking the playfulness LGBTQ culture brought to club music or the prowess of the Black women we honor. The KLF had these attributes. So did M People and Pizzicato Five. Björk still does.

Yet for much of the '90s, queer spirit mostly came through female rockers, such as Ani Di Franco or 4 Non Blondes, who earlier would've remained LGBTQ secrets. The latter's 1993 worldwide smash "What's Up" enabled its lesbian singer, Linda Perry, to become one of the prime architects of early twenty-first-century pop, producing and often writing hits for Pink, Christina Aguilera, Gwen Stefani, and many more. The US record industry may have put its muscle into alternative rock as a preemptive strike against gay-championed dance music overtaking straight dudes with guitars as it had in the '70s, but our women still sometimes came out on top.

⏭

Chapter Fifty-Eight

Bikini Kill, Green Day, Pansy Division, and Suede

In the 1980s and early '90s, two overlapping punk movements were more read about than heard yet soon rippled into the mainstream and bettered it. These were riot grrrl, a third-wave feminist movement centered in Olympia, Washington; and queercore, a geographically diverse LGBTQ crusade of bands similarly fed up with patriarchal bullshit. Both grew out of zines, strove to self-sanction musicians and fans, and created validation not forthcoming from the neo-chauvinists who had infiltrated punk. These were pre-internet means for us to talk with one another and say, *No, you're* not *subhuman. You're a potential warrior of truth. Learn an instrument, write a song about it, and tell the others.*

If Bikini Kill's 1993 riot grrrl manifesto "Rebel Girl" had been recorded twenty years earlier by guys, it would simply be considered headbanging rock. But leader Kathleen Hanna's first-person lyric about her awe for a stalwart outcast operates on levels simultaneously sexual and sororal. The first verse situates the song in childhood's innocence; the second in the physical manifestation of adolescence's ideals. "In her kiss, I taste the revolution" ranks among the greatest lines cited in this book, for it encapsulates everything feminism and LGBTQ pride represent. Is this crush platonic, or something more? "They say she's a slut," Hanna sings in some renditions. But on the supercharged single, "slut" becomes "dyke." That switch might be a tip of the hat to Joan Jett, who produces, plays guitar, and sings backup on that version. The single's lyric sheet even crosses out the former word and adds the latter. Future Le Tigre frontwoman Hanna defies naysayers through a friendship that can't be delineated or defined because it's total. Riot grrrl is remembered for its rage, but "Rebel Girl" rises above the movement's fury through its all-encompassing opposite. Sisterhood is punk, it says. So is loving all girls through another one.

Queercore's brush with the mainstream came through Pansy Division's inclusion on Green Day's 1994 tour right when that punk-pop trio's breakout, *Dookie,* started selling millions. Outsiders didn't take Green Day seriously, despite its origins in the same queer-positive East Bay scene. Yet thirty years before Green Day's 2024 bisexual love song "Bobby Sox," *Dookie* includes "Coming Clean," in which its teen protagonist comes out. When Billie Joe Armstrong sings "I found out what it takes to be a man," he subverts the stale notion of equating virility with machismo and instead situates it within the bravery demanded of those who can't be what their parents expect and society rewards. Those who look down upon us think sex between men is sissified, yet it engages our masculinity on every level. Their hate ensures we'll "man up" and fight back.

That's what Green Day did by aligning itself with Pansy Division, a San Francisco band that epitomizes queercore with insurgent gayness. On 1994's *Deflowered,* "Denny" describes an AIDS-stricken porno actor on death's brink. "I want them to see/What they've done to me," Jon Ginoli sings. More often, Pansy Division battles homophobia through humor. When the two bands reunited for a free healthcare benefit in Oakland in 1995, the opening act walked onstage and said, "Hi, we're Pansy Division, and we're big fags for all you jocks who can't handle it." The kids first pogoed madly, then froze as

Pansy's gayness sank in. When goons flipped the band off, bassist Chris Freeman challenged them to meet him backstage. Do you see what I mean about queerness fostering manliness?

Back then, Armstrong came out as bisexual and spoke about his gay uncle with AIDS in *The Advocate*. At the 2009 Berkeley opening of *American Idiot*, the musical theater incarnation of Green Day's same-named smash album from 2004, I ended up hanging out with Armstrong's mom. She explained that her son looked up to her brother. Their friendship as well as her brother's death impacted Billie profoundly. So much in that moment made sense: Armstrong witnessed what happened to his uncle and aimed to spare others. This, too, is how revolution tastes.

Hungry for another Kurt Cobain, the suits went on an alt-rock spending spree that made disco's post-*Fever* excess seem sensible. Despite Cobain's allyship, gay, bi, and gender-blurred men were this time left largely on the shelf. And although 1980s-originated musicians like Bob Mould and Pet Shop Boys upped their queer content in the wake of coming out in the 1990s, few gay-connected newcomers of that decade could climb any higher than queercore's underground.

One exception sparked Britpop, England's most overground '90s rock movement. Led by epicene vamp Brett Anderson, Suede conveys dismay and drama rooted in glam's rift from what's quotidian. "I'm a bisexual man who's never had a homosexual experience," he famously declared in the early '90s—a quote some considered opportunistic then but now seems prescient. While proclaiming solidarity with the band's gay drummer Simon Gilbert, Anderson's statement pushes beyond the few LGBTQ delineations that existed.

Suede's first single, 1992's "The Drowners," extols male-on-male intimacy.

"We kiss in his room to a popular tune," Anderson swooningly croons. It's all but stated that his protagonist surrenders to anal intercourse, as concluding handclaps signal consent—not just his, but also Suede's audience's. "You're taking me over," the chorus repeats to affirm that butt-fucking between guys is jolly good indeed.

In the band's 1993 UK Top Ten hit "Animal Nitrate," the narration shifts to second person but describes similar participants. Its pun on amyl nitrate again alludes to anal sex—the drug's muscle-relaxing effect facilitates it. The situation remains consensual, although barely, but turns violent. "So in your broken home, he broke all your bones/Now you're taking it time after time," Anderson sings, repeating that "Drowners" verb to again emphasize the passive partner's receptivity. Alternatingly orgasmic and agonized, Anderson's sobbing vocal emphasizes his identification with an implicitly male subject. Enchanted by this brute, he's abandoned for being over twenty-one, then the age of homosexual consent and, therefore, no longer criminally desirable.

That year on the Brits—the UK Grammy equivalent—Anderson bookended "Animal Nitrate" by literally aiming his backside at the English music industry and striking his microphone audibly hard against his bottom, as if he, too, were taking it time after time. Four decades after Little Richard and two after Bowie, Suede at its buggery-boosting best made homosexuality dangerously rock 'n' roll all over again. Anderson said *fuck you* by pantomiming *fuck me.*

Featuring a cover image of two women kissing from the 1991 book *Stolen Glances: Lesbians Take Photographs*, 1993's *Suede* entered the UK chart at Number One, selling faster there than any debut in a decade. What became known as Britpop prompted mixed-gendered and modern bands like Elastica, Echobelly, and Pulp, but turned laddish and retrograde when Oasis became the movement's biggest seller. The lesbian singer also known as Suede sued Sony for trademark infringement, forcing the group to be billed in North America as the London Suede, starting with its also homoerotically packaged and Bowie-influenced 1994 successor, *Dog Man Star.*

The most compositionally advanced UK guitarist since Johnny Marr, Bernard Butler left before that album's release and paired with David McAlmont—

that phenomenal gay Black singer I'd mentioned chapters ago—and created 1995's "Yes," a swanky collision of indie rock and symphonic soul that went Top Ten in the UK. This duo, McAlmont & Butler, also clicked in Europe, where Suede remains successful, but they never had a chance here. The US music biz has long since forgotten that when white, Black, straight, and gay musicians last united, for disco, it created a four-billion-dollar industry.

⏭

Chapter Fifty-Nine

Queen Latifah and Hip-Hop

You may've wondered: *Why has he only tangentially mentioned hip-hop?* I was an early champion, but I've held off writing about hip-hop in this book until now because it and LGBTQ culture have had a problematic relationship. A few initial, disco-leaning rap hits, like Kurtis Blow's "The Breaks" from 1980, played in gay clubs. The 1982 breakdance favorite "Hip Hop, Be Bop (Don't Stop)" came courtesy of Man Parrish, the same gay gent who created the title song for that year's virile porn classic *Heatstroke*. But hip-hop was otherwise more popular in alternative spaces that attracted arty queers like me than on exclusively gay dancefloors.

Some of this had to do with racism. Many mainstream clubs had overtly racist (and transphobic) door policies and by the 1990s covertly racist music programming as well. So did ours. R&B of one form or another soundtracked much of our revolution, but as house turned poppy and European or trance-y and vocal-deficient, Black acts comprised a shrinking percentage of our playlists. When we were most discriminated against, we sometimes did the same to others, and even ourselves.

The rest comes down to another indisputable truth: Hip-hop—even the otherwise outstanding kind—was often antigay and misogynist. I beelined to buy Grandmaster Flash and the Furious Five's 1982 game-changing "The Message" because I loved every bit of it . . . except its use of "fag hag," "undercover fag," and other lines about prison rape culminating in suicide. I had to remind myself that this is how the story ends for many because of institutionalized racism. But those lyrics didn't do LGBTQ listeners any favors, and a part of me died inside every time I danced to them. Others that followed were worse. In "Live at Union Square, November 1986," on 1988's triple-platinum *He's the DJ, I'm the Rapper* by DJ Jazzy Jeff and the Fresh Prince, actor/rapper Will Smith cajoles fans into cheering by yelling at them, "All the homeboys that got AIDS be quiet! All the girls out there that don't like guys be quiet!" Even the Beastie Boys, who came up through Danceteria, had to be talked out of titling their debut album *Don't Be a Faggot.* By the mid-'90s, I couldn't stomach any more "hos" and "homos."

Before queer hip-hop could come out, women had to clear the way. Gay and lesbian clubs that wouldn't touch Public Enemy embraced Salt-N-Pepa's "Push It" in 1987, while LGBTQ hip-hop hotspots emerged. In San Francisco, lesbian DJ Page Hodel hosted the Box, a pan-racial, pan-queer club in which she combined rap with funk, electro, and other genres left behind when house swept gay dancefloors. It was there where I first saw a performance by a woman who epitomized the Box, Queen Latifah.

This Newark MC came up in a late-'80s moment when hip-hop evolved from the starkness and shouting of Run-D.M.C. Like Deee-Lite, Latifah's early records are awash with waves of samples that she rode with nobility. In "Ladies First," a 1989 duet with London-born MC Monie Love, a fellow member of NYC's individualistic Native Tongues collective, the pair trade feminist verses that demonstrate women can be as lyrically and percussively intricate as their male counterparts, and sing better, too.

Released as a single weeks before Madonna's "Vogue," 1990's "Come into My House" combines hip-house with elements of the Peech Boys' Larry Levan–mixed Paradise Garage classic "Don't Make Me Wait" on a track tailormade for ballroom dance battle. Its video further emphasizes Latifah's inclusivity through traditional African and Asian dancing and costuming, as well as through contemporary clubbers vogueing in male-on-male silhouette. "Give me body!" Latifah commands us.

All this made it a major gay event when Latifah performed at the Box on New Year's Eve 1989. Everything from the dignified way she held herself to her knack for making pro-female, pro-Black lyrics personable said she'd soon be a star. The one time during her Box set when her regal bearing cracked was when she spotted a pal. It was that awkward-but-hilarious moment when one closeted person encounters another in a queer space and, while realizing their friend is gay, suddenly fathoms this other person is drawing identical conclusions about them.

After achieving pop success with 1993's misogyny-crushing, Motown-released "U.N.I.T.Y.," Latifah sang in LGBTQ-relevant musicals such as 2007's *Hairspray* and 2015's *Bessie*. When receiving BET's 2021 Lifetime Achievement Award, she thanked "her love," Eboni Nichols, and their son, Rebel, and wished the crowd a happy Pride. But when I mentioned her Box appearance during an early '90s phone interview, our Queen abruptly hung up. She didn't need to explain why.

⏭

Chapter Sixty

RuPaul (and a little more Sylvester)

From the start, RuPaul mixed punk and drag with the impishness of a much earlier gender magician: Bugs Bunny. Yet RuPaul's ingenuity first emerged not on a stage or in the recording studio but for the camera's hungry eye. In his appearances on Atlanta public access television's *The American Music Show*, 1980s RuPaul was a jester's version of what Sylvester had been doing with the Hot Band, occupying multiple musical genres while not fully in drag or cisgendered. Drawing from the diversity of the variety shows he watched obsessively as a kid, Ru forged for himself a free zone in which he could mix male, female, straight, gay, comedy, social commentary, and DIY glitz. Even in this early stage, RuPaul solely defined RuPaul. That's a big deal for us who have labels thrown at us soon after our difference seeps out, because these names are usually not very nice.

As one must if born Black, gay, and other things thought substandard, this polyglot prankster broke out of multiple boxes, and propelled himself into the mid-'80s East Village drag of the Pyramid Club. Even gayer than Danceteria but aesthetically akin, the Pyramid scene combined gender illusionists with gender benders, giving every kind of queen space to create serious craft while seemingly just kidding around. Lady Bunny (a winsome comedian who also came up through Atlanta), Lypsinka (a lip-sync maestro who draws from vintage Hollywood dialogue), and John Kelly (a tremendous performance artist with a delicate Joni Mitchell act) all occupied the same drag continuum there.

When RuPaul traded the Pyramid's mutability for the purely female glamazon he perfected in the early '90s, he maintained his eccentricities but funneled them through the discipline of his idol, Diana Ross. Adopting Ross's Cheshire cat smile, Ru parted the curtains of a world that hadn't welcomed James Baldwin's scowl. Ru took the AIDS-fed negativity gobbling up clubland like Ms. Pac-Man, switched it to positivity, and sashayed right on in.

With 1992's "Supermodel (You Better Work)," Ru made his manifesto. *Sanford and Son*'s LaWanda Page monologues his character's fictional backstory: Headhunted by an *Ebony* fashion scout, this Detroit girl, not coincidentally from the same Brewster projects that nurtured Miss Ross, becomes a modeling sensation. She "works" in the conventional sense yet also as one does in the Black LGBTQ ballroom scene, where "working it" is how one unleashes inner truths reined in within the straight white world. "It don't matter what you wear/They're checkin' out your savoir faire," RuPaul sings in a bridge that musically modulates his cover girl upward. Doing the right thing in any occasion without concession, she turns work into play by breathing life into what burns out others.

In the video, directed by Randy Barbato of the LGBTQ production company World of Wonder, Ru enacts this story while adding a gay metanarrative. Overwork means this supermodel loses her sanity, like so many women, LGBTQ people, and other minorities forced to sacrifice mental health to prove their worth. Her strain builds until Ru re-creates the fabulously psychotic face made by *Sunset Boulevard*'s Gloria Swanson when the faded starlet she's playing declares that she's ready for her closeup while being arrested for murder. Just as comics aspire to "kill," drag artists aim to "slay"—even sweet ones like Ru, who breaks character with a giggle.

"Supermodel" wore down radio's resistance to dance music this queer through welcoming slogans, nonstop hooks, and RuPaul's innate charm. MTV pumped the clip far more than anything else drag-related that wasn't Madonna, while Ru did the same talk shows that welcomed Melissa Etheridge. All this added up to a respectable number forty-five on *Billboard*'s Hot 100, higher chart placements in Europe, and half a million in worldwide sales.

Many gay club hits followed 1993's hairstyling spiritual "Back to My Roots," yet Ru's pop trajectory faltered, even as his cultural profile further ascended when in 1994 M·A·C Cosmetics made him the first drag spokesperson. In 1996, VH1 gave him *The RuPaul Show*, which he co-hosted with former Seduction singer Michelle Visage, also then his morning cohort on WKTU. Lesbian director Jamie Babbit's 1999 satire of LGBTQ conversion therapy camps, *But I'm a Cheerleader,* proved his panache even as a male actor, but 2007's self-written spy spoof *Starrbooty* committed a drag felony: It wasn't funny. Few at the time would have predicted that Ru's greatest achievement still lay ahead.

Reality TV has much to answer for: ghastly pop idols, history's worst president, and the resulting near-collapse of civilization. On the bright side, there's *RuPaul's Drag Race.* Beginning in 2009 on queer Logo TV, this ongoing series and its many spinoffs coalesce all that RuPaul represents, not merely "Charisma, Uniqueness, Nerve, and Talent." Mama Ru's drag boot camp teaches those whom society deems the lowest of the low how to rise and shine their brightest through communally shared self-love and a truckload of sequins.

The effects of this are monumental. At age forty eight, Ru created an LGBTQ platform that bypassed the usual cultural bouncers to validate us. Despite little to no airplay, gays and their friends know RuPaul's "Cover Girl," "Sissy That Walk," "I'm a Winner, Baby," and other *Drag Race* mainstays. Moreover, Ru raised drag beyond a regional and sometimes regressive folk craft into politically progressive art. By demystifying its creation on TV, making it accessible to those who'd never venture into a gay bar, and championing its competitors not as failed men but as triumphant entertainers, Ru not only revolutionized drag but also how the world perceives it.

It wasn't long ago that the general public thought gays and lesbians yearned to be like straights of the opposite sex. All gay guys secretly wear frilly tulle dresses, it believed; all lesbians live in double-breasted gangster suits. Our adversaries have long believed that by controlling what we wear, they can make us invisible or be just like them. We've challenged these misconceptions, which meant in Stonewall's immediate wake that many gay and lesbian activists opposed traditional drag. That's why freeform gender deviation became an LGBTQ signifier of rock 'n' roll rebellion through resisters such as David Bowie and Joan Jett.

Right when gender-bending guys temporarily faded from pop, Ru brought drag back. His show revived it so successfully that drag is once again a focus for the far right in its renewed war against us—especially trans folk—and its revived conspiracy theories about LGBTQ people grooming kids for recruitment and corruption. *Drag Race* testifies that we're the ones who have been debased—especially those of us who as kids were taunted, beaten, and thrown out of our homes for being gay or trans. In high school, a friend of mine ended up on a street corner when his parents found women's clothes in his bedroom. Prostitution was the only way many homeless LGBTQ teens could survive in the 1970s. In much of the world, that's still the case.

While writing this book, I watched plenty of *Drag Race* to remind myself what life is like for pop's young queer audience, especially for those who diverge from all norms, whether they are sexual, gender, or racial. It's these kids who capture what it means to be LGBTQ, because they're the queerest: the ones who'll never fit into corporatized compromises of mainstream gay culture. They're the most artistic and least inhibited, which enables them to tell all our stories, no matter what hue we occupy on the gay and racial rainbow. We don't recognize the universality of this multiplicity as we should.

When I was coming of age, clones defined gay culture. Yet the queer figure most beloved of that era's macho-aspirant population was the singer who most stood outside its conformity: Sylvester. Shortly after his 1986 hit "Someone Like You" was released with a Larry Levan mix and a Keith Haring sleeve, I saw him perform at the Red Parrot, an upscale Manhattan club, where Tony Bennett walked out as I walked in. Eager to elevate the club's largely straight crowd onto the exalted plane that he embodies on 1985's ecstatic "Take Me to

Heaven," Sylvester asked for volunteers to dance with him, so I did. Moments like that one are why I came out, and why it's been worth it.

Sylvester is the reason I live in San Francisco. When during SF's 1988 Pride march he joined the People with AIDS contingent in a wheelchair, Sylvester became the first music celebrity to do the hardest work of humanizing the disease: simply volunteering that he had it. I wanted to honor this valor while he was still alive, so I convinced the *Voice* to let me profile him.

Not even the early loss of my father and several friends had prepared me for being face-to-face with someone who had embodied so much of gay life yet was so close to death. He asked me to watch the *Donahue* talk show with him because drag entertainers like Jimmy James guested that afternoon. My eyes, however, kept drifting to the details in his museum-like home, which included a framed collection of gloves, many Aunt Jemima salt and pepper shakers, and a giant "Free South Africa" poster by Haring that hung above his bed—all signifiers of Sylvester's and his people's complicated but proud history. Yet our conversation focused on his present, which never got any better.

"When I came home from the hospital, I weighed 140 pounds," he told me of his bout with AIDS-related pneumocystis pneumonia. "Now I'm at 167, but my normal weight was 190 to 200 pounds. Thank God I always had a great fashion sense and knew how to make myself look thinner. I was always on a diet. This wasn't quite the way I wanted to do it."

While visiting San Francisco, I also applied for a job at the *Examiner*, where I ended up working for nine years. Since late 1988, I've lived in the Castro a few blocks from where Sylvester did. He's still SF to me, much like Madonna will always be my New York. But it's painful to remember that my time here started when Sylvester was gravely ill, even though he did make me smile during our interview whenever "honey," "child," or "Miss Thing" fell from his chapped gray lips. I've cried so many times while writing our stories here that I only want to remember Sylvester bathed in rouge, covered in sequins, and showered by shimmering disco lights.

It's cliché to commemorate a beloved club's closing or a quintessential star's passing by declaring it "the end of an era." But when the Paradise Garage shuttered in 1987, the Saint followed the next year, and Sylvester—the sole figure to epitomize both venues—perished that December from the disease that had claimed his collaborator Patrick Cowley in 1982 at the epidemic's beginning, it felt as though most everything LGBTQ nightlife represented for nearly two decades after Stonewall went with them.

RuPaul can't replace all that. His talents are different from Sylvester's, and *Drag Race* isn't perfect. Too often its contestants spar with one another when they could be uniting to overthrow the patriarchy.

But for decades RuPaul has carried Sylvester's gay baton. Like Sylvester, Ru unites all LGBTQ audiences with straight ones by extolling and not compromising our queerness. He represents aspiration without assimilation. And I can verify that he's Sylvester's student. In 2004, when I spoke alongside Martha Wash and others at a New York University conference about Sylvester, I struggled to keep my cool when I looked into the audience and spotted natty-suited Ru. He knows our history. That's why he's able to nurture our future like few others.

RuPaul's imprimatur is all over twenty-first-century LGBTQ culture: Janelle Monáe, Big Freedia, Lil Nas X, Chappell Roan, and others have made his queer fearlessness their own. Decades after Warhol and "Walk on the Wild Side," drag queens and those schooled by them are pop stars.

When social media began allowing everyone to interact with minimal mediation, music stopped being the primary means for LGBTQ people to hear one another. We no longer need bars, discos, or bathhouses to meet, which is a good thing, because many of our neighborhoods have been gentrified out of existence. Dance clubs of any sort are few, and lesbian bars are nearly extinct. We still need our designated safe spaces where we can revel in the glory of our music together as one and feel the power of our collectivity. The validation I received from an all-night marathon at the Paradise Garage cannot be obtained on any phone. I work out nearly every day, so when I do have the rare chance to dance in public to the music of my gay generation, I'm ready.

Today's virtual connections create a pressure for us to mimic one another that is greater than even that of the clone era I endured. That's why I'm closing by sharing my gratitude for how RuPaul promotes the exquisiteness of individual expression. As fans well know, every episode of *Drag Race* episode ends with his mantra: "If you can't love yourself, how in the hell are you gonna love somebody else?" And although it goes unstated, he means the very thing about us that we're taught to despise. This is a lesson of paramount importance: We must love what sets us apart for it fuels our music *and* our essence.

Our queerness remains our mightiest realness.

Acknowledgments

This journey began with the 1990 passing of Vito Russo, the activist, scholar, and friend who wrote the first and still definitive LGBTQ take on film, *The Celluloid Closet*. I couldn't have created *Mighty Real* without him and other queer homesteaders on the far side of the rainbow.

Nor could I have completed it without the love of the living. Three homo Hail Marys for my agent David Dunton at Harvey Klinger Inc., who stayed by my side during eight years of writing, waiting, and wailing; and to matchmaker Regina Joskow, who knew her ex-husband was fit for the task. Thank you Rick Kot, who signed my book but retired after Barbra Streisand's. I salute my editor, Allison Lorentzen, who took over and taught me what to cut, cut, cut. I tip my bowler to copy editor Cliff Corcoran, who helped this AP-style guy obey Chicago house rules. My compliments to Andrea Schulz, for upgrading *Mighty Real* from a Penguin paperback to a Viking hardcover, to cover designer Colin Webber, for following my instructions to the groove-encircled letter, and to interior designer Alexis Sulaimani, for making *Mighty Real*'s insides as stylish as its outsides.

What have I done to deserve a truckload of help from my former editor, Michael Azerrad? Thank you for being the greatest grammatical ally of which a gay boy could ever dream.

I applaud further fellow critics Rob Sheffield, Michaelangelo Matos, Will Hermes, Ann Powers, Bill Brewster, Chris Molanphy, Dave DiMartino, Bill Holdship, Kurt Reighley, Smith Galtney, David Nathan, and Jason King for their access and advice. I'm grateful to Joe Keyes, Craig Marks, Jessica Hopper, and others who assigned articles that begat chapters. Bravo to the editors who helped me write queerly, especially my *Village Voice* bosses of the 1980s: Robert Christgau, Doug Simmons, Richard Goldstein, Barbara O'Dair, Karen Durbin, and Kit Rachlis.

Praises to JD Doyle for preserving our history online at Queer Music Heritage.

I'm beholden to everyone I interviewed for this book but also to those whose LGBTQ music conversations with me over the last fifty years informed it.

Mighty Real wouldn't have been possible without my kin and clan of choice, especially Jim, Eric, Frankie, Beth, and Patty Salveson; Joanne LaFreniere, Luna Osleger, my sister Linda and her husband, Bob Elliott, Scott Montgomery, Marc Rand, Kelly Lawrence, Jerry Bonham, Marga Gomez, Jens Peterson Hällefors, Eva Hällefors, Rio Vizmanos, Johnny Ray Houston, Jenni Olson, Pete Moruzzi, Lauren LeBaron, Deena Davenport, Laurel Gude, Liz Ortiz, Paul Wolf, Steven Herrick, Greg Prevost, Jim Hirsch, Jim Castronovo, Joe DeBell, Mike Russello; and Brad, Aleta, and Matt Allen. Special thanks to my dad, Elmer, who bought me Bowie and all the rest but didn't live to see how it helped me survive and even thrive.

Blessed are the libraries, record stores, bookstores, concert halls, discos, psychotherapy offices, and other sacred queer spaces.

Thank fucking god for the right teachers, particularly Kevin Griffith, Paul Menges, and Terry Brennan.

Huzzah to Rainer Geissler, who encouraged me to make all this realness personal.

And as always, cheers to Vince Aletti for opening a closing door.

Discography

All US chart positions are from *Billboard*. All UK chart positions are from The Official UK Charts Company Limited. Each number represents peak chart positions. For album entries, the first number is for the *Billboard* 200. For single entries, the first number is from the *Billboard* Hot 100. If a single that is part of an album cited here was released in a year previous to its inclusion, that year is noted. If a single charted two or more years after its album, that year is also stated.

Over the course of several years, *Billboard*'s club music charts underwent multiple name changes that downplayed the word "Disco," starting with its March 27, 1982, issue and ending in its September 19, 1987, issue, when the word dropped out of its "Dance" music chart titles entirely. Therefore, "Disco" in these listings refers to songs that entered *Billboard*'s Disco chart before March 27, 1982, and "Dance" refers to what followed.

Preface

- The Partridge Family, "I Think I Love You" (1970: #1, UK #18)

Chapter One: The Velvet Underground and Lou Reed

- Lou Reed, *Sally Can't Dance* (1974: #10)
- The Velvet Underground and Nico, *The Velvet Underground & Nico* (1967: #171)
- The Velvet Underground, *White Light/White Heat* (1968: #199)
- Van Morrison, *Astral Weeks* (1968: UK #55)
- The Velvet Underground, *The Velvet Underground* (1969; 1985 rerelease: #197)
- Mott the Hoople, *All the Young Dudes* (1972: #89, UK #21)
- The Velvet Underground, *Loaded* (1970)

- Lou Reed, *Transformer* (1972: #29, UK #13), including "Walk on the Wild Side" (#16, UK #10)
- Lou Reed, *Coney Island Baby* (1975: #41, UK #52)

Chapter Two: Laura Nyro

- Laura Nyro, *More Than a New Discovery* (1967)
- Laura Nyro, *Eli and the Thirteenth Confession* (1968: #181)
- Laura Nyro, *New York Tendaberry* (1969: #32)
- Blood, Sweat & Tears, "And When I Die" (1969: #2)
- Three Dog Night, "Eli's Coming" (1969: #10)
- Barbra Streisand, *Stoney End* (1971: #10), including "Stoney End" (1970: #6, UK #28), "Time and Love" (#51), and "Flim Flam Man" (#82)
- The 5th Dimension, "Stoned Soul Picnic" (1968: #3, R&B #2)
- The 5th Dimension, "Sweet Blindness" (1968: #13, R&B #45)
- The 5th Dimension, "Wedding Bell Blues" (1969: #1, R&B #23, UK #16)
- The 5th Dimension, "Blowing Away" (1969: #21)
- The 5th Dimension, "Save the Country" (1970: #27, R&B #41)
- Laura Nyro, *Smile* (1976: #60)
- Laura Nyro, *Mother's Spiritual* (1984: #182)
- Laura Nyro: *Laura: Live at the Bottom Line* (1989)
- Laura Nyro, *Walk the Dog and Light the Light* (1993)
- Carole King, *Tapestry* (1971: #1, UK #4)

Chapter Three: Janis Joplin

- Big Brother and the Holding Company, "Ball and Chain" from *Monterey Pop* documentary (1968)
- Big Brother and the Holding Company, "Down on Me" (1967: #43)
- Janis Joplin, *In Concert,* (1972, #4, UK #30)
- Big Brother and the Holding Company, *Cheap Thrills* (1968: #1)
- Janis Joplin, *Pearl* (1970: #1, UK #20)

Chapter Four: Motown

- Jackie Shane, "Any Other Way" (1962)
- The Miracles, "Shop Around" (1960: #2, R&B #1)
- The Temptations, "My Girl" (1964: #1, R&B #1, UK #43)
- The Marvelettes, "Forever" (1963: #78, R&B #24)
- The Supremes, "Where Did Our Love Go" (1964: #1, R&B #1, UK #3)
- Martha and the Vandellas, "Heat Wave" (1963: #4, R&B #1)

- The Supremes, "Baby Love" (1964: #1, R&B #1, UK #1)
- Diana Ross and the Supremes, *Love Child* (1968: #14, R&B #3, UK #13)
- The Miracles, "The Tracks of My Tears" (1965: #16, R&B #2, UK #9)
- Smokey Robinson and the Miracles, *Make It Happen* (1967: #28, R&B #3), including "The Love I Saw in You Was Just a Mirage" (#20, R&B #10) and "The Tears of a Clown" (1970: #1, R&B #1, UK #1)
- The Miracles, *City of Angels* (1975: #33, R&B #29), including "Love Machine" (#1, R&B #5, UK #3, Disco #20)
- Jim Stafford, "My Girl Bill" (1974: #12, UK #20)
- Smokey Robinson, *A Quiet Storm* (1975: #36, R&B #7)
- The Dynamic Superiors, *The Dynamic Superiors* (1975: R&B #36), including "Shoe Shoe Shine" (1974: #68, #16 R&B)
- The Dynamic Superiors, *Pure Pleasure* (1975)
- Ashford & Simpson, "Solid" (1984: #12, R&B #1, Dance #15)
- Valentino, "I Was Born This Way" (1975)
- Lady Gaga, "Born This Way" (2011: #1, UK #3, Dance #1)
- The Trammps, "That's Where the Happy People Go" (1976: #27, R&B #12, UK #35, Disco #1)
- Carl Bean, "I Was Born This Way" (1978: Disco #15)

Chapter Five: The Kinks

- The Beatles, *Sgt. Pepper's Lonely Hearts Club Band* (1967: #1, UK #1)
- The Kinks, "You Really Got Me" (1964: #7, UK #1)
- The Kinks, "All Day and All of the Night" (1964: #7, UK #2)
- The Beatles, *Help!* (1965: #1, UK #1)
- The Kinks, "See My Friend" (1965: UK #11)
- The Kinks, "Dedicated Follower of Fashion" (1966: #36, UK #4)
- The Kinks, "I'm Not Like Everybody Else" (1966)
- The Kinks, *Something Else by the Kinks* (1967: #153, UK #35)
- The Kinks, "Waterloo Sunset" (1967: UK #2)
- The Kinks, "Lola" (1970: #9, UK #2)

Chapter Six: David Bowie and Glam

- David Bowie, *Blackstar* (2016: #1, UK #1)
- David Bowie, *The Man Who Sold the World* (1970; 1972 rerelease: #105, UK #24)
- T. Rex, "Children of the Revolution" (1972: UK #2)
- David Bowie, *Hunky Dory* (1971: UK #3), including "Changes" (#66; 1975 rerelease: #41)
- David Bowie, "Space Oddity" (1969: UK #5; 1973 US rerelease: #15; 1975 UK rerelease: #1)

- Mott the Hoople, "All the Young Dudes" (1972: #37, #3 UK)
- David Bowie, *The Rise and Fall of Ziggy Stardust and the Spiders from Mars* (1972: #75, UK #5), including "Starman" (#65, UK #10) and "Rock 'n' Roll Suicide" (1974: UK #22)
- David Bowie, *Diamond Dogs* (1974: #5, UK #1)
- Everyday People, "I Like What I Like" (1972)
- Argent, "Hold Your Head Up" (1972: #5, UK #5)

Chapter Seven: Bette Midler

- Bette Midler, *The Divine Miss M* (1972: #9), including "Do You Want to Dance" (#17), "Boogie Woogie Bugle Boy" (#8), and "Friends" (#40)

Chapter Eight: Labelle

- Patti LaBelle and the Bluebells, *Over the Rainbow* (1966: R&B #20)
- Labelle, *Nightbirds* (1974: #7, R&B #4), including "Lady Marmalade" (#1, R&B #1, UK #17, Disco #7)
- The Eleventh Hour, *The Eleventh Hour's Greatest Hits* (1974)
- Labelle, *Chameleon* (1976: #94, R&B #21)
- Patti LaBelle, "New Attitude" (1984: #14, R&B #3, Dance #1)
- Sarah Dash, "Sinner Man" (1978: R&B #70, Disco #9)
- Nona Hendrix, *Nona* (1983: #83, R&B #25), including "Keep It Confidential" (#91, R&B #33, Dance #23) and "Transformation" (R&B #40)

Chapter Nine: Elton John

- Elton John, *Tumbleweed Connection* (1970: #5, UK #2)
- Elton John, "Your Song" (1970: #8, UK #7)
- Elton John, *Madman Across the Water* (1971: #8, UK #41)
- Elton John, *Honky Château* (1972: #1, UK #2), including "Rocket Man" (#6, UK #2) and "Honky Cat" (#8, UK #31)
- Elton John, *Don't Shoot Me I'm Only the Piano Player* (1973: #1, UK #1), including "Daniel" (#2, UK #4) and "Crocodile Rock" (#1, UK #5)
- Elton John, *Goodbye Yellow Brick Road* (1973: #1, UK #1), including "Saturday Night's Alright for Fighting" (#12, UK #7), "Goodbye Yellow Brick Road" (#2, UK #6), "Bennie and the Jets" (#1, R&B #15), and "Candle in the Wind" (UK #11)
- Elton John, "The Bitch Is Back" (1974: #4, UK #15)
- Aretha Franklin, "Border Song (Holy Moses)" (1970: #37, R&B #5)
- Elton John, "Candle in the Wind 1997" (1997: #1, UK #1)

Chapter Ten: Lavender Country

- Lavender Country, *Lavender Country* (1973)
- Various Artists, *Strong Love: Songs of Gay Liberation 1972–1981* (2012)
- Lavender Country, *Blackberry Rose* (2022)

Chapter Eleven: Olivia Records and Women's Music

- Roberta Flack, *First Take* (1969: #1, R&B #1)
- Cris Williamson, *Cris Williamson* (1971)
- Carly Simon, "That's the Way I've Always Heard It Should Be" (1971: #10)
- Carly Simon, "You're So Vain" (1972: #1, UK #3)
- Helen Reddy, "I Am Woman" (1972: #1)
- Joni Mitchell, *Blue* (1971: #15, UK #3)
- Joni Mitchell, *Court and Spark* (1974: #2, UK #14), including "Free Man in Paris" (#22)
- Various, *The Queen Is in the Closet* (1964)
- Meg Christian/Cris Williamson, "Lady"/"If It Weren't for the Music" (1974)
- Meg Christian, *I Know You Know* (1974)
- Cris Williamson, *The Changer and the Changed* (1975)
- Margie Adam, *Songwriter* (1976)
- Margie Adam, *We Shall Go Forth!* (1982)
- Janis Ian, *Between the Lines* (1975: #1), including "At Seventeen" (#3)
- Janis Ian, *Miracle Row* (1977: #45)
- Linda Shear, *A Lesbian Portrait* (1975)
- Various, *Lesbian Concentrate: A Lesbianthology of Songs and Poems* (1977)
- Holly Near, *Imagine My Surprise!* (1978)
- Teresa Trull, *Let It Be Known* (1980)

Chapter Twelve: Queen

- Queen, *Queen II* (1974: #49, UK #5)
- Queen, "Killer Queen" (1974: #12, UK #2)
- Queen, *Day at the Races* (1976: #5, UK #1), including "Good Old-Fashioned Lover Boy" (UK #17)
- *Queen, News of the World* (1977: #3, UK #4), including "We Are the Champions" (#4, UK #2)
- Queen, *Jazz* (1978: #6, UK #2)
- Queen, "Body Language" (1982: #11, UK #25)
- Queen, "I Want to Break Free" (1984: #45, UK #3)
- Queen, "These Are the Days of Our Lives" (1991: UK #1)

- Queen, "Who Wants to Live Forever" (1986: UK #24)
- Queen, *A Night at the Opera* (1975: #4, UK #1), including "Bohemian Rhapsody" (1975: #9, UK #1; 1991 UK rerelease: UK #1; 1992 US rerelease: #2)

Chapter Thirteen: Patti Smith

- Patti Smith, *Horses* (1975: #47)
- Patti Smith Group, *Easter* (1978: #20, UK #16)
- Patti Smith, "People Have the Power" (1988)

Chapter Fourteen: *The Rocky Horror Picture Show*

- Original London Cast, *The Rocky Horror Show* (1973)
- Various, *The Rocky Horror Picture Show* soundtrack (1975: #49)

Chapter Fifteen: Disco's Birth

- Stevie Wonder, "My Cherie Amour" (1969: #4, R&B #4, UK #4)
- Marvin Gaye, "Too Busy Thinking About My Baby" (1969: #4, R&B #1, UK #5)
- The Four Tops, "Don't Bring Back Memories" (1969)
- Shirley Bassey, "This Is My Life" (1968)
- Chris Montez, "The More I See You" (1966: #16, UK #3)
- Spiral Staircase, "More Today Than Yesterday" (1969: #12)
- Sly and the Family Stone, "Stand!" (1969: #22, R&B #14)
- The Edwin Hawkins Singers, "Oh Happy Day" (1969: #4, R&B #2, UK #2)
- Henry Mancini, His Orchestra and Chorus, "Love Theme from *Romeo & Juliet*" (1969: #1)
- The Beatles with Billy Preston, "Get Back" (1969: #1, UK #1)
- Jerry Butler, "Only the Strong Survive" (1969: #4, R&B #1)
- Harry Nilsson, "Everybody's Talkin'" (1968: #6)
- Sam Cooke, "Twistin' the Night Away" (1962: #9, R&B #1, UK #6)
- Little Richard, "Tutti Frutti" (1955: #17, R&B #2)
- Chicago Transit Authority, "I'm a Man" (1969: #48, UK #8)
- Little Sister, "You're the One" (1970: #22, R&B #4)
- Manu Dibango, "Soul Makossa" (1972: #35, R&B #21)
- Kool & the Gang, "Jungle Boogie" (1973: #4, R&B #2)
- Ian Matthews, "Da Doo Ron Ron (When He Walked Me Home)" (1972: #96)
- The Hues Corporation, "Rock the Boat" (1974: #1, R&B #2)
- George McCrae, "Rock Your Baby" (1974: #1, R&B #1)

- Gloria Gaynor, *Never Can Say Goodbye* (1975: #21, R&B #21), including "Never Can Say Goodbye" (1974: #9, R&B #34, UK #2, Disco #2)
- Double Exposure, "Ten Percent" (1976: #54, R&B #63, Disco #2)
- Evelyn "Champagne" King, *Smooth Talk* (1977: #14, R&B #8), including "Shame" (#9, R&B #7, Disco #8)
- Chic, "Dance, Dance, Dance (Yowsah, Yowsah, Yowsah)" (1977: #6, R&B #6, UK #6, Disco #1)
- Rod Stewart, "Do Ya Think I'm Sexy" (1978: #1, R&B #5, UK #1, Disco #1)
- Instant Funk, "I Got My Mind Made Up" (1978: #20, R&B #1, Disco #1)
- Candi Staton, "Young Hearts Run Free" (1976: #20, R&B #1, Disco #8)
- Chaka Khan, "I'm Every Woman" (1978, #21, R&B #1, UK #11, Disco #30)
- Jackie Moore, "This Time Baby" (1979: R&B #24, Disco #1)

Chapter Sixteen: Donna Summer

- Donna Summer, "Love to Love You Baby" (1975: #2, R&B #3, UK #4, Disco #1)
- Donna Summer, *A Love Trilogy* (1976: #21, R&B #16, UK #41), including "Try Me, I Know We Can Make It" (#80, R&B #35, Disco #1), and "Could It Be Magic" (#52, R&B #21, UK #40, Disco #3)
- Donna Summer, *Four Seasons of Love* (1976: #29, R&B #13, Disco #1)
- Donna Summer, *I Remember Yesterday* (1977: #18, R&B #11, UK #3, Disco #1), including "I Feel Love" (#6, R&B #9, UK #1, Disco #3)
- Silver Convention, "Fly, Robin, Fly" (1975: #1, R&B #1, Disco #1)
- Donna Summer, *Once Upon a Time . . .* (1977: #26, R&B #13, UK #24, Disco #1), including "I Love You" (#37, R&B #28, UK #10), and "Rumour Has It" (#53, R&B #21, UK #19)
- Donna Summer, *Bad Girls* (1979: #1, R&B #1, UK #23), including "Hot Stuff" (#1, R&B #3, UK #11, Disco #1), and "Bad Girls" (#1, R&B #1, UK #14, Disco #1)
- Donna Summer, "Last Dance" (1978: #3, R&B #5, UK #51, Disco #1)
- Donna Summer and Barbra Streisand, "No More Tears (Enough Is Enough)" (1979: #1, R&B #20, UK #3, Disco #1)
- Donna Summer, *Live and More* (1978: #1, R&B #4, UK #16), including "MacArthur Park" (#1, R&B #8, UK #5, Disco #1) and "Heaven Knows" (#4, R&B #10, UK #34)
- Donna Summer, "She Works Hard for the Money" (1983: #3, R&B #1, UK #25, Dance #3)
- Donna Summer, *The Wanderer* (1980: #13, R&B #12, UK #55)
- Donna Summer, *Donna Summer* (1982: #20, R&B #6, UK #13)

- Donna Summer, *Another Place and Time* (1989: #53, R&B #71, UK #17), including "This Time I Know It's for Real" (#7, UK #3, Dance #5) and "Love's About to Change My Heart" (#85, UK #20, Dance #3)

Chapter Seventeen: Village People and Their LGBTQ Kin

- Disco Tex and the Sex-O-Lettes, "Get Dancin'" (1974: #10, UK #8, Disco #3)
- Alicia Bridges, "I Love the Nightlife (Disco 'Round)" (1978: #5, R&B #31, Disco #2)
- The Edgar Winter Group, "Free Ride" (1973: #14)
- Dan Hartman, "Instant Replay" (1978: #29, R&B #44, UK #8, Disco #1)
- Dan Hartman, "Vertigo/Relight My Fire" (1979: Disco #1)
- Take That featuring Lulu, "Relight My Fire" (1993: UK #1)
- Amanda Lear, *I Am a Photograph* (1977), including "Blood and Honey" and "Queen of China-Town"
- Amanda Lear, *Sweet Revenge* (1978)
- Amanda Lear, "Fabulous (Lover, Love Me)" (1979)
- Various, *Thank God It's Friday* soundtrack (1978: #10, R&B #6, Disco #1), including Paul Jabara, "Disco Queen"
- Barbra Streisand, "The Main Event/Fight" (1979: #3, Disco #13)
- The Weather Girls, "It's Raining Men" (1982: #46, R&B #34, UK #2, Dance #1)
- The Ritchie Family, "Brazil" (1975: #11, R&B #13, Disco #1)
- Village People, *Village People* (1977: #54, R&B #36, Disco #1), including "San Francisco (You've Got Me)" (UK #45)
- Village People, *Macho Man* (1978: #24, R&B #31, Disco #4), including "Macho Man" (#25)
- Village People, *Cruisin'* (1978: #3, R&B #5, UK #24), including "Y.M.C.A." (#2, R&B #32, UK #1, Disco #2)
- Village People, *Go West* (1979: #8, R&B #14, UK #14)
- Various, *Can't Stop the Music* soundtrack (1980: #47, UK #9)

Chapter Eighteen: Sylvester

- Sylvester and the Hot Band, *Sylvester and the Hot Band* (1973)
- Sylvester and the Hot Band, *Bazaar* (1973)
- Sylvester, *Sylvester (1977)*, including "Over and Over" (Disco #18)
- Sylvester, "Dance (Disco Heat)" (1978: #19, R&B #4, UK #29, Disco #1)
- Sylvester, "You Make Me Feel (Mighty Real)" (1978: #36, R&B #20, UK #8, Disco #1)
- Cheryl Lynn, "Got to Be Real" (1978: #12, R&B #1, Disco #11)

- Sylvester, "I (Who Have Nothing)" (1979: #40, R&B #27, UK #46, Disco #4)
- Chic, "Good Times" (1979: #1, R&B #1, UK #5, Disco #3)
- Frankie Valli, "Swearin' to God" (1975: #6, UK #31, Disco #4)
- Walter Murphy and the Big Apple Band, "A Fifth of Beethoven" (1976: #1, R&B #10, UK #28, Disco #10)
- The Michael Zager Band, "Let's All Chant" (1978: #36, R&B #15, UK #8, Disco #1)
- Various, *Saturday Night Fever* soundtrack (1977: #1, R&B #1, UK #1)
- Various, *Grease* soundtrack (1978, #1, UK #1)
- Various, *Fame* soundtrack (1980, #7, UK #1)
- Lipps, Inc. "Funkytown" (1980: #1, R&B #2, UK #2, Disco #1)

Chapter Nineteen: Blondie and Punk

- New York Dolls, *New York Dolls* (1973: #116)
- The Runaways, *The Runaways* (1976: #194)
- Ramones, *Ramones* (1976: #111)
- Rod Stewart, "The Killing of Georgie (Part I and II)" (1976: #30, UK #2)
- Blondie, *Parallel Lines* (1978: #6, UK #1), including "Heart of Glass" (#1, UK #1, Disco #58), and "Sunday Girl" (UK #1)
- Blondie, *Eat to the Beat* (1979: #17, UK #1)
- Blondie, *Blondie* (1976: UK #75)
- Blondie, "Rapture" (1981: #1, UK #5, Disco #1)
- Blondie, "Maria" (1999: #82, UK #1, Dance #9)
- Blondie featuring Beth Ditto, "A Rose by Any Name" (2013)
- Buzzcocks, "Orgasm Addict" (1977)
- Buzzcocks, "Ever Fallen in Love (With Someone You Shouldn't've)" (1978: UK #12)
- Pete Shelley, "Homosapien" (1981: Disco #14)
- The Tom Robinson Band, *Power in the Darkness* (1978: #144, UK #4), including "2-4-6-8 Motorway" (1977: UK #5)

Chapter Twenty: The B-52s

- The B-52s, *Mesopotamia* (1982: #35, UK #18, Disco #13)
- The B-52s, *The B-52s* (1979: #59, UK #22, Disco #24), including "Rock Lobster" (#56, UK #37)
- The B-52s, *Wild Planet* (1980: #18, UK #18, Disco #5)
- The B-52s, *Whammy!* (1983: #29, UK #33, Dance #9), including "Legal Tender" (#81)
- The B-52s, *Bouncing Off the Satellites* (1986: #86, UK #74), including "Summer of Love" (Dance #3)

- The B-52s, *Cosmic Thing* (1989: #4, UK #8), including "Channel Z" (UK #61), "Love Shack" (#3, UK #2, Dance #7), and "Deadbeat Club" (#30)
- Was (Not Was), "Tell Me That I'm Dreaming" (1981: Disco #3)
- The Temptations, "Psychedelic Shack" (1969: #7, R&B #2, UK #33)
- Rough Trade, "Crimes of Passion" (1982)
- The Parachute Club, "Rise Up" (1983: Dance #26)
- The Psychedelic Furs, "Pretty in Pink" (1981: UK #43; 1986 re-recording #41, UK #18)
- The Psychedelic Furs, "Love My Way" (1982: #44, UK #42, Dance #40)

Chapter Twenty-One: Talking Heads and Post-Punk

- Tom Tom Club, "Genius of Love" (1981: #31, R&B #2, Disco #1)
- Talking Heads, *More Songs About Buildings and Food* (1978: #29, UK #21)
- Talking Heads, "Psycho Killer" (1978: #92)
- Lavender Jane, *Lavender Jane Loves Women* (1973)
- Alix Dobkin, *Yahoo Australia! Alix Live from Sydney* (1990)
- LiLiPUT, "Die Matrosen" (1980)
- Book of Love, *Book of Love* (1986), including "Boy" (1985: Dance #7)
- Au Pairs, "It's Obvious" (1980: Disco #37)
- Bush Tetras, "Too Many Creeps" (1980: Disco #57)
- Rough Trade, "High School Confidential" (1981)
- Rough Trade, *For Those Who Think Young* (1981), including "All Touch" (#58)

Chapter Twenty-Two: Judas Priest

- Judas Priest, *Killing Machine* (1978: UK #32), released in North America as *Hell Bent for Leather* (1978: #128), including "Take on the World" (UK #14)
- Judas Priest, *Sin After Sin* (1977: UK #23)
- Judas Priest, *Stained Class* (1978: #173, UK #27)
- Judas Priest, *Defenders of the Faith* (1984: #18, UK #19)

Chapter Twenty-Three: Prince and Wendy & Lisa

- Prince, *Controversy* (1981: #21, R&B #3), including "Controversy" (#80, R&B #3, Disco #1)
- Prince, "Soft and Wet" (1978: #92, R&B #12)
- Prince, *Prince* (1979: #22, R&B #3), including "I Wanna Be Your Lover" (#11, R&B #1, UK #41, Disco #2)

- Prince, *Dirty Mind* (1980: #45, R&B #7), including "Dirty Mind" (R&B #65) and "Uptown" (R&B #5, Disco #5)
- The Time, "Get It Up" (1981: R&B #6, Disco #16)
- Prince, "1999" (1982: #12, R&B #4, UK #25, Dance #1; 1985 UK rerelease: #2).
- Prince and the Revolution, *Purple Rain* (1984: #1, R&B #1, UK #7), including "I Would Die 4 U" (#8, R&B #11, UK #58)
- Prince and the Revolution, *Parade* (1986: #3, R&B #2, UK #4)
- Prince, *Sign "O" the Times* (1987: #6, R&B #4, UK #4), including "Sign 'O' the Times" (#3, R&B #1, UK #10, Dance #2) and "If I Was Your Girlfriend" (#67, R&B #12, UK #20)
- The Family, *The Family* (1985: #62, R&B #17)
- Wendy & Lisa, *Wendy and Lisa* (1987: #88, UK #84), including "Waterfall" (#56, UK #66)
- Wendy & Lisa, *Eroica* (1990: UK #33)
- Prince, *The Black Album* (1994: #47, R&B #15, UK #36)
- Prince, *Lovesexy* (1988: #11, R&B #5, UK #1)
- Prince and the New Power Generation, "Cream" (1991: #1, UK #15)
- [symbol], "The Most Beautiful Girl in the World" (1994: #3, R&B #2, UK #1)

Chapter Twenty-Four: Joan Jett and the Go-Go's

- Suzi Quatro, *Suzi Quatro* (1973: US #142, UK #32)
- The Beatles, *Please Please Me* (1963: UK #1)
- The Germs, *(GI)* (1979)
- Joan Jett, *Bad Reputation* (1981: #51), including "Do You Wanna Touch Me (Oh Yeah)" (#20)
- Peaches, *Fatherfucker* (2003)
- Leslie Gore, "You Don't Own Me" (1963: #2)
- Joan Jett and the Blackhearts, "I Love Rock 'n' Roll" (1982: #1, UK #4, Disco #31)
- Joan Jett and the Blackhearts, "Crimson and Clover" (1982: #7)
- Joan Jett and the Blackhearts, *Album* (1983: #20)
- Gloria Gaynor, "I Am What I Am" (1983: R&B #82, UK #13, Dance #3)
- Joan Jett and the Blackhearts, "I Hate Myself for Loving You" (1988: #8, UK #46)
- Joan Jett and the Blackhearts, *Pure and Simple* (1994)
- Joan Jett and the Blackhearts, *Sinner* (2006: UK #56)
- Joan Jett and the Blackhearts, *Greatest Hits* (2010: #141)
- Go-Go's, *Beauty and the Beat* (1981: #1), including "Our Lips Are Sealed" (#20, UK #47, Disco #10) and "We Got the Beat" (#2, Disco #35)

- Josie Cotton, "Johnny Are You Queer?" (1981: Disco #38)
- Go-Go's, "Turn to You" (1984: #32)

Chapter Twenty-Five: Diana Ross and Luther Vandross

- Diana Ross, "Ain't No Mountain High Enough" (1970: #1, R&B #1, UK #6)
- Diana Ross, "Remember Me" (1970: #16, R&B #10, UK #7)
- The Supremes, "My World Is Empty Without You" (1965: #5, R&B #10)
- Diana Ross, "Love Hangover" (1976: #1, R&B #1, UK #10, Disco #1)
- Diana Ross, *The Boss* (1979: #14, R&B #10, UK #53, Disco #1), including "The Boss" (#19, R&B #12, UK #40, Disco #1)
- Diana Ross, *diana* (1980: #2, R&B #1, UK #12), including "Upside Down" (#1, R&B #1, UK #2, Disco #1) and "I'm Coming Out" (#5, R&B #6, UK #13, Disco #1)
- Diana Ross and Lionel Ritchie, "Endless Love" (1981: #1, R&B #1, UK #7)
- Diana Ross, "Muscles" (1982: #10, R&B #4, UK #15)
- David Bowie, "Young Americans" (1975: #28, UK #18)
- Luther, "Funky Music (Is a Part of Me)" (1976: R&B #34)
- Various, *The Wiz* original cast album (1975: #43)
- Bionic Boogie, "Hot Butterfly" (1978: Disco #8)
- Change, *The Glow of Love* (1980: #29, R&B #10, Disco #1), including "The Glow of Love" (R&B #49)
- Luther Vandross, *Never Too Much* (1981: #19, R&B #1), including "Never Too Much" (#33, R&B #1, UK #41, Disco #4)
- Aretha Franklin, *Jump to It* (1982: #23, R&B #1), including "Jump to It" (#24, R&B #1, UK #42, Dance #4)
- Luther Vandross, *Busy Body* (1983: #32, R&B #1, UK #42)
- Luther Vandross, *The Night I Fell in Love* (1985: #19, R&B #1, UK #19), including "If Only for One Night" (1986: R&B #59)
- Luther Vandross, "Any Love" (1988: #44, R&B #1, UK #31)
- Luther Vandross, "Here and Now" (1989: #6, R&B #1, UK #43)
- Luther Vandross, "Your Secret Love" (1996: #52, R&B #5, UK #14)
- Luther Vandross, *I Know* (1998: #26, R&B #9, UK #42)

Chapter Twenty-Six: Grace Jones

- Grace Jones, "I Need a Man" (1975; 1977 rerecording: #83, Disco #1)
- Grace Jones, "Sorry"/"That's the Trouble" (1976: Disco #7)
- Grace Jones, *Portfolio* (1977: #109, R&B #56), including "La Vie en Rose" (Disco #10)

- Grace Jones, *Fame* (1978: #97, R&B #57), including "Do or Die" (Disco #3)
- Grace Jones, *Muse* (1979: #158, including "On Your Knees" (Disco #28)
- Grace Jones, *Warm Leatherette* (1980: #132, UK #45, Disco #20)
- Yoko Ono, "Walking on Thin Ice" (1981: #58, Disco #13)
- Taana Gardner, "Heartbeat" (1981: R&B #10, Disco #6)
- Grace Jones, *Nightclubbing* (1981: #32, R&B #9, UK #35), including "Pull Up to the Bumper" (R&B #5, UK #53, Disco #2; 1985 rerelease: UK #12)
- Grace Jones, *Slave to the Rhythm* (1985: #73, R&B #25, UK #12), including "Slave to the Rhythm" (R&B #20, UK #12, Dance #1)
- Grace Jones, "Love on Top of Love" (1989: Dance #1)
- Grace Jones, *Hurricane* (2008: UK #42)

Chapter Twenty-Seven: Michael Jackson

- Jackson 5, "I Want You Back" (1969: #1, R&B #1, UK #2)
- Jackson 5, "ABC" (1970: #1, R&B #1, UK #8)
- Jackson 5, "I'll Be There" (1970: #1, R&B #1, UK #4)
- Jackson 5, "The Love You Save" (1970: #1, R&B #1, #7)
- Michael Jackson, "Ben" (1972: #1, R&B #5, UK #7)
- The Jacksons, "Shake Your Body (Down to the Ground)" (1979: #7, R&B #3, UK #4, Disco #20)
- Michael Jackson, *Off the Wall* (1979: #3, R&B #1, UK #3), including "Don't Stop 'Til You Get Enough" (#1, R&B #1, UK #3, Disco #2) and "Off the Wall" (#10, R&B #5, UK #7)
- Michael Jackson, *Thriller* (1982: #1, R&B #1, UK #1, Dance #1), including "The Girl Is Mine" (#2, R&B #1, UK #8), "Wanna Be Startin' Somethin'" (#5, R&B #5, UK #8), "Billie Jean" (#1, R&B #1, UK #1, "Beat It" (#1, R&B #1, UK #3), and "Thriller" (1984: #4, R&B #3, UK #10, Dance #44)
- Jackson 5, "Never Can Say Goodbye" (1971: #2, R&B #1, UK #33)
- Various, *The Little Prince* soundtrack (1974)
- The Jacksons, *Victory* (1984: #4, R&B #3, UK #3), including "State of Shock" (#3, R&B #4, UK #14, Dance #3)
- Janet Jackson, *Control* (1986: #1, R&B #1, UK #8)
- Michael Jackson, *Bad* (1987: #1, R&B #1, UK #1, Dance #22), including "Smooth Criminal" (1988: #7, R&B #2, UK #8, Dance #10)
- Michael Jackson, *Dangerous* (1991: #1, R&B #1, UK #1), including "Black or White" (#1, R&B #3, UK #1, Dance #1), "In the Closet" (#6, R&B #1, UK #8, Dance #1), and "Gone Too Soon" (UK #33)
- The Simpsons, "Do the Bartman" (1990: UK #1)

- Michael Jackson, *HIStory: Past, Present and Future, Book 1* (1995: #1, R&B #1, UK #1), including "Scream" (#5, R&B #1, UK #3, Dance #1), "You Are Not Alone" (#1, R&B #1, UK #1, Dance #3), and "They Don't Care About Us" (#30, R&B #10, UK #4, Dance #27)

Chapter Twenty-Eight: Wendy Carlos and Kraftwerk

- Wendy Carlos, *Switched-On Bach* (1968: #10)
- Various, *Stanley Kubrick's A Clockwork Orange* soundtrack (1971, #146)
- Kraftwerk, *Autobahn* (1974: #5, UK #4)
- Kraftwerk, *Radio-Activity* (1975: #140)
- Kraftwerk, *Trans-Europe Express* (1977: #140), including "Showroom Dummies" (UK #25)
- Kraftwerk, *The Man-Machine* (1978: #130, UK #9, Disco #39), including "The Model" (1981: UK #1)
- Kraftwerk, *Computer World* (1981: #72, UK #15, Disco #13), including "Numbers" (R&B #22)
- Kraftwerk, "Tour de France" (1983: UK #22, Dance #4)
- Kraftwerk, *Electric Café* (1986: #158, UK #58)

Chapter Twenty-Nine: Iggy Pop and David Bowie in Berlin

- Iggy and the Stooges, *Raw Power* (1973: #183)
- Iggy Pop, *The Idiot* (1977: #72, UK #30)
- David Bowie, *Low* (1977: #11, UK #2)
- David Bowie, *"Heroes"* (1977: #35, UK #3), including "'Heroes'" (UK #12)
- Big Ben Tribe, "Heroes" (1983)
- David Bowie, *Lodger* (1979: #20, UK #4), including "Boys Keep Swinging" (UK #7)
- David Bowie, *Scary Monsters (And Super Creeps)* (1980: #12, UK #1), including "Ashes to Ashes" (UK #1) and "Fashion" (#70, UK #5, Disco #21)
- David Bowie, *Let's Dance* (1983: #4, R&B #21, UK #1), including "China Girl" (#10, UK #2, Dance #51)

Chapter Thirty: Gary Numan

- Tubeway Army, *Replicas* (1979: #124, UK #1), including "Are 'Friends' Electric" (UK #1)
- Gary Numan, "Cars" (1979: #9, UK #1)

Chapter Thirty-One: Duran Duran and the New Romantics

- Visage, "Fade to Grey" (1980: UK #8)
- Visage, "The Anvil" (1982)
- Spandau Ballet, "To Cut a Long Story Short" (1980: UK #5, Disco #28)
- Spandau Ballet, "Muscle Bound" (1981: UK #10)

- Spandau Ballet, "Chant No. 1 (I Don't Need This Pressure On)" (1981: UK #3, Disco #17)
- Spandau Ballet, "True" (1983: #4, R&B #76, UK #1)
- Duran Duran, "Planet Earth" (1981: UK #12, Disco #26)
- Spandau Ballet, *Diamond* (1982: UK #15)
- Duran Duran, *Rio* (1982: #6, UK #2), including "Save a Prayer" (UK #2; 1985: #16)
- Duran Duran, "The Reflex" (1984: #1, UK #1, Dance #14)
- Duran Duran, "The Wild Boys" (1984: #2, UK #2, Dance #27)
- Adam and the Ants, *Kings of the Wild Frontier* (1980: #44, UK #1), including "Dog Eat Dog" (UK #4), "Antmusic" (UK #2, Disco #19), and "Kings of the Wild Frontier" (UK #2)
- Adam and the Ants, "Beat My Guest" (1981)
- Adam and the Ants, "Prince Charming" (1981: UK #1)
- Adam Ant, "Goody Two Shoes" (1982: #12, UK #1)
- Culture Club, *Kissing to Be Clever* (1982: #14, R&B #24, UK #5), including "Do You Really Want to Hurt Me" (#2, R&B #39, UK #1), "Time (Clock of the Heart)" (#2, R&B #34, UK #3), "I'm Afraid of Me" (Dance #34), and "I'll Tumble 4 Ya" (#9, R&B #70, Dance #14)
- Culture Club, *Colour by Numbers* (1983: #2, R&B #7, UK #1, Dance #3), including "Church of the Poison Mind" (#10, UK #2), "Karma Chameleon" (#1, R&B #67, UK #1), "Victims" (UK #3), and "Miss Me Blind" (#5, R&B #8, Dance #10)
- Moe & Joe, "Where's the Dress" (1984: Country #8)
- Elton John, *Captain Fantastic and the Brown Dirt Cowboy* (1975: #1, UK #2), including "Someone Saved My Life Tonight" (#4, UK #22)

Chapter Thirty-Two: Kate Bush

- Kate Bush, *The Kick Inside* (1978: UK #3), including "Wuthering Heights" (UK #1) and "The Man with the Child in His Eyes" (#85, UK #6)
- Kate Bush, *Lionheart* (1978: UK #6), including "Wow" (1979: UK #14)
- Kate Bush, *Never for Ever* (1980: UK #1)
- Kate Bush, *The Dreaming* (1982: #157, UK #3), including "Sat in Your Lap" (1981: UK #11)
- Kate Bush, *Hounds of Love* (1985: #30, UK #1), including "Running Up That Hill" (#30, UK #3, Dance #17), and "Cloudbusting" (UK #20)

Chapter Thirty-Three: Dolly Parton

- Dolly Parton, *The Fairest of Them All* (1970: Country #13)

- Dolly Parton, "Dumb Blonde" (1966: Country #24)
- Dolly Parton, "Jolene" (1973: #60, Country #1; 1976: UK #7)
- Dolly Parton, "I Will Always Love You" (1974: Country #1)
- Dolly Parton, *All I Can Do* (1976: Country #3)
- Dolly Parton, "Here You Come Again" (1977: #3, Country #1)
- Dolly Parton, "Two Doors Down" (1978: #19) backed with "It's All Wrong, but It's All Right" (Country #1)
- Dolly Parton, *9 to 5 and Odd Jobs* (1980: #11, Country #1), including "9 to 5" (#1, UK #47, Country #1, Disco #77)
- Various, *The Best Little Whorehouse in Texas* soundtrack, (1982: #63, Country #5), including "I Will Always Love You" (#53, Country #1)
- Dolly Parton, *The Great Pretender* (1984: #73, Country #7)

Chapter Thirty-Four: Soft Cell and Eurythmics

- Gloria Jones, "Tainted Love" (1965)
- Soft Cell, *Non-Stop Erotic Cabaret* (1981: #22, UK #5, R&B #55), including "Tainted Love" (#8, UK #1, Disco #4), "Bedsitter" (UK #4), "Sex Dwarf" (Dance #65), and "Say Hello, Wave Goodbye" (UK #3)
- Coil, "Tainted Love" (1985)
- Soft Cell, "Torch" (1982: UK #2)
- Soft Cell, *Non Stop Ecstatic Dancing* (1982: #57, UK #6, Dance #31)
- Soft Cell, *The Art of Falling Apart* (1983: #84, UK #5), including "Numbers" (UK #25)
- The Doors, *L.A. Woman* (1971: #9, UK #28)
- Soft Cell, *This Last Night . . . in Sodom* (1984: UK #12)
- Soft Cell and Pet Shop Boys, "Purple Zone" (2022)
- Eurythmics, *Sweet Dreams (Are Made of This)* (1983: #15, R&B #36, UK #3), including "Sweet Dreams (Are Made of This)" (#1, UK #2, Dance #2) and "Love Is a Stranger" (1982: #23, UK #6, Dance #7)
- Eurythmics, *Touch* (1983: #7, R&B #35, UK #1), including "Who's That Girl?" (#21, UK #3) and "Here Comes the Rain Again" (#4, UK #8, Dance #4)
- Eurythmics, *1984 (For the Love of Big Brother)* (1984: #93, UK #23), including "Sexcrime (Nineteen Eighty-Four)" (#81, UK #4, Dance #2) and "Julia" (UK #44)
- Eurythmics, *Be Yourself Tonight* (1985: #9, UK #3), including "Would I Lie to You?" (#5, UK #17, Dance #14) and "Sisters Are Doin' It for Themselves" with Aretha Franklin (#18, R&B #66, UK #9, Dance #10)
- Aretha Franklin, "Respect" (1967: #1, R&B #1, UK #10)
- Aretha Franklin, "I Never Loved a Man (The Way I Love You)" (1967: #9, R&B #1)

- Eurythmics, *Revenge* (1986: #12, UK #3), including "Missionary Man" (#14, UK #31, Dance #6)
- Eurythmics, *Savage* (1987: #41, UK #7), including "Beethoven (I Love to Listen To)" (UK #25) and "I Need a Man" (#46, UK #26, Dance #6)
- Eurythmics, *We Too Are One* (1989: #34, UK #1)
- Annie Lennox, *Diva* (1992: #23, UK #1), including "Why" (#34, UK #5), "Walking on Broken Glass" (#14, UK #8), and "Little Bird" (1993: #43, UK #3, Dance #1)

Chapter Thirty-Five: Frankie Goes to Hollywood and Bronski Beat

- The Buggles, "Video Killed the Radio Star" (1979: #40, UK #1)
- Frankie Goes to Hollywood, *Welcome to the Pleasuredome* (1984: #33, UK #1), including "Relax" (1983: #10, UK #1, Dance #20), "Two Tribes" (#43, UK #1, Dance #3), "The Power of Love" (UK #1), and "Welcome to the Pleasuredome" (#48, UK #2, Dance #31)
- Frankie Goes to Hollywood, *Liverpool* (1986: #88, UK #5)
- Holly Johnson, "Love Train" (1989: #65, UK #4)
- Holly Johnson, "Legendary Children (All of Them Queer)" (1994: UK #85)
- Paul Rutherford, "Oh World" (1989: UK #61, Dance #45)
- Deniece Williams, "Let's Hear It for the Boy" (1984: #1, R&B #1, UK #2, Dance #1)
- Evelyn Thomas, "High Energy" (1984: #85, UK #5, Dance #1)
- Hazell Dean, "Searchin' (I Gotta Find a Man)" (1983: UK #6, Dance #8)
- Bronski Beat, *The Age of Consent* (1984: #36, UK #4, Dance #20), including "Smalltown Boy" (#48, UK #3, Dance #1), "Why?" (UK #6, Dance #27), and "It Ain't Necessarily So" (UK #16)
- Bronski Beat and Marc Almond, "I Feel Love (Medley)" (1985: UK #3)
- John Leyton, "Johnny Remember Me" (1961: UK #1)
- The Tornados, "Telstar" (1962: #1, UK #1)
- Bronski Beat, "Hit That Perfect Beat" (1985: UK #3, Dance #7)
- Patrick Cowley, "Menergy" (1981: Disco #1)
- Harold Melvin & the Blue Notes, "Don't Leave Me This Way" (1976: UK #5, Disco #3)
- Thelma Houston, "Don't Leave Me This Way" (1977: #1, R&B #1, UK #13, Disco #1)
- The Communards, *Communards* (1986: #90, UK #7), including "Don't Leave Me This Way" (#40, UK #1, Dance #1)
- The Communards, *Red* (1987: #93, UK #4), including "Never Can Say Goodbye" (#51, UK #4, Dance #2),

"For a Friend" (UK #28), and "There's More to Love" (UK #20)

- Jimmy Somerville, "Read My Lips (Enough Is Enough)" (1990: UK #26)

Chapter Thirty-Six: Boy George

- Culture Club, *Waking Up with the House on Fire* (1984: #26, R&B #55, UK #2)
- Culture Club, *From Luxury to Heartache* (1986: #32, UK #10)
- Boy George, *Sold* (1987: #145, UK #29)
- Boy George, *High Hat* (1989: #126)
- Jesus Loves You, *The Martyr Mantras* (1990: UK #60), including "Generations of Love" (UK #35, Dance #11) and "No Clause 28" (1988: UK #57)
- Boy George, "The Crying Game" (1992: #15, UK #22)

Chapter Thirty-Seven: R.E.M.

- R.E.M., *Murmur* (1983: #36)
- R.E.M., *Reckoning* (1984: #27, UK #91), including "So. Central Rain (I'm Sorry)" (#85)
- R.E.M., *Lifes Rich Pageant* (1986: #21, UK #43), including "Fall on Me" (#94)
- R.E.M., *Document* (1987: #10, UK #28), including "The One I Love" (#9, UK #51; 1991: UK rerelease: #16)
- R.E.M., *Green* (1988: #12, UK #27)
- R.E.M., *Out of Time* (1991: #1, UK #1), including "Losing My Religion" (#4, UK #19) and "Shiny Happy People" (#10, UK #6)
- R.E.M., *Automatic for the People* (1992: #2, UK #1), including "Drive" (#28, UK #11), "Man on the Moon" (#30, UK #18), "Nightswimming" (UK #27), and "Everybody Hurts" (#29, UK #7)
- David Essex, "Rock On" (1973: #5, UK #3)
- R.E.M., *Monster* (1994: #1, UK #1), including "What's the Frequency, Kenneth?" (#21, UK #9) and "Crush with Eyeliner" (1995: UK #23)
- R.E.M., *Collapse into Now* (2011: #5, UK #5)

Chapter Thirty-Eight: The Smiths and Morrissey

- The Smiths, *The Smiths* (1984: UK #2), including "Hand in Glove" (1983), "This Charming Man" (1983: UK #25, 1992 UK #8 rerelease:) and "What Difference Does It Make?" (UK #12)
- The Smiths, *Meat Is Murder* (1985: #110, UK #1), including "How Soon Is Now?" (1985: UK #24, 1992: UK #16 rerelease)
- The Dead Milkman, "Instant Club Hit" (1987)
- The Smiths, *The Queen Is Dead* (1986: #70, UK #2), including "The Boy with the Thorn in His Side" (1985: UK #23), "Bigmouth Strikes

Again" (UK #26), and "There Is a Light That Never Goes Out" (1992: UK #25)

- The Smiths, *Louder Than Bombs* (1987: #62, UK #38), including "Heaven Knows I'm Miserable Now" (1984: UK #10), "William, It Was Really Nothing" (1984: UK #17), and "Sheila Take a Bow" (UK #10)
- The Smiths, *Strangeways, Here We Come* (1987: #55, UK #2)
- Morrissey, *Bona Drag* (1990: #59, UK #9), including "Piccadilly Palare" (UK #18) and "Hairdresser on Fire" (1988)
- Morrissey, *Vauxhall and I* (1994: #18, UK #1)
- Morrissey, "The Boy Racer" (1995: UK #36)
- Morrissey, "Roy's Keen" (1997: UK #42)
- Morrissey, *You Are the Quarry* (2004: #11, UK #2)
- Morrissey, *Ringleader of the Tormentors* (2006: #27, UK #1)

Chapter Thirty-Nine: Hüsker Dü and Bob Mould

- Hüsker Dü, *Candy Apple Grey* (1986: #140)
- Hüsker Dü, *Zen Arcade* (1984)
- Hüsker Dü, "Eight Miles High" (1984)
- Hüsker Dü, *Warehouse: Songs and Stories* (1987: #117, UK #72)
- Hüsker Dü, *New Day Rising* (1985)
- Hüsker Dü, *Flip Your Wig* (1985)
- Hüsker Dü, "Love Is All Around" (1985)
- Bob Mould, *Workbook* (1989: #127)
- Sugar, *Copper Blue* (1992: UK #10)
- Grant Hart, "2541" (1988)
- Morel, "True (The Faggot Is You)" (2000: UK #64)
- Blowoff, *Blowoff* (2006)
- Bob Mould, "It's Too Late" (1990)

Chapter Forty: *Grease* and Olivia Newton-John

- Olivia Newton-John, "I Honestly Love You" (1974: #1, UK #22)
- Various, *Grease* soundtrack (1978: #1, UK #1), including John Travolta and Olivia Newton-John, "You're the One That I Want" (#1, UK #1) and Frankie Valli, "Grease" (#1, UK #3)
- Olivia Newton-John, *Physical* (1981: #6, R&B #32, UK #11), including "Physical" (#1, R&B #28, UK #7, Disco #22)
- Olivia Newton-John, "Soul Kiss" (1985: #20, UK #100)
- Olivia Newton-John, *The Rumour* (1988: #67), including "The Rumour" (#62, UK #85, Dance #17)

Chapter Forty-One: ABBA

- ABBA, "Dancing Queen" (1976: #1, UK #1)
- Barry Manilow, "Copacabana (At the Copa)" (1978: #8, Disco #15)

- ABBA, "Lay All Your Love on Me" Disconet remix (1981: UK #7 for album version, Disco #1)
- Jimmy Ruffin, "Hold on (To My Love)" (Disconet remix 1980: #10, R&B #29, UK #7 for single version)
- ABBA, "The Visitors" Hot Tracks remix (1982: #63 for single version, Disco #8)
- Diana Ross, "Swept Away" (1984: #19, R&B #3, Dance #1)
- Lime, "Babe, We're Gonna Love Tonight" (1982: Dance #6)
- Patrick Cowley featuring Sylvester, "Do Ya Wanna Funk" (1982: UK #32, Dance #4)
- ABBA, *ABBA Gold: Greatest Hits* (1992: #25, UK #1), including "Waterloo" (1974: #6, UK #1), "SOS" (1975: #15, UK #6), "Fernando" (1976: #13, UK #1), "Mamma Mia" (1976: #32, UK #1), "Knowing Me, Knowing You" (1977: #14, UK #1), "Gimme! Gimme! Gimme! (A Man After Midnight)" (1979: UK #3), and "The Winner Takes It All" (1980: #8, UK #1)
- ABBA, "I Do, I Do, I Do, I Do, I Do" (1975: #15, UK #38)
- Madonna, "Hung Up" (2005: #7, UK #1, Dance #1)
- ABBA, *Voyage* (2021: #2, UK #1)

Chapter Forty-Two: Cher

- Sonny & Cher, "I Got You Babe" (1965: #1, UK #1)
- Cher, "Gypsys, Tramps & Thieves" (1971: #1, UK #4)
- Cher, "The Way of Love" (1972: #7)
- Cher, *Half-Breed* (1973: #28), including "Half-Breed" (#1)
- Cher, *Dark Lady* (1974: #69), including "Dark Lady" (#1, UK #36)
- Cher, "Take Me Home" (1979: #8, Disco #2)
- Cher, "If I Could Turn Back Time" (#3, UK #6)
- Cher, *It's a Man's World* (1995: #64, UK #10)
- Cher, *Believe* (1998: #4, UK #7), including "Believe" (#1, UK #1, Dance #1)

Chapter Forty-Three: Cyndi Lauper

- Cyndi Lauper, *She's So Unusual* (1983: #4, UK #16), including "Girls Just Want to Have Fun" (#2, UK #2, Dance #1), "She Bop" (#3, UK #46, Dance #10), and "Time After Time" (#1, UK #3)
- Cyndi Lauper, *True Colors* (1986: #4, UK #25), including "True Colors" (#1, UK #12)
- Dionne & Friends, "That's What Friends Are For" (1985: #1, R&B #1, UK #16)
- Cyndi Lauper, *Hat Full of Stars* (1993: #112, UK #56)
- Cyndi Lauper, "Hey Now (Girls Just Want to Have Fun)" (1994: #87, UK #4)
- Cyndi Lauper, "Ballad of Cleo and Joe" (1997: Dance #36)

- Original Broadway Cast, *Kinky Boots* (2013: #51)

Chapter Forty-Four: Madonna

- Madonna, *Madonna* (1983: #8, R&B #20, UK #6), including "Everybody" (1982: Dance #3), "Burning Up" (Dance #3), "Holiday" (#16, R&B #25, Dance #1; 1985 UK rerelease: #2), "Lucky Star" (#4, R&B #42, UK #14, Dance #1), and "Borderline" (#10, Dance #4; 1986 UK rerelease: #2)
- Loose Joints, "Is It All Over My Face?" (1980: Disco #23)
- Stephanie Mills, "Never Knew Love Like This Before" (1980: #6, R&B #12, UK #4, Disco #5)
- Madonna, *Like a Virgin* (1984: #1, R&B #10, UK #1), including "Like a Virgin" (#1, R&B #9, UK #3, Dance #1) and "Material Girl" (#2, R&B #49, UK #3, Dance #1)
- Madonna, "Into the Groove" (1985: UK #1, Dance #1)
- Peter Brown, "They Only Come Out at Night" (1984: R&B #50, Dance #1)
- Cheyne, "Call Me Mr. Telephone" (1985: R&B #62, Dance #1)
- Madonna, *True Blue* (1986: #1, R&B #47, UK #1), including "Live to Tell" (#1, UK #2), "Papa Don't Preach" (#1, UK #1, Dance #4), and "Open Your Heart" (#1, UK #4, Dance #1)
- Regina, "Baby Love" (1986: #10, R&B #30, UK #50, Dance #1)
- Alisha, "Baby Talk" (1985: #68, R&B #75, Dance #1)
- Madonna, *Like a Prayer* (1989: #1, R&B #55, UK #1), including "Like a Prayer" (#1, R&B #20, UK #1, Dance #1), "Express Yourself" (#2, UK #5, Dance #1), "Cherish" (#2, UK #3), and "Oh Father" (#20; 1995: UK rerelease #16)
- Madonna, *I'm Breathless: Music from and Inspired by the Film Dick Tracy* (1990: #2, UK #2), including "Vogue" (#1, R&B #16, UK #1, Dance #1)
- Sylvester, "Stars" (1979: UK #47, Disco #4)
- Natalie Cole, "Pink Cadillac" (1988: #5, R&B #9, UK #5, Dance #1)
- Madonna, *The Immaculate Collection* (1990: #2, R&B #81, UK #1), including "Justify My Love" (#1, R&B #42, UK #2, Dance #1)
- Madonna, "This Used to Be My Playground" (1992: #1, UK #3)
- Madonna, *Erotica* (1992: #2, UK #2), including "Erotica" (#3, UK #3, Dance #1), "Deeper and Deeper" (#7, UK #6, Dance #1), and "Bad Girl" (1993: #36, UK #10)
- Minnie Riperton, "Inside My Love" (1975: #76, R&B #26)
- Madonna, *Bedtime Stories* (1994: #3, UK #2), including "Take a Bow" (#1: R&B #40, UK #16)
- Madonna, *Evita* soundtrack (1996: #2, UK #1), including "Don't Cry for Me Argentina" (#8, UK #3, Dance #1)

- Madonna, *Ray of Light* (1998: #2, UK #1), including "Frozen" (#2, UK #1, Dance #2), "Ray of Light" (#5, UK #2, Dance #1), and "Drowned World/ Substitute for Love" (UK #10)
- Madonna, *Music* (2000: #1, UK #1), including "What It Feels Like for a Girl" (#23, UK #7, Dance #1)
- Madonna, "Hollywood" (2003: UK #2, Dance #1)

Chapter Forty-Five: Wham! and George Michael

- Wham!, *Fantastic* (1983: #83, UK #1), including "Wham Rap! (Enjoy What You Do)" (1982: UK #8), "Young Guns (Go for It)" (1982: UK #3, Dance #21), and "Club Tropicana" (UK #4)
- Wham!, *Make It Big* (1984: #1, UK #1), including "Everything She Wants" (#1, R&B #12, UK #2, Dance #7), "Wake Me Up Before You Go-Go" (#1, UK #1, Dance #27), and "Careless Whisper" (#1, R&B #8, UK #1)
- Wham!, "Last Christmas" (1984: UK #2)
- Wham!, "I'm Your Man" (1985: #3, R&B #55, UK #1, Dance #42)
- Wham!, "Battlestations" (1986)
- George Michael, *Faith* (1987: #1, R&B #1, UK #1), including "I Want Your Sex" (#2, R&B #43, UK #3, Dance #2), "Faith" (#1, UK #2), "Father Figure" (#1, R&B #13, UK #11, Dance #13), and "One More Try" (#1, R&B #1, UK #8)
- Queen, "Crazy Little Thing Called Love" (1979: #1, UK #2)
- George Michael, *Listen Without Prejudice Vol. 1* (1990: #2, R&B #61, UK #1), including "Praying for Time" (#1, UK #6) and "Freedom! '90" (#8, UK #28, Dance #16)
- Various, *Red Hot + Dance* (1992: #52, UK #6), including "Too Funky" (#10, UK #4, Dance #20)
- George Michael, *Older* (1996: #6, UK #1), including "Jesus to a Child" (#7, R&B #22, UK #1), "Fastlove" (#8, R&B #44, UK #1), "Spinning the Wheel" (UK #2, Dance #44), and "You Have Been Loved" (UK #2)
- Patrice Rushen, "Forget Me Nots" (1982: #23, R&B #4, UK #8, Dance #2)
- George Michael, "Outside" (1998: UK #2, Dance #3)

Chapter Forty-Six: Whitney Houston

- Cheryl Lynn, "Star Love" (1979: #62, R&B #15, Disco #11)
- Original Broadway Cast, *Dreamgirls* (1982: #11, R&B #4), including Jennifer Holliday, "And I Am Telling You I'm Not Going" (#22, R&B #1, UK #32)
- Cissy Houston, "Think It Over" (1978: R&B #32, Disco #5)
- Chaka Khan, "Clouds" (1980: R&B #10, Disco #31)

- Whitney Houston, *Whitney Houston* (1985: #1, R&B #1, UK #2), including "You Give Good Love" (#3, R&B #1, UK #93) and "How Will I Know" (#1, R&B #1, UK #5, Dance #3)
- Whitney Houston, *Whitney* (1987: #1, R&B #2, UK #1), including "So Emotional" (#1, R&B #5, UK #5, Dance #1)
- Whitney Houston, *I'm Your Baby Tonight* (1990: #3, R&B #1, UK #4), including "I'm Your Baby Tonight" (#1, R&B #1, UK #5, Dance #17)
- Various, *The Bodyguard* soundtrack (1992: #1, R&B #1, UK #1), including Whitney Houston, "I Will Always Love You" (#1, R&B #1, UK #1)
- Various, *Waiting to Exhale* soundtrack (1995: #1, R&B #1, UK #8)
- Whitney Houston, *The Preacher's Wife* soundtrack (1996: #3, R&B #1, UK #35)
- Whitney Houston, *My Love Is Your Love* (1998: #13, R&B #7, UK #4), including "Heartbreak Hotel" featuring Faith Evans and Kelly Price (#2, R&B #1, UK #25, Dance #1) and "It's Not Right but It's Okay" (#4, R&B #7, UK #3, Dance #1)
- Whitney Houston, *Whitney: The Greatest Hits* (2000: #2, R&B #3, UK #1) including "If I Told You That" with George Michael (UK #9)
- Destiny's Child, "Say My Name" (2000: #1, R&B #1, UK #3, Dance #39)

Chapter Forty-Seven: Depeche Mode, Yaz, and Erasure

- Depeche Mode, "People Are People" (1984: #13, UK #4, Dance #44)
- Depeche Mode, *Speak & Spell* (1981: #192, UK #10), including "Just Can't Get Enough" (UK #8, Disco #26)
- Blancmange, "That's Love, That It Is" (1983, UK #33, Dance #16)
- Depeche Mode, "Master and Servant" (1984: #87, UK #9, Dance #49)
- Depeche Mode, "Shake the Disease" (1985: UK #18)
- Depeche Mode, *Black Celebration* (1986: #90, UK #4), including "A Question of Lust" (UK #28)
- Depeche Mode, *Music for the Masses* (1987: #35, UK #10), including "Never Let Me Down Again" (#63, UK #22, Dance #12)
- Depeche Mode, *Violator* (1990: #7, UK #2)
- Depeche Mode, "Blasphemous Rumours" (1984: UK #16)
- Depeche Mode, *Songs of Faith and Devotion* (1993: #1, UK #1)
- Yaz, *Upstairs at Eric's* (1982: #92, UK #2), including "Situation" (#73, R&B #31, Dance #1)
- Erasure, "Who Needs Love Like That" (1985: UK #55, Dance #8)
- Erasure, *The Circus* (1987: #190, UK #6)
- Erasure, *The Innocents* (1988: #49, UK #1), including "Chains of Love"

(#12, UK #11, Dance #4) and "A Little Respect" (#14, UK #4, Dance #2)

- Erasure, "Blue Savannah" (1990: UK #3, Dance #44)
- Erasure, "Love to Hate You" (1991: UK #4, Dance #17)
- Gloria Gaynor, "I Will Survive" (1978: #1, R& B #4, UK #1, Disco #1)
- Erasure, *Abba-esque* (1992: #85, UK #1), including "Take a Chance on Me" (Dance #10)
- Erasure, "Always" (1994: #20, UK #4, Dance #6)

Chapter Forty-Eight: New Order

- Joy Division, "Love Will Tear Us Apart" (1980: UK #13, Disco #42)
- New Order, "Blue Monday"/"The Beach" (1983: UK #9, Dance #5)
- New Order, "1963" (1987)

Chapter Forty-Nine: Pet Shop Boys, Dusty Springfield, and Liza Minnelli

- Wayne County & the Backstreet Boys, "Max's Kansas City" (1976)
- Divine, "Native Love (Step by Step)" (1982: Dance #21)
- Pet Shop Boys, *Please* (1986: #7, UK #3), including "West End Girls" (1985: #1, UK #1, Dance #1) and "Opportunities (Let's Make Lots of Money)" (#10, UK #11, Dance #3)
- Pet Shop Boys, *Actually* (1987: #25, UK #2), including "It's a Sin" (#9, UK #1, Dance #3), "What Have I Done to Deserve This?" with Dusty Springfield (#2, UK #2, Dance #1), and "Rent" (UK #8)
- Eighth Wonder, "I'm Not Scared" (1988: UK #7)
- Dusty Springfield, *Reputation* (1990: UK #18), including "Nothing Has Been Proved" (1989: UK #16) and "In Private" (1989: UK #14)
- Charles Aznavour, "Comme ils Desent" (aka "What Makes a Man") (1972)
- Liza Minnelli, *Results* (1989: #128, UK #6), including "Losing My Mind" (UK #6, Dance #26)
- Pet Shop Boys, *Introspective* (1988: #34, UK #2), including "Always on My Mind," (1987: #4, UK #1, Dance #8), "Domino Dancing" (#18, UK #7, Dance #5), and "Left to My Own Devices" (#84, UK #4, Dance #8)
- Noel, "Silent Morning" (1987: #47, Dance #6)
- Pet Shop Boys, *Behavior* (1990: #45, UK #2), including "Being Boring" (UK #20)
- Pet Shop Boys, "Your Funny Uncle" (1989)
- Kylie Minogue, "Better the Devil You Know" (1990: UK #2)
- Pet Shop Boys, *Very* (1993: #20, UK #1), including "Can You Forgive Her?" (UK #7, Dance #1), "Go West" (UK #2, Dance #1), and "Liberation" (UK #14)

- Pet Shop Boys, *Nightlife* (1999: #84, UK #7), including "New York City Boy" (UK #14, Dance #1)
- Pet Shop Boys, "Somewhere" (1997: UK #9, Dance #19)

Chapter Fifty: Tina Turner and Bonnie Raitt

- Ike and Tina Turner, "Proud Mary" (1971: #4)
- Heaven 17, "Let Me Go" (1982: #74, UK #41, Dance #4)
- Tina Turner, *Private Dancer* (1984: #3, R&B #1, UK #2), including "Let's Stay Together" (1983: #26, UK #6, Dance #1), "What's Love Got to Do with It" (#1, UK #3, Dance #21), "Better Be Good to Me" (#5, UK #45, Dance #16), and "Private Dancer" (#7, R&B #3, UK #26)
- Tina Turner, "I Don't Wanna Fight" (1993: #9, R&B #51, UK #7)
- Bonnie Raitt, *Give It Up* (1972: #138)
- Bonnie Raitt, *Takin' My Time* (1973: #91)
- Bonnie Raitt, *Nick of Time* (1989: #1, UK #51)
- Bonnie Raitt, *Luck of the Draw* (1991: #2, UK #38), including "Something to Talk About" (#5) and "I Can't Make You Love Me" (#18, UK #50)
- George Michael, "I Can't Make You Love Me" (1997: UK #3)

Chapter Fifty-One: Phranc and k.d. lang

- Phranc, *Folksinger* (1985)
- Phranc, *I Enjoy Being a Girl* (1989)
- Phranc, *Positively Phranc* (1991)
- Phranc, *Goodyfoot* (1995)
- k.d. lang and the Reclines, *A Truly Western Experience* (1984)
- Frances Faye, "Frances and Her Friends" (1959)
- Rusty Warren, *Knockers Up!* (1960)
- k.d. lang and the Reclines, *Angel with a Lariat* (1987: Country #53)
- k.d. lang, *Shadowland* (1988: #73, Country #9)
- k.d. lang and the Reclines, *Absolute Torch and Twang* (1989: #69, Country #12)
- Various, *Red Hot + Blue* (1990: #38, UK #6)
- k.d. lang, *Ingénue* (1992: #18, UK #3), including "Miss Chatelaine" (UK #68) and "Constant Craving" (#38, UK #15)
- k.d. lang, *Even Cowgirls Get the Blues* soundtrack (1993: #82, UK #36)
- k.d. lang, *All You Can Eat* (1995: #37, UK #7), including "Sexuality" (Dance #3) and "You're OK" (UK #44)
- k.d. lang, *Drag* (1997: #29, UK #19)
- k.d. lang, *Invincible Summer* (2000: #58, UK #17), including "Summerfling" (Dance #25)

Chapter Fifty-Two: Sinéad O'Connor

- Sinéad O'Connor, *The Lion and the Cobra* (1987: #36, UK #27), including "I Want Your (Hands on Me)" (1988 remix with MC Lyte: UK #77)
- Sinéad O'Connor, *I Do Not Want What I Haven't Got* (1990: #1, UK #1), including "Jump in the River" (1988: UK #81) and "Nothing Compares 2 U" (#1, UK #1)
- Sinéad O'Connor, *Am I Not Your Girl?* (1992: #27, UK #6)
- Sinéad O'Connor, *Faith and Courage* (2000: #55, UK #61)

Chapter Fifty-Three: Tracy Chapman

- Tracy Chapman, *Tracy Chapman* (1988: #1, UK #1), including "Fast Car" (#6, UK #4), "Talkin' 'bout a Revolution" (#75, R&B #78, UK #85), and "Baby Can I Hold You" (#48)
- Two Nice Girls, *2 Nice Girls* (1989)
- Joan Armatrading, "Love and Affection" (1976: UK #10)

Chapter Fifty-Four: Indigo Girls

- Indigo Girls, *Indigo Girls* (1989: #22), including "Closer to Fine" (#52)
- Indigo Girls, *Rites of Passage* (1992: #21)
- Indigo Girls, *Swamp Ophelia* (1994: #9, UK #81)
- Bruce Springsteen, "Streets of Philadelphia" (1994: #9, UK #2)
- Michael Feinstein and Cheyenne Jackson, *The Power of Two* (2009)
- Various, *Jesus Christ Superstar: A Resurrection* (1994)
- Indigo Girls, *Shaming of the Sun* (1997: #7, UK #81)

Chapter Fifty-Five: Melissa Etheridge

- Melissa Etheridge, *Melissa Etheridge* (1988: #22), including "Similar Features" (#94)
- Melissa Etheridge, *Brave and Crazy* (1989: #22, UK #63)
- Trisha Yearwood, "You Can Sleep While I Drive" (1995: Country #26)
- Melissa Etheridge, *Never Enough* (1992: #21, UK #56)
- Melissa Etheridge, *Yes I Am* (1993: #15), including "Come to My Window (1994: #25) and "I'm The Only One" (#8)
- Melissa Etheridge, *Your Little Secret* (1995: #6, UK #85), including "I Want to Come Over" (1996: #22) and "Nowhere to Go" (1996: #40)
- The Byrds, "Triad" (recorded 1967, first issued on *Never Before,* 1987)
- Jefferson Airplane, *Crown of Creation* (1968: #6)
- Crosby, Stills, Nash & Young, *4 Way Street* (1971: #1, UK #5)
- Melissa Etheridge, *Breakdown* (1999: #12)
- Melissa Etheridge, *Skin* (2001: #9)

Chapter Fifty-Six: Nirvana and Hole

- Nirvana, *Nevermind* (1991: #1, UK #5), including "Smells Like Teen Spirit" (#6, UK #7, Dance #14)
- Nirvana, *Incesticide* (1992: #39, UK #14)
- Nirvana, "All Apologies"/"Rape Me" (1993: UK #32)
- Sweet 75, *Sweet 75* (1997)
- Hole, "Teenage Whore" (1991)
- The Breeders, "Cannonball" (1993: #44, UK #40)

Chapter Fifty-Seven: C+C Music Factory, Deee-Lite, and House Music

- Steve "Silk" Hurley, "Jack Your Body" (1986: UK #1, Dance #25)
- Rick Astley, "Never Gonna Give You Up" (1987: #1, UK #1, Dance #1)
- C+C Music Factory, "Gonna Make You Sweat (Everybody Dance Now)" featuring Freedom Williams (1990: #1, R&B #1, UK #3, Dance #1)
- Deee-Lite, *World Clique* (1990: #14, R&B #34, UK #14), including "Groove Is in the Heart" (#4, R&B #28, UK #2, Dance #1)
- Deee-Lite, *Infinity Within* (1992: #67, UK #37)
- 4 Non Blondes, "What's Up" (1993: #14, UK #2)

Chapter Fifty-Eight: Bikini Kill, Green Day, Pansy Division, and Suede

- Bikini Kill, "Rebel Girl" (1993)
- Green Day, "Bobby Sox" (2024)
- Green Day, *Dookie* (1994: #2, UK #13)
- Pansy Division, *Deflowered* (1994)
- Suede, *Suede* (1993: UK #1), including "The Drowners" (1992: UK #49) and "Animal Nitrate" (UK #7)
- Suede, *Dog Man Star* (1994: UK #3)
- McAlmont & Butler, "Yes" (1995: UK #8)

Chapter Fifty-Nine: Queen Latifah and Hip-Hop

- Kurtis Blow, "The Breaks" (1980: #87, R&B #4, Disco #9)
- Man Parrish, "Hip Hop, Be Bop (Don't Stop)" (1982: R&B #66, UK #41, Dance #4)
- Grandmaster Flash and the Furious Five, "The Message" (1982: #62, R&B #4, UK #8, Dance #12)
- DJ Jazzy Jeff and the Fresh Prince, *He's the DJ, I'm the Rapper* (1988: #4, R&B #5)
- Queen Latifah featuring Monie Love, "Ladies First" (1989: R&B #64, Dance #38)
- Queen Latifah, "Come into My House" (1990: R&B #81, Dance #7)
- Queen Latifah, "U.N.I.T.Y." (1993: #23, R&B #7)

Chapter Sixty: RuPaul (and a little more Sylvester)

- RuPaul, "Supermodel (You Better Work)" (1992: #45, UK #39, Dance #2)
- RuPaul, "Back to My Roots" (1993: UK #40, Dance #1)
- RuPaul, "Cover Girl" (2009)
- RuPaul, "Sissy That Walk" (2014: Dance #55)
- RuPaul, "I'm a Winner, Baby" (2021)
- Sylvester, "Someone Like You" (1986: R&B #19, Dance #1)
- Sylvester, "Take Me to Heaven" (1985: Dance #6)

Notes

Preface

xiv **"I will sue":** Donald Padgett, "The Village People Will Sue You for Saying 'YMCA' Is About Gay Sex," *Out*, September 23, 2020, out.com/music/2020/9/23/village-people-will-sue-you-saying-ymca-about-gay-sex.

One: The Velvet Underground and Lou Reed

1 **"That's what was recommended":** Legs McNeil and Gillian McCain, *Please Kill Me: The Uncensored Oral History of Punk* (Grove Press, 2016).

1 **While in high school:** Howard Sounes, *The Life of Lou Reed: Notes from the Velvet Underground* (Doubleday, 2015).

1 **"If it's not dark":** Todd Haynes, dir., *The Velvet Underground* (Apple Original Films, 2021), dailymail.co.uk/news/article-10092807/New-Velvet-Underground-doc-reveals-Lou-Reed-fired-Andy-Warhol-drug-induced-battle-egos.html.

3 **"I like to think":** Victor Bockris and Gerard Malanga, *Up-Tight: The Velvet Underground Story* (Cooper Square, 2003).

4 **Morrison denied his epic:** Peter Mills, *Hymns to the Silence: Inside the Words and Music of Van Morrison* (Continuum, 2010), 296.

4 **As art historian:** Benjamin H. D. Buchloh, "Andy Warhol's One-Dimensional Art: 1956–1966," in *Andy Warhol: A Retrospective*, ed. Annette Michelson (MIT Press, 2001), 28.

6 **According to Reed biographer:** Victor Bockris, *Transformer: The Lou Reed Story* (Simon & Schuster, 1994), 214.

6 **"The gay life at the moment":** Lou Reed and Chris Roberts, *Lou Reed: Walk on the Wild Side: The Stories Behind the Songs* (Hal Leonard, 2004), 46.

7 **"He should forget":** Nick Tosches, review of *Transformer* by Lou Reed, *Rolling Stone*, January 4, 1973, rollingstone.com/music/music-album-reviews/transformer-89126.

8 **Reed's soon fell hard:** Bockris, *Transformer*, 314.

Two: Laura Nyro

13 **"I stopped writing songs":** Richard Williams, "Lady Lightning," *Guardian*, April 1, 2005, theguardian.com/music/2005/apr/02/popandrock.

Three: Janis Joplin

14 **"I think she wanted kids":** Alice Echols, *Scars of Sweet Paradise: The Life and Times of Janis Joplin* (Henry Holt, 2000), 87.

16 **"You fly up there":** Echols, *Scars of Sweet Paradise*, 251.

16 **"I was stark naked":** Peggy Caserta and Dan Knapp, *Going Down with Janis* (Lyle Stuart, 1973).

Four: Motown

23 **After Lindsey was diagnosed:** Ericka Blount Danois, "Play Another Slow Jam: An Oral History of the Quiet Storm," *Essence*, updated November 4, 2020, essence.com/entertainment/play-another-slow-jam-cathy-hughes-remembers-creating-the-quiet-storm.

Five: The Kinks

34 **"The song is about homosexuality":** Johnny Rogan, *Ray Davies: A Complicated Life* (Vintage, 2016), 238.

34 **Yet it impressed:** Dave Davies, *Kink: An Autobiography* (Hyperion, 1996), 76.

35 **Following the Kinks':** Michael James Roberts, *Tell Tchaikovsky the News: Rock 'n' Roll, the Labor Question, and the Musicians' Union, 1942–1968* (Duke University Press, 2014), 188.

35 **American Federation of Television:** Thomas M. Kitts, *Ray Davies: Not Like Everybody Else* (Routledge, 2008), 61.

35 **"In his apartment":** Rob Jovanovic, *God Save the Kinks: A Biography* (Aurum, 2013).

36 **"All the Kinks":** Nick Hasted, *You Really Got Me: The Story of the Kinks* (Omnibus, 2011).

36 **In his autobiography, Dave:** Davies, *Kink*, 52–53.

Six: David Bowie and Glam

38 **"It was such a seminal":** George Hencken, dir., *Soul Boys of the Western World* (IFC Films, 2014).

39 **"All that filters":** Seth Abramovitch, "Pet Shop Boys on Their Favorite Hollywood Memories: 'So Gorgeous. So Elegant,'" *Hollywood Reporter*, April 25, 2024, hollywoodreporter.com/news/music-news/pet-shop-boys-madonna-liza-minnelli-kylie-minogue-collab-1235881378.

40 **"It's a Gay Anthem!":** Simon Goddard, *Ziggyology: A Brief History of Ziggy Stardust* (Ebury, 2014), 226.

41 **"A song has to":** Craig Copetas, "Beat Godfather Meets Glitter Mainman: William Burroughs Interviews David Bowie," *Rolling Stone*, February 28, 1974, rollingstone.com/feature/beat-godfather-meets-glitter-mainman-william-burroughs-interviews-david-bowie-92508.

Seven: Bette Midler

44 **Ostrow claimed to have:** Tim Lawrence, *Love Saves the Day: A History of American Dance Music Culture, 1970–1979* (Duke University Press, 2004), 63.

47 **"It wasn't bizarre":** Kevin O'Donnell, "Bette Midler's 'The Divine Miss M' Reissue: Hear an Alternate Version of Superstar," *Entertainment Weekly*, October 19, 2016, ew.com/article/2016/10/19/bette-midler-divine-miss-m-reissue.

Eight: Labelle

49 **"If one wanted to":** John Rockwell, "The Pop Life: Labelle at Met: Sequins, Regions and Acoustics," *New York Times*, October 11, 1974, nytimes.com/1974/10/11/archives/labelle-at-met-sequins-regions-and-acoustics-the-pop-life.html.

Eleven: Olivia Records and Women's Music

62 **"A socialist venture":** Andrew Male, "'Our Sound Engineer Got a Death Threat': How Lesbian Label Olivia Shook Up Music," *Guardian*, July 19, 2020, theguardian.com/music/2020/jul/19/lesbian-record-label-olivia-linda-tillery-californian-feminists-death-threat-music.

70 ***The Village Voice*'s Robert Christgau:** Robert Christgau, review of *The Deadly Nightshade* by the Deadly Nightshade, in *Christgau's Record Guide: Rock Albums*

of the '70s (Pantheon Books, 1990), 104, robertchristgau.com/get_artist.php?name=The+Deadly+Nightshade.

Twelve: Queen

75 **Even before the single:** Rock History, "Eric Hall, Killer Queen," rockhistory.co.uk, November 9, 2012, youtube.com/watch?v=aHbJW5xrDB0.

77 **"The hint of it":** Jim Sullivan: "He Wants to Break Free: Brian May at 75," *Rock and Roll Globe*, July 19, 2022, rockandrollglobe.com/rock/he-wants-to-break-free-brian-may-at-75.

Thirteen: Patti Smith

81 **Years later, this:** Ray Padgett, "The Story Behind Patti Smith's 'Gloria,'" *Cover Me*, August 4, 2014, covermesongs.com/2014/08/the-story-behind-patti-smiths-gloria.html.

83 **When hiring fellow:** Patti Smith, *Just Kids* (Ecco, 2010), 181.

Fourteen: *The Rocky Horror Picture Show*

86 **In the late '70s:** "1978 News Report on the *Rocky Horror* Craze Captures a Teenage Michael Stipe in Drag," *Open Culture*, June 9, 2016, openculture.com/2016/06/1978-news-report-on-the-rocky-horror-craze-captures-a-teenage-michael-stipe-in-drag.html.

Fifteen: Disco's Birth

88 **Consider what the Stonewall:** Willson Lee Henderson, "Songs of the *Original* Stonewall Club Jukebox," accessed May 6, 2024, stonewallvets.org/songsofStonewall-1.htm.

90 **Even in LGBTQ clubs:** Hugh Ryan, "How Dressing in Drag Was Labeled a Crime in the 20th Century," *History*, June 25, 2019, updated September 14, 2023, history.com/news/stonewall-riots-lgbtq-drag-three-article-rule.

90 **Although the club wasn't gay:** Angela Taylor, "Arthur, Once a Hairdo, Is Now a Discotheque; Club's Debut Separates the Ins from the Outs," *New York Times*, May 7, 1965, nytimes.com/1965/05/07/archives/arthur-once-a-hairdo-is-now-a-discotheque-clubs-debut-separates-the.html.

91 **What distinguished Arthur:** Bill Brewster and Frank Broughton, *Last Night a DJ Saved My Life: The History of the Disc Jockey* (Grove, 2000), 75.

91 **"Many people would come up":** Bill Brewster, "Interview: Terry Noel," Red Bull Music Academy, March 31, 2016, original interview, DJHistory.com, October 1998, redbullmusicacademy.com/2016/03/terry-noel-interview.

91 **Sanctuary started out straight:** Lawrence, *Love Saves the Day*, 20.

93 **After Mancuso shared:** Peter Shapiro, *Turn the Beat Around: The Secret History of Disco* (Faber and Faber, 2005), 35.

94 **In its July 1:** Mark Jacobson, "Hollyw-o-o-o-d! The Return of the New York Disco," *New York*, July 1, 1974.

95 **Florence Greenberg of Scepter:** "Radio Complaints Just Too Bad: Gregory," *Billboard*, February 7, 1976, 24, worldradiohistory.com/Archive-All-Music/Bill board/70s/1976/Billboard%201976-02-07a.pdf.

Sixteen: Donna Summer

98 **"I do not sing":** Donna Summer with Marc Eliot, *Ordinary Girl: The Journey* (Villard, 2003), 102.

98 **Whereas soul stars:** Summer and Eliot, *Ordinary Girl*, 125.

99 **"I have heard the sound":** Rob Sheffield, "Dim All the Lights for Donna Summer," *Rolling Stone*, May 17, 2012, rollingstone.com/music/music-news/dim-all-the-lights-for-donna-summer-242108.

101 **"I let go long enough":** "Show Business: Sex Rock," *Time*, December 29, 1975, https://content.time.com/time/subscriber/article/0,33009,945456,00.html.

103 **The slogan "God made":** Zach Schonfeld, "The Surprising History of the Phrase 'Adam and Eve, Not Adam and Steve,'" *Newsweek*, July 1, 2015, newsweek.com/surprising-history-phrase-adam-and-eve-not-adam-and-steve-348164.

104 **"We make gay records":** Edwin J. Bernard, "The Great Renegade," *Record Mirror*, October 18, 1986.

Seventeen: Village People and Their LGBTQ Kin

108 **In 2016, Italy's:** Simone Vazzana, "I 70 Anni (ma Anche No) di Amanda Lear, Storia di un Mistero," *La Stampa*, November 19, 2016, lastampa.it/spettacoli/showbiz/2016/11/19/news/i-70-anni-ma-anche-no-di-amanda-lear-storia-di-un-mistero-1.34773035.

108 **As Dalí's protégé and muse:** Ian Gibson, *The Shameful Life of Salvador Dali* (W. W. Norton, 1998), 582–83.

110 **"Morali was openly gay":** Robert Hofler, *Party Animals: A Hollywood Tale of Sex, Drugs, and Rock 'n' Roll, Starring the Fabulous Allan Carr* (Da Capo, 2010), 94.

110 Enthralled by Felipe Rose: Ken Emerson, "The Village People: America's Male Ideal?," *Rolling Stone,* October 5, 1978, in *The Rolling Stone Encyclopedia of Rock & Roll,* eds. Jon Pareles and Patricia Romanowski (Rolling Stone Press/Summit Books, 1983).

111 According to Jones: Jeff Pearlman, "'Y.M.C.A.' (An Oral History)," *Spin,* May 27, 2008, www.spin.com/2008/05/ymca-oral-history.

112–13 In the spring of 1979: Hofler, *Party Animals*, 96.

113 Shafting LGBTQ authenticity: Hofler, *Party Animals*, 112.

113 Only their showstopping: Hofler, *Party Animals*, 113.

113 Bombing everywhere but: Hofler, *Party Animals*, 127.

113 Village People have continued: Ellie Harrison, "Trump Ends Presidency to Soundtrack of 'YMCA' and 'Gloria,'" *Independent*, January 20, 2021, independent.co.uk/arts-entertainment/music/news/trump-white-house-ymca-gloria-dont-stop-believin-b1790094.html.

113 President Donald Trump: Matt Baume, "Donald Trump's 8 Worst Attacks on the LGBTQ+ Community," *Them*, August 27, 2020, them.us/story/donald-trump-worst-lgbtq-attacks.

Eighteen: Sylvester

119 No wonder Dahl's on-air: Frank Rose, "Discophobia! Rock & Roll Fights Back," *Village Voice*, November 12, 1979, https://www.frankrose.com/essays/discophobia.

123 Bowie's influence meant: Trish Bendix, "Why Is Joan Jett's 'Bad Reputation' Playing Outfest When She's Not Out?," *INTO*, July 18, 2018, intomore.com/culture/why-is-joan-jetts-bad-reputation-playing-outfest-when-shes-not-out.

123 The next year, the entire: Bendix, "Why Is Joan Jett's 'Bad Reputation' Playing Outfest When She's Not Out?"

124 *Ramones*'s fleshiest narrative: Christopher Keeley, *Addict Out of the Dark and Into the Light* (Xlibris, 2007), tunlaw.org/deedeer.htm.

124 In 1996, researchers: H. E. Adams, L. W. Wright Jr., and B. A. Lohr, "Is Homophobia Associated with Homosexual Arousal?," *Journal of Abnormal Psychology* 105, no. 3 (1996): 440–45, https://doi.org/10.1037/0021-843X.105.3.440.

124 In 2012, researchers: Richard M. Ryan and William S. Ryan, "Homophobic? Maybe You're Gay," *New York Times*, April 27, 2012, nytimes.com/2012/04/29/opinion/sunday/homophobic-maybe-youre-gay.html?src=recg, https://www.eurekalert.org/news-releases/849246.

125 They illustrate this hypothesis: Tim Fitzsimons, "Homophobia Linked to Latent Same-Sex Attraction: Study," *World*, April 29, 2012, theworld.org /stories/2012-04-29/homophobia-linked-latent-same-sex-attraction-study-video.

125 "The 'Blondie' character": Debbie Harry, *Face It: A Memoir* (Dey Street Books, 2019), 105.

126 During the band's appearance: Michael McKenzie, "Grand Punk," *Mandate*, October 1977, 24, cowboyfrank.men/PDF/Mandate/1977-10-Mandate.pdf.

127 "We used to do 'Heart'": "500 Greatest Songs of All Time (2004)," *Rolling Stone*, December 11, 2003, rollingstone.com/music/music-lists/500-greatest-songs -of-all-time-151127/blondie-heart-of-glass-51117.

127 Sure enough, Harry divulged: Chris Hastings, "My 'Sensual' Nights with Women, by Debbie Harry: Blondie Star Reveals She Is Bisexual Despite Relationship with Bandmate," *Daily Mail*, April 5, 2014, updated April 6, 2014, dailymail .co.uk/tvshowbiz/article-2597774/My-sensual-nights-women-Debbie-Harry -Blondie-star-reveals-bisexual-despite-relationship-bandmate.html.

128 Shelley sang nearly all: Mark Freitas, "Buzzcocks: The Queer Punk Interview," *Outpunk* #6, queermusicheritage.com/jul2009qg11.html.

128 Years later, Shelley divulged: Freitas, "Buzzcocks: The Queer Punk Interview."

129 Yet when *Outpunk*: Freitas, "Buzzcocks: The Queer Punk Interview."

130 Closer to Bruce Springsteen: JD Doyle, "Tom Robinson Interview," Queer Music Heritage, aired August 23, 2004, on Houston, TX: KPFT, web.archive.org /web/20070705004226/http:/www.queermusicheritage.us/aug2004s.html.

Twenty: The B-52s

135 I learned this firsthand: Royal Scribe, "The Castro Sweep: Martial Law in the Castro," *SF Gay History*, October 6, 2014, sfgayhistory.com/2014/10/06/the -castro-sweep-martial-law-in-the-castro.

Twenty-One: Talking Heads and Post-Punk

138 She'd met drummer Frantz: Adam Jacques, "How We Met: Chris Frantz & Tina Weymouth," *Independent*, March 17, 2013.

139 Guitarist Marlene Marder: Jess Scott, "Blast from the Past: Kleenex," *Maximum Rocknroll*, May 2010, posted July 9, 2015, maximumrocknroll.com/blast -from-the-past-kleenex.

139 New York yielded Bush Tetras: Dakota Brown, "Cynthia Sley - Bush Tetras," *The Self Portrait Gospel*, theselfportraitgospel.com/interviews/cynthia-sley-bush-tetras.

139 This isn't a ladylike: Guy Trebay, "Talking Heads: L'Apres-Midi d'un Tetra," *Village Voice*, December 10, 1980.

141 "It's basically addressed": Bill Holdship, "The Psychedelic Furs: Sugar Cubes for the New Depression," *Creem*, February 1983, rocksbackpages.com/Library/Article/the-psychedelic-furs-sugar-cubes-for-the-new-depression.

Twenty-Four: Joan Jett and the Go-Go's

156 Updating the pansexual freedom: Dave Thompson, *Bad Reputation: The Unauthorized Biography of Joan Jett* (Backbeat, 2011), 25.

156 Jett refrained from formal wording: Evelyn McDonnell, "Joan Jett," *Interview*, February 20, 2010, interviewmagazine.com/film/joan-jett-the-runaways.

158 Based on Fear's: "Josie Cotton: The Story of '80s New-Wave Hit 'Johnny, Are You Queer?'," *Magnet*, September 9, 2006, magnetmagazine.com/2006/09/09/josie-cotton-the-story-of-'80s-new-wave-hit-"johnny-are-you-queer".

Twenty-Five: Diana Ross and Luther Vandross

163 In recent years, Rodgers: Nile Rodgers, "#LGBTQhistory is what inspired us to write Diana Ross' 'I'm Coming Out,'" TikTok, February 4, 2021, tiktok.com/@nilerodgersandchic/video/6925348748902092038.

168 He said that this was: Dawn Porter, dir., *Luther: Never Too Much* (Giant Pictures, 2024).

169 Patti LaBelle, who'd known Vandross: *Watch What Happens Live with Andy Cohen*, aired December 6, 2017, on Bravo, yahoo.com/entertainment/patti-labelle-says-luther-vandross-never-came-didnt-want-upset-world-193806171.html.

Twenty-Six: Grace Jones

171 Back in 1979: Lynn Norment, "The Outrageous Grace Jones," *Ebony*, July 1979.

171 She didn't have many: Grace Jones and Paul Morley, *I'll Never Write My Memoirs* (Gallery, 2015), 48.

Twenty-Seven: Michael Jackson

183 In 1979, Jackson's future biographer: J. Randy Taraborrelli, *Michael Jackson: The Magic and the Madness* (Birch Lane, 1991), 199.

185 A 2020 UCLA study: "LGBT People Nearly Four Times More Likely Than Non-LGBT People to Be Victims of Violent Crime," Williams Institute, UCLA,

October 2, 2020, williamsinstitute.law.ucla.edu/press/ncvs-lgbt-violence-press-release.

185 As the UN has noted: United Nations Human Rights Council, "Homophobic and Transphobic Violence," Free & Equal Fact Sheet, unfe.org/en/know-the-facts/challenges-solutions/lgbtiq-youth-bullying-and-violence-at-school.

185 According to the University of Arizona's: Hilary Burge, Zami T. Hyemingway, Adela C. Licona, "Gender Non-Conforming Youth: Discipline Disparities, School Push-Out, and the School-to-Prison Pipeline," Gay-Straight Alliance Network, September 2015, arcusfoundation.org/wp-content/uploads/2015/09/Gender-Nonconforming-Youth-Discipline-Disparities-School-Push-Out-and-the-School-to-Prison-Pipeline.pdf.

187 In contrast, he vowed: "Michael Jackson Reacts to Gay Rumors," *Detail*, September 2, 2021, youtube.com/watch?v=F65aDGFSuMk.

187 In his autobiography, *Moonwalk*: Michael Jackson, *Moonwalk* (Harmony, 2009), 265.

189 The creative team behind: Marlow Stern, "'The Simpsons' Boss Al Jean: Michael Jackson Used the Show to 'Groom Boys,'" *Daily Beast*, March 13, 2019, thedailybeast.com/the-simpsons-boss-al-jean-michael-jackson-used-the-show-to-groom-boys.

189 Madonna had previewed: Don Shewey, "The Saint, the Slut, the Sensation . . . Madonna," *Advocate*, May 7, 1991.

189 But when she got back: Adam White, "Madonna Told Michael Jackson to 'Dress Like a Girl' for Music Video, Producer Babyface Claims," *Independent*, April 22, 2020, independent.co.uk/arts-entertainment/music/news/madonna-michael-jackson-babyface-in-the-closet-video-teddy-riley-instagram-a9477446.html.

191 most of the dates: Randy Taraborrelli, *Michael Jackson: The Magic, the Madness, the Whole Story*, 1958–2009 (Grand Central, 2009), 510–20.

191 In early 1994: Rochelle Steinhaus, "Jackson Settlement from 1993 Allegations Topped $20 Million," CNN, June 16, 2004.

191 In 2020, Kelly: Sonia Moghe and Dakin Andone, "R. Kelly Sentenced to 30 Years in Prison for Federal Racketeering and Sex Trafficking Charges," CNN, June 30, 2022, cnn.com/2022/06/29/us/r-kelly-sentencing-racketeering-sex-trafficking/index.html.

192 In 2023, he was additionally: Eric Levenson and Bill Kirkos, "R. Kelly, Already Serving 30 Years for Sex Trafficking, Sentenced to 20 Years in Federal Child Porn Case," CNN, February 23, 2023, cnn.com/2023/02/23/entertainment/rkelly-chicago-child-porn-sentence/index.html.

192 "You left in your wake": Moghe and Andone, "R. Kelly Sentenced."

192 "It all happened": Terry Gross, "Reporter Who Broke R. Kelly Story: Abuse Was in 'Full View of the World,'" *Fresh Air*, aired June 4, 2019, on NPR, npr

.org/2019/06/04/729539206/reporter-who-broke-r-kelly-story-abuse-was-in-full-view-of-the-world.

Twenty-Eight: Wendy Carlos and Kraftwerk

194 **While beginning her transition:** Susan Nunziata, "Wendy Carlos Goes 'Bach' and Forward All at Once with New Reading of Old Set," *Billboard*, August 15, 1992.

Twenty-Nine: Iggy Pop and David Bowie in Berlin

202 **In a 1983 *Rolling Stone*:** Kurt Loder, "David Bowie: Straight Time," *Rolling Stone*, May 12, 1983, rollingstone.com/music/music-news/david-bowie-straight-time-69334.

202 **There he explained:** Clark Collis, "Dear Superstar: David Bowie," *Blender*, August 2002, bowiewonderworld.com/press/00/0208dearsuperstar.htm.

Thirty-One: Duran Duran and the New Romantics

207 **"A seedy gay club":** Chris Sullivan, "New Romantics Could Be Heroes—Just for One Night," *Times*, November 21, 2012. thetimes.com/sunday-times-rich-list/profile/article/new-romantics-could-be-heroes-just-for-one-night-pk7bfdql8rm.

209 **The US record company:** Nile Rodgers, *Le Freak: An Upside Down Story of Family, Disco, and Destiny* (Spiegel & Grau, 2011), 214.

213 **Director Julien Temple:** Rob Tannenbaum and Craig Marks, *I Want My MTV: The Uncensored Story of the Music Video Revolution* (Dutton, 2011), 99.

Thirty-Three: Dolly Parton

221 **"I look one way":** Randy L. Schmidt, ed., *Dolly on Dolly: Interviews and Encounters with Dolly Parton* (Chicago Review, 2017), 202.

223 **"We're all Harold":** Erika Milvy, "Bud Cort," *Salon*, September 4, 1999, salon.com/1999/09/04/cort.

Thirty-Four: Soft Cell and Eurythmics

226 **When the duo appeared:** Patrick Clarke, "Non-Stop Erotic Cabaret: An Oral History of Soft Cell's Debut Album," *Quietus*, November 26, 2021, thequietus.com/articles/30878-soft-cell-non-stop-erotic-cabaret-oral-history-dave-ball-marc-almond-interview.

228 In the song and video: Daniel Dylan Wray, "The Story Behind the 'First Ever Ecstasy Song,'" *Vice*, November 10, 2021, vice.com/en/article/v7dmdd/soft-cell-memorabilia-anniver-first-ever-ecstasy-song.

230 As he wrote in his memoir: Dave Stewart, *Sweet Dreams Are Made of This: A Life in Music* (New American Library, 2016), 90.

231 After their domestic split: Lucy O'Brien, *Annie Lennox: Sweet Dreams Are Made of This* (Pan Macmillan, 1991), 64, 73.

232 The single's picture sleeve: Rebecca Winters, "Q&A with Annie Lennox," *Time*, February 16, 2004, time.com/vault/issue/2004-02-16/page/117.

233 During the recording, Stewart: Stewart, *Sweet Dreams Are Made of This*, 139–40.

234 Donning a feathered headpiece: Barbara Rosen, "For Rent: 150 Years of Stars' Costumes," *New York Times*, August 25, 1998, nytimes.com/1998/08/25/style/IHT-for-rent-150-years-of-stars-costumes.html.

Thirty-Five: Frankie Goes to Hollywood and Bronski Beat

236 Even *Rolling Stone*: David Thomas, "England's Crazy About Frankie Goes to Hollywood," *Rolling Stone*, October 11, 1984, zttaat.com/article.php?title=145.

236 "We used the gay bit": Thomas, "England's Crazy About Frankie Goes to Hollywood."

237 The entire band: Ben Gilbert, "How We Made: Relax by Frankie Goes to Hollywood," *Guardian*, August 2, 2021, theguardian.com/music/2021/aug/02/how-we-made-relax-by-frankie-goes-to-hollywood-sex-mix-gay-clubs.

238 "It was only when": Richard Buskin, "From ABC to ZTT: The Amazing Career of Trevor Horn," *Sound on Sound*, August 1994, web.archive.org/web/20060411044321/http://www.soundonsound.com/sos/1994_articles/aug94/trevorhorn.html.

238 As Johnson explained: Neil Tennant, "Frankie Goes to Hollywood in the War Game," *Smash Hits*, April 26, 1984, zttaat.com/article.php?title=55.

239 KROQ listeners voted: "KROQ Top 106.7 of 1984," RockLists.com, rocklists.com/kroq-1984.html.

240 The *Voice*'s Robert Christgau: Robert Christgau, review of *Welcome to the Pleasuredome* by Frankie Goes to Hollywood, *Village Voice*, robertchristgau.com/get_artist.php?name=Frankie+Goes+to+Hollywood.

240 *Rolling Stone*'s David Fricke: David Fricke, review of *Welcome to the Pleasuredome* by Frankie Goes to Hollywood, *Rolling Stone*, January 17, 1985, web

.archive.org/web/20020129075413/http://rollingstone.com/recordings/review .asp?aid=70996&cf=724.

241 **Rutherford advanced with:** Paul Waller, "Frankie Goes to Hollywood: Interview with Paul Rutherford," *Pennyblackmusic*, March 24, 2013, pennyblackmusic .co.uk/Home/Details?id=20988.

241 **The week of June 10:** "Official Singles Chart: 9 June 1984–15 June 1984," Official Charts, officialcharts.com/charts/singles-chart/19840610/7501.

241 **The straightest act:** Howard Jones (@hoawardjones), "As a proud Father of 2 gay sons the #LGBT issue is very close to my heart. Let's continue to fight for equality for all," Twitter, June 30, 2016, 12:39 pm, twitter.com/howardjones /status/748556625858957312.

243 **Recalling Steinbachek getting:** Steve Bronski, "The Beginning of Bronski Beat," *History Bronski Beat*, jimmysomerville.de/history/steve_beginning_en.htm.

244 **Bronski Beat was picked:** Steve Gett, "The Communards Reject Rock's Stereotypes," *Billboard*, December 20, 1986, 22, worldradiohistory.com/Archive-All -Music/Billboard/80s/1986/BB-1986-12-20.pdf.

245 **"Our aim was to bring":** "The Communards—Don't Leave Me This Way | The Story Behind the Song | Top 2000 a gogo," Top 2000 a gogo, 2021, posted to YouTube, January 6, 2022, youtube.com/watch?v=1J-gqqJ0HZU.

Thirty-Six: Boy George

247 **Right after its release:** Michael Goldberg, "Boy George's Nightmare," *Rolling Stone*, August 28, 1986, rollingstone.com/music/music-news/boy-georges-nightmare -42205.

248 **Thatcher-era laws:** Local Government Act 1988, c.9, part IV, sec. 28, legisla tion.gov.uk/ukpga/1988/9/section/28/enacted.

Thirty-Seven: R.E.M.

251 **In 2008, the singer revealed:** Michael Azerrad, "R.E.M.: R.E.Born," *Spin*, April 2008, 61.

252 **Stipe later countered:** David Fricke, "Michael Stipe: The Rolling Stone Interview," *Rolling Stone*, March 5, 1992, rollingstone.com/music/music-news/mi chael-stipe-rolling-stone-interview-195878.

253 **With no effective treatment:** "Current Trends Mortality Attributable to HIV Infection/AIDS—United States, 1981–1990," *Morbidity and Mortality Weekly Report* 40, no. 3 (January 25, 1991), 41–44, cdc.gov/mmwr/preview/mmwrhtml /00001880.htm.

254 **Its director, Tarsem:** Eric Ducker, "The Making of R.E.M.'s Iconic 'Losing My Religion' Video," *Rolling Stone,* March 11, 2016, rollingstone.com/music/music-news/the-making-of-r-e-m-s-iconic-losing-my-religion-video-55002/2.

255 **"I thought that I was going":** Hrishikesh Hirway, host, *Song Exploder,* podcast, episode 125, "R.E.M.—Try Not to Breathe," Radiotopia from PRX, December 20, 2017, songexploder.net/transcripts/rem-transcript.pdf.

256 **On "Try Not to Breathe":** Hirway, *Song Exploder,* "R.E.M.—Try Not to Breathe."

256 **"I had watched, intimately":** Hirway, *Song Exploder,* "R.E.M.—Try Not to Breathe."

256 **Kaufman's weirdness spoke:** Zach Schonfeld, "Michael Stipe Reflects on R.E.M.'s 'Automatic for the People,': 'It Was F—king Dark Times,'" *Newsweek,* November 2, 2017, newsweek.com/2017/11/10/rem-michael-stipe-automatic-people-698161.html.

257 **In the 2014 biography:** Bob Zmuda and Lynne Margulies, *Andy Kaufman: The Truth, Finally* (BenBella, 2014), 117.

257 **told her he was gay:** Zmuda and Margulies, *Andy Kaufman,* 119.

257 **The book even speculates:** Zmuda and Margulies, *Andy Kaufman,* 169.

258 **"Half the population":** Zach Schonfeld, "Reclaiming 'Monster': Reflecting on R.E.M.'s Most Misunderstood Album with Michael Stipe," *Newsweek,* September 26, 2014, updated March 1, 2016, newsweek.com/reclaiming-monster-reflecting-rems-most-infamous-album-michael-stipe-273408.

258 **"I'm an equal opportunity lech":** Marcus Gray, *It Crawled from the South: An R.E.M. Companion* (Da Capo, 1997), 427.

258 **Having had relationships:** Sean O'Hagan, "Michael Stipe: 'I Often Find Myself at a Loss for Words,'" *Guardian,* March 5, 2011, theguardian.com/music/2011/mar/06/michael-stipe-rem-collapse-interview.

Thirty-Eight: The Smiths and Morrissey

260 **Introducing himself as:** James Henke, "The Smiths: Out to Save Rock & Roll," *Rolling Stone,* June 7, 1984, rollingstone.com/music/music-features/the-smiths-out-to-save-rock-roll-62389.

260 **"Unfortunately, I am not homosexual":** "Morrissey Says He's 'Humasexual,' Not Homosexual, *Guardian,* October 21, 2013, theguardian.com/music/2013/oct/21/morrissey-humasexual-not-homosexual-autobiography.

260 **Way back in 1984:** Henke, "The Smiths: Out to Save Rock & Roll."

260 **a declaration the singer:** Simon Goddard, *Mozipedia: The Encyclopedia of Morrissey and the Smiths* (Plume, 2010), 168.

263–64 **Morrissey argued that celibacy:** Goddard, *Mozipedia,* 68.

266 **Even in his teens:** Goddard, *Mozipedia,* 127.

267 Hyperbole has always been: Simon Armitage, "Morrissey Interview: Big Mouth Strikes Again," *Guardian*, September 3, 2010, theguardian.com/music/2010/sep/03/morrissey-simon-armitage-interview.

267–68 Then he supported: Will Humphries, "Ukip Loser Anne Marie Waters Will Start Far-Right Party," *Times*, October 12, 2017, thetimes.co.uk/article/ukip-loser-anne-marie-waters-will-start-far-right-party-fsgps673r.

268 the unfortunately lesbian leader: Benjamin Butterworth, "Lesbian Ally of the EDL's Tommy Robinson Standing to Be UKIP Leader," *PinkNews*, June 14, 2017, thepinknews.com/2017/06/14/lesbian-ally-of-the-edls-tommy-robinson-standing-to-be-ukip-leader.

268 of her now-defunct: Fiona Dodwell, "This Is Morrissey: An Interview," *Tremr*, June 5, 2018, tremr.com/Fiona-Dodwell/this-is-morrissey-an-interview.

Thirty-Nine: Hüsker Dü and Bob Mould

270 Not surprising, speed: Michael Azerrad, *Our Band Could Be Your Life: Scenes from the American Indie Underground* (Little, Brown, 2001), 192.

270 At the end of the group's: Azerrad, *Our Band Could Be Your Life*, 193.

270 Hart's methadone leaked: Azerrad, *Our Band Could Be Your Life*, 194.

270 The latter was a subject: Azerrad, *Our Band Could Be Your Life*, 192.

270 It wasn't until months after: Azerrad, *Our Band Could Be Your Life*, 195.

274 Mould's official disclosure: Steve Kandell, "The SPIN Interview: Bob Mould," *Spin*, February 1, 2008, spin.com/2008/02/spin-interview-bob-mould.

274 Rightfully feeling pressured: Dennis Cooper, "Real Personal," *Spin*, October 1994.

Forty: *Grease* and Olivia Newton-John

279 According to *Billboard*: Gary Trust, "Olivia Newton-John's 'Physical' Crowns Billboard's Top Songs of the '80s Chart," *Billboard*, April 15, 2019, billboard.com/pro/olivia-newton-john-physical-tops-billboards-top-80s-songs-chart.

Forty-Three: Cyndi Lauper

292 But by dropping its: "Robert Hazard Sets the Record Straight," *Morning Call*, October 2, 2021, mcall.com/1986/11/22/robert-hazard-sets-the-record-straight.

292 At the height of *Unusual*'s: David Remnick, "Pensive, with Orange Hair," *Washington Post*, September 6, 1984, washingtonpost.com/archive/lifestyle

/1984/09/07/pensive-with-orange-hair/a5cd332f-a8ca-4746-bae6-c8e1b2d0b537.

294 **"I wanted to sing it":** Cyndi Lauper with Jancee Dunn, *Cyndi Lauper: A Memoir* (Atria, 2012), 163.

294 **Enkindled by rock's inclusivity:** Gilbert Baker, *Rainbow Warrior: My Life in Color* (Chicago Review, 2019), 36–37.

295 **Packed with drag queens:** Lauper and Dunn, *Cyndi Lauper*, 230.

295 **Epic's dance-music department:** Lauper and Dunn, *Cyndi Lauper*, 249.

295 **Her gay friend Gregory's:** Keaton Bell, "Cyndi Lauper Discusses Virtual Benefit Concert and Her Mission to End LGBTQ Youth Homelessness," *Vogue*, December 8, 2020, vogue.com/article/cyndi-lauper-virtual-benefit-concert-to-end-lgbtq-youth-homelessness.

Forty-Four: Madonna

301 **In 2010, she spoke:** Gus Van Sant, "Madonna," *Interview*, May 3, 2010, interviewmagazine.com/music/madonna.

302 **Many didn't, like her gay:** J. Randy Taraborrelli, *Madonna: An Intimate Biography* (Simon & Schuster, 2001), 122.

303 **Her most seditious move:** Erin Clements, "Flashback: Madonna Premiered Controversial 'Like a Prayer' Pepsi Ad 25 Years Ago," *People,* March 2, 2014, https://web.archive.org/web/20140305043732/http://www.people.com/people/article/0%2C%2C20791901%2C00.html.

303 **While many TV stations:** Taraborrelli, *Madonna*, 167.

304 **Pepsi withdrew its sponsorship:** Taraborrelli, *Madonna*, 167.

307 **Many of the tour's:** Jerry Nunn, "Legendary Choreographer Vincent Paterson's 'Smooth' Moves," *Windy City Times*, April 29, 2014, windycitytimes.com/lgbt/-Legendary-choreographer-Vincent-Patersons-Smooth-moves-/47212.html.

309 **"I was thinking of":** Vince Aletti, "Never Can Say Goodbye," *Village Voice*, September 8, 1992, postimg.cc/Lh2qPxvs.

310 **"Of course, some of us":** Caryn James, "The Empress Has No Clothes," review of *Sex* by Madonna, *New York Times*, October 25, 1992, nytimes.com/1992/10/25/books/the-empress-has-no-clothes.html.

313 **When the antiviral cocktails:** Timothy Rodrigues, "No Obits," *Bay Area Reporter*, August 13, 1998, archive.org/details/BAR_19980813.

314 **Right before recording:** Mary Gabriel, *Madonna: A Rebel Life* (Little, Brown, 2023), 475.

317 **"I am the mommy":** "Madonna: Daughter Asked if Mom's Gay," CBS News, March 7, 2006, cbsnews.com/news/madonna-daughter-asked-if-moms-gay.

Forty-Five: Wham! and George Michael

319 **Ridgeley's gracious 2019 memoir:** Andrew Ridgeley, *Wham!, George Michael & Me: A Memoir* (Dutton, 2019), 67.

319 **Find yourself a record contract:** Ridgeley, *Wham!, George Michael & Me*, 119.

319 **Like the narrator:** James Gavin, *George Michael: A Life* (Abrams, 2022), 6.

320 **While filming the "Club Tropicana":** Neil Forsyth, "The Incredible Story of Tony Pike, the Man Who Built the Club Tropicana Party Hotel—and His Own Legend," *Shortlist*, May 25, 2018, shortlist.com/news/tony-pike-ibiza-club-tropicana-freddie-mercury-manumission-grace-jones.

321 **"I was supremely confident":** Andrew Johnson, "George Michael: Why I Had to Keep My Homosexuality Secret," *Independent,* September 30, 2007, independent.co.uk/news/uk/this-britain/george-michael-why-i-had-to-keep-my-homosexuality-secret-403989.html.

322 **Enchanted by what:** Chris Smith, dir., *Wham!* (Netflix, 2023).

323 **In the satin-sheeted:** Gavin, *George Michael*, 86.

323 **The truth was:** Gavin, *George Michael*, 101–2.

323 **Some stations wouldn't play it:** "Remembering Casey Kasem," *Billboard*, June 20, 2014, billboard.com/music/music-news/remebering-casey-kasem-6128593.

323 **Having already demanded cuts:** "Michael: Latest Song Isn't About Casual Sex," *Orlando Sentinel*, July 5, 1987, orlandosentinel.com/1987/07/05/michael-latest-song-isnt-about-casual-sex.

328 **Years later, *Older* co-producer:** Gavin, *George Michael*, 238.

Forty-Six: Whitney Houston

333 **We'd recognized both:** Clive Davis with Anthony DeCurtis, *The Soundtrack of My Life* (Simon & Schuster, 2013), 545–48.

333 **whereas Griffin just joked:** Lola Ogunnaike, "In the Chatting Olympics, Look for Merv Griffin," *New York Times*, May 26, 2005, nytimes.com/2005/05/26/arts/television/in-the-chatting-olympics-look-for-merv-griffin.html.

335 **"Because of their easy intimacy":** Richard Corliss, "The Prom Queen of Soul," *Time*, July 13, 1987, time.com/time/subscriber/article/0,33009,964980-5,00.html.

335 **Crawford's 2019 memoir:** Robyn Crawford, *A Song for You: My Life with Whitney Houston* (Dutton Books, 2019), 74–76.

337 By this point, the public: "Bobby Brown Faces DUI Charge in Hollywood," *Sun Sentinel*, December 24, 1996, sun-sentinel.com/1996/12/24/bobby-brown-faces-dui-charge-in-hollywood.

337 while she endured: "Whitney Miscarries Third Time," *New York Daily News*, December 21, 1996, nydailynews.com/1996/12/21/whitney-miscarries-third-time-2.

338 In her memoir, Crawford relates: Crawford, *A Song for You*, 111.

338 "I'd never seen her": Crawford, *A Song for You*, 260–61.

344 When Crawford discussed: Crawford, *A Song for You*, 262.

344 Soon after our interview: Crawford, *A Song for You*, 265–66.

Forty-Seven: Depeche Mode, Yaz, and Erasure

346 Unlike the bulk of this: Jason Newman, "Depeche Mode Reject Alt-Right Leader's Band Praise," *Rolling Stone*, February 23, 2017, rollingstone.com/music/music-news/depeche-mode-reject-alt-right-leaders-band-praise-124411.

346 Years later, Gore explained: Brandon Voss, "Masters of 'The Universe,'" *David*, May 7, 2009, brandonvoss.com/blog/depeche-modes-martin-gore-masters-of-the-universe.

349 Soon after Depeche: Keith Cameron, "Dead Man Talking," *New Musical Express*, January 18, 1997, davegahandevotion.com/articles/print_media/nme_1997jan18.php.

349 Gore struggled another decade: Dorian Lynskey, "Depeche Mode: 'We're Dysfunctional. Maybe That's What Makes Us Tick,'" *Guardian*, March 28, 2013, theguardian.com/music/2013/mar/28/depeche-mode-interview-delta-machine-dysfunctional.

352 "I'd had enough": Dave Simpson, "Andy Bell: 'I'd Had Enough of Being Bullied,'" *Guardian*, July 30, 2014, theguardian.com/culture/2014/jul/30/andy-bell-erasure-hiv-cocaine-interview.

353 It's now estimated: Jude Rogers, "The Silent Partner Speaks: Vince Clarke Interviewed," *Quietus*, October 5, 2023, thequietus.com/articles/33464-vince-clarke-interview-2.

353 his HIV-positive diagnosis: "Erasure's Bell Reveals HIV-Positive Status," *Billboard*, December 15, 2004, billboard.com/music/music-news/erasures-bell-reveals-hiv-positive-status-65282.

353 Way back in 1991: Bill Wyman, "Chorus," *Entertainment Weekly*, November 22, 1991.

Forty-Eight: New Order

356 At two million copies: Andre Paine, "The Story Behind New Order's Blue Monday—the UK's Biggest-Selling 12-Inch Single," *Music Week*, March 7,

2023, musicweek.com/talent/read/the-story-behind-new-order-s-blue-monday-the-uk-s-biggest-selling-12-inch-single/087537.

Forty-Nine: Pet Shop Boys, Dusty Springfield, and Liza Minnelli

361 **Despite having recorded:** Emanuel Levy, *Vincente Minnelli: Hollywood's Dark Dreamer* (St. Martin's, 2009), 112.

364 **A 2014 BBC poll:** "Pet Shop Boys' Always on My Mind Tops Cover Version Vote," BBC, October 27, 2014, bbc.com/news/entertainment-arts-29791820.

367 ***PSBVA* quotes my review:** Chris Heath, *Pet Shop Boys Versus America* (Viking, 1992), 101–3.

367 **Near the song's end:** Chris Heath, Liner notes for *Very/Further Listening* by Pet Shop Boys. Parlophone 0190295809164, 2018, compact discs.

367 **It happened after Lowe:** Chris Heath, Liner notes for *Very/Further Listening* by Pet Shop Boys.

368 **In 1994, Tennant came out:** Paul Burston, "Attitude Archive: Neil Tennant's 1994 Coming Out Interview," *Attitude*, September 7, 2017 (original in August 1994 issue), attitude.co.uk/uncategorised/attitude-archive-neil-tennants-1994-coming-out-interview-288047.

368 **"The 1990s has been":** Mireille Silcott, "The Pet Shop Boys, Obsessively," *Montreal Mirror*, November 11, 1999, web.archive.org/web/20120204040754/http://www.montrealmirror.com/ARCHIVES/1999/111199/music1.html.

Fifty: Tina Turner and Bonnie Raitt

374 **When a mid-'80s skiing accident:** Mark Bego, *Bonnie Raitt: Just in the Nick of Time* (Carol, 1995), 124–27.

375 **When Eikhard died:** Brad Wheeler, "New Brunswick Singer-Songwriter Shirley Eikhard Wrote Hit Song 'Something to Talk About,'" *Globe and Mail*, December 22, 2022, theglobeandmail.com/arts/music/article-new-brunswick-singer-songwriter-shirley-eikhard-wrote-hit-song.

Fifty-One: Phranc and k.d. lang

379 **On the title cut:** Nick Krewen, "Owen Bradley Interview 1988—Shadowland and k.d," *Hamilton Spectator*, June 28, 1988, susandoddblog.wordpress.com/2013/07/27/owen-bradley-interview-1988-shadowland-and-k-d.

380 **And when in 1990:** Richard Harrington, "Cattle Country's Beef with k. d. lang," *Washington Post*, July 1, 1990, washingtonpost.com/archive/lifestyle/1990/07/

02/cattle-countrys-beef-with-kd-lang/7dd680b4-ecf0-407a-aed5-b6120b879d38.

382 In real life, she'd been: Brendan Lemon, "A Quiet Life," *Advocate*, June 16, 1992, kdlang.org/the-advocate-1992-t1073.html.

Fifty-Two: Sinéad O'Connor

385 In the August 2000: Diane Anderson-Minshall, "No Man's Woman," *Curve*, August 2000, curvemag.com/blog/no-mans-woman.

385 She'd later qualify: Chris Azzopardi, "Q&A: Sinéad O'Connor on How Gays Changed Her Life & Getting Her 'D*ck Hard,'" *Pride Source*, July 22, 2014, updated August 20, 2023, pridesource.com/article/67109-2.

387 *Time* grilled O'Connor: Janice C. Simpson, "People Need a Short, Sharp Shock: Sinéad O'Connor," *Time*, November 9, 1992, content.time.com/time/subscriber/article/0,33009,976937,00.html.

387 Years later she reflected: Sinéad O'Connor, *Rememberings* (Houghton Mifflin Harcourt, 2021), 181.

Fifty-Three: Tracy Chapman

390 In 2022, Walker published: Alice Walker, *Gathering Blossoms Under Fire: The Journals of Alice Walker,* ed. Valarie Boyd (Simon & Schuster, 2022), 397.

Fifty-Five: Melissa Etheridge

399 Her friend k.d. lang: Melissa Etheridge with Laura Morton, *The Truth Is . . . My Life in Love and Music* (Villard, 2001), 133–34.

400 Despite this, she received: Andrew Male, "'Our Sound Engineer Got a Death Threat': How Lesbian Label Olivia Shook Up Music," *Guardian*, July 19, 2020, theguardian.com/music/2020/jul/19/lesbian-record-label-olivia-linda-tillery-californian-feminists-death-threat-music.

400 Her eventual boss: Etheridge and Morton, *The Truth Is*, 85.

400 "I want the girl": Etheridge and Morton, *The Truth Is*, 97.

401 Written about her open relationship: Etheridge and Morton, *The Truth Is*, 81.

401 As they parted: Etheridge and Morton, *The Truth Is*, 106.

402 Etheridge's first autobiography: Etheridge and Morton, *The Truth Is*, 88–89.

406 Soon after they: Etheridge and Morton, *The Truth Is*, 184.

406 "It was the first time I felt": Etheridge and Morton, *The Truth Is*, 185.

406 "I really drank that in": Etheridge and Morton, *The Truth Is*, 185.

Fifty-Six Nirvana and Hole

409 "If we were in San Francisco": Steve Appleford, "L7 on Broken Arms, Lesbian Fans, Twerking, Biting New Album '*Scatter the Rats*,'" *Revolver*, May 9, 2019, revolvermag.com/music/l7-broken-arms-lesbian-fans-twerking-biting-new-album-scatter-rats.

Fifty-Seven: C+C Music Factory, Deee-Lite, and House Music

412 "The president of the label": "Matty's Celebrates 4 Years with Lady Kier," *Hotspots*, August 23, 2012, hotspotsmagazine.com/2012/08/23/mattys-celebrates-4-years-with-lady-kier.

Fifty-Nine: Queen Latifah and Hip-Hop

420 When receiving BET's: Mia Mercado, "A Very Happy Pride to Queen Latifah," The Cut, June 28, 2021, thecut.com/2021/06/queen-latifah-thanked-her-love-eboni-at-the-bet-awards.html.